Whose Land, Whose Law

In 1976 an Aboriginal community returned to Noonkanbah Station in Australia's far north-west as the new owners.

But, the people's return coincided with an exploration boom that saw their land overrun by miners, and blanketed by mineral claims. However, rather than accept this invasion, the people decided to fight for their land.

Their struggle became focused around the defence of a particular piece of sacred ground against a proposed wild cat oil well. And so began an extraordinary battle involving the Noonkanbah people, the miners and the Western Australian Government. Aboriginal groups from around Australia, the trade union movement and the Australian Government, and even the United Nations were drawn into the dispute as it escalated.

The climax to the struggle was a national event, seen on television screens and recorded in headlines across Australia. A juggernaut convoy of trucks loaded with mining equipment, running a gauntlet of union pickets, and descending on Noonkanbah as police break up a blockade by a small group of Aborigines sitting in a river bed, singing for their country.

'The best theatrical drama provides profound insights into its characters by placing them in extreme situations… On rare occasions a community or a nation will throw up, as if by chance, a set of circumstances that provides similar insights and revelations about itself. Noonkanbah was such an occasion.'

Noonkanbah was a drama which has become a landmark in the modern history of Aboriginal Australia. Steve Hawke's highly-readable text and Michael Gallagher's vivid photographic images recreate that extraordinary drama with great power and sensitivity.

Cover photograph by Michael Gallagher, hand-coloured by Chris Dosser.

This is the Pea Hill, Umpampurru. That's the hill.

An' this one here, this is the place for Goanna, Malaji. Any people – might be Joe – or even me, when I dream, I can grab 'em Goanna from here.

An' 'nother Malaji here, that's the same Kakaji [Goanna].

But I know from my mother, 'is name Alice Tinjinalla, he b'long a that area. This area 'is name Kurji. That's the area now.

Old station – Noonkanbah. One road go through to Irralapajan [Hill].

That's the one billabong now.

This one road, go to Warrimbah through Number One bore.

An' this is the place we bin have 'em argument all the time.

That's the same Kurji. This is the same area now, this is the area goin' from here to Pea Hill.

Bob Mululby, 1988

Noonkanbah

Whose Land, Whose Law

STEVE HAWKE   MICHAEL GALLAGHER

FREMANTLE ARTS CENTRE PRESS

First published 1989 by
FREMANTLE ARTS CENTRE PRESS
1 Finnerty Street (PO Box 891), Fremantle
Western Australia, 6160.

Consultant Editor B.R. Coffey.
Designed by Fremantle Arts Centre Press – John Douglass, Helen Idle,
                        B.R. Coffey, Ian Templeman.
Production Manager Helen Idle.

Typeset in 10/11 pt Garamond by Caxtons, Perth, Western Australia, and printed on 115
gsm Primatrend by Globe Press, Melbourne, Victoria.

National Library of Australia
Cataloguing-in-publication data

Hawke, Stephen, 1959- .
    Noonkanbah.

    Bibliography.
    Includes index.
    ISBN O 949206 55 5.

    (1). Aborigines, Australian – Western Australia – Noonkanbah – Government
    relations. (2). Aborigines, Australian – Western Australia – Noonkanbah – History. (3).
    Passive resistance – Western Australia – Noonkanbah. I. Gallagher, Michael, 1949- . II.
    Title.

323.1'19915

To the Noonkanbah mob,
and especially to Ginger Nganawilla,
a man of vision who is sadly missed.

CONTENTS

LIST OF MAPS

All maps are drawn by W.S. Hart. Maps 5 are re-drawn from Western Australian Mines Department maps; Maps 4 and 6 are sketch maps adapted from sketch maps by Kingsley Palmer, 1978; Map 7 is adapted from a map by Peter Bindon, 1979.

ACKNOWLEDGEMENTS

The support that we have had in bringing this book to life has come from many quarters, and in many forms.

Particular recognition is due to the Aboriginal Arts Board of the Australia Council, the Department of Aboriginal Affairs, and the Australian Institute of Aboriginal Studies, which all provided financial assistance for the project at various stages; and to the Yungngora Community of Noonkanbah and the Marra Worra Worra Aboriginal Corporation of Fitzroy Crossing who sponsored funding applications to these bodies.

Thanks go to Maggie Bourne for helping to organise the map/drawing by Bob Mululby on pages 2 and 3 and for taking down his story about it; to Bill Hart for drafting the maps; to Amanda Curtin for producing the index; and to Kim Akerman for the photograph on page 108, Lyn McLeavy for the photograph on page 127, Bobby Kogolo for the photograph on page 248, The J.S. Battye Library of West Australian History for the photographs on page 53 and West Australian Newspapers for the photographs on pages 134, 278 and 288.

We are indebted to the Western Australian Government for granting significant but restricted access to Government files and records. (Cabinet documents and decisions were not made available.)

To families, friends, individuals and organisations that provided support, information, assistance, facilities, feedback and criticism: we thank you sincerely. You are too many to mention by name.

But most of all, and most important, we wish to thank and pay tribute to the people of Noonkanbah, for supporting this project, and agreeing to let their story be told. We would not, and could not have done it without you.

Steve Hawke and Michael Gallagher
April 1989

The creative writing program of Fremantle Arts Centre Press is assisted by the Australia Council, the Australian Government's arts funding and advisory body.

Fremantle Arts Centre Press receives financial assistance from the Western Australian Department for the Arts.

Canberra

Darwin

Wyndham
KIMBERLEY

Victoria River
Downs

Derby

Hooker's Creek
(Lajamanu)

Broome

Halls Creek

NOONKANBAH

Balgo

Northern Territory

Port Hedland

Great Sandy Desert

Strelley

Karratha
Roebourne

PILBARA

Western Australia

• Mt Newman

GASCOYNE
Carnarvon

South Australia

MURCHISON

Geraldton

Eneabba

Perth

Route of convoy

0 100 200 300 400 500
Kilometres

Projection – Bonne.

**WESTERN AUSTRALIA INCLUDING PART OF
THE NORTHERN TERRITORY**

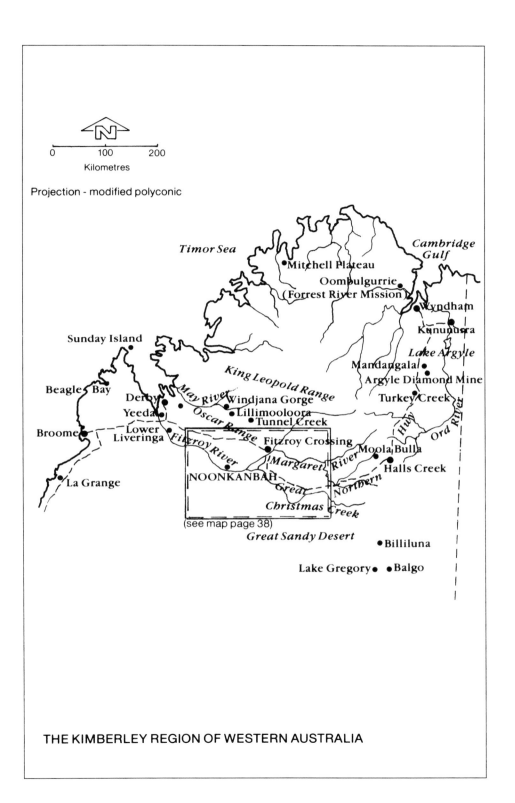

N

| 0 | 100 | 200 |

Kilometres

Projection - modified polyconic

Timor Sea

Cambridge Gulf

•Mitchell Plateau

Oombulgurrie
(Forrest River Mission)

•Wyndham

•Kununurra

Sunday Island

Lake Argyle

Mandangala•
Argyle Diamond Mine

Beagle Bay

King Leopold Range

Derby
•Windjana Gorge

May River

Turkey Creek

Yeeda•
•Lillimooloora

Oscar Range

•Tunnel Creek

Broome

Lower
Liveringa

Fitzroy River

Fitzroy Crossing

Moola Bulla

Margaret River

Hann

Ord River

NOONKANBAH

Great

Northern

Halls Creek

La Grange

Christmas Creek

(see map page 38)

Great Sandy Desert

•Billiluna

Lake Gregory• •Balgo

THE KIMBERLEY REGION OF WESTERN AUSTRALIA

13

The drill site, Noonkanbah, 1989. Top: The steel plate marking the abandoned drill hole, with Pea Hill in the background. Bottom: Close-up of the steel plate marker.

INTRODUCTION

There is a rusty steel plate welded to a crowbar hammered into the hard ground, now leaning at a precarious angle. The inscription on the plate, roughly lettered with solder, is only just decipherable. It reads:

FITZROY RIVER NO 1
PLUGGED NOV 23 1980
ABANDONED OCT 25 1983
LAT 18 DEG 29' 39" E
LONG 124 DEG 52' 50" S
TOTAL DEPTH 3133.8 MET

This is the only memorial of a drama that was at the centre of public attention in Australia for almost two years.

The remains of a *Cyclone* wire fence and a sludge dam with eroded walls and a cracked, hard surface are the only other signs of the drilling activity. The site is on a gravel and spinifex plain, relieved only by occasional bushy shrubs, alone or in small clumps. A low, gnarled, ancient-looking range stretches along the southern horizon, standing above a thick belt of trees in the middle distance. The only other noticeable feature is a small cone-shaped hill with a knobby top; it is about two kilometres away in the east, but looks much further.

The two-metre high posts and sagging wire of the *Cyclone* fence are the only indication that this might have been any different from the dozens of other wildcat wells drilled in the frenetic exploration of the Canning Basin since the mid-1970s. The construction of security fences around a wildcat well is not normal practice in the Kimberley.

This particular well was different. The drilling rig belonged to a subsidiary of Colonial Sugar Refineries (CSR), one of Australia's largest companies. It was the subject of trade union bans, and manned by a specially recruited 'scab' crew; and most remarkably, it had been temporarily taken over by the State Government. The Minister for Mines, not the exploration consortium, was the legal driller of the well.

The rig was brought to the site in a two-thousand-kilometre convoy of over fifty trucks with specially issued numberplates, and many of the drivers were wearing face masks to hide their identities. It was escorted by a large contingent of police, with logistic support provided by the State Emergency Service. The convoy's journey north was marked by demonstrations and arrests and intense media coverage.

These events took place in 1980. The cone-shaped hill with a knobby top is called Pea Hill. The gravel and spinifex plain is on the Noonkanbah Pastoral Lease. The government was the State Government of Western Australia, led by Sir Charles Court.

The wildcat well was part of an oil exploration program for a consortium led by an Australian subsidiary of the American corporate giant, Amax.

This book tells the story of Noonkanbah, Amax, and the Western Australian Government.

The book has been the result of collaboration between myself and Michael Gallagher. Both of us were involved with the Community at Noonkanbah during the drama of 1979 and 1980.

I first met the Community leaders at Broome late in 1978, and then spent a week at Noonkanbah. I returned at the Community's request in May 1979 and spent the next two years working for them in the capacity of liaison officer during their struggle with Amax and the State Government. My main duties were to assist the Community with the preparation and distribution of press releases and correspondence, and to act as a link between the Community and the various organisations that were supporting it.

Since the events of 1979-80 I have stayed on in the Kimberley, and am still working with the Noonkanbah people and other communities in the Fitzroy area.

Michael Gallagher is a freelance photographer who spent much of 1979 and 1980 in the Kimberley, and particularly at Noonkanbah, at the invitation of the Community. He has maintained his involvement with Aboriginal people in a number of capacities, most recently as a historian for the Western Desert Aborigines. He was responsible for the initial research and much of the compilation of source material that went into this book, as well as most of the photographs.

We have had the support of the Noonkanbah Community throughout our work on the project, which we gratefully acknowledge. But the book itself is our work, and the responsibility for opinions and judgements expressed is mine, as author of the text.

A large part of the story is told in the words of the Noonkanbah people themselves, using interviews and transcripts of meetings, and letters and press releases of the time. Where transcripts are used, they have in most cases been edited in order to make the Aboriginal English of the people more easily accessible to a wider audience. Aboriginal English has its own vocabulary and rules of grammar that can be confusing or misleading to the unpractised ear. But apart from this grammatical editing the words are as spoken by the people themselves.

I am sure that many readers will notice the absence of women's voices and participation in the action. I mean no disrespect to the women of Noonkanbah. On the whole they were very supportive of the stance taken by the Community and articulated by the leaders. Due to the nature of the dispute, particularly some of the religious aspects involved, and the way the Community operated at the time, the women of the Community were directly involved only on rare occasions. And my work and contact with the Community, at the time of the mining dispute and subsequently, has been almost exclusively with the men. If this means that one dimension of the Community's perspective is missing, I can only say that it is dictated by circumstances, and that the dispute was treated by the Community as being primarily men's business.

The Noonkanbah drama became one of the most significant episodes in the history of Aboriginal/European relations in Australia. It is generally acknowledged as a landmark of modern Aboriginal history.

The old saying that 'history is written by the winners' reflects the truth that there is always more than one perspective on a given set of events. Noonkanbah especially is an example of this phenomenon, for more than anything else, it was a clash of two realities, two different ways of interpreting the world. Noonkanbah generated intense passions and opinions on both sides. Although the primary issues were clear cut, the unfolding of the drama was such a complex, and at times confusing, saga that it cannot be claimed that there is one true version of events. Noonkanbah 1979-80 was history in the making. Like all history, it is open to interpretation.

The aim of this book is to document and explain the events of 1979 and 1980 at Noonkanbah, and the history that lies behind them. We make no claim to an objective or impartial analysis; as participants, supporters and sympathisers, we have attempted to present the story from the perspective of the Aboriginal community at Noonkanbah at the time of the dispute.

Steve Hawke
1989

1

WHOSE LAND, WHOSE LAW?

Now this is the way that we are thinking – to pull the white man from
the ears to listen to what the Aboriginal Law will say.

Dicky Skinner, Noonkanbah, November 1978.

In November 1978 a group of about forty men made the journey from Noonkanbah and surrounding communities to Broome, four hundred kilometres away. They were Elders and Lawmen and community leaders. They were there to witness the first skirmish in a two-year-long drama that became known around Australia as 'The Noonkanbah Conflict', or more simply, 'Noonkanbah'.

The Mining Warden's Court had been convened to hear objections by the Yungngora Community of Noonkanbah to mining claims on their land. The courtroom made a most unusual sight; rows of old men with stern faces in the public benches at the back, listening with earnest attention, but virtually no comprehension, to the Queen's Counsels and the Magistrate at the front. During each recess there would be a quick exit, and a huddle would form on one of the wide verandahs, or under the spreading trees of the courthouse gardens, to listen to the progress reports and explanations of the lawyers.

The old men were there fighting to save a dream that had become a reality just two years earlier, when in August 1976 the Commonwealth Government had purchased the Noonkanbah Pastoral Lease for the Yungngora Community.

This was one of a number of such purchases for Aboriginal groups in northern and central Australia around that time. To the Government it was one step in a larger scheme of implementing new and bolder policies in the field of Aboriginal affairs. To those of the public who noticed or cared, the policy of purchasing land for Aboriginal people was mostly accepted as fair and just in the political mood that prevailed. Amongst the pastoral community in the north the purchase of Noonkanbah in particular caused something of a stir, because unlike most of the other new Aboriginal properties, it was in good pastoral country, and in its prime it had been a famous sheep station.

The purchase of Noonkanbah was more than simply a homecoming to the Yungngora people, it was the culmination of a ninety-year struggle. It meant a return to their home; the home of their forefathers, the home of their childhood, and perhaps most importantly, the home of their spirits and their spirituality: the home of their dreams.

This return followed five years of exile as fringedwellers in the rural slums of Fitzroy Crossing. To the people the return to their land had little to do with the details of pastoral leasehold as compared to freehold title, or any of the mechanics of the white man's law. To them it was a return to country, and, finally, recognition of the legitimacy of their rights to the country. This belief was one that had a great bearing on the events that were to follow.

The people had taken enormous steps towards establishing a cohesive community with a sense of purpose and direction in the two years that they had been back on their own land. Community management structures were in place. A Community operated school had been established to provide education for their children. They had made significant inroads into the task of re-establishing a famous pastoral property that had been virtually derelict on their return, after suffering years of neglect without the input of the Aboriginal labour that had made it what it was in its prime.

It was also a time of hope and optimism, and the flexing of newly found political muscles for Aboriginal people throughout the Kimberley. The Commonwealth Government's land purchase policies; Land Rights legislation in the Northern Territory; active participation in hotly contested and disputed State election campaigns; a growing ability to articulate their feelings and positions on issues; a growing sense of their capacity to exercise their own power, both at a local community level and on the wider scene: these were all factors contributing to a new mood in the Kimberley.

Among the people of Noonkanbah, this mood, or sense of power, was largely channelled into the station property and Community. The Community was in many senses isolationist – having returned to their country they wanted to live on it by themselves, and for themselves. They had firmly rejected the efforts of the Commonwealth's Department of Aboriginal Affairs (DAA) to install a resident manager to assist with the operation of the cattle station, preferring to handle affairs themselves. In 1978 they recruited two white teachers in order to get their Community school off the ground, but as a rule they did not encourage or welcome the presence of outsiders beyond what was strictly necessary.

The main shadow hanging over the Community's optimistic outlook in 1978 was the uninvited presence of the men and machinery working for oil and mineral exploration companies. Although a quick education was to follow, the Noonkanbah people initially had no appreciation of the technicalities of the Mining Act vis-a-vis the Lands Act that gave these strangers virtually an unfettered right to enter and work on the station. In their experience the owner of a pastoral lease was the lord of all he surveyed. And hence, both in their own terms and in their understanding of the white man's ways, the presence of the miners was not right.

In 1978 the hectic race to claim ground in the oil and diamond boom that hit the Kimberley was at its height. The Canning Basin was seen as highly prospective for oil. C.R.A Exploration (CRA), a subsidiary of the mining giant Conzinc Riotinto Australia, had found diamonds at Ellendale just to the north of Noonkanbah, and was starting to appreciate what it had found at Argyle in the East Kimberley. Noonkanbah Station was blanketed by five hundred odd mining leases, and by Exploration Permit Number 97, the oil lease held by a consortium led by Amax. There had been a number of incidents relating to the activities of the miners that had upset the people of Noonkanbah.

The most prominent amongst the holders of the mining leases on Noonkanbah, in terms of sheer numbers, was CRA. Company operatives had approached the Community to discuss an exploration program.

Concerned by the activity of the miners, and the threat which they felt was posed to the progress the Community was making, and particularly by the threat to sacred sites, the Community called in the Aboriginal Legal Service (ALS) in June 1978, and instructed it to take any legal steps available to stop further exploration on the Station.

The only avenue available was the provisions of the Mining Act allowing for objections to the granting of mineral claims. Many of those on Noonkanbah had already been approved, and were not open to objection. However the ALS was able to file objections in the Broome Mining Warden's Court to claims recently lodged by CRA and others.

Objections to ninety-five claims pegged by CRA between May and July 1978 came before the Mining Warden as a test case in November. The grounds of objection lodged by the ALS were that:

(a) One mining company had already been given mineral rights on the property and the activities of a multiplicity of mining companies could not be satisfactorily monitored by the Aboriginal lessees and occupiers;

(b) The sacred sites of the Aboriginal people would be endangered by such occupation;

(c) Such occupancy would deprive the Aboriginal occupiers of the land from enjoying newly found self-dependence and freedom from alien cultural pressure; and

(d) Such occupation would interfere with their pastoral business and subsistence, cause roads and tracks necessary to their livelihood to deteriorate and generally cause the deterioration of scenery and environment.

From a legal point of view it was never a strong case, as legal precedent held that the Mining Warden's jurisdiction extended only as far as the technical aspects of pegging and compliance with regulations; furthermore the Warden had only the power to recommend, with any final decision resting in the hands of the State Government's Minister for Mines.

The hearing lasted two days. Magistrate David McCann, who was also the Mining Warden, explained that he could not allow the objections grounded in concerns about social or pastoral enterprise effects, but did agree to hear arguments regarding the danger to sacred sites. Most of the hearing revolved around the evidence of anthropologist Kingsley Palmer, who had undertaken a fifteen-day site survey of the CRA claims on behalf of the ALS in August.

Palmer's evidence consisted of general information about the nature of Aboriginal religious belief, and the relationship of that belief to the land, followed by an inventory of the sites and areas of significance he had mapped during his August survey.

In his written judgement[1], McCann said of Palmer's evidence:

> Some few sites were located within areas which were the subject of claims by the Applicant Company. Some additional sites were adjacent to areas claimed and Mr Palmer stated that those areas claimed were within the *sphere of influence* of those sites. [Emphasis added.]

McCann also commented that as Palmer's evidence proceeded it became apparent that his information on features and sites was incomplete after a study of only fifteen days, and said:

> ...it would appear that a much longer and more thorough period of research is necessary to allow matters to be established with certainty.

Two Community representatives, Elder Nipper Tabagee and Spokesman Dicky Skinner, also gave evidence, but handicapped by their Aboriginal English and the courtroom atmosphere, they were unable to get their message across. McCann said in his judgement:

> I do not doubt that they were truthful and sincere but I was unable to derive any help from their evidence.

Magistrate McCann's final recommendation was that all but two of CRA's claims should be unconditionally approved, and that these two should be approved subject to the condition that no mining should take place until action was taken under the Aboriginal Heritage Act to identify, and where necessary protect, places and objects within them.

He heard the case carefully and compassionately, but the result was inevitable:

> As Mr Kennedy [CRA counsel] pointed out the issues raised in these

proceedings are merely a continuation of the problems posed when the first white man came to settle in Australia. In this case there is a conflict between the desire of the Mining Company to explore and exploit the land and the wish of the aboriginal people, as is expressed in the Form of Objection, to enjoy independence and freedom from the pressure of a culture other than their own.

Just as these issues were raised long ago, so too was the decision made. In coming to Australia, the white man brought his form of law. That law stands and cannot be over-ridden by moral or spiritual arguments.

The Noonkanbah people headed home from Broome with a keener appreciation than ever of the fact that the white man's law was not on their side, but also with a determination that this was not the end of the matter.

The case was the first step on a path that the Noonkanbah people were to follow with clarity and consistency over the next two years; they would reason with the white man, his law and his government, but they would not bow to him. Unlike Magistrate McCann they were of the opinion that white law could and should be overridden by moral and spiritual arguments.

Although the significance was not appreciated at the time, the evidence and McCann's judgement raised two issues that were to assume vital importance in the later conflict with Amax. Firstly, Palmer, on the basis of information gathered from his informants at Noonkanbah, raised the concept and importance of 'spheres of influence' around specific sites; a concept that the people and anthropologists were later accused of inventing for the purpose of frustrating Amax. Secondly, having listened to Palmer's evidence McCann unreservedly accepted the complexity of the task of researching and mapping information relating to sacred/religious sites, and recognised the need for time and care 'to allow matters to be established with certainty'. This foreshadowed the Community's later request for a moratorium on mining activity to allow such mapping, and became a condemnation of the practices employed by Amax, and the demands that were to be made by the Government.

In the final paragraphs of his judgement McCann also made a prophetic warning:

> I have written at some length rather than summarily dismiss the matters raised by the Objectors. It would be insensitive not to recognise the sincere and deep interest of these Aboriginal people in the land they see as theirs. It is clear that they are worried and, to a degree, feel threatened by the mining development in the area. This concern and worry has manifested itself in the objections made to these claims. It is a matter of comfort that this manifestation has taken a lawful, as distinct from an illegal and hostile, form.
>
> If only as a matter of self-interest, the Government, the Mining Companies and the community at large would do well to look at the issues raised in these proceedings and take positive steps to attempt to abate the concern expressed by the Aboriginal people.

Tragically, this warning was not heeded, and was in fact blatantly disregarded. The consequences of this failure were to become apparent to 'the Government, the Mining Companies and the community at large' within a matter of six months.

I had been flown down from Darwin by the Kimberley Land Council (KLC) for the court case in Broome. The KLC, then in its infancy, was trying to assist the Community by drawing public attention to the situation at Noonkanbah and the issue of intrusion onto Aboriginal land by mining companies. I had been writing on Aboriginal issues as a freelance journalist for the *Nation Review,* a weekly newspaper that has since closed down. It was my first trip to the Kimberley.

After the hearing I went to Noonkanbah and recorded a series of interviews as background material for the article I was to write. For the first two days at Noonkanbah I was left in the company of one of the white teachers at the Community school.

It was to become clear that the people were giving careful thought to the matter of what they should say to me. This was some six months before Noonkanbah first became a public issue. It was the first visit to the Community by a journalist, and the first time the members of the Community had sat down to express to an outsider, in a considered way, their feelings on the situation they were facing.

The people did not talk only about the immediate problems they were facing with CRA and other mining companies. The older men in particular felt the need to clearly establish their right and authority to speak. Each of them would talk at length about his and the Community's history, or relate stories from his land and Dreaming, before making any comment about the current situation.

In the interviews, as can be seen in the excerpts included here, all the major issues, themes and concerns that dominated the debate over the next two years were anticipated and discussed by the people of Noonkanbah. Coupled with the evidence of Kingsley Palmer in court at Broome regarding sites and spheres of influence, and the prophetic warning of Magistrate McCann to the Government and miners, it is clear that the scene was set for what was to come. The people of Noonkanbah knew what they were about, and why they were about it.

On my third day at Noonkanbah, I was summonsed to a meeting under a bough-shade that had been built just outside the homestead yard. There were about a dozen men there. All were middle-aged or elderly, except for Ivan McPhee, the young Community Secretary. Those who spoke included Hanson Boxer, Nipper Tabagee, Dicky Skinner, and Friday Muller, who had been the leader of the Community during its time in Fitzroy Crossing and when it first returned to Noonkanbah.

I was not aware that in the intervening couple of days, two representatives of CRA had visited Noonkanbah unannounced to offer some employment to Community members in the exploration program it planned to conduct on the station. Hanson Boxer opened the interview by referring to this visit.

> Two men came on Saturday, Saturday afternoon. They were looking for two men; they wanted Dicky Skinner and they wanted Nipper Tabagee, to talk to them about Aborigines working with them in the mining. Six or twelve men they want to work with them in the mine. I didn't know what this was all about, but I didn't ask questions, like how much money they are going to work for there. I just held myself not to ask questions.
>
> This is, I think, maybe a trick. Aborigines go and work amongst the gudias* over there in the mining so that they might send a report back to their big man and tell him, 'Oh, Aborigines agree, they are working in the mine with us, in the mining job, so why the people say they don't want mining'.
>
> So now these two men they came here, they want Aboriginal people to

---

* Gudia: the term used by Aboriginal people throughout the Kimberley as the name for a white person. It appears with various spellings, including gudiya, gadiya, kartiya.

Dicky Skinner.

work. But Aborigines say that we don't want to work amongst those white men in the mine. Now I'm going to ask these people if they agree. Now Nipper, do you agree to send six men to work with those gudia in the mine? What do you say, yes or no?

Tabagee: I say no, because we've got good work.

Boxer: Okay, we'll wait till everybody gets together before we do something about it; say yes, or say no. I think people say no. They are the CRA men, those two men who came here to talk to Dicky and Nipper.

Skinner: They are just getting whatever stone they can find, the rich stones in the ground. They just go down and pick them up. They just don't worry about Aborigines. That's the way white people keep Aborigines down all the time. We want to try to talk up for our own citizens, for our own land, because we know that we've been losing half our ground before, and the Aboriginal people have been left with nothing. They make money from the tribal area and they don't worry about Aboriginal people.

It looks like there's two laws, white man law and Aboriginal Law. The white man law is not believing in the Aboriginal Law. Same way, this Aboriginal Law is not believing in the white man's side. This is the way the people are thinking, they are quite happy and say they think Aboriginal Law is very good, and this is the way it has stood from the beginning. White man law just comes over and is trying to put one over on Aboriginal Law. But we want to get that Aboriginal Law up, and make some people think what the Aborigine is, and what the tribal area is.

Maybe that white man law knows everything in this Kimberley, he's got it all in the map. But what about the Aboriginal map? This is the way. With the police; if he wants to arrest a man, he fills the warrant and arrests a person. The same in the Aboriginal way, if we want to arrest somebody we fill our own warrant. Same thing. A lot of these gudia say that we just make up the story, but this thing has been going on for a thousand hundred years back.

Same with the pastoralist company. This land is owned by the Aboriginal Lands Trust.[2] Our question back to these people; why did they get this land when the white man came into this place. Did he say to the tribal people, 'I'll buy these acres from you?' Maybe six or ten million acres, or something like that. We didn't see that. We didn't hear about that. We never had that money in the finger. White man just came and lay the concrete floor down, and Aborigines were just peeping out from the bush and wondering what that house was doing in his tribal area.

I reckon every white man in this country is making money from minerals in tribal areas. My Law says they are still renting. They never bought this land off Aboriginal tribal people.

After this initial discussion centred around mining and the two laws there was a short break, and then Friday Muller spoke about their fight to obtain Noonkanbah Station, which led on to a discussion of country, Aboriginal Law, and back to mining.

Well I'm going to talk about this problem from the start when we've been going for this Noonkanbah. I've been fighting for Noonkanbah for so long; through two men, Duncan Beaton and Jim Cooper. Duncan Beaton and his wife owned this place, and then Jim Cooper was manager. First I was just

Friday Muller.

asking for that Millijidee outstation back down the other side of the river, where that Kadjina is. All them DAA [Department of Aboriginal Affairs] men in Perth asked me, 'What do you want to get that place for?' Well that's our place. That's the answer. We wanted to try to get ourselves a place there. Start there, from the desert, right up to Millijidee. From there on, if this Noonkanbah would be for sale, I would be fighting through for this one. That goes back about six years, maybe more, ten years.

From there, Canberra tells me he was going to get that Quanbun Downs Station. But we didn't want that one, Quanbun's too small. We wanted Noonkanbah. We fight for Noonkanbah all the time. They tried to push us into Quanbun. We've got more stories here on the culture side and the background side. We've kept that from the old days.

Skinner and Muller told the story of the creation of the Fitzroy River by Unyupu and the two water snakes, and then explained how this related to their view of the country.

Skinner: From where those snakes started at Mijirrikan every deep waterhole has got a name. That's not written in the white man's map. The white man says, 'I'm holding the land'. Does he know that Aboriginal background? Nothing. This is the way that we think about it.

Muller: That's true. This river has got the Law, it's got the background.

Skinner: This station is a million acres in the gudia map. Well from Mijirrikan, that's my father's country, right up to Parrparrkarra we've got a boundary there.

Muller: Just like the boundary between Noonkanbah and Paradise Station.

Skinner: In the same way we have a boundary. That's my area from Mijirrikan to that pool we call Parrparrkarra.

Muller: From there, Kurji, that's all my country, my tribal area, to where the crossing is today. And all the gudia have been bringing bulldozers and everything, cutting up all my country. That road coming in, they cut it this way, then cut it this way. They come everywhere like this.

Skinner: Now Friday owns that area. Before I go into his area I have to get authority from him. We are talking about spirits, living spirits and Dreams and tribal areas. In my spirit time I came from my father's side. The same with younger generations, kids born again. When my kids are born their spirit comes from that area.

If there's any minerals or diamonds in that country, it could be my spirit living around there in a mineral site, because some tribal things are brought up from under the ground. A lot of gudias talk about land as if there's nobody owning it underneath the ground.

My Law can ask the white man's law a question. If that diamond or mineral inside under the ground has got CRA's name written on it, he is allowed to go down and get it. If it hasn't got CRA written on the minerals, that means there's nobody owning it. It is for the tribal land, for the tribal people.

This is the way we are thinking about it. We've got a map, the same as the gudia have a map. We've got a map in certain areas, and certain people come out from the different areas. This is the way they feel that their spirit likes to live. Gudia come along and try to kill people, mine. Their feelings are knocked back.

We are looking at that, way back from the beginning until today. We want to teach our children, remind them to think about their own culture, from their father's side and their grandfather's side. I think our people are upset about this, all this mining and drilling going round.

Muller: We started to think about this government, because before we didn't receive anything. We only just get this paper here – that's your money. You worship that thing. You want to buy something and hold it – in that paper. His citizen's there too [on paper]. And so everything that we think about, and how we want to get our country back, that's all been held up. [Paper] is the thing been sitting on it, you know.

Well I've got my citizenship in my background; they don't know anything about Aboriginal Law. They brought their citizenship from overseas, and they're on my island now. And from there on they put this paper, that citizenship, and that money; and drink. A good lot of good things. They make you happy – down on the paper.

The gudia might say I'm just a nothing up here in the head. I'm all right up here, but I grew up in the stockcamp, I got nothing to bring it out with.

He can drill a bore, and cut my roads, and make his roads with a bulldozer. But what happened to my tree here. I've got that tree here, I was born under that tree. That's my background in that tree. For so many years it was standing there, for so long.

Skinner: A little bit of money we need, but land is very important for us. This ground is not changing every year, this ground is staying this way. That white man's law is changing every year.

We vote for a government, we put him in the top seat. The government goes down to Parliament, and it makes the law a different way. That doesn't change this ground; this ground is left this way. That's the way we're talking about our spirit – to live in the country, like where we've been living before, where our old people were living. The ground doesn't change, this ground is sitting here.

We are walking on top of our old people's bodies. We haven't got any other bit of land. We can't go anywhere else. If we go down to Canberra or New Guinea or somewhere like that, that isn't our country. Other people say, you can move around, you can move from here to Fitzroy, or into Derby. But the people just think about their own place, Noonkanbah. People think about their spirit, and their old people who lived in this area.

The Government says that it owns underneath the ground. But how far does it know that Aboriginal tribal background? My Law says, it is written in my map; every tree, every fish, every animal has a name. We know from the beginning in the stories, from our spirit side. The land has been taken from the Aboriginal tribal people to the whites. The ground should not be taken from this place to overseas.

I could let the miners in, but what about my tribal people. They would tell me, 'Why are you letting this land go, are we going to let the white man have this land back?' I'm putting it for the people; this land should not be taken over. And under the ground should not be taken out either, it's the same. They reckon we own the land on top of the ground, but our tribal side comes up from under the ground to the top of the ground. It's got a meaning.

This time the white man can't go first. He must think. He must go to the tribal people. Same as the Government gives him authority to take this ground to look for minerals, we think he should come to the tribal people and find out what they want to say. If the tribal man says, 'No I can't let you do this, you might be cutting my area', all right.

As soon as the people think we are owning the land, another lot of gudia say, 'Right, we own the land'. I don't think we'll just let this happen. We are fighting for our land. We don't think we'll let the white man take this land away. They've been doing that before, but this time Aboriginal Law will catch white man's law.

Gudia law is very strong. His law was standing up from that day as soon as the white man came in. They just don't believe in Aboriginal Law. Now this is the way that we are thinking – to pull the white man from the ears to listen to what the Aboriginal Law will say.

For a long time Aboriginal people didn't mention this sort of thing, didn't put it through to the white man. They were frightened of the white man. If the people gave a white man a hiding the gudia used to come round with a gun and shoot Aboriginal people. This is why they were frightened and didn't talk about their own Law. Now this time we can say, 'Why were you doing this before, shooting our people in this country? You must have thought you were settling wild Aboriginal people in this country.' They were not wild. They were living as their own citizens.

This is the time we want to pull this white man and put him on the right track. We want them to listen to Aborigines. We are looking for something to be changed. We can talk to people, make them understand what the Aborigine is.

They talk in the Parliament for making laws. They've been pushing laws onto Aboriginal people. Now we are looking for a law – a law we can put up that can help people.

The white man's law was registered from as soon as the white man came to this place. And he knows that his law was registered. Laws for pegging and things like that. I think that Aboriginal people are starting to wake up. Some gudia have started to explain to our people what was happening before, and that's going to make everything very changed.

Noonkanbah Station was bought by the Government for Aboriginal people; and the same people [Government] say, 'All right, we'll try and drill a hole in the Noonkanbah area'.

Some of our old people just can't understand the white man.

Over the next few days some of the most prominent Elders in the Community spoke individually about their experiences and their feelings.

The first was Friday Muller, the former leader of the Community. He had a younger man drive us over the river crossing to Tatju Hill, a rocky outcrop on the plain between the river and the St George Range. As we drove he explained that CRA had been pegging mining tenements on the plain. When we got there, he spent a quiet minute watching the hill, to address the spirits there, and as if to examine it and gather his thoughts. Then he spoke:

Now I'm giving this message. That is an old sacred ground, a main sacred ground at Tatju Hill. Some surveyors went through here a few years back, and they took all the secret boards away from this hill down to Melbourne. I came down with the sergeant from Fitzroy Crossing and Kevin Johnson from Native Welfare in Derby.[3] I brought them down here and showed them. All our old boards had been taken away – about twenty of them – from this hill, Tatju Hill. The other ones they broke up around here, broke them up into pieces.

This is our main sacred ground from the old people until today. We've got it now. We shifted everything [the recovered boards] away from here to the other side of the river near the station, where we can watch it.

The boards that Muller refers to are of profound religious importance to the Noonkanbah people. They embodied the essence, and power of particular stories, sites and tracts of country. They were of central importance in certain ceremonial activity, and in the Community they were a source of great prestige and power to their owners.

Those boards that were not broken were later recovered, but the sacrilege of the theft, the loss of the broken boards, and the distress of the long wait for the others to be returned had deeply offended Muller and the other Elders.

Muller then turned and pointed to the flood plain between Tatju Hill and the river, and though he named CRA, he was in fact describing the seismic work carried out by Amax earlier that year.

They went across there that CRA mob. They brought a bulldozer down, about two miles west from here. They cut all the way around those old dead bodies, all around that place where we took those old people. That's nearly all sacred ground through there too.

From Tatju Hill Muller directed the car back towards Noonkanbah, but he stopped it on the river crossing, at the foot of the north bank. There were two deep gouges in the river bank, within one hundred and fifty metres of each other. One was the normal river crossing; where previously the road had come down at a relatively gentle gradient, it had become a steep and slippery ascent. The other was a seismic cut line.[4] Both had been made by Amax contractors during their 1978 seismic program.

Again the old man looked for a minute, this time at the cut in the bank just upstream from the crossing, before he spoke:

We are stopped right at the middle of the river. This is the main place where that surveyor went across. Two times the surveyors went across. He cut the road here and made it bad for us. And there's another one just across there where I was born. I am talking where I was born. I belong to here. This is where that mob put a bulldozer across my place, our sacred ground. This is a place we people don't want to get messed up, here, right in the middle of the tribal area that's been used from the early days by old people.

The Amax bulldozer had gone through sacred ground, damaging an old, old dancing ground, and the tree which had contained the old man's spirit, under which he was born. This incident had occurred in May, during a dance festival attended by over fifteen hundred people from throughout the Kimberley and northern Australia, for which Muller had been the principal host. This festival was also the occasion of the inaugural meeting of the Kimberley Land Council.

Another of the old men to talk that week was Nipper Tabagee. Tabagee is a Dreamer. He talks of seeing things, and of things that have come to him. He is not so involved in the day-to-day affairs of the Community as some of the others who spoke, but he is passionate about the land; his land and his people's land. He has been an active member of the executive of the KLC since its inception at Noonkanbah. He spoke of the land, the spirits of the land, the early days, and the miners, and of why and how the people had come to their position.

> I was pretty sick the other day, so I couldn't talk to you in that first meeting, to come out with the problem we've been talking about. We were talking about Marrala and Tanggapa [in the court]. We call that place Puntirliman, where Tanggapa and Marrala fought. That country was full of Aboriginal people in the first place before the Europeans came. It's still the same, from the Dreamtime to today. That Marrala was a big boss in the Dreamtime, and the same with Tanggapa.

Tabagee's evidence in the courthouse in Broome had been about the Dreamtime story of Marrala and Tanggapa. Many of CRA's claims had covered the country where these two figures had fought and, in their struggle, made the land as it is now. Tabagee and the other Elders were distressed that he had not been able to convey the story and its import properly. He told me the story, concluding with the fate of one of the other characters in the saga: a man called Wumina, who had been killed in this fight, and transformed into a boab tree on the station. Then he continued:

> All those mining companies are walking round there now, running round that boab tree where Wumina is. But they don't know he's there. That's Wumina's place.
> We've got a lot of stories about that Wumina, and those two, Marrala and Tanggapa. He's still walking around – his spirit – that Tanggapa. I saw him once when I stopped at the old dam over that way. He came there with his five boys. He had a corroboree with them, and they showed me. Last year.
> He's a man, a real man, when we Dream. Those ant beds there walk like a man in the afternoon. That was all his people. If you go over there, at six o'clock or sometime like that, you can see all the ant beds moving, starting to move. They turned into ant beds from men, all Tanggapa's people.
> A lot of these people think we are liars. But we have a story from the everlasting. It's not a lie, what we think. That's why we want to try to keep these people out from some places, but they just don't take any notice.

> Another olden days story now for that country where Friday took you. All round that [Tatju] hill.
> When I was a Dreamtime kid running round as a spirit – we call that spirit raii – I was playing all round that plain; from the other side to this side, from far away right down to the river, from Tamparkutayi to Irrtar. Irrtar Creek, that's where my father used to live. That's where I ran around before I was born.
> There's plenty of people [raii spirits] there now. I've got one girl that came out from that country, that creek, and one boy. They came out from that part of the country, and were born. One lives here, and one is in Derby.
> There are stories all around in that plain, before you come to Tatju Hill. When people were walking in the early days they had big meetings in that Tatju Hill. All the people came from everywhere. That's a main place belonging to everywhere. Everybody came to have a meeting, if they had a kid they had to make a man, they go in there.

Nipper Tabagee.

And that place we call Kurliti is the main place for all the people belonging to the Puntirliman country. There's a lot of spirits walking round there.

And those mining companies always go round there. Pegs all over the place. We saw it when we went mustering. All Toyotas and Landrovers all over the place. They don't think our way. They only think, 'They only hold the top of this place, nobody owns the bottom'.

All those things we talked about are very important things. We don't like people to damage our country. All these stories coming out, that we're giving you now, are all from the country round here. All the same story.

That place Parlil, that hill near the road coming in, that's a snake place. That snake came up from a place called Jangalajarra to Parlil. That's a woman snake, she came over here when she had her babies. She was looking for a place to lay her eggs. When she came to that place she stopped. She spread all the little snakes everywhere, from that Parlil. If we let them [the miners] come to that place what will happen? Those poison snakes will eat all the people.

It's very important all these things we're talking about. We don't like to lose our country. If we let the Europeans take a place when they find minerals, they want to come more, a little bit more. Pushing, pushing, pushing – hunt the people out; we can't have a station. That's why we're trying to put a stop on them if we can. If we don't, well...you know that bloke

I was talking to [the CRA representative who called to see Skinner and Tabagee], well he just doesn't care.

They should have more brains. They're just like little kids running round. You tell a little kid to get away from a place, and he comes back again a second time. We'd like to see it happen that once we tell them, they keep out.

If I go into their place, Derby or Perth or anywhere in those big cities; if I want to get minerals or diamonds if I find things there; what will they tell me? That's what we're telling them. It's just like that. He can't let me come in. He might tell me, 'Where's your bloody country?'

If the Queen died in England, and I went there and cut that tree there alongside the Queen; that's too bad for me, somebody might come up and shoot me there. They don't see that.

I know a story from [the time of] the German war, the first war that started in King Edward's time. White man came on top of the Aboriginals. We didn't fight back. The white man just came and took the land. We didn't know what they were doing. They were doing a little bit of a robbery, hey.

White people came into the Aboriginals and give him a hiding. We did their work, in our own land, in Aboriginal land. God gave the Europeans another land. When they came here they had to make themselves a big boss. We used to work for them. I worked for them. It come to my mind a few years ago, when I was in Derby. I worked it out, what they were doing, and what we were doing.

Then we asked for the land. They said, 'You can't take it, this is for the white people'. One bloke said to me like that, 'This is for the white people'.

I said, 'Where were you born? What language are you talking? This is the Walmatjari people's country. You don't talk Walmatjari, you talk the European language. You must be careful.' He said to me, 'Who taught you that?'

'I'm big enough to think about it.'

We never did anything about this lot of white people, what they make, or what they try to do. They've done a lot of wrong things.

If a man had a good young woman the boss would take him away, and shoot him out that way in the bush. And when he came back he would say, 'Oh, he ran away'. After he'll have that woman for himself. Nobody ever cared about that. Every house, every station, doesn't matter where, they used to do that. We don't want them to do that again this time.

They used to knock us around. And shift us from place to place. We like to stay in one place, that's how we are talking today.

They reckon the Aboriginals are mad talking this way. But we only just worked this thing out. I went to Halls Creek to talk about this thing, and Margaret River [KLC meetings], before we came to the court in Broome.

I am worried about my land, that they don't take it away. It doesn't matter what they think.

We don't like to have an argument about these sort of things. If they wanted to be friends with the people, they should have come up and talked first. We might say yes or no. But they don't care that Aboriginals have got the country, this station now. They just come over as if they own the country.

They want to just come in, they're worried for money, that's all. It's a silly idea really. People get mad from thinking about what they're going to do to the country. We don't want it any more. They make us upset, make people worry, knock us around. They just don't care.

The final interview that week was with Dicky Skinner, the Community's spokesman and leader in its dealings with the outside world. As a younger man than the Elders who gave him direction – about thirty years old at the time – he felt his responsibilities very keenly; particularly the traditional obligations to safeguard the country, which rested largely on his shoulders as spokesman; and the need to impress upon the young people of Noonkanbah, and upon the outside world, the strength and continuity of his culture.

He began by talking about the skin system, through which all the people of the area belong to one of eight groups, or skins, with a totem, a place within society, and a relationship to all other people of the area. And he explained how this related to the animals, the geography and the Dreaming of the country. Against this background he then spoke of his and his people's values.

I must go through the old people. I think about what my father was telling me before. He was telling me the stories that we call Ngarranggani, which means a long time ago. Stories like the emu who was a man, and the turkey who was a man, and those little birds around here that were men. And the same with the blue tongue lizard, and the blackhead snake; they were men. And they turned into spirits. This was a long time ago. They were travelling around like human beings. Everything can change, but the spirit for the people, it stays that way.

If a woman is trying to have a baby, the spirit will point to a person, maybe the father. The spirit will say to that man, 'I'll be a snake'. Then we might kill a snake, a man or a woman snake. That means a baby will be born. If the snake we kill is a man snake, well that means the baby will be born a little boy. We know that spirit will be born again.

It is the same with trees. You see those trees when they get dry. The tree has a seed, good flowers and seed. The seed gets old and falls down to the ground. Maybe we don't have a good year, and the tree will be dry, and is very old. But when a good year comes, maybe the rains come, and it grows that seed up. That means the seed is the spirit of the tree, and it grows up the same tree again. It keeps on and on like this.

This is the way we look at it on the tribal side. I don't know much on the white man's side, but I know the Aboriginal side, and this is the way we look at it. The old people start teaching younger people. They might send them hunting to kill meat for the old people. They start to teach young fellows, and point to the lessons on the tribal side – what the spirit is, what the spirit does, how the spirit is close to the people.

The person with a spirit, he gives the signal first. Say he might be sent a kangaroo. We know that kangaroo is Jakarra. They are all Jakarra, it doesn't matter where. If the kangaroo was Jakarra, all the kangaroos must be Jakarra, kangaroos and the people [people of the Jakarra skin].

The same if it's a brolga. She's a Nyapurru. It doesn't matter where, they are all Nyapurru, and nobody can change it round. In the white man's law they have their second name, and next minute they change their second name again. Now this name – the skin name – will be forever.

I think this is very important for tribal people. And the same with the land. The land doesn't change every year. Every waterhole doesn't change; they might be dry, but still the billabong lives there. In a big floodwater a sandbank might be washed out, but still the sand will be there. Maybe a tree gets old and dies, but the same tree comes up again from the seed.

This is the way that my father was teaching me and telling me, way back from the old days. He told me, 'When you grow up big you must think about this. You might have a son or daughter; you must tell your son the same way that I'm telling you.'

And every time I tell my sons and daughters. They talk English, they were in at Fitzroy for a couple of years. We put our kids in a government school, and they didn't really pick up their own language. But as soon as we came out to Noonkanbah we got a school here – our independent school – and everybody starts to talk their own language now.

They think now. They see what's happening, and what happened in the past. They read in the book and in the paper that everything changes, but from the tribal side they see that everything's not changed, it's still the same.

I don't think this land is changing every year. I think it stays like this, and the spirit stays that way too – in the tribal way. This is what my father was telling me and I tell my kids.

When the white man came along and said, 'You can send your kids to school, and your kids will read and write', a lot of things went wrong. I know how many people got away from Noonkanbah, they went up to high school. And they don't have respect for their own people. Because they know this and that, and they're educated and read and write, they can do what they like.

The tribal people are just standing up and fighting for their own citizens, for their own way of living, in their own country.

In these words from the people of Noonkanbah can be found the view of past, present and future that motivated them for the next two years. Perhaps the most impressive is the complex religious outlook in which people and spirits, animals and plants, and the country from the depths underground to the anthills above are interwoven and interdependent in a system where the natural changes and cycles are part of an eternal continuity.

The original theft of the land by the pastoralists is seen as being repeated by the mining companies. The contempt of the early settlers is seen to be repeated by the attitude of the Government and the miners. The horror of the first decades of the station era and the humiliation that followed may be repeated in some new form. The people had been scared of the white man, and aware of his power, and at times his brutality. But this time they were to make a stand, not only for themselves as a community, but for their culture and beliefs.

The people of Noonkanbah, and in particular their major spokesman Dicky Skinner, had an ability to talk about large issues simply and powerfully, and to bring a discussion or argument back to their own terms. That is, they talked about their own view of the world.

The position articulated by the Noonkanbah people in November 1978 had four main themes.

They did not trust the mining companies, the police or the white man's law. Through long and hard experience they had learnt that these and other agencies of white culture were there to protect white interests. The interests of Aboriginal people were at best tolerated, or in a situation of conflict, suppressed.

They did not see their ownership of the Noonkanbah Pastoral Lease and their occupation of the station as a gift for which to be grateful, but as a right finally recognised. Accordingly, they believed that they should be able to live in the country in peace and use it as they saw fit.

Their value system, their code of conduct, their approach to the management of their affairs and their dealings with the world were determined by their own Law and culture. They saw this as a continuation of something eternal and unquestioned, and an obligation that they were not free to ignore. Furthermore, they absolutely refused to accept the notion that their values and their Law were in any way inferior to or subject to the white law. White law was regarded as something imposed without consent, and as an ever changing, expedient, 'paper' law. Their own, in contrast, had a basis in religion and the land, and a stability which underlined its worth.

These attitudes to the two laws led them to say that they believed they were not obliged to accept, and in fact were duty bound to oppose, the imposition of activities such as mining exploration, where these infringed upon their own code of Law.

In essence, this is what Noonkanbah was about; a conflict between two laws.

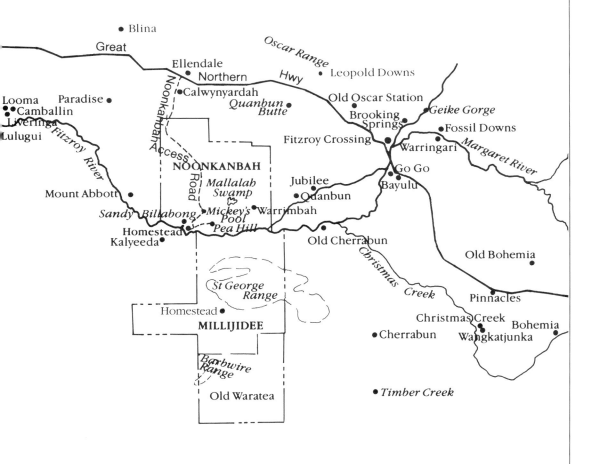

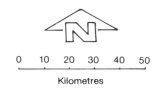

Projection – modified polyconic

NOONKANBAH AND THE FITZROY RIVER AREA

2

A LOT OF MISCHIEF

A long, long time before this country was marked by white people the Aborigines lived on this country. It was a free land. In our way we have looked at this country; and now we talk about it, we have a meeting, and we fight for land. We fight for land because this country was a free land before.

The old people were living in this country. They passed away; old grandfather, mother, and grandmother, gone and finished...All over the place; round the desert, through this river, right around over this land was full with the native people.

George Bell, Noonkanbah, 1979.

The history of Noonkanbah that can be traced through documents and archives begins in 1886, with the arrival of Isadore Emanuel and his sheep. The one hundred years of recorded history that has followed is, of course, but a tiny fraction of this land's human history, which stretches back to either the Dreamtime, or forty thousand odd years, depending on whether one takes an Aboriginal or a European perspective.

The land that was to become known as Noonkanbah is dominated by two features. There is the Fitzroy River, with its headwaters more than a hundred and fifty kilometres to the north-east in the King Leopold Ranges, which grows from a peaceful and plentiful series of billabongs in the dry season, to an awesome torrent spreading out onto the surrounding plains in the wet. A few kilometres to the south, running parallel to the river, is Kalijidi, or the St George Range, as it was named by the newcomers; an ancient, weathered range that has a beauty all its own.

On either side of the river stretch plains that were once reminiscent of the African savannah – tall grasses and scattered trees, supporting abundant wildlife – until the land was denuded beyond recognition by the erosion caused by the hard-hoofed stock of the invaders. South of the river the plains, scattered with soaks, springs and creeks, run up against Kalijidi. On other side of the range the sandhills begin, growing in frequency and size as the pastoral country merges into the Great Sandy Desert. To the north the country becomes poorer as the river plains give way to pindan and wattle scrub.

The people that first occupied these plains, ranges and deserts were of four language groups. The Djaba lived on the river country around today's Noonkanbah homestead. They are nowadays referred to as the 'light' Nyigina, a branch of the proper, or 'heavy' Nyigina, who roamed the western reaches of Noonkanbah, and downstream towards the river mouth. The Bunaba occupied the King Leopold and Oscar Ranges further north, but came as far south as the northern parts of Noonkanbah. And the Walmatjari were a desert people who hunted as far north as Kalijidi and the Fitzroy River.

Today these language groups are often called tribes, but in fact the social organisation was more decentralised than this term implies. The country was held by family clans, each with its own estate, or range, to which it had rights and obligations inherited through the Law. These rights and obligations were bound up with the creation stories of the Dreamtime – or the Ngarranggani, as the Noonkanbah people call it – which were the source of the Law, and the common heritage that bound the neighbouring clans together.

The Law also laid down the rules and conventions that formed the basis of relationships between and within clans. Marriages that tied the clans together were governed by this Law. Ceremonies to celebrate and renew the Law, the land and its creatures, and to mark the rites of passage through life, brought the people together.

And the land and the Law were inextricably tied together. Each was a manifestation of the other. Each was dependent on the other.

The Aboriginal people of today talk of the life of their forebears – only one or two generations ago for most of the adults – as one of bounty and harmony. In George Bell's words, which are echoed by many others, they were a free people in a free land.

Whilst life at a material level was basic, culturally, and in the day-to-day social life, it was extremely rich. No doubt there were times of hardship; and perhaps an objective history, if it were available, would show that life and environment were not as perfectly balanced and unchanging as Aboriginal belief held it to be. There is no doubt, however, that it was a stable society in which people were secure, and by all accounts happy.

If civilisations and cultures are judged by values such as durability, equity and peacefulness that western society holds up as ideals, then Aboriginal Australia is one of the most successful in all history.

Into such a world, with their cultural blinkers firmly in place, arrived Isadore Emanuel and his contemporaries. Their belief in their own destiny and moral superiority, and above all, their commercial motivation, did not allow for any reflection upon the consequences of their arrival for the true owners of the land. The cultural blinkers they wore were never removed, and are still worn by many of their successors.

The establishment of Noonkanbah by the Emanuels was the first permanent white presence in the area, and in 1886 represented the eastern frontier of the gradual thrust of the pastoral invasion pushing up the Fitzroy from the newly established port of Derby at the rivermouth. But they were not the first whites into the area.

Alexander Forrest, younger brother of John who was to become Western Australia's first Premier, had travelled up the Fitzroy on an exploratory expedition in 1879. His glowing and somewhat exaggerated reports had started a feverish land grab by speculators and 'map graziers'; including the English Duke of Manchester, who was the first holder of the Noonkanbah Pastoral Lease, when it was nothing more than lines on a roughly drawn map.

There is strong evidence that Forrest had been preceded by pearlers on blackbirding expeditions. The pearling masters were particularly notorious, even by the standards of those days, for their brutal and cynical exploitation of Aborigines as prostitutes and short-term, low cost divers. Some were known to pitch their captives overboard as soon as they had been worked beyond the point of usefulness, or showed any signs of venereal disease. They would have been a particularly gross introduction to the new and alien culture for the inhabitants of the area.

The Emanuel and Durack families were successful entrepreneurs with pastoral interests in the Goulburn region of New South Wales, and in Queensland. They joined forces to investigate the potential of the Kimberley on hearing of Forrest's reports. Isadore Emanuel's young brother Sydney was a member of a party that made its way in 1882 from the Cambridge Gulf in the East Kimberley, up the Ord River and down the Fitzroy, coming out at Yeeda, the first of the sheep stations established in the region.

Eighteen eighty-two was also the year of the first recorded white death in the Kimberley. In December Tony Cornish, who had come with the party that established Yeeda, was found speared to death. This resulted in the first police patrol to the Kimberley, despatched early the next year from Roebourne in the Pilbara, and the first official act of revenge, when one of the alleged Aboriginal perpetrators was subsequently hanged at Rottnest Island prison.[1]

The Duracks decided to go into cattle in the East Kimberley, starting their empire with stock overlanded from Queensland. The Emanuels, with the shrewd business sense they continued to show for the next one hundred years, plumped for sheep in the West

Kimberley, swayed by the marketing advantages of wool in bales as against live cattle, and the access provided by Derby.

They were by far the best financed and best organised of the new settlers to that date. Certainly they were pioneers in European terms, but they were not operating on a prayer and a wish. They invested heavily in a calculated gamble that was to reward them handsomely.

Isadore Emanuel started at May River near Derby in 1885 with a flock of nearly three thousand sheep shipped from Perth. But later that year the flock encountered disease problems, and a decision was made to seek cleaner country inland. The family patriarch, Solomon, in Goulburn, negotiated the acquisition of Noonkanbah and Lower Liveringa from speculators in Sydney (the Duke of Manchester had already fallen by the wayside), and in August 1886 Isadore and his sheep headed upriver.[2]

The year before, gold had been found at Halls Creek, nearly six hundred kilometres inland from Derby. The port of Wyndham had not yet been established, so the only access for the first two years of the rush was from Derby, up the Fitzroy. With a voracious speed which is almost incomprehensible given the communications and transport systems of the time, the goldseekers flocked in. In the second half of the 1880s thousands made the journey.

There is very little documentation of the effects of this sudden invasion through the river country, apart from odd mentions of 'trouble with the natives', but the evidence there is and the logic of the Australian experience suggest that the Nyigina and other river tribes did not escape lightly.

Apart from the vast central deserts, the Kimberley was the last major region of Australia to be invaded by Europeans, lying as it does at the north-west extremity of a continent that has been dominated by the south-east corner since the arrival of the First Fleet. Sydney had been established for ninety years, and Perth for fifty years by the time Forrest made his survey. By the 1880s Darwin was an established, if small and ramshackle town, and the Northern Territory was dotted with pastoral leases. From Perth the Western Australians had pushed up through the Murchison, the Gascoyne and into the Pilbara. The Kimberley was the last frontier of a young nation with federation on the horizon.

The Colony of Western Australia had not yet achieved self-government. And in the process of the northward pastoral expansion it had acquired a notorious reputation for its treatment of Aboriginal people. In 1886 the Reverend J.B. Gribble had created an Australia-wide furore, with repercussions in England, through his public campaign in Perth and his writings alleging slavery, kidnapping and maltreatment of the worst kind on stations in the Murchison.[3] In the debate which raged, the Colony's dirty linen was aired at a time that was most inconvenient for the local politicians, who were negotiating with the Colonial Office the terms of self-government. Gribble himself was ostracised to the extent that he was effectively hounded out of the Colony.

This well-justified perception of Western Australia led to a unique provision being inserted in the Constitution Act of 1889 that granted self-government to the Colony. Under Section 70 of the Act, all power over Aboriginal affairs was vested in the Aboriginal Protection Board, under the direct control of the Governor as the representative of the British Crown; thus removing the responsibility from the new Government. Also, under the same section, a fixed percentage of the State's revenue was to be set aside to fund the work of the Aboriginal Protection Board. Such provisions had not applied to any of the other colonies in Australia when they were granted self-government. It was a clear statement of concern and rebuke by the British Crown, and a source of indignant outrage and continuing protest by the colonists.

Nevertheless, both pre- and post-self-government the pastoral lobby exerted enormous influence in Perth. This was due to a number of factors, including the perceived need to settle and populate the State, which led a somewhat fragile existence until the Kalgoorlie goldrush of the 1890s, and the public's view of the pastoralists as battling pioneers forever having to contend with hardships and savages. The most important factor, though, was a massive gerrymander that gave the sparsely settled country north of Geraldton a disproportionate representation in the Perth Parliament.

Through the exercise of this political power the pastoralists were the main lobbyists for, and beneficiaries of, a series of oppressive laws relating to Aboriginal affairs, and especially the use of Aboriginal labour. The details of these laws and their frequent amendments are well documented elsewhere.[4] First a contract system, and from 1905 a permit system with harsh penalties that gave the police the role of enforcers, established a regime that resembled the accepted definitions of slavery in all but the auction block and the legal status of persons as property.

The pastoralists made no bones about it; they were dependent on Aboriginal labour, and Aboriginal labour without wages. Beginning with Alexander Forrest in the report of his 1879 expedition onwards, they saw the Aboriginal people of the Kimberley as a potential labour pool to be pacified and brought into service under their self-appointed masters.

There were two sets of contradictions – the need to protect the Colony's tarnished reputation in matters Aboriginal from further damage, versus placating the pastoral lobby and protecting the beleaguered graziers; and the dependence on Aboriginal labour, versus the fear of Aborigines and the basic motive of self-preservation. These two sets of contradictions were to lead to curious tensions and inconsistencies in government policies and public attitudes as Aboriginal resistance to the invasion and appropriation of land mounted in the 1890s.

These problems of the whites were, of course, not appreciated by the Aboriginal population. They were confronted by an alien and powerful culture, the theft of their land and destruction of their lifestyle, and an even more pressing problem of self-preservation.

The strategy of the pastoralists when establishing a new station was, by one means or another, to create a community of Aborigines large enough to supply its labour needs and sufficiently dependent on the station to ensure that the people would remain there. This was achieved in a variety of ways: from negotiation and the provision of commodities such as tea, sugar, flour and tobacco, for which people developed cravings that bordered on addiction; through to wholesale slaughter followed by the importation of Aboriginal labour from elsewhere.

Once this was achieved the technicalities of the labour laws had little relevance in the Kimberley. Rather, 'there was a sort of code of honour among the pastoralists not to interfere with each others' Aborigines, a runaway stockman had usually no choice but to return to his station'.[5]

There is no evidence available as to exactly how Isadore Emanuel established an Aboriginal camp at Noonkanbah. The oral tradition of the people does not specifically deal with the very first years of the station. Certainly the Djaba, and the Nyigina as a whole, would have already suffered severe culture shock, and probably a significant level of disease and death, from the goldseekers on the road to Halls Creek. The impression gained from the few historical sources is that the river people, living on the open plain country, had no refuge from the invaders, and the survivors of the first years of the invasion could not remain independent of the new stations.

For this reason, the river tribes were regarded by the white settlers as 'quiet'. In 1886 the Derby police made their first report of 'native trouble...just beginning to occur here', referring to the Lennard and Lillimooloora Stations, in the foothills of the ranges due east of Derby, well north of the Fitzroy River country.[6] In fact the records show that the main determinant of the level of Aboriginal resistance to the pastoral invasion was geographical; that is, where there were hills and ranges that offered protection and refuge, there was serious resistance. Hence the protracted struggle of the Bunaba led by Jandamarra/Pigeon in the Oscar and Leopold Ranges.

On Noonkanbah the station run for the first thirty odd years was limited to the natural waters of the river frontage and the spring country to the south, so the territory of the Bunaba to the north was not affected. But the St George Ranges, which effectively formed the southern boundary of Noonkanbah, whilst not large enough to sustain a population through a prolonged resistance, did provide a refuge to the bushmen, which proved a significant hindrance to the station.

In 1887 two white men named Isdell and Carey travelled through the St George Range whilst searching for a stock route from the Fitzroy south to the Pilbara. They found the remains of two white prospectors. Carey described how, when they camped at the head of a creek in the range,

> [we] managed to get one old man to appear and talk with us. We told him we were going to camp there for a few days and for all other natives to clear off or we would shoot them. We believed the natives had hostile intentions. We camped there, but the natives stayed in caves. We ordered them to go away or we would kill them. The old man who we had talked to ordered the others to stay. He began throwing rocks at us.

Carey then fired shots over his head, but the old man would not move. So Carey shot him, 'as an example to the others'.[7]

Isdell observed that many of the people spoke a few words of English, and assumed that some must have worked for the pearlers. He said it was not safe to travel in the district of the ranges, and suggested, 'it will require a strong party to go out and shoot down about fifty of them...informing the others of the reason for doing so'. (It is a curious feature of this, and many other similar reports 'from the frontier', that the authors often specify the number of people that need to be killed to administer the appropriate lesson, as with a doctor determining the correct dosage for a prescription.) The Commissioner of Police, on the basis of Isdell's report, ordered the Derby Inspector to 'bring the offenders to justice'. It is assumed he meant the killers of the prospectors, not Carey and Isdell.[8]

Presumably it was incidents such as this, as well as significant losses of stock from spearing, that caused Isadore Emanuel in 1888 to be 'in the forefront of a demand for stronger police protection and sterner measures against Aboriginal resistance'.[9] In response to these demands, in 1889 the West Kimberley police force was expanded from eight to twenty-one men, with three new permanently staffed posts being created, including one at Mount Abbott, which was then on Noonkanbah, but now lies just outside the western boundary, on Paradise Station, an outstation of Liveringa.

With another twenty-seven officers based in the East Kimberley, forty-eight police, out of a total force of two hundred and five men, were now stationed in the Kimberley. The white population of the region was just a few hundred at that time, in fact a half of one percent of the total population of the Colony of Western Australia. This meant that almost a quarter of the police force was devoted to protecting one two hundredth of the people, and in particular, just a handful of pastoralists.

The new police posts had only one real function: to safeguard the pastoralists and their economic interests, by suppressing Aboriginal resistance and enforcing the control of Aboriginal labour. Labour control was enforced through the recapture of workers and families who had left stations, done at the request of station owners and in the course of regular patrols. The tracking and raiding of groups of people living in the bush was usually prompted by reports of stock killing. As will be seen in the oral accounts of the Noonkanbah people, the police work was conducted in a brutal and ruthless manner.

Through the late 1880s and early 1890s the lower Fitzroy region, including Noonkanbah, appears to have been relatively quiet, although there is no doubt that stock killing continued, both for food and as a tactic used to disrupt the stations. Further up the Fitzroy, where the Emanuels had expanded into beef on Go Go Station and the McDonalds had established Fossil Downs Station, and in the country bordering the ranges to the north, it was a different story. The Bunaba were inflicting heavy losses on the northern stations, threatening their existence, and preventing any further expansion of the industry in that direction. There is no doubt that the Kimberley pastoralists felt anything but secure.

Alexander Forrest had become the first parliamentary member for the West Kimberley in 1887; he also had interests in stations in the region. In 1894 he and the Emanuels formed a company which monopolised the shipping and marketing of West Kimberley cattle. In 1893 he supported the member for East Kimberley in calling for the use of Queensland style native troopers against the 'savage and destructive hill tribes', concluding his speech with the rhetorical question, 'I ask whether the life of one European is not worth one thousand natives as far as the settlement of the country is concerned'.[10]

Isadore Emanuel, at an election meeting in Derby for Forrest in July 1894, claimed that the hands of the local police were tied in regard to 'the native question', and called for greater discretionary powers for the local Inspector.[11] In that era the phrase 'discretionary powers' was a euphemism for removing all the normal controls over the police, giving them open slather to use whatever methods they and the pastoralists deemed necessary; in effect, as was to be seen within a year, it meant a licence to kill at will.

The next month a tracker named Longooradale, attached to Constable Pilmer at the newly established Fitzroy Crossing Police Post, absconded from Mount Abbott during a patrol, after unsuccessfully trying to free sixteen chained prisoners, who had presumably been arrested on the stations along the river. Like most other trackers Longooradale would have originally been arrested as a cattle spearer, and then put into service. He made his way from Noonkanbah back to the hills behind Fitzroy Crossing, from where he sent messages threatening to kill Pilmer and burn down the telegraph station.[12]

The tension the settlers felt was obviously rising. The Derby correspondent of the *North West Times* wrote in October, 'It would be a good time for the Western Australian Government to shut its eyes for say three months and let the settlers up here have a little time to teach the nigger the difference between thine and mine...it would only have to be done once and once done, could easily be forgotten about.'[13]

Within days of this call to arms being published police tracker Pigeon shot and killed Constable Richardson at Lillimooloora Police Station and released a group of cattle spearers from the chain. Jandamarra, as he was known to his people, and his band then ambushed three whites attempting to push through the Leopold Range at nearby Windjana Gorge to establish a new station in the heart of Bunaba country. They killed two, and seized weapons and ammunition and a wagonload of supplies.[14]

According to information the police obtained from captured Bunaba women the group's plan was to sweep through the stations along the foothills of the ranges, and on to Derby, driving the white settlers before them. On news of the uprising reaching Derby the local police were immediately granted the discretionary powers they and the settlers had been seeking. Reinforcements were sent from the Pilbara, and 'special constables' were recruited locally. A force of twenty-eight attacked Jandamarra and his people at Windjana Gorge, killing some, and injuring many more. The police believed that they had killed Jandamarra, but in fact he had escaped with most of the key members of his band.

For the next two and a half years, until Jandamarra was finally killed, a siege mentality operated amongst the whites in the region, with all blacks under suspicion, whether station or bush people. Jandamarra was described as the black Ned Kelly; the uprising was seen by the locals and the politicians, press and public of Perth as the most serious yet in Australia, due to the use of arms, and Jandamarra's military style tactics. In their efforts to capture Jandamarra and secure their position of domination, the police and their special constables, and the private 'punitive expeditions', wrought havoc on the Aboriginal people.

After the battle at Windjana Gorge police patrols scoured the ranges from the Barker and Lennard Rivers near Derby, to Geike Gorge, a few kilometres upriver from Fitzroy Crossing, killing many, 'dispersing' others. Some were from Jandamarra's band, but many were not.

In mid-December 1894 Inspector Lawrence of Roebourne, who had been brought in to command the campaign against Jandamarra, left Derby to conduct 'operations' in the Fitzroy River valley with a force of ten men. Included as a special constable was Joe Blythe, who had come in from Brooking Springs Station above Fitzroy Crossing, claiming it was no longer safe there. Before going to Brooking Springs Blythe had been the first manager appointed at Noonkanbah by Isadore Emanuel. In 1893 his son Lindsay had died of thirst on Noonkanbah after getting lost. Blythe had refused to accept that his son could get lost in the bush, and had insisted on a coronial inquiry. The inquiry returned a finding of death by misadventure.

According to Lawrence's reports he travelled straight up the Fitzroy, gathering information from pastoralists about any problems they were experiencing, but taking no action. He found that Pilmer had already taken 'effective' action in clearing the area since Blythe's departure.

Before riding out from Fitzroy Crossing he telegraphed the Commissioner in Perth to say, 'extreme measures have to be taken. Dispersing them is simply useless...they would return and commence depredations that are worse'.

With Blythe providing local knowledge and advice, the party headed up the Margaret River, a tributary of the Fitzroy that formed the boundary between Go Go and Fossil Downs. A day's ride out they came across a group of thirty to forty people in the river bed. Eleven were shot, and surviving women and children ordered to disperse, on pain of shooting. After further skirmishes in this area, the party was split into two, with Lawrence leading one group down the north side of the Fitzroy, and Blythe another group down the south side.

The wet had arrived, making tracking difficult. According to Lawrence, Blythe's group killed two people on Christmas Creek, and another two on Go Go, whilst his party killed one person on Quanbun, and on Noonkanbah twenty people were found hunting on the river, and when the trackers opened fire to disperse them, one was killed.

Lawrence returned to Derby believing Jandamarra to be dead, and that he and his colleagues had done enough to cow the Aboriginal population of the West Kimberley into submission.

But they were to be proved wrong. In mid-1895 the police discovered from a man arrested near Lillimooloora that Jandamarra was still alive, and with two of his lieutenants was headed for the Fitzroy River to try to capture arms and ammunition. Word went out throughout the West Kimberley that settlers should hide all their arms and ammunition.

Then in 1896 there was a shortlived uprising on Noonkanbah. The police received reports in late July 'that the natives on the Fitzroy were giving trouble'[15], and set out to investigate. On the first of August 'a telegram was received from William Cox (the manager at Noonkanbah) that Duncan boundary rider had been speared by natives who were stealing sheep and who had threatened to take Cox's life'.[16]

Alex Duncan had been speared by a group led by Noomoodie, or Albert, a man who had already served time for killing stock, and was now back in his country, using the St George Range as his stronghold.

By the time the police party reached Liveringa on the fifth of August, 'the country for miles around had been fired by runaway station natives who had stirred up the bush natives to join them. The fire had been started on the Fitzroy, and on the 5th instant was close to Derby...the natives had cleared out from several stations taking sheep.'[17]

The police came upon the tracks of the group, and followed them for forty kilometres, but were only able to arrest one, before the rest escaped into the ranges, beyond the reach of the patrol's horses.

The next report from Sub Inspector Ord in charge of the police patrol stated:

> Myself, Constables Phillips and Pilmer, six trackers and a Volunteer met 'Alberts' gang on the 11th instant on the Fitzroy, when they attempted to surround us in the river bed. Shot 3 dead rest escaped in cane break, followed them to almost inaccessable stronghold in St George Range; scaled it at night, and at dawn on the 14th instant surprised camp, natives attempted resistance but we had gained summit; dispersed mob killing six and wounding two. Mob is completely broken and scattered...Raiding and burning of paddocks has ceased anticipate no further trouble.[18]

As a result of this uprising, and the continued presence of Jandamarra, the police patrols remained out in full force. Noomoodie was captured later that year, and sentenced to ten years' imprisonment at Rottnest Island. Jandamarra, after leading the police a merry dance, during which he stole a revolver from Lillimooloora Police Station, returned again and stole stores, led an attack on Oscar Range Station in which a white stockman was shot and killed, and made some miraculous escapes from the posses pursuing him, was finally killed and beheaded at Tunnel Creek in March 1897.

The Elders who led the Noonkanbah people through the trials of 1979 and 1980 are only one generation removed from the 1890s, the era of Jandamarra, Noomoodie and the massive police response. Most of their parents would have been young adults at the time. And of course these events live in the oral tradition of the people.

The two versions of Noonkanbah's history – the oral account of the people, and the records from government archives – do not always make a neat fit. There are different memories, different interpretations, and different emphases, which is hardly surprising. And perhaps both sides, in the first tellings of stories and the writing of reports, have glossed the truth on occasions for reasons which we can only guess at now.

One interesting aspect is that Aboriginal accounts tend to play down the resistance that obviously did take place. The Aboriginal orthodoxy runs along the lines of, 'the white man came in and took the country, and we couldn't or didn't fight back'.

The oral tradition tells of a series of massacres all along the Fitzroy and Margaret Rivers, and in the St George Range, carried out by parties led by Constable Pilmer. Pilmer was based at Fitzroy Crossing from 1894. He was definitely involved in patrols that killed numbers of Aboriginal people. But his name has assumed almost legendary status amongst Aboriginal people, and it seems likely that virtually all killings by police are now attributed to him.

One of the main keepers of this oral tradition at Noonkanbah was Ginger Nganawilla. He was never a public spokesman for the Community, but he had been one of their key leaders for many years. He was a staunch traditionalist, with a keen sense of historical perspective. Yet perhaps more than any of the other leaders at Noonkanbah, he combined this with a clear vision of the direction he wanted the Community to take. To this end, he had channelled much of his energy into his role as founding Chairman of the board that controlled the Community school.

To Nganawilla, an understanding of the Community's past was essential to understanding its present position. When I first visited the Community in 1978, he spent the better part of two days talking about this past. He was extremely earnest, mostly looking into the middle distance as he talked, occasionally emphasising a point by chopping one hand into the palm of the other. Only at the grimmest points in his stories would he allow a small exclamation, or a rueful laugh, as if deflecting an internal grimace.

This is one of his stories. Similar versions are told by many Aboriginal people in the Fitzroy area.

> Not too long ago a white man had his son working on a dam on Quanbun Station. He had a bullock team, and all the working bullocks got away. He chased them from Quanbun right out bush. There were no fences. They didn't have fences on Noonkanbah or Quanbun then.
>
> He was a young bloke. He was chasing those bullocks from early morning. And he had no water. It was hot weather time, hot, and he couldn't get a drink. There was one waterhole there, Mallalah, a big billabong. But he was coming across, and he missed it.
>
> Well, he stopped, took the saddle off the horse, put him in the shade and hobbled him. He got a paper and pencil from his pocket, and he wrote, 'I'm finished'. He broke a stick and split it, and he put that paper under a tree. He went in the shade, went to sleep, and...finish. One old Aboriginal man named Sam chased him from his tracks. He chased him all the way along, he saw where he missed that Mallalah and cut across. Then he found him, dead.
>
> He got off his horse and picked up that paper, and took it back to Quanbun. Old man Rose was there, Geoff Rose. [The owner of Quanbun.] Sam didn't give the father that letter, he gave it to old Geoff Rose, and he read it. Before Rose showed that letter to the father he hid his rifle and knife, and then showed him.
>
> His father was jumping around, looking for revolver, rifle, knife – nothing. He showed the mother that letter. She started crying. All the Aboriginal women gave her a hand, they all cried.
>
> Next morning they got a sulky and put it in the yard. They made a long box very quickly and chucked it in under the sulky. They went out, his father, Mr Rose, and Sam, to where he was near Warrimbah. Sam showed them. They picked him up and put him in that box, and took him back to Quanbun. Next morning they took him to Fitzroy Crossing. They rang up from there for a plane. They tied him up underneath that plane with a big belt, that dead man. And they took him back to his place where he was born.
>
> That man was thinking about what he was going to do for his son. He was a Lawman, that father. He knew about the Law belonging to Aboriginal people. He thought we must have sung his son. He thought, 'This is what I have to do. I can start off Pilmer.'

Ginger Nganawilla.

Pilmer started off from that Liveringa Police Station. And he had a camp on Paradise, just the other side of the Noonkanbah boundary. [The Mount Abbott Police Post.] Pilmer put a house there, and a house at the Liveringa Police Station. Every loading train [the old donkey wagons] dumped all the cartridges [ammunition] there.

A big mob of people were along the river. A big mob. Not many were on the job, nobody was living here [at Noonkanbah], working.

Pilmer started shooting from somewhere near Yeeda Station, right through. That man who lost his son, and thought the people had sung him, made him shoot all those people.

He very near shot my father. He chained him, and took him to Quanbun. And the Quanbun boss, Mr Rose, said, 'That's my boy, I sent him on holiday not long ago'. They said, 'That's your boy?' 'Yes.' 'All right.' They gave Rose the key and took him out of the chains. He very near got shot, my father.

He was shooting all along this river. We can show you anytime, you know. Bones laying just like rubbish. Right along. When he got short of cartridges he got them from this Paradise place. And from there he came shooting.

Pilmer would go one side of the river, and another policeman would go the other side. If the boys jumped over from the other side of the river, they got shot here. Two policemen, and all the Sunday Island police boys, not from this country. Right along, right along the Fitzroy. That's no good, hey. Just like rubbish.

If Pilmer came out along a big mob of people, he'd just shoot, straight in. He shot more people than we've got living here [at Noonkanbah]. There were only a few people working at the station, but a big mob were living on the river.

They came through shooting. Then they camped half way, and started again in the morning. Camp again, all the way along. From here to Jubilee, from there to Fitzroy, from Fitzroy to Fossil Downs. After that they went back shooting in the St George Range. Killed the whole lot. Nothing left.

That's what Pilmer did in the old days.

It seems likely that the Aboriginal version of the massacres along the Fitzroy is a combined recollection of the patrols of Lawrence and Blythe in 1894/95, and Ord in 1896. The detail is sufficiently similar, with the two parties on either side of the river, the locations extending as far as Fossil Downs, where Lawrence killed members of the group he found in the bed of the Margaret River, and Nganawilla describing them returning later to the St George Range, which would parallel Ord's hunt for Noomoodie.

Presumably Lindsay Blythe, son of Joe, has become the son of a worker on Quanbun; the character of Blythe, who refused to believe that his son could have got lost and died of thirst, and who was more closely identified with the police patrols than any other private citizen, matches that of the father in the oral account, obsessed by the death of his son.

The most notable discrepancy in the two versions is in the number of people killed. Lawrence's and Ord's reports list a total of twenty-six dead, whereas Nganawilla spoke of well over a hundred, perhaps even two hundred. But it is worth bearing in mind the work of Queensland historian Professor Henry Reynolds, and others, where detailed investigations of specific historical episodes with similar discrepancies between the two sides of the story have shown that the true numbers of deaths are often much nearer to the Aboriginal accounts than the official records.[19]

In March 1895, while Jandamarra was still believed dead, the police stationed at Lillimooloora had been reprimanded by the Commissioner for 'unjustifiably' killing four people in a raid[20], indicating that whilst they believed the situation was under control the authorities were trying to rein in some of the excesses of the force. It is not inconceivable, for instance, that Lawrence gave a less than full description of the efforts of his Special Constable Blythe.

A few years of relative calm for the pastoralists followed the massive police operations of 1894 to 1897. It is doubtful that the Aboriginal people saw any more real hope of regaining control of their country. But in the 1906 report of the Aborigines Department it is clear that they had not yet been completely subjugated:

> Mr Annear [the Fitzroy Crossing telegraphist, and local agent of the Department] reports an alarming increase [in cattle killing] since the commencement of leniency to natives in the Derby Court, and also that the manner of the natives towards the whites have changed, he says: –
> > It is admitted by all that the natives have the upper-hand of the police in the district; that the police cannot cope with the trouble.
> There seems to be an opinion that 'it will take years to again get the natives under.' He goes on to say: –
> > ...[after describing the loss of thousands of cattle driven off their grazing grounds on Fossil Downs]...and since then there are other reports of killing close here, and in other directions...I have also heard of cases of robbing camps, and the blacks tell the whites in very rough language, 'I don't care for you or the police.' Such remarks are bad. There is no doubt about it the blacks are becoming saucy; they are also becoming useless. They will seldom earn their living by work, but when hungry will ask for work, get clothing, blankets, etc., and in a few days clear out with the lot. Many fear there will be serious trouble later on.[21]

Annear's comments regarding the Aboriginal attitude to employment on the stations show that the people used their own tactics against the pastoralists' strategy of making them dependent. Many would work only as long as it suited them, or long enough to obtain commodities they needed or wanted. Reports of a patrol from Halls Creek, down the Margaret and Fitzroy Rivers to Derby by one of the Department's travelling inspectors in 1910 show that he encountered nearly as many people living in the bush as were living at the stations.[22]

Annear's report makes clear that this situation did not meet with the approval of the pastoralists and police, but that they just did not have the manpower and resources to enforce the level of control they desired. It seems clear that much of the stock killing that continued at least until the late 1920s in the Fitzroy Crossing district was done by people who moved in and out of the stations, as well as by the bushmen who had not yet come, or been forced in.

Ginger Nganawilla had first hand experience of the way such people were treated when they were caught, in an incident that must have taken place sometime in the 1920s.

> My father, he was working on Quanbun Station. He went away from the station a little bit, he got sick and tired of work and he went away. Old man Rose [the owner of Quanbun] put him in to the police. They chased him along and found him half way to Cherrabun, and grabbed him there.
> Right; tie him up. They tied up his legs, and tied up his two hands, to a tree. They got a big lump of stone, and hit him all round. All around

the face, all around the ribs, low on the back. They made him proper crippled, he couldn't walk around.

I ran, crying. The police grabbed me by the neck and took hold of me right there, crying for my father.

After that, my mother. He got her on the ground, and tied her up with her hands behind her back. He put his hand on her neck, and put his foot on her; stopped her crying. She was worried for her husband. He didn't like her crying, and stopped her from crying.

They crippled him properly, my father. He was cut all round. They hit him with a stick after. They just put him on a horse, and took him up and put him on the station.

I was a big boy, good middle size, when the policeman did that to my father. I couldn't do anything, because I was frightened. I'm black colour; I'm frightened of the white, that he wanted to try to kill my father or mother.

After telling that story, he went from the personal, to the general experience:

Sometimes the police would come along as soon as it was daylight. Sometimes he would come in on a galloping horse – the men would jump up from sleep. Sometimes they sneaked up softly, had a look, tied a man up while he slept. He wouldn't feel it. Put the handcuffs on everyone. Then fire a shot. Everybody got up – in the chain. Too late.

Then he'd go down the house and tell the boss. The boss comes down. He tells one of the police boys to get a stick. He didn't take the bark off. Gave them a good hiding, leave them half dead.

We were frightened. The old people never touched gudia. But the gudia didn't like them. Gudia didn't like my skin. He said it's rubbish. That's the way they were doing before. The gudia were doing a lot of mischief to blackfellows; policemen, manager gudias, and working gudias.

It took up until about 1930, nearly fifty years after the first stations were established, for the settlers to finally subdue the river tribes whose country they had usurped; to bring an end to cattle spearing, and force everyone into permanent residence on the station camps.

Of this fifty year period, the first fifteen had been marked by widespread slaughter, and a regime of terror continued well after this, as Nganawilla's experience testifies. There were also annual epidemics of the flu and worse diseases that took their toll. Whole tribes were wiped out, and others brought to the edge of extinction, including the Djaba of Noonkanbah, whose few remaining members died in a flu epidemic on Quanbun during the Second World War.[23] The survivors inherited a legacy of fear that took decades to come to terms with, and bitter memories that are still alive.

The struggle for control of the country did not unduly affect the economic side of the Emanuels' operation at Noonkanbah. The sheep thrived on the rich river country, numbers increasing at a rapid rate. The family's solid finances enabled them to weather a decline in wool prices in the late 1880s and 1890s that sent many of their neighbours bankrupt. Noonkanbah and its western neighbour, Upper Liveringa, became famous as the largest sheep properties in Australia, shearing eighty-five thousand, and one hundred and three thousand sheep respectively in the 1903 season.

One result of this huge flock, all concentrated on the river frontage, was the destruction of the river ecology in less than twenty years. The first survey of the area by the State's

Early years. Top: Noonkanbah Station, 1915. Bottom: Aboriginal prisoners, 1894. *(Battye Library 67243P, 67238P, 5225P)*

Agriculture Department in 1905 reported that 'the effect [of erosion] was so disastrous that all pastures along the [Fitzroy] river frontages had completely disappeared for the time being'.[24]

But this did not affect the rise in the Emanuels' fortunes. As well as the partnership with the Forrests and the expansion into cattle at Go Go Station, which was later subdivided into three properties, they bought and sold properties in the East Kimberley, and the giant Victoria River Downs Station in the Northern Territory. At one stage, 'Either singly or in partnership the Emanuel brothers controlled more than 20,000 square miles in the Kimberleys and the adjacent part of the Northern Territory. It was a considerable achievement in twenty years, and a long way from Goulburn.'[25] The 'free land' the people of Noonkanbah had known had provided the foundation of a family empire and fortune for the Emanuels.

Isadore Emanuel spent less and less time in the Kimberley, acquiring property in Perth, and the surrounding countryside, supervising his spreading business interests, and becoming a prominent figure in Perth society, even representing Western Australia at the Paris International Exhibition of 1900.

During the 1890s and 1900s Forrest, Emanuel & Co. were involved in a long running controversy in which they were accused of being one of the main parties in the 'meat ring', which allegedly kept the price of meat in Perth and on the goldfields artificially high. Isadore vehemently denied this before a Royal Commission in 1908, but by this time he was looking to greener pastures. In 1909 the sale of Victoria River Downs brought a handsome profit. In 1910 and 1911 State and Federal Labor Governments were elected. Isadore had contributed to a fighting fund to defeat Labor, which was hardly surprising as they were vocal critics of the 'meat ring' and advocated limiting the size of pastoral holdings.

In 1912 Isadore moved permanently to London. But he was still actively involved, via the telegraph, in the management of his Australian interests, including the Kimberley stations. The 1910s were not good years for the sheep industry, the effects of long-term overgrazing were taking their toll at Noonkanbah. In 1922 the station was sold to the Perth firm of Mawley and Sims.

During the 1920s Noonkanbah was the first station in the West Kimberley to sink bores, opening up the country back from the river, and enabling the sheep numbers to climb back towards the levels of the early years of the century. From the owners' point of view the period from the 1920s to the mid-1960s was a time of steady and secure income, from a well-established property, with the 1940s, and especially the 1950s, being boom years, as they were for sheep farmers all around the country.

The major development in the Aboriginal community at Noonkanbah during this period of prosperity for the station was the continuing influx of desert people.

The Walmatjari were a desert tribe. Before the arrival of the Europeans the St George Range was the northern boundary of their territory, though they would move further north in dry times, and for ceremonial business. The northern clans would have come into conflict with the settlers very early on. It is quite likely that Noomoodie was a Walmatjari man. But the Walmatjari from further south, and their neighbours, came into Noonkanbah and the other stations on the desert fringe over a long period. The biggest influx was in the 1930s, but the Roses on Liveringa were still 'recruiting desert natives from the West of the Fitzroy River' in 1946.[26] And the Noonkanbah manager spoke of two people 'picked up out back by a police patrol' in 1953.[27]

The causes of the gradual movement of people in from the desert are not entirely clear. The truth probably lies in a combination of the various theories advanced. It is believed that there was a prolonged dry cycle in the desert regions in the first half of the century,[28] which would have forced people towards the periphery seeking water. Encounters with explorers, and drovers on the Canning Stock Route, and rumours of the strange happenings in the north, from the wonders of the white man's commodities to the plentiful supply of sheep and cattle, must have caused enormous curiosity, as well as apprehension. But strongest of all must have been the gradual pull of each group's desire for news of and contact with relatives in the last group that had been drawn in.

It must also be realised that it was not a matter of just walking in from the desert to live in a station camp. For most it was a step-by-step movement, in which they gradually came closer in, establishing contact with relatives in the station camps while still living in the bush. For some the final step into the station was voluntary, others were found on the station runs by police or station workers and brought in, and still others never

Mick Nicki.

made it, the victims of raids and patrols seeking stock killers.

Mick Nicki, still living at Noonkanbah, told the story of his introduction to the new world on arrival from the desert.

> A big mob of us were coming along, and we came out at Timber Creek – that's the gudia name, Timber Creek. [Near the southern boundary of Cherrabun Station, south-east of Noonkanbah.] A good place that one, good country. We killed three bullocks, speared them.
>
> That gudia was coming along, white man, cheeky feller. He found our tracks. 'Oh Christ, big mob here.'
>
> We were following the creek, chasing cattle, oh, good fresh ones. We all came along, and then made a camp.
>
> Two blokes came along, found us. 'Oh Christ, big mob of people here.' They went back and told that gudia.
>
> The next night, a long way before daylight they came. One station gudia, mob of police boys, and Christmas Creek boys.
>
> Finish.
>
> I got out, I was a little one. My old man took me away, we ran up a hill. Oh, we heard shots. Bang, bang. They started shooting all the people.
>
> With the little kids they only used a stick. Kill them, hit them on the head.
>
> I was a young feller then. I was hiding in the hills. We looked that way. Oh Christ, people lying down finished, from shooting.
>
> One old man got up, he was running. Bang. He fell down before he was shot. They only shot a stone, and thought, 'I got that one'.
>
> Aaaahhh, finish.
>
> They used kerosene, burned them up. Big mob of people. Too much, too much, too much. Like that camp there and this camp here. [Pointing to two camps at Noonkanbah containing fifty to sixty people.] Too much.
>
> That Timber Creek is on Cherrabun. Right, we went bush, finish, no come back. We ran round here, Kalijidi [St George Range]. No flour; only kirlilpaja – that's our tucker – and that marlpaja, and kirriri and parta and karnakun and kumupaja and wirrpun. We were living on this tucker. And hill kangaroo, goanna, pussycat, that's all.
>
> They used only the rifle this side. [Meaning the Fitzroy Crossing region, and the stations to the south.] That side [south-east towards the desert and the Canning Stock Route, where many more Walmatjari people came in] they used poison. On the stock route they used poison. They put poison in the meat.
>
> Poor fellers, we fell down all round. Little ones. Little kids say give me, give me meat. Fall down right there. No good. Too much.
>
> Near Billiluna one gudia handed poison meat to a man and wife and a little kid, only two or three. He watched them die straightaway.
>
> They used poison that side. This side shot.

Mick Nicki's estimated date of birth in Native Welfare records in 1925. He is definitely younger than Ginger Nganawilla, who was born on Noonkanbah Station in 1916. The earliest possible date for the Timber Creek massacre that he escaped would be about 1923, but it is likely to have been nearer to, or even after, 1930.

The Forrest River massacre of 1926 in the north-east Kimberley caused a public outcry.* The nation was shocked by the revelations, thinking it had left that era behind. But it is clear from the oral accounts that massacres continued at least into the 1920s on the stations of the desert fringe south of Fitzroy Crossing, particularly Cherrabun, Christmas Creek and Bohemia Downs. It seems that they were mainly perpetrated by station staff rather than the police, principally in revenge for stock killings by the people moving in from the desert.

Ginger Nganawilla provided corroboration of this, with stories from his mother's country on Christmas Creek.

> A big mob of people were on Quanbun Station one time. They stole some flour and sugar and tea from the station, and took it down to Quanbun Hill. The same man, Pilmer, went after all that mob. Shot the whole lot. We can show you the bones there, all stacked up. Kids and all, boys. The station manager made him shoot those boys. This is the way they did it before, in the early days.
>
> And on Christmas Creek it was the same. And on that place, Bohemia Downs. There's a hill halfway between Christmas Creek and Bohemia Downs. One day the bush boys killed a bullock. A big mob of bush boys were there. When the manager came mustering around he saw the bones of the bullock and followed the tracks. He followed them up, just rounded them up, and shot them like kangaroos.
>
> The same fellow chained them up, tied them up to a tree, and started a fire when the cartridges were finished. They took kerosene in a backpack and chained the people up. When they got to the camp they started fires [piled wood] all around a tree. A boy took them there inside and tied them up. They got the kerosene and chucked it all around, chucked it on the fire [on the wood piles], chucked it on the boys too. Right, get a match... [He lit a match, threw it to the ground, raised his eyebrows, and shrugged.]
>
> A station manager did this, after Pilmer, old Bert Smith on Christmas Creek Station. That's bad, hey. I was here then, at Noonkanbah, about that high. [He placed his hand about four feet from the ground, suggesting that he was about ten years old, dating the incident around 1925.] They told me about this story. Everyone knows; Nipper knows, and Friday. They burnt them all, and they took all the women to the station, no boys. When the boys were finished they threw water everywhere, and took the chains off.
>
> Bert Smith and another man from Bohemia Downs, when they started mustering, they used to meet up together. They would see cattle bones, follow the tracks and chase them round till they came out on the place where those boys were living, eating bullocks. Round them up...no one got away. That's the way they were doing it.

It seems that the massacre stories in which burning of the bodies feature, as opposed to those where the bones were left where they can still be seen, were the more recent ones, and they occurred in the southern country on the desert fringe. This suggests that the stations were perhaps acting without the official sanction of the earlier massacres, and were trying to destroy the evidence of their deeds.

Mick Nicki also told the story of his early years, following the Timber Creek massacre. He and the people he had joined up with in the St George Range, like the river people

---

* Following the spearing of a white man on a station adjoining the Forrest River Reserve in 1926, a party of police and private citizens launched an expedition that resulted in the massacre of about thirty Aboriginal people. Reverend Gribble of the Forrest River Mission led a campaign to investigate the incident that resulted in a Royal Commission of inquiry the next year; but no one was charged.

before them, were far from willing to settle down on the stations. For a number of years they kept returning to the hills.

We were knocking those sheep. Oh, too much, sheep, sheep, sheep. We went one way, 'Oh no, we'll go that way'. Too much sheep, they were strung up along the fence.

We took only the best kind. Just kill them, kill them. Just cut their guts; 'Any fat?' 'Nothing, little bit fat.' 'Oh, leave him.'

Well we went that way and grabbed another lot. Right, we just split their guts. 'Oh Christ, he's no good.' All along.

When we saw a fat one, all right, take him. That's the way we did it, killed them all along, all along the fence. No brains, sheep. You know lambs, just put them in our [hair] belt, little feller.

We had dinner camp in the creek. Cooked them right there. In the afternoon we went to the hills – a big place there, home. Oh, great tucker that one, sheep.

A gudia came along, a contractor bloke. He found all the tracks. 'Oh, what are they doing here, what's this lot? Oh Christ, big mob here. What happened to these sheep?'

They found two or three. 'Oh Christ, more that way yet.' Three or four, oh, all along. Too much. He went, that gudia.

He came along here [to Noonkanbah homestead]. He rang up from here for the police. We were sitting down there eating sheep.

That policeman got a plane and landed here. He got horses here. He came along that policeman, and made a camp at a big rockhole. Plenty fellers, they got some from here, another lot. He came to our camp then, a long way before daylight.

All right, we were getting up. 'What's this one, got a makarti [hat]? What's this one?' We looked that way. 'Oh Christ, another one there got a makarti.' We looked another way. 'Oh Christ, another one.' All around, they were there.

All the policemen got up, and ran towards us. We sat down. Only one old man went in a hole, where there was a crack in the stone. He went in there and got that grass, and put it over his head.

We went then. He was a proper cheeky feller that gudia. When we walked slow he hit us with a stick. Chain on the neck.

We got in here to the old contractor's camp, next to the river. 'Who's the boss? Who made you fellers go those sheep? This old man here?' It was old man Jumbo. 'All right, come on, I want you.'

Big, big feller [as in important], old, old feller; finish. They took him away. I stayed here [presumably because he was still a child]. The other lot went that way, to Broome or somewhere, to gaol.

They came back after that. They walked, starting from Broome. No motorcar, they walked right through to here. We went back to the hills then.

We only got bullocks, speared bullocks. We went the other way, not on this Noonkanbah side. [To the Cherrabun end of the ranges.] They grabbed us there, at a big hill.

We were eating a kidney, the last kidney from a bullock, when a policeman came along. 'What's this, what's this? No bullock? Oh good. Good show boys.'

He rounded us up and put the chain on. We came back this way. We sat down here, tied up in this horse stable.

They rang up for a motorcar, but no motorcar. They walked. They all went, and they got a motorcar at Jubilee. I stopped here. They all went straightaway to gaol in Broome.

Later, when I was a man, I took the chain. I had one bloke with me; one chain, we walked away together. From Jubilee all along the river, through here to Noonkanbah.

An old man sang out right here to we two. He took the chain off us. We all went across the river, and were sitting down there.

That policeman came along here to the station. 'Any bush blokes there?' 'Yeah, that way.' 'Good, I want that lot.'

He chased us out there. He tied us up. Three old men, and us two young fellers. From there, we went right through to Fitzroy.

Lot of times the policeman was chasing us mob.

This period of Nicki's life, with spells in the bush between arrests, and enforced stays at Noonkanbah waiting for his relatives to return from gaol, would have been during the 1930s, possibly into the 1940s. Neck chains were used on Aboriginal prisoners in the Kimberleys as late as 1956.[29]

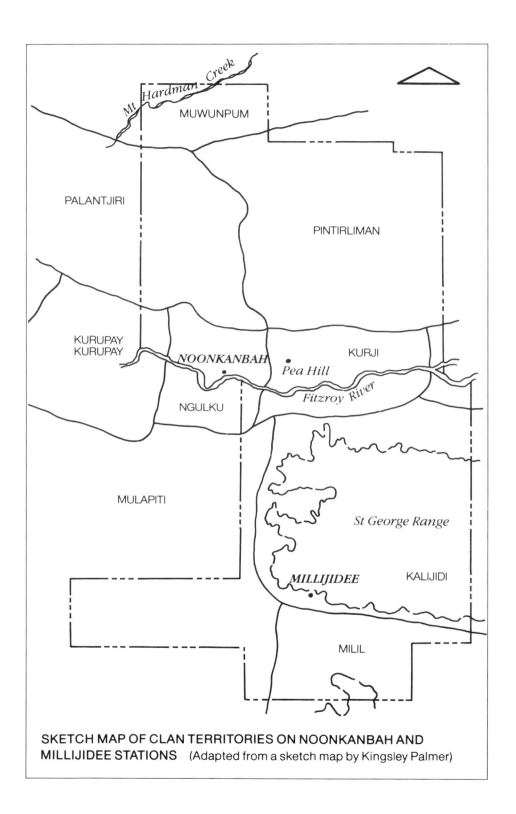

SKETCH MAP OF CLAN TERRITORIES ON NOONKANBAH AND MILLIJIDEE STATIONS (Adapted from a sketch map by Kingsley Palmer)

3

GIVE NO CHEEK

The people that came behind those first gudia don't know...They think the gudia was doing good in the early days. But they were doing very bad.

Ginger Nganawilla, Noonkanbah, November 1978.

The river tribes and the desert people had notably different experiences in their respective collisions with white power, though for both groups it was a time of crisis and tragedy. The survivors of the river tribes living in the station camps in the 1930s could not be described as a whole people: in addition to the physical losses, their culture and their Law had not been immune from the overall effects of the invasion. The desert people came into country that was not theirs in either white or Aboriginal terms. But they brought a gift to the river people: a Law that was still fresh, strong, and whole.

Erich Kolig, an anthropologist who worked with the Noonkanbah people in the 1970s, described the process this way:

> The fragments of traditional [river] culture were revived through the infusion of the vitality of belief and lore of the Desert people...For much of the indigenous river culture any revival came largely too late, as this culture had been irretrievably lost. But as wave after wave of Desert Aborigines arrived, with their culture still untouched by disintegrative processes of westernisation, the needed boost was provided for Aboriginal culture per se to survive...The revivifying impact of Desert Aborigines holds distinctly true for Noonkanbah. Here the vitality of the southerners not only stopped the agonising decline of river culture, but by a happy marriage of the two sides shaped the station into a religious centre and its Aboriginal community into a mainstay of traditional culture in the area.[1]

Thus the people who made it in from the desert replenished the Noonkanbah Community not only numerically, but spiritually. It is not as if the two groups were complete strangers, nor was it a matter of a 'desert takeover'. The Walmatjari and the Nyigina were neighbours in pre-European times, and would have had much in common, in terms of the creation stories and the practice of the Law.

The intimate details of the 'happy marriage', in which the complexities of land inheritance, the combination of the two peoples and their Laws, and the variations of the resultant mix from the original state of affairs can be analysed and discussed, are the stuff of anthropological dissertations. Some of these points will be examined later in relation to the specific issues raised by the conflict with the miners. However, in broad terms, the Nyigina and the Djaba, until the last of them passed away at Quanbun Station in the 1940s, contributed the intimate knowledge of country, sites and local creation stories which forms the bedrock of the Law, and this was enhanced by the ritual and ceremonial knowledge and prestige brought by the Walmatjari.

As they intermarried, and ultimately merged into 'the Noonkanbah mob', they were able to retain and weld together these two strains, and become a centre of religious knowledge and power.

George Bell of Noonkanbah described it this way:

> Noonkanbah, he's a big country, big place. The Law-ground. From Christmas Creek, Cherrabun, Leopold – all round these stations – Fossil Downs, Brooking Springs; we used to go for corroboree to Noonkanbah. We used to have a big dance. We used to take the kids, take them in the Law at Noonkanbah. We used to walk miles when I was a young man. My father used to take me down there.[2]

But its role as a Law centre was by no means limited to the initiation ceremonies described by Bell. Kolig explains its significance in a larger network:

> The highly religious character of the Noonkanbah people is beyond doubt. Fairly early, it seems, the matured know-how of the river people and continuing Desert vitality combined to produce a highly respected religiosity, respected by Aborigines throughout the southern Kimberleys. There are only a few places which can match the reputation of the Noonkanbah community as a religious centre, a place with a 'yini bulga' [big name], its significance carefully nursed over many years ...Noonkanbah became an important link in the religious exchange network that spans the entire Southern Kimberleys, from the coast of the Eighty Mile Beach to the border of the Northern Territory and beyond.[3]

It was this recourse to Law, culture and spirituality that provided the positive balance to the bleak years of the entrenched white regime at Noonkanbah. And it was the strength found in this refuge which gave them the determination in later years, first to fight for the return of their country, and then to fight to protect it from further damage.

Throughout this period of the influx of desert people, and the building of Noonkanbah as a Law and cultural centre, the daily grind of life as station workers continued.

Noonkanbah was typical of the large, big name, big money stations that dominated the Western Australian pastoral industry. It was to a very large extent a self-contained community, with a large vegetable garden and meat killed from station stock regularly. Supplies and equipment that were needed from outside were brought in by wagons that could carry ten-tonne loads hauled by teams of forty and more donkeys. Until they were eventually replaced by trucks these donkey wagons would also take out the bales of wool, stacked seven and eight high, to Derby for shipping.

Of course, the indispensable foundation on which this busy and profitable community was built was the unpaid Aboriginal labour. The power of the Australian Workers Union, which had an unabashed policy of protecting its white members from Aboriginal competition, ensured that the shearing was done by teams of white workers who would come up for the season, but apart from this there was very little white labour. The Aboriginal people worked as shepherds, stockmen, shed hands, drovers, horsebreakers, gardeners, domestics, nannies, butchers, fencers, carpenters and builders, and whatever else was demanded by the manager.

The lifestyle that developed for the Community around their labour for the station was not totally alien, nor all unremitting hardship. The work kept them moving around the station run, in touch with the country, the sites and the Dreaming. Until the mid-

Joe Wunmah.

1950s the Community was relatively stable and secure, with a strong sense of identity and cohesion; though this security could be, and was at times, shattered for individuals or the Community as a whole by arbitrary management actions. And of course, each wet season when the station work wound down there was the great cycle of ceremonial and religious activity: a time of renewal and independence, usually involving friends and relations from all the surrounding stations.

Also the people took real pride in much of their work on the station, and in their skills. The old people of today will describe just how they laboured to build a post and rail fence or yard, to break a horse, to muster a mob of sheep, and compare this scornfully to the slipshod, time and labour-saving methods used on stations today. And they will speak with respect, and occasionally affection, of individual whites who worked with them on a friendly basis, or taught them particular skills well.

At its best it could be said that a station culture developed which retained a great deal of the traditional culture and values, and adapted to the demands and routines of the pastoral regime. The best of the white managers and workers had some sort of feel for this positive side, and a respect for the input the people made to the station; the two longest reigning managers at Noonkanbah, Bill Henwood, from 1922 to 1950, and Duncan Beaton, from 1950 to 1969, particularly the former, seem to have been of this type, compared to some of the hard-nosed bosses on other stations. Certainly the Noonkanbah people, while full of bitter memories, and resentful of their exploitation over the years, compare their own lot relatively favourably to that of many other station communities.

But for any good that can be found, there is tragedy, misery and oppression aplenty to counterbalance it. The most determined attempts to put a positive light on the station experience come up against the hard facts of the lives of the old people at Noonkanbah. Perhaps this is best summed up by one of these old people, Joe Wunmah, who told of how he was 'given a good hiding' by his parents, so that 'when gudia tell me to do rough work, give no cheek, do it'.

Acceptance of the white man's terms, at least in external appearances, was the price of survival. This business of 'give no cheek', and jumping to do the white man's bidding, whatever it was, goes some way to explaining how many of the station managers were able to convince themselves that the people were happy with their lot. Perhaps it also gives a clue to the gradual suppression of the stories of resistance in the Aboriginal oral tradition, in all but the most dramatic instances, such as Jandamarra.

The American slaves created a rich and vibrant sub-culture in their captivity; but these days no one suggests that they enjoyed the captivity, or that it was beneficial to them, as some still try to say of Aboriginal people on the great pastoral leases.

The basic demand made of the Community was the supply of labour. In addition to this, most of the white men who worked on the station, and many of those who passed through, expected the right of access to the women of the Community. The other constant was the continual requirement of the owners in Perth that any expenditure of station money on food, clothing and other supplies be kept to the absolute minimum needed to keep people alive and working.

Bill Henwood's long reign at Noonkanbah was relatively benevolent. But before he arrived, and well after this time on many other stations, the control over labour, and the claiming of the right of sexual access to the women were brutally enforced. Ginger Nganawilla's story of his father's treatment by the police when he was caught after walking off Quanbun illustrates this, but just as often matters were handled within the station.

In 1910 an inspector on patrol for the Aborigines Department arrived at Noonkanbah to find that a seventeen-year-old boy had been 'put on the chain [for five days] by the manager as a punishment for running away from a team whilst on the road from Derby'.[4] The manager was actually charged with assault and fined five pounds in the

Derby court, but how frequently this form of 'punishment' was practised can only be guessed.

When Ginger Nganawilla told the story of the shootings and burnings on Christmas Creek and Bohemia Downs Stations, I asked whether similar things had happened on Noonkanbah:

> No, it was never really bad on Noonkanbah. They just pinched the women from the boys. Pinched the women and kept them in the house. The Aborigines never said anything, they were frightened of gudia. My mother did that; I've got a half-caste sister.

He went on to describe how, on some stations, it was more than just a matter of 'pinching the women':

> The people that came behind those first gudia don't know. These other people don't know. They think the gudia was doing good in the early days. But they were doing very bad, shooting people. That's no good.
>
> When anybody made trouble at the station they would lock him up, give him a hiding there inside, and kill him after. They were having black women, those gudia. They made it wrong. Her husband made a row. That woman came back from the job, and her husband asked, 'What's going on?' 'He's been pinching me from you', his wife told him. And that man came up to the manager, he came up to the store, and walked inside there. At night time. They belted him, killed him, and took him away at night time.
>
> That was in my time. I put everything in my brain. I know what every manager was doing, on the stations all around.
>
> When he belted that man inside the house, he took him away at night time. He shot an old bullock or cow, slit the guts, picked up that man and shoved him inside. He turned it over, and nobody could see. That's what the gudia were doing before. You ask Nipper and he'll tell you, and Friday. This is the story from Cherrabun, Christmas Creek and Bohemia Downs, all around. We've got plenty of stories that say what the gudia was doing before.

The horrifying story of the method used to hide and dispose of bodies in the guts of dead cattle was indeed confirmed in the stories of other old people. Again, the oral tradition at Noonkanbah attributes this practice to the Christmas Creek/Bohemia Downs locality, but the abduction and rape of women was common to all stations. Though it must be said that there was also a parallel sexual trade between the races in which Aboriginal women participated either willingly or out of economic necessity.

In yet another cruel twist of policy that must have seemed incomprehensible to the people, it was decided that the children fathered by the invaders must be removed from their mothers and families. This policy was enforced from the turn of the century, at least into the 1960s. All the families at Noonkanbah have lost members, taken by force to institutions in the south, and to Beagle Bay, Moola Bulla and Forrest River; most were never seen again. Ginger Nganawilla, well into his sixties, still spoke of the sister he had lost as a young boy.

At government level this policy was based on the assumption that any children with white blood were inherently more intelligent and more deserving than their brothers and sisters (though definitely still not on a par with whites).

An Aborigines Department inspector charged with rounding up these children on a patrol through the West Kimberley in 1908 wrote enthusiastically:

I was glad to receive telegraphic instructions...to arrange for the transport of all half-castes to the Beagle Bay Mission...With regard to the paternity of these waifs, very few will admit it, and it is very difficult to prove...In collecting and transporting these waifs the question of separating them from their mothers against their wish is sure to crop up...I am convinced from my own experience and knowledge that the short-lived grief of the parent is of little consequence compared with the future of the children. The half-caste is intellectually above the aborigine, and it is the duty of the State that they be given a chance to lead a better life than their mothers. I would not hesitate for one moment to separate any half-caste from its aboriginal mother, no matter how frantic her momentary grief might be at the time. They soon forget their offspring.[5]

The policy was also welcomed by the white men on the stations, who, as the inspector noted, were reluctant to admit paternity, and were even more reluctant to take any responsibility. It is interesting to observe that most, if not all of the grand families who made their fortunes in the pastoral industry, and have exerted such a powerful and continuing influence on Western Australian society and politics, have Aboriginal blood relatives scattered around the State, largely unacknowledged.[6]

Like colonists the world over, the pastoralists and their handful of white employees could see nothing to fault in the regime they had imposed on the original owners of the land. Many of them were even able to put forward contorted arguments and justifications to the effect that they were the benefactors of the Aboriginal people. From the most brutal to the most benevolent, the universal assumption that allowed them to profit from the regime, and still sleep easy at nights, was that blacks were inferior beings who were somehow less than human, or at least less human than the white man. And they saw no reason why this should not continue indefinitely.

The Kimberley was the last region of Australia to introduce cash wages for Aboriginal employees, in 1950. And even then it was done reluctantly, and with ill grace. From the time of Gribble's allegations of slavery and maltreatment in 1886, attacks on the pastoral industry continued to surface in Perth, the eastern states and England every few years, raising essentially the same charges. These were never seriously addressed by governments, who continued to be influenced by the power of the pastoral lobby.

Between 1910 and 1928 five separate proposals emanating from the Aborigines Department to compel the payment of a minimum cash wage on pastoral stations were sabotaged before they even came to a vote in the Parliament. The historian Peter Biskup, in describing these attempts, wrote of the Department:

[It] was one of the least important agencies, politically, and one of the smallest as well...The department had little 'pull' in the corridors of political power...the aborigines, except during brief flare-ups of public interest occasioned by violence on either side or a sensational newspaper article, came always last in the calculations of the politicians.[7]

He compared this to the power of the pastoralists:

During the thirty years [1906-1935] five groups influenced, or attempted to influence, aboriginal policy and administration in Western Australia: the pastoral lobby, organised labour, local government authorities, parents' and citizens' associations, and the humanitarians...the pastoralists wanted to preserve the status quo...[and were] the most effective and at the same time the least conspicuous interest group: the northern pastoralists had always possessed an influence out of all proportion to their members. Like other groups concerned with the preservation of the status quo, the pastoral lobby did not require a tight organisation to express its influence: it operated subtly through powerful allies in parliament, the civil service, and the press. L.R. Marchant, writing in 1954, assessed the influence of the pastoralists between 1886 and 1905 in the following words:

> From the time of the first Aborigine Act of 1886 the application of the law has been affected by a legislative body that found itself idolizing the pioneer spirit of the settlers. Whenever this spirit was at odds with a desire to protect the natives, the Aborigines Acts were modified accordingly.[8]

In 1946 most of the Aboriginal workers on the stations of the Pilbara went out on strike. Token wages were already being paid there, but the people were demanding increases and improved conditions. The strikers were led by a white man, Don McLeod, and two inspiring black organisers, Dooley Bin Bin and Clancy McKenna. After a bitter three year struggle, which saw McLeod and many of the strikers gaoled repeatedly, significant gains were made. But the hard core of the strikers never went back to the stations. With the continuing help of McLeod they shaped an independent life, living by mining activities and pearl shelling, and eventually buying stations of their own. They became known as the Strelley mob, after the station which became their headquarters. They were to play a crucial role in the Noonkanbah dispute thirty years later.[9]

At the time of the strike, drastic action by the authorities prevented Don McLeod and the strikers from extending their influence beyond the Pilbara, but in 1948 there were reported rumours of plans for a strike of Aboriginal workers in Derby. The Kimberley pastoralists, who were still paying no wages at all, and were beginning to experience labour problems, must have seen the writing on the wall, but continued to resist the inevitable.

A Department of Native Welfare patrol officer's report of 1946 is revealing in this regard. The officer first visited Upper Liveringa, where the size of the station's Aboriginal camp had declined from one hundred to forty people in a few years, attributed by the owner 'to an increase in deaths over births'.[10] (A rather dramatic increase that makes one wonder what the reasons may have been.)

The report continues, quoting the owner:

> Mr. Rose stated that he had done all in his power short of offering wages in cash to attract native labour to his station but without success, he has at times recruited desert natives from the West of the Fitzroy River but they are not inclined to stay as it is out of their tribal country.
> Mr. Rose is of the opinion that the time has arrived at Liveringa when the changeover from the old system of wages in kind will have to be replaced by cash payments and or the introduction of white labour, he is reluctant to offer wages in cash to local natives on the grounds that it would upset the labour situation on neighbouring stations some of whom are not on the sound financial basis of Liveringa, but is quite willing to pay reasonable wages and provide decent living conditions for half-castes from Broome or elsewhere if they will accept station work.[11]

The next day the officer arrived at Noonkanbah, where he:

Discussed native matters with Mr. Henwood the Manager who states that Noonkanbah is not experiencing any shortage of native labour...Mr. Henwood has a number of half-castes employed who are paid wages in cash but the station natives still receive food, clothes and tobacco as in the past and Mr. Henwood is not favourable to a changeover as he is of the opinion that the station natives are happier and more contented under the present system than they would be if receiving cash, as the vices of drinking and gambling would inevitably follow such a procedure, he is in sympathy with the Manager of Upper Liveringa in his labour problem but expresses the opinion that a changeover to payments in cash would not solve the problem as other stations would be forced to follow suit and any natives who had been attracted to Upper Liveringa by such payments would then return to the original station from where they came.[12]

The astonishing mental gymnastics that underpinned the colonial style pastoral regimes are revealed when one sees the Noonkanbah manager saying in the one breath that his workforce is happier and more contented receiving no wages, and then that they would leave to go elsewhere if cash wages were on offer, and that he would be forced to follow suit.

Three years later, as white Australia was entering an unprecedented era of prosperity and self-confidence, the Commissioner of Native Welfare in Perth was writing to the local suppliers of 'native stick tobacco',

...making representation on behalf of the managements of Noonkanbah and Ashburton Downs Stations [who were having difficulty obtaining supplies]...as I understand the native stockmen and other employees are becoming restless because of their difficulty in obtaining their tobacco ration. The labour situation in the pastoral industry is a problem these days, chiefly because of the high rate of wages offering in other forms of employment and the Stations are suffering accordingly.[13]

Still in the Kimberley the pastoralists clung to the era of food, clothes and tobacco in lieu of wages, and expected and obtained the assistance of the authorities in administering this regime.

But by this time the pastoralists were fighting a losing battle. A 1948 inquiry into Aboriginal affairs had publicised the fact that the Kimberley was the only region in the country not paying wages. A 1949 Department of Native Welfare survey of Kimberley working conditions recommended the immediate introduction of a nominal cash wage, and compulsory provision of housing of a minimum standard. The Pastoralists' Association attacked these recommendations as 'unsuited to the present development of the natives in the Kimberleys'.[14] But the next year they did voluntarily agree to the introduction of wages. One suspects that this may have been to avoid legislation which may have required them to invest in the much larger capital costs involved in the provision of housing. The rate agreed to was one pound per month for stockmen, and half a pound per month for domestics.

Department of Native Welfare reports of patrols to Noonkanbah, covering most of the years from 1950 until the people walked off in 1971, provide interesting information on the state of the Community, and the response of the owners and management to the changes that began with the introduction of cash wages in 1950.[15]

At that time the permit system still applied, and in 1950 the new manager, Duncan

Noonkanbah Station. Top: Horse-mustering and stockmen. Bottom: Horse-breakers – Steven Laurel, Patrick Nargoodah, David Yungabun and Leo Thirkall.

Beaton, paid the Department fifty-two pounds for a 'General permit for ninety natives to be employed on Noonkanbah Station'. Reports list fifty-two people employed, from an Aboriginal population of one hundred and eighteen people, with wages ranging from five shillings, up to two pounds per month for a head stockman. The patrol officer reported:

> This station in time has every indication of becoming one of the best in the district, if the ideas and the work planned by the manager for the natives is put into effect.

But things appeared to go downhill from there. Beaton appears to lose his enthusiasm for improvements to the people's conditions fairly quickly, and the owners are certainly not interested. In 1955 the patrol officer reported:

> In comparison, this station has the worst conditions for their natives than many others. Many natives have already left for employment elsewhere and the Manager informed me that further native staff cuts are likely for economy reasons.
>
> I was able to discuss native welfare matters with Mr. G. Mawley, the Managing Director, and Mr. D. Beaton, Manager. The former is inclined to have very definite views on native matters, which are rather outmoded under present policy. However the usual promises of better conditions were made, but from previous experience I am not hopeful of quick results.

The same report numbered the Aboriginal population at eighty-four people, with fifty-nine on wages, and said that,

> [the] camp rationed natives complained bitterly about shortage of food...the matter was taken up by me with Manager, Mr. Beaton, who contended [that the ration issued] was sufficient, and no satisfaction obtained.

Over the next few years the total population continued to decline, while the number of workers stayed about the same. There was a clear policy on the part of the station to get rid of dependants, particularly old people, who they were still obliged to feed without being able to extract any labour. Promises of improved accommodation were still being made in 1960.

In the late 1950s and early 1960s wages were increased, but the workforce reduced. In 1961 there were two patrols: the first in April found forty people, with twenty-two on wages; by November it was down to twenty-eight people with eighteen on wages. Both reports commented that the wages were good in comparison to other stations, but that the employees were expected to work very hard. By 1962 'the general impression at this station was that the natives are not very content. They all complained that they are worked too hard.' This should not have been surprising, as fifteen workers were employed to do what had taken fifty-two people only twelve years before.

In the 1960s Aboriginal people finally became entitled to claim social security benefits, including pensions and child endowment. This immediately became a source of controversy. The system operating at Noonkanbah, and many other stations, was described in a 1963 report following a joint patrol by Native Welfare and Social Security officers:

> Mr. Davies [Social Security] discussed pension matters with Mr. D. Beaton, manager and Mr. Morley [Mawley] Director of Noonkanbah Pastoral Co. The pensioners at Noonkanbah are all direct pension payments. However, Mr. Beaton cashes the cheques and gives them pocket money component laid down by PGA [Pastoralists and Graziers Association]. The balance, which he said was for housing, food, etc., is sent to [their head office in] Perth. Mr. Morley intimated that they did not want pensioners on the station and it was their policy to get rid of them...Mr. Morley made it clear that he had no time for the DNW and that it was the policy of their station to cut down on the natives employed there.

This controversy was still going on in 1966, when the senior officer with Native Welfare in Derby felt constrained to write to his Commissioner, seeking an inspection of the company's books at head office in Perth in an effort to establish what was happening to the pensioners' money:

> This Station [Noonkanbah] was visited in company with Mr. M. Davies of the Social Services Department on 25th May, 1966. We received a very hostile reception from Mr. Morley, owner of the Station, who snarled at us from behind a wire door, and did not even have the courtesy to step outside to speak or to invite us in...
>
> An inspection of the Station and natives presented deplorable and extremely depressing conditions. The natives were found to be in a very low state.
>
> Sanitation and toilet facilities were not existent. A stand pipe and two halves of 44 gallon drums appeared to represent laundry facilities.
>
> One Quonset hut with a dirt floor was occupied by at least eight families...The rest of the accommodation consisted of breakwinds and bough shades. There were no tents in evidence on my visit.
>
> ...it was ascertained that the pensioners were not obtaining the full benefit of their pensions, and the Station was doing very little for the workers and their dependants.
>
> It would appear that the native pensioners, who are on direct payment, take their cheques to the Manager who gives them varying amounts of pocket money ranging from $1.00 to $3.00 per week from petty cash and keeps the cheque.
>
> The pensioners further allege that they purchase food from the store with their pocket money. This seems necessary as the rations provided seem quite inadequate.
>
> The figures quoted by Mr. Roberts [the bookkeeper at Noonkanbah] for rations total $3.59 and even if each pensioner received the sum of $3.00 pocket money, which is hardly likely, there is still a deficiency of $10.82 per fortnight, and as no records can be produced it is not known if balances exist.

On these calculations the station would have been making a profit in the vicinity of three hundred dollars per year from each pensioner on the grounds of making deductions for housing that was non-existent, and food that was totally inadequate. Furthermore, another report later that year mentioned that 'all the pensioners capable of any work are required to perform some duties'. In the Northern Territory this practice was known amongst the pastoralists as 'nigger farming'.

The response of the owners to the pressure from Native Welfare was to displace yet more people. Beaton obviously felt somewhat uneasy about this when he wrote to the Department early in 1967 saying, 'I have been instructed by my Directors to cut down on number of Natives on Noonkanbah. As you will realise this is not easy to do.'

These years that paralleled the boom in wool prices which lined the pockets of farmers around the country, including no doubt the owners of Noonkanbah, were hard ones for the Noonkanbah people. Their community, which up until the mid-1950s had always numbered well over one hundred, was slowly whittled away and dispersed by deliberate station policy. Conditions and morale appeared to gradually deteriorate. But at least the annual conduct of Law business in the wet season provided respite, and a renewal of pride and a sense of worth and purpose.

Even their religion, though, was not safe from the intrusions of the white man. In 1963 a group of white shearers stole a number of sacred boards from the cave in which they were stored, on Tatju Hill south of the river. When the people complained to Beaton he ordered the return of the boards, and warned the shearers off. But one returned and once again stole some of them. He made the mistake of taking them to the Museum in Perth for valuation. After enquiries, he was eventually charged with theft, and the boards were returned.

There was a repeat of this incident, described by Friday Muller in the first chapter, in 1970. This time the thief was an employee of the Stockdale Exploration Company, which had a camp on Noonkanbah involved in diamond exploration. This time the boards, stolen again from Tatju Hill, were sent to the anthropology museum at Monash University in Melbourne. It took fifteen months of pressure from Native Welfare, following complaints by the Noonkanbah people, before the boards were returned. The most curious feature of this was that the thief had acquired the status of owner, with the museum claiming it was unable to return the boards until it had his written permission as the donor.

In 1969 two very significant things happened. Firstly, the standard pastoral award became applicable to Aboriginal station hands, putting them at last on an equal basis with white employees. Secondly, Duncan Beaton's twenty-year reign as manager came to an end, and he was replaced by Jim Cooper. The combined effects of these two developments dramatically altered the status quo on the station.

There is some confusion in the available records as to the station's response to the introduction of the award, but it certainly seems that many, if not all, of the workers were put on twenty dollars a week and keep under the slow workers provision that was inserted in the award. Aboriginal people recall a drop in wages from Beaton's time to Cooper's, so perhaps Beaton paid the award for the short time it applied before he left, and then Cooper invoked the slow workers provision.

Cooper is not remembered at all fondly by the Noonkanbah people. He is recalled as a hard man, a 'rough boss' who exploited them, and had none of the respect that was a part of Beaton's rule. By October 1970 the size of the Aboriginal camp was down to nineteen people, from forty-four in mid-1969. In December a Liveringa man who was closely associated with the Noonkanbah people delivered a note to the Native Welfare office in Derby, complaining that, 'Noonkanbah Station people don't get their pay and their [social security] cheques; Don't get much rations, only a little bit; Girls who work in the house don't get their pay'.

In the upheavals that followed introduction of the pastoral award Aboriginal people had already walked off or been evicted from most of the stations in the area, congregating in the previously tiny settlement of Fitzroy Crossing. In 1971 the Noonkanbah people joined them.

The particular spark for the walkoff from Noonkanbah is not clear. It happened on the eighteenth of August, the culmination of two years of tension. A Native Welfare patrol was visiting the station that day. Four days earlier,

> On Saturday 14th August an old woman...had died. She had come from Derby a month previously, and had been sick then. There is currently an investigation taking place to determine if there were negligence, or callous indifference on the part of the Management.

The report of the officer attributed the walkoff to an industrial dispute:

> There had been trouble brewing on this station for a long time due to the Management's attitude to the labour, and disputes over pay. About a week before the Inspection, the Manager's wife had sacked Domestic Biddy Ngidering for wasting water on the lawn sprinkler (she received her keep and clothes). Mickie Mick [Mick Nicki] organised the labour force to take

the stand that if Biddy was sacked, they would all walk off. The Manager agreed and offered transport, but this was refused; two men set off to Fitzroy Crossing hoping to borrow the Mission lorry. They had not been seen since. On leaving the station, the Inspecting Officer took aboard the Toyota one family. George Bell was met on the way in driving Billy Bryant's ramshackle lorry, and behind this in another rickety car came Friday Muller. By night-fall, the entire labour force had been evacuated.

In their recollections, today's Noonkanbah people (many of whom had left the station before 1971) provide a variety of reasons for the walkoff; including disputes over pay, the shooting and poisoning of camp dogs, and an argument over the use of a tractor for collecting firewood. Obviously life on the station under Jim Cooper had become intolerable for them, and the walkoff was inevitable.

They became uneasy and unwilling fringedwellers in Fitzroy Crossing. For the first time in many thousands of years, for the first time since the heroes of the Dreaming had created the land, the true owners were no longer living on and caring for the country.

4

EXILE AND RETURN

Lots of my people are under fear of trouble, because of drinks and women selling to whites and children are fatherless and single mothers are battling to look after their children. That's why we are asking for this area near Noonkanbah Station where we can live and work and call something our own belonging.

Friday Muller, leader of the Noonkanbah people, writing to the Minister for Aboriginal Affairs, February 1974.

The move from Noonkanbah did not bring relief to the people. Indeed, the time that followed in Fitzroy Crossing is remembered, especially by the older people, as the low point in their lives.

Fitzroy Crossing was not their country; the spirits of the land and of the river's waterholes were unfamiliar, and a source of fear. The creation stories and religious lore which had provided the basic fabric of life through good times and bad could not be properly separated from the country which gave it meaning. The soul of the Community had been left behind, along with the sacred boards, the symbols of faith and power, which could not be lightly removed from their caches in the caves of the Noonkanbah hills.

The Community established a camp on the banks of the Fitzroy, about a kilometre and a half from the main road. The camp went under various names, but was most commonly known as the River Reserve. Most of the Noonkanbah people lived in this camp, though some with family ties in Derby drifted in to the reserve there, and some who had left the station before 1971 were living in the other fringedweller camps.

Humpies were cobbled together from pipe, timber and corrugated-iron scrounged from the tip. Some lived under bough-shades constructed of bush-timber and spinifex, and slept in derelict car bodies when the rains came. Conditions were abysmally poor; it was a prime example of the poverty-stricken fringe camp that is one of the most sordid images of modern Aboriginal Australia.

The river camp of the Noonkanbah people was the last of three major fringedwellers' camps established between 1969 and 1971 near Fitzroy Crossing. The others were known as Fig Tree Reserve and Windmill. At Fig Tree were some of the people who had left Noonkanbah earlier, and other people mostly from Quanbun, Jubilee and Cherrabun Stations. Windmill was the camp of the Christmas Creek mob; they had been the first of the large groups to leave the stations, in January 1969. All three camps were contained within a Native Welfare Reserve that had been created in February 1969 to cater for the influx of people from the stations, following the introduction of the pastoral award.

Some of the Christmas Creek and Cherrabun people moved into the United Aborigines Mission camp, located on another reserve several kilometres further along the old highway, nearer to the school and other facilities. In just a few years the Aboriginal population in Fitzroy Crossing grew from about one hundred to almost a thousand.

The tight internal discipline and traditional authority structures of the station camps struggled to survive in the trauma of the Fitzroy Crossing camps. The station regimes, harsh and restrictive as they were, had provided something of a shield, or at least a physical isolation, from many of the vices of the wider world that inevitably afflict the poor and the oppressed. In Fitzroy Crossing the shields, the isolation, were removed abruptly, and for all but the strongest and clearest of mind the circle of drink, dependence

Hairpin Marner and Wadgie Thirkall, Fitzroy Crossing, 1979. This dwelling was home for Thirkall and his large family for ten years.

and poverty closed in.

Drinking and alcoholism became an enormous problem very quickly. The younger people were the worst affected, but not the only ones. Some people succumbed completely, whilst others drifted in and out of the degradation centred around the pub. With the drinking came the associated social problems. Rules and conventions that had governed the communities all their lives were flouted in the camps by the drunks, much to the consternation of the Elders and traditionalists. The worst aspects of cowboy and pub culture, such as drunken brawling, began to emerge. Young men and women began to ignore the traditional laws governing sex and marriage. The drinkers' children were often neglected and malnourished.

The communities as a whole suffered enormously. Those who were healthy carried the drunks and their children. The women of the communities were the main source of stability in the midst of this turmoil. The leaders struggled to keep their people together and, against all odds and the seeming indifference of the white world, to provide a sense of purpose and direction.

A lot of effort was put into two small enterprises; a vegetable garden at the River Reserve, and a piggery at the Fig Tree camp run by some of the Cherrabun people who were emerging as a younger generation of leaders and entrepreneurs. Both projects had a fitful existence. Much love and labour was lavished on them. But they were never seen as important enough to take precedence over other demands, such as the need to travel for Law business. And an inadequate capital equipment base and a lack of any real management expertise prevented them from ever achieving real success. Some of the men found work in the mustering season on stations or in contract teams, but nearly all the people were dependent on welfare payments.

One of the positive lights for the people in this era was the growth and extension in Law activity. In the early 1970s the Fitzroy mob had managed to scrape together the money to acquire a few vehicles. And some of the larger groups in the vast chain

Fitzroy Crossing Races.

of communities from La Grange, south of Broome, through Looma, Balgo and into the Northern Territory had also become mobile. Whereas people had previously been limited to travelling by foot to the annual ceremonial activities, a cycle began to develop where people and ceremonies moved each year throughout this network. The Noonkanbah people of the River Reserve were centrally involved in this activity. Again the Law was providing a source of strength and refuge in difficult times, although the nature of these travelling ceremonies was different from those that had been held on the station, where the whole community was always involved.

Early in 1972, under the leadership of Friday Muller, the people of the River Reserve and Fig Tree camps formed a loose alliance which they called the Karjunna Tribe. The choice of the name was highly significant. Karjunna (or Kadjina) is one of the major players in the creation stories of the Dreaming for the Noonkanbah country. His spirit resides high on a hill in the St George Range, where the figure of a black man holding a stone axe in his left hand can be seen against the surrounding red rock. He is significant in both Walmatjari and Nyigina Dreaming. Hence the name served to identify the people with their tradition and Law, and with the Noonkanbah country; and it was also a symbol of the unity of the Walmatjari and the Nyigina in their new life and in their plans for the future.

It was under the Karjunna umbrella that the fringedwellers made the first steps in a long and continuing struggle to forge a new lifestyle and identity as independent people. The garden and piggery enterprises were one aspect of this struggle, but the real focus was a determined campaign to reclaim their land.

The commitment to this goal of a return to their land is the hallmark of the exile of the Noonkanbah people. The campaign had in fact begun before they ever walked off Noonkanbah, and continued until they returned triumphant in 1976.

While still living on Noonkanbah, Friday Muller had asked the station management to make available a small area for him and his group to establish their own settlement. This had been refused outright. Early in 1972 he again approached the station seeking the use of the abandoned Warrimbah outstation and two surrounding paddocks on the Quanbun boundary, again with no success.

In Fitzroy Crossing the Karjunna leaders made contact with an anthropologist employed by the Aboriginal Affairs Planning Authority (AAPA), and officers of the Department for Community Welfare (DCW)[1], and enlisted their aid in the campaign.

At about the same time the newly elected Federal Labor Government of Gough Whitlam established the Department of Aboriginal Affairs, and established the Woodward Commission to investigate ways and means of introducing Land Rights legislation in the Northern Territory. The Land Rights movement was gathering strength Australia wide. The Noonkanbah leaders attended meetings in Derby and Broome, and Muller went to a Land Rights conference in Darwin. They became aware for the first time that there were potential allies out there in white society, and heard of landmarks such as the Gurindji's claim to Wattie Creek in the Northern Territory. Their determination was increased, and expectations and horizons were broadened.

The first documented land claim, in July 1972, focused on the Millijidee outstation, in the southern foothills of the St George Range, and the surrounding country. The claim extended south to the unused Waratea lease, which was held under the same ownership as Noonkanbah. It was channelled through the Derby office of the AAPA, which was supportive, but felt the claim was unrealistic. The local officer wrote:

> I cannot see these people getting their land back and therefore a letter directed to the group should be sent as soon as possible explaining the reasons.
> Furthermore I think we should all realise how much these people have come to believe that they are going to have their land back simply by officers of the Department going out to such places and simply plotting out with the group, the land being sought after.[2]

But the people were more persistent and more optimistic than the bureaucrats. In January 1973 the AAPA anthropologist, Erich Kolig, helped the people to update and resubmit their proposal, claiming much the same country. Kolig provided an impressive substantiation of the claim in terms of traditional rights and historical affiliations, and attempted to convince his superiors of the determination and abilities of the group. He also pointed out the derelict condition of the land in question under the existing Noonkanbah management.

Still there was no response from higher up the ladder. In June of the same year Kolig wrote another report trying to prompt some response. Having discussed with the people the apparent futility of trying to acquire land from the Noonkanbah lease, which included Millijidee outstation, this report focused on a more remote outstation within the Waratea lease that had been abandoned after a short and unsuccessful attempt at settlement at least twenty years earlier. It was clear that the people were desperate to obtain a land base somewhere in their traditional country, in order to leave Fitzroy Crossing and attempt to create an independent community. However Kolig also noted that:

> [Muller] has articulated a claim to the whole of the group's traditional land. This comprises most of the present Noonkanbah lease and extends south to the fringe of the desert.[3]

He also observed that,

In general, land claims of Aborigines become more and more articulate and at the same time dissatisfaction with administration's inefficiency and slowness to comply with Aboriginal wishes increases. In the present case, there can be little doubt that the group may eventually undertake more drastic steps if their repeated effort to re-gain their land, or part of it, is continuously frustrated.[4]

At this time there was no procedure for assessing or dealing with Aboriginal land claims, and in a sense the bureaucrats were right in pouring cold water on the people's ambitions, for compulsory acquisitions of land seemed unlikely, and if the pastoralist was not interested in selling, nothing could be achieved.

The nature of the claims to the Millijidee and Waratea areas was interesting in that they did not nominate specific boundaries for the area they wanted, and they made it clear that the people were flexible in their demands. They gave first priority to the Millijidee area, which was known traditionally as 'woradia' or 'waratea' (causing some confusion with the Waratea lease, which was actually further south) and had the Kadjina manifestation in the ranges at its spiritual centre. But they also nominated alternative areas in the vicinity. These areas, as with woradia, were each traditionally named and associated with particular aspects and figures from the Dreaming. Clearly the claim to land was intimately interwoven with the religious knowledge of the land.

Throughout 1974 the people kept the pressure on the authorities with a succession of letters. The first was from Muller to the Federal Minister for Aboriginal Affairs, Senator James Cavanagh, on February 4:

> As far as my memory can take me back, that white man in this country were made rich by us native people. So, this once again I'll say, just let us try our own native to native, but I know myself they work as hard as they worked for white man...
>
> So sir, I beg you to come over to Fitzroy Crossing Reserve to see and to prove for yourself about how many people I have in my hand, also my old people would like to meet you so badly. Lots of my people are under fear of trouble, because of drinks and women selling to whites and children are fatherless and single mothers are battling to look after their children. That's why we are asking for this area near Noonkanbah Station where we can live and work and call something our own belonging.
>
> In early days our people were like slaves and were working harder because it was easy way for a white man to make money quicker and faster...Now lots of our boys know how to handle stock work better than any other white man. Now I want you and any member of Governments to help us just for start. For sure we will work as good as any other station.[5]

This was followed by others to the Department of Aboriginal Affairs in Canberra:

> February 18, 1974: We want some lands for our people and have got the maps marked out. We badly need these lands for us and for our children in the future.

> July 31, 1974: We...received [your] letter back saying that you had asked the W.A. Director to investigate if any of our tribal land would be available for purchase. An officer was to contact us but he has not done so yet. Could you tell us when he will come to help us as we want to be able to get our people settled on our land as soon as we can.

October 9, 1974: Still waiting to hear about the land Millijidee Station, if you do hear more about this station could you please let me know as soon as possible. We want houses on our Reserve for our old pensioners and also for our own families we are still living in tents built under bough shelters and also sleeping against windbreaks, we do not like the way we are living.[6]

Throughout this time the people continued to visit and pass through Noonkanbah. Friday Muller and his lieutenants visited Millijidee and Waratea a number of times with Erich Kolig and AAPA and DCW staff who assisted in preparing and pressing their land claims. On one occasion in 1972 a potentially nasty incident developed when the manager, Jim Cooper, and his son found them camped south of the river one night, and during an acrimonious encounter, warned them to keep away from the Millijidee homestead.

In 1973 a few of the Noonkanbah people returned to work for Cooper during the cattle season. But this lasted only a couple of months before there was another argument, and the workers returned to the River Reserve in Fitzroy Crossing. The station started to go into decline, as Cooper could not attract labour. Cattle turnoff was maintained at reasonable levels, but there was virtually no branding, and windmills, tanks and fences were not maintained.

In May 1974 Cooper came in to Fitzroy Crossing, and offered some of the people at the River Reserve work at Noonkanbah. He was refused. Two days later he was back in, and confronted the local DCW officer to 'express his concern at not having [the Noonkanbah people] back for work'.[7] He said that there was no way they would get the Waratea land. Cooper and the officer went to the reserve, where the people again refused an offer of work from Cooper. It was a tense scene, according to the officer's report, with Cooper claiming, 'You can be sure there will be trouble over this, I'm not going to take this I'll let them know in Perth what you are doing'.[8] He demanded to see Friday Muller, and when he was found, told the people that they would not get Waratea. But he went away without any workers.

In October 1974 the Federal and State Ministers with responsibility for Aboriginal Affairs, Senator Cavanagh and Norman Baxter, and their departmental heads, visited Fitzroy Crossing during a tour of the Kimberley. It appears that they were genuinely shocked at the conditions they encountered, and impressed by what the people had to say to them, including the demand for land that was articulated most strongly by the Karjunna leaders. Undertakings were given to take action to improve conditions in the town camps, and to see what could be done about the land claims.

The response of the State's Department for Community Welfare was to produce startling results. By early 1975 a team of community development workers employed by the Department was at work in Fitzroy Crossing. The brief for the team was broad in its scope; with the blessing of the Department Head they took on the task of establishing a close working relationship with the people in the fringe camps, assisting them to identify goals and development programs, and working as activists to help them achieve the goals and implement the programs. This was a radically different concept to that of the traditional welfare officer employed to that time by the Department and its predecessor, Native Welfare. The approach drew an immediate and enthusiastic response from the people; 1975 proved to be a watershed year in the lives of the Fitzroy Crossing people, the Noonkanbah mob included.

Within a few months four of the Fitzroy Crossing groups had become legally incorporated. A range of small-scale social, economic and self-help projects were underway, with new ideas constantly coming up. Particularly successful were the homemaker programs, which helped the women of the camps organise all sorts of self-help projects, from feeding pensioners and schoolchildren, to dressmaking. More funds were starting to flow in from the recently established DAA office in Derby, and land claims were being lodged with the Aboriginal Land Fund Commission (ALFC) in Canberra.

The Karjunna had become the Kadjina Community Incorporated, with Muller as Chairman, and two younger men from the Fig Tree Reserve, Charlie Rangi and George Bell, as Secretary and Treasurer. The Kadjina were the most responsive and active of the newly emergent communities. In July 1975, the leader of the DCW team wrote:

> We are more than impressed with the purposefulness, cohesion and determination of the [Kadjina] group. There has been nothing their leaders have decided to do that they have not carried out.[9]

Still the main focus during this year of development was the campaign for land; this time centred around the hope of purchasing Quanbun Downs, a relatively small property with Fitzroy River frontage, on the eastern boundary of Noonkanbah.

News that Quanbun was available for sale had come through in November 1974, the month after the Ministers' visit. There was some debate amongst the people and the public servants and advisers working with them as to whether a bid should be made for the station. The Kadjina response was that some of their members had strong links to Quanbun, and they were making no progress with their claims for land on Noonkanbah, so yes, try to buy it. But they made it clear that this was a step towards their real goal, rather than an end in itself: 'Quanbun first, then Noonkanbah', was their statement.

Negotiations between the Commonwealth and the owners dragged on for a year, with the differences over price complicated by the fact that the ALFC was still in the process of being formally established as a government authority. At one point, frustrated by the lack of progress, the Community wired a hundred dollars to the Minister of Aboriginal Affairs, asking that he use it as a deposit for the purchase.

Many of the Kadjina people, in a move designed to demonstrate their determination and pressure the Government, moved out of town and established a squatters' camp on Quanbun. Of course, this was also prompted by the desire to get out of the oppressive conditions of the town camps. The Quanbun owner, whilst far from easy about the camp, was prepared to allow it, as he was eager for a sale on his terms, and could see the advantages of their presence. He also used the negotiations with the Community over the camp as an opportunity to secure some cheap labour.

The Quanbun camp lasted nearly a year, from February 1975 to January 1976. At its peak there were about one hundred people living there. As in Fitzroy Crossing, there was a physical separation maintained between the River Reserve and Fig Tree groups. The Community established a system of 'chuck in' from social security funds to finance Community business, including the purchase of a second-hand truck. They also ran an informal Walmatjari school under the control of George Bell, and operated a store.

As the negotiations dragged on, and a favourable settlement began to appear unlikely, the differences between the two halves of the Community became accentuated. The younger leaders, Rangi and Bell, led the Fig Tree mob back to Fitzroy Crossing where they set up camp at the River Reserve in Fitzroy Crossing, whilst Muller and the bulk of the Noonkanbah people stayed on at Quanbun. They moved their camp nearer to the homestead; unsure of their future, but unwilling to return to Fitzroy Crossing.

The group that remained at Quanbun took over the management of their own affairs and finances, and soon assumed the name of the Yungngora Association. Yungngora was another Dreamtime figure, a dog, whose spirit home lies in the Sandy Billabong, site of the main Noonkanbah stockyards, several kilometres north of the homestead. In fact, in the stories of the country Yungngora had fought with Kadjina in the St George Range before returning to Sandy Billabong. So the naming of the group could be taken at one level as a clear statement of their differences with the Kadjina; and there is no doubt that significant tensions existed between the two groups and continued for some years.

Nevertheless, as late as December 1975, both groups participated in meetings with ALFC commissioners, insisting that they wished to jointly acquire and manage Quanbun Station. But in early January 1976 the owner of Quanbun formally advised that the ALFC's final offer was unacceptably low. The ALFC was not prepared so early in its existence to pay Quanbun's asking price, which was well above their valuations, for fear that it would establish a precedent and acquire a reputation amongst pastoralists as an easy mark.

The time at Quanbun was a failure in its specific objective of acquisition of the lease, and to this extent it was another frustration for the people. It also saw the breakup of the previously united Kadjina into two groups. But it was also a positive learning experience. With the support of the DCW staff, the people began to develop ideas and models of self-management that they would take with them when they returned to Noonkanbah. A younger group of men, within Yungngora, as well as the Kadjina leaders, were gaining more experience and confidence in articulating their needs and demands and in conducting the communities' business.

In retrospect the failure to acquire Quanbun was a blessing in disguise for both the Yungngora and the Kadjina, as it would have been most unlikely, given the land needs of Aboriginal people around the country, that the ALFC would have been prepared to negotiate another acquisition for them immediately afterwards. But following the disappointment over Quanbun, when Noonkanbah and Waratea were advertised for sale on 1 January 1976, the ALFC was bound to respond.

On hearing that Noonkanbah was for sale the people wasted no time. The chairmen of Kadjina and Yungngora immediately telegrammed the ALFC to express their interest and ask that purchase of the leases be investigated. The ALFC, trying not to raise hopes too much, advised that the asking price was unrealistically high, but commenced the process of getting valuations done and negotiations underway.

The Yungngora moved from Quanbun Station back into Fitzroy Crossing, where they established a new camp, separate from the Kadjina, who were now in occupation of the River Reserve. The Kadjina had been able to acquire funds from DAA to purchase a contract mustering plant, and secured a contract on Blina Station, north of Noonkanbah. The two groups, to the surprise of advisers, who thought they were at loggerheads, co-operated closely in this venture, with the bulk of workers on the contract team being drawn from Yungngora's membership.

Friday Muller made the Community's feelings about Noonkanbah clear in a letter early in March to the new Minister for Aboriginal Affairs (by now this was the Liberal, Ian Viner; the Whitlam Labor Government had been ousted in December 1975):

> People [are] going to move to that station as soon as the road is dry...When we were in Quanbun Station we were there only for a short time. But when we go back to Noonkanbah this time we are not coming back to Fitzroy again, because when we were asking for Quanbun we didn't get that station, so this time when we go into Noonkanbah we are not coming back any more.[10]

Later that month – before the road had dried out – the ALFC was able to advise that it had 'virtually reached agreement with vendors for purchase of Noonkanbah Station'.[11] So as the contracting team headed out for Blina Station, the leaders in Fitzroy

Crossing postponed their plans to move out and squat, and started to plan for the move back to their beloved Noonkanbah as the owners.

One of the first decisions they made in their planning – a decision that they were to implement successfully – was that there would be no grog allowed on the station. Noonkanbah was to be a dry camp.

The finalisation of the sale actually took another five months. It was a tense and frustrating period for the Community, sitting in Fitzroy Crossing. They started to become cynical as to whether this would be yet another let down.

One factor in the delay was the insistence of the State Government that the Federal Government, via the ALFC, should not be in any part a holder of the title. The approval of the Western Australian Minister for Lands, Mr Alan Ridge, who was also the member for Kimberley, was required before any transfer of the leases could take place. He had supported much of the Community development work in the Fitzroy Crossing area, and the proposed Noonkanbah purchase. But in freezing the Commonwealth out of any ownership role he reflected his government's anti-Canberra phobia.

The solution reached was that the ALFC's money was used to purchase the companies – Noonkanbah Pty Ltd and Waratea Pty Ltd – that owned the leases and station assets. These companies were then placed in the hands of the State's Aboriginal Lands Trust (ALT), which appointed its secretary and nominees of the communities as directors of the companies. The ownership role the State obtained at no cost in this way was to prove highly significant four years later.

As finalisation of the deal approached, two matters emerged as the focus of difficulties in planning the takeover. Firstly there was the division of the spoils. Friday Muller and his followers insisted that the whole of Noonkanbah was their country; they were the Noonkanbah mob, he had led the fight to regain it, and the Kadjina mob, as far as he was concerned, should try and get land on Cherrabun or elsewhere. Naturally the Kadjina were not agreeable to this. They could not dispute the primacy of the traditional claims of Muller and the Yungngora Elders, but they maintained that they also had claims on the country, and a right to share in the land.

The Kadjina, with the support of the DCW officers and the DAA office in Derby, proposed that the station should be divided in two, with the Yungngora taking and working the portion north of the Fitzroy River, and themselves having the southern portion. This would give them a larger area of land, but in cattle terms the pasture north of the river was of better quality and better serviced by bores and fences, and much of the southern portion was occupied by the economically barren ranges.

At one point a large meeting was held, in which a number of senior Lawmen argued the legitimacy of the Kadjina case, and ultimately this view won the day. But Muller never happily accepted the compromise, and continued sniping at the Kadjina.

The second issue, on which the two groups were united, was the plan, advocated by DAA, that a white manager be appointed at Noonkanbah to help them run the properties. Both groups were adamantly opposed to this proposal, even to the extent of threatening not to go back to Noonkanbah if a manager were installed against their will. They were confident of their own ability, and absolutely sure that they wanted to return as their own masters. They feared, with good reason, that a white man, whether called manager or adviser, would finish up as the boss.

With the assistance of the Community Welfare staff they drew up their own management proposal which centred around a Management Committee comprising their own leaders and cattlemen, assisted by two local station managers who agreed to act as advisers when needed, and attend as members of the Management Committee. After extensive discussions, including a session with the Federal Minister, Ian Viner, when he visited Fitzroy Crossing, they were successful in having their plans approved by the Department.

Finally, on 20 August 1976, all the negotiations, inspections and documentation were completed. An officer of the ALT formally handed over responsibility for management of the properties to the Yungngora and Kadjina Communities. The total price to the ALFC was $540,544. Two Kadjina nominees became directors of Waratea Pty Ltd, and two Yungngora nominees had the same role with Noonkanbah Pty Ltd.

The people were home and free. Ninety hard years after the arrival of Isadore Emanuel they were once again masters of their own land, and owners of a cattle station to boot. They now had a future to believe in.

The destiny, the future, the vision that the Noonkanbah Community held was not spelt out in any charter, not even articulated in specific terms, and perhaps not even shared by all the Noonkanbah Community; but it was there in the mind's eye of the old men who were the powerhouse and the spiritual leaders of the group.

Certainly it included the notion of a successful cattle station, and a concept of self-management and self-determination, the phrases so overworked by the politicians and bureaucrats. The people had already demonstrated their determination to do things their own way in resisting the idea of a white manager for the station. In fact, when they first returned to Noonkanbah, for the first eighteen months there was not a single white person living on the property, a marked departure from the pattern of management adopted by or forced upon most Aboriginal communities. But these things were not at the heart of the vision.

At the heart lay the old people's love of and faith in the Law, the culture, the Aboriginal way of life as they knew it. This was not the traditional life of the days before the white men, which had passed before their time, for all except a couple of the old desert folk like Mick Nicki. It was the life of their youth and middle-age in the station camps in the relatively secure period from the 1930s to the 1950s, when outside the labour demands of the station, the Law was supreme, Noonkanbah was a renowned centre of the Law, children were born and reared to the Aboriginal way, the young people lived by the Law, went through the ceremonial cycles, and respected the Elders.

The vision related to a picture of a community which lived by these principles, in which the oppressive power of the white boss was removed, and in which the people's labour was for their own benefit. The important elements in this vision were internal social and cultural ones, not economic; bringing the younger people back to the Law, making sure they married the right way, making sure that they spoke Walmatjari before they spoke English, caring for the land, conducting the ceremonies.

Whether such a future was ever achievable to the extent that the Elders hoped is highly debatable, given the changes that had been wrought by the years in Fitzroy Crossing, the different perspective of the younger generation, and the compromises that were required with the new world.

It was a vision of conservatives, who yearned for an old and familiar order. It was assumed by the Elders, and grasped to a lesser extent by the younger people in the Community. But it affected the way the Community conducted its affairs, and the decisions it made. It called for an internal strength, and a determination to swim against the tide of the bureaucracy and government policy that in practice regarded such values as admirable, but somewhat quaint and dated – not really relevant to the important issues of development and administration.

By the time the people moved back onto Noonkanbah in September 1976 the cattle season was nearly over. The station plant was mostly in very poor condition, and

Horse-breaking, Noonkanbah.

the horse plant* had gone bush. There was only one working bore on Noonkanbah, and none on Millijidee. Obviously the place had been allowed to deteriorate as the sale negotiations dragged on. This came on top of years of neglect following the changeover from sheep to cattle, which had just preceded the walkoff of the mob in 1971. The only fences were the old sheep fences, now in a state of disrepair. The station was in effect open range, with cattle concentrated on the river frontage and seasonal swamps, in which many would die as the swamps grew boggy and then dry. The station the people took over was but a shadow of the rich and productive enterprise they had once laboured to maintain.

With horses from the Kadjina plant that were worn out from the hard but successful Blina contract, and the handful of working horses that could be mustered on Noonkanbah, the two groups set to, each mustering their own side of the river. Within two weeks of occupying the station they had managed to muster and truck over three hundred and fifty head of cattle to the meatworks. But the return from this was not sufficient to cover their planned operations through to the next season, so with most other stations in the area closing down for the year they kept going, and after a couple of fruitless attempts, the two groups combined forces for a joint muster of the Millijidee river frontage, and were able to truck a last load north to Wyndham, as the local West Kimberley meatworks had by now closed for the year. They were also making running repairs to windmills, trying to keep stock alive. It was a busy few months.

In his first report on the new enterprise the DCW officer working with the Communities was able to write:

Of course one would expect some difficulties in such a new venture, but

---

* Horse plant: herd of working horses kept by a station or contract musterer.

at the same time I believe that the people did a remarkable job in coping with the number of difficulties which they found.[12]

The difficulties were not only of the practical kind. DAA and DCW were competing for influence in the two Communities, and offering markedly different advice. And the tensions between Yungngora and Kadjina continued to flare up regularly, especially in arguments over the use and control of the sparse plant and equipment.

Over their first wet season back on the station the people abandoned the joint Management Committee on which both Communities had been represented in favour of separate ones for each station, and from 1977 on, the two operated as separate entities, though the cycle of co-operation and antagonism continued. Also, by the time the 1977 season started, the departmental disputes were brought largely under control, with the DCW staff, and their philosophical approach of community development, providing the primary advisory input.

With the land and the cattle enterprise firmly in their hands, and settled back in their home country, the next two years were good ones for the Noonkanbah mob. Development of the station continued, with over fifteen hundred head of cattle trucked, and the long program of rehabilitation of bores and construction of cattle fences started up. It was not the perfect cattle station, but it was certainly operational, and improving, more than could be said for many Kimberley properties at the time. The people were proud of their achievements, and seemed to have won the grudging respect of many of the local pastoralists, some of whom continued to help with advice, and practical input, such as assistance with aerial mustering.

The other major initiative was the establishment in 1978 of a Community run school. In 1977 most of the children had stayed in Fitzroy Crossing to attend school, under the care of a few of the women and Elders. For family, social and cultural reasons the Community found this intolerable, and determined to change the situation. They were far from impressed with what they had seen of the government school system in Fitzroy Crossing. Not only did they feel that it did not produce results, and in fact was a negative influence on their children, they were most concerned at the fact that the kids were losing their traditional language in favour of English.

Late in 1977 a delegation from the Community set off south to the unknown territory of the Pilbara, to visit the Strelley mob and inspect their school. The Strelley mob were the strikers of the 1940s – still on strike they claimed. After years of keeping their children out of the government schools, they had finally attracted sufficient money to establish their own independent school system. Their emphasis was on reinforcement of Aboriginal Law and culture, appropriate teaching materials and methodology, and most importantly, a bilingual approach in which priority was given to fluency and literacy in the traditional languages, with subsequent transfer of these skills to English.

The theory and practice of this type of education struck a deep chord in the Noonkanbah people. Having seen it they were in no doubt that this was what they wanted. With substantial financial assistance from Nomads – the operational organisation of the Strelley mob – and their own 'chuck in' money, they made an incredible effort to get their own school up and running in the old shearing shed for 1978, and bring their kids back home. The school was actually operated under the Nomads umbrella, with administrative and educational support coming from Strelley; but control was exercised by a school board comprising Noonkanbah Community members led by Ginger Nganawilla, which would meet weekly with the two white teachers who were employed. All this was done in double quick time despite the opposition and cynicism of the Education Department, which initially refused to register the school, and DAA, which refused requests for financial support.

The pride and enthusiasm generated by the successful establishment of the school

Kulkarriya Community School. Top: Pre-primary class. Bottom: Primary class.

were a tangible thing in the Community. There were Community members on staff, actively engaged in the teaching. Old people were teaching language and telling stories. Some women were running the kindergarten on their own, others were cooking lunches for the kids. The students attended regularly – a far cry from the truancy and negativity associated with the Fitzroy Crossing school. Conditions and educational facilities were crude by any description, but the spirit was high. More than anything else that happened in the Community, this school was the manifestation of the vision of the Elders of a truly Aboriginal Community of Aboriginal values.

In this period there were also significant changes in the power structures of the Community. This revolved around the removal of Friday Muller as Chairman, and his loss of power and influence. He had lost some of his credibility and prestige during his losing battle to keep the whole of the old Noonkanbah and Waratea lease under

Yungngora's control. During 1977 and 1978 he was very ill, spending long periods in hospital, eventually losing one leg to gangrene. And when he was on the station his individualistic, and at times autocratic, style began to rub some of the Community the wrong way. It did not sit easily with the broad participation, and communal decision-making style encouraged by the Community development model that was operating at Noonkanbah. By the end of 1978 he had been eased out of power, and the Management Committee that had been established to run the station enterprise had been expanded and revamped to become responsible for the whole of the Community's affairs.

Muller's unwilling slide from power was a sad phenomenon. Two years later the State Government tried to present it as a coup by a younger generation of non-traditionalists, replacing the only man with the true right to speak for the country. This was far from the truth, as the new system had the involvement and support of the other Noonkanbah Elders, who had seen, and either supported or quietly accepted the need for change. The new spokesman for the Community, Dicky Skinner, was certainly a much younger man, and one more at ease and familiar with the mechanics of the government system. But he was also a 'maban man' (a traditional healer), a believer in the Aboriginal way with the teachings of his father echoing in his mind. In his own way he shared the vision of the Elders, as can be seen from his words in the first chapter.

The other issue that demanded the attention of the Community leaders, old and new, during these first years was the ever increasing presence of the miners, and the growing evidence of their effect on the land, the station enterprise, and the Community's new found feeling of security.

It had been a problem right from the start, when the minutes of the very first Management Committee meeting on the station, on 10 September 1976, recorded that 'The presence of the Mining Company on Noonkanbah and Millijidee was discussed. It was pointed out that there was no action which could prevent the entry and exploration going ahead.' From there it had escalated to the point where the Community instructed the Aboriginal Legal Service to lodge the objections to mining claims that led to the Broome hearing of November 1978.

D espite the spectre of the miners, Noonkanbah was a confident community at the close of that year. The cattle season had wound down; their school had broken up for its first Christmas holiday, leaving not a white face on the property; the wet season closed in, and it was time for Aboriginal business – dancing, singing and ceremonies.

There were nearly two hundred people in the Community. Most were living in camps that were not a lot better than those of the old days or the fringe camps, though some families occupied the buildings formerly reserved for the white staff and the shearers. But this was not a cause for undue concern; it was expected that decent housing would come in due course. And at least now they could spread out into separate camps for each of the clans, instead of all being crowded on top of each other.

They were the custodians of the land, steeped in its Law and Dreamtime stories; and now the owners of the white man's pastoral lease as well. They had a proud reputation that stretched from the Pilbara, throughout the Kimberley, and into the Northern Territory as 'properly strong Lawmen'. They were proud Aboriginal people, they planned to stay that way, and bring their children up the same way.

And they were strong. They had won the fight for their land. They had won the fight to run and manage the land their way, and were doing it well. They had won the fight to teach their children in their own school, in the way they believed to be right.

They believed in themselves and their own power. And there was a spirit abroad in the Kimberley communities that what the Noonkanbah mob had done could be done by others, and that together they had the capacity to change the present and build for the future. The pendulum was swinging back their way after ninety long years.

The anthropologist Kingsley Palmer sensed the mood at Noonkanbah, and described it this way in the conclusion to his report prepared for the Broome court case:

> Noonkanbah has emerged as a distinct Aboriginal community, which has attempted to solve some of the problems confronting Aborigines in the Kimberley today. The community is independent and progressive, providing a safe, quiet camping place, a home without violence and social disintegration that so often accompanies alcohol in urban settlements. It is an expression of Aboriginal determination to do something to ameliorate the situation. This aspect of the Noonkanbah community is obviously of the utmost importance. The establishment of mining close to Noonkanbah community would undoubtedly present the Aborigines with many serious problems, and would be a direct threat to the peace and continued existence on Noonkanbah as it exists today.[13]

5

DIFFERENT DREAMS

We have been saying 'yes Boss' and 'yes Father' for too long.

Tommy Edgar of Broome, at the first Kimberley Land Council meeting. Noonkanbah, May 1978.

By the second half of the 1970s Aboriginal people all over the Kimberley were beginning to emerge from the trough of despondency that had followed the dislocations of the previous ten years. New ideas, new influences and new attitudes were at work. Most importantly, there was a greater preparedness to challenge accepted wisdoms and practices.

Many factors contributed to this new assertiveness. Land Rights legislation just across the border in the Northern Territory had created a precedent, and a goal to aim at. Federal Government funding programs had made people more aware of the possibilities of change. The community development policies of the Department for Community Welfare, first applied in the Fitzroy Crossing area, began to spread to their other offices in the region, though never with quite the same effect or success. There was a sprinkling of white workers in government departments and Aboriginal organisations and communities willing to promote the new attitudes, and to take on the role of advocates and activists, rather than be merely administrators of government policy.

But these factors only assisted and shaped a development that was bound to come sooner rather than later. The living conditions that the vast majority of Kimberley people suffered were a shameful anachronism in the Australia of the 1970s. An era of absolute subservience on the cattle stations had given way to an equally depressing and destructive fringedwelling life. A reaction against the circumstances in which they found themselves was inevitable.

The issue that first clarified and hardened attitudes on all sides was the battle for the seat of Kimberley in the 1977 State Election. Until that time the great mass of Aboriginal people either were not on the electoral roll, or voted at the direction of the station bosses, as Dicky Skinner described:

> Man was going round campaigning, telling people 'Right, you've got to vote for me, I'll help you, help you as much as I can.' Soon as the election comes, the station manager used to come down, and he said, 'Right, you've got to vote for that good man so he can help us'.[1]

But in 1977 the sitting member, the Liberal Minister for Lands, Alan Ridge, faced a strong challenge from the Australian Labor Party (ALP) candidate, Ernie Bridge. Bridge was an Aboriginal pastoralist, and a previous President of his home town shire of Halls Creek. He was well-known and popular in Aboriginal communities through his work on the Aboriginal Lands Trust and the Aboriginal Land Fund Commission, and he ran a strong campaign, travelling throughout the region in his light plane.

On election day the Liberal Party flew in five Perth lawyers to act as scrutineers

Noonkanbah store.

at strategic polling booths, and instructed their local workers for the other booths where Aboriginal people would be voting. 'The Plan' they implemented called on the scrutineers to require the polling booth officials to use a literal interpretation of the Electoral Act when ascertaining the identity, address and right to vote of Aboriginal people coming into the booth. The questions used for this purpose, as set out in the Act, are full of legal jargon. As the Liberals anticipated, many potential Aboriginal voters became confused or frustrated, and were either ruled ineligible when unable to answer the questions as put, or walked out of the booths in despair.

Where this ploy did not succeed, the written instructions the Liberals provided to the lawyers advised them that when a voter presented a How to Vote card they were to 'intervene and demand that the voter be questioned to find out whether he knows what a How to Vote card is...Require the letter of the law to be carried out...use the technicalities of the law to the full extent.'[2]

Ridge won by ninety-three votes. Bridge challenged the result in the Court of Disputed Returns. The sordid detail and cynicism of 'The Plan' were revealed, as were some of the other tricks used, including the deliberate deception of a returning officer by a Liberal scrutineer. The Court, after conducting hearings throughout the Kimberley, found that at least ninety-seven Aboriginal people were unjustly prevented from casting votes for Bridge, and declared the result invalid.

But the evidence in the hearings that most offended Aboriginal people was a post-election letter Ridge wrote to one of his constituents in which he stated:

> It was a degrading experience to have to campaign amongst the Aborigines to the extent I did and it offended me to know that whilst I was concentrating my efforts on these simple people...I was neglecting a more informed and intelligent section of the community...It is indeed a travesty of justice that a comparative handful of such ill-informed people who can be used like pawns in a game by unscrupulous opportunists, should have the right or power to determine the future of our State.[3]

Ridge won the re-run of the election, this time by two hundred and five votes, after a bitter campaign. Three independents stood, effectively acting as dummy candidates for the Liberals, by taking a few votes from Bridge in their localities, and increasing the informal vote.

The electorate was deeply polarised. The controversy generated by the dispute, the public exposure of Alan Ridge's private attitudes, and the subsequent inquiry into the

Electoral Act did much to politicise the Aborigines of the Kimberley and set them against the ruling Liberal Government. By the time the next election came round in 1980 there were enough new Aboriginal voters on the rolls to ensure that Ridge had no chance of re-election.

In 1978 the pace of events quickened, with new controversies and developments in the Kimberley throughout the year.

The most significant initiative for Aboriginal people was the formation of the Kimberley Land Council (KLC), in May at Noonkanbah. The occasion was a cultural festival funded by the Aboriginal Cultural Foundation of Darwin.

A month earlier, at a smaller planning meeting near Halls Creek, Mark Moora of the Balgo Community had set the tone, when he appealed to people to come to Noonkanbah:

> I'm calling the people from everywhere who hear my voice. Now I'm saying all this word, what we come here for – because we've come here for talking about things that have been took away from us. And meaning that we're going to try to bring these things back for our country. And white people from all over Australia they took our country away – that's what we've come here for; to have a meeting amongst ourselves – to help us. That's what we've called all these people for – to give us more power.[4]

There were people from thirty Kimberley and five Northern Territory communities in attendance at Noonkanbah. Many delegations included large dance groups for the cultural festival, as well as community leaders. The two Kimberley members of the National Aboriginal Conference (NAC), Jimmy Bieunderry and Reg Birch, and Ernie Bridge were there, as well as Galawurry Yunupingu of the Northern Land Council. Apart from strictly ceremonial gatherings, it was the largest and most significant meeting of Aboriginal people of the Kimberley to that time.

In two days of talks, punctuated by nights of dancing and social activity, the decision was made to form a Land Council for the Kimberley. Of course, it was a very different kettle of fish from Yunupingu's statutory and well-funded organisation in Darwin; but there was no doubt that it belonged to the people, and they invested great hopes and expectations in it.

The major issues were the need for land and Land Rights legislation; concern and anger over the activity of mining companies throughout the Kimberley; social issues such as housing, drinking and community organisation; and a desire to learn from people such as Bridge and Yunupingu about how to organise and run a Land Council effectively. There was a strong anti-State Government undercurrent, balanced by a mood of determination, best expressed by the Broome delegate Tommy Edgar when he stated: 'We have been saying "yes Boss" or "yes Father" for too long'[5]; and Yunupingu, when he said:

> We have a victory to win. We have to believe in ourselves ... Big talks are to come...don't think Councillor's job will be easy, don't make this mistake. It's the hardest job any Aboriginal can face. It's a long job. It means talking sharp and strong and straight.[6]

Over the rest of that year the KLC was involved in supporting a number of communities in disputes that attracted public attention. It was operating with virtually no funds or facilities, surviving mainly through the assistance provided by the NAC members. In these circumstances it was not able to do much in terms of field-work with communities, policy development or pursuit of a clear political strategy. However, it supported communities in their individual fights, and was able to develop a public profile through association with these issues, and tours of delegates to Perth and eastern cities.

The pressure from the Kimberley people was increasing. There was no clear focus or defined platform for their energies yet, but their silence of ninety years in the public forums of Western Australia was clearly over.

It was pure coincidence that this surge of Aboriginal activism arose at the same time as a mineral exploration boom in the Kimberley. Unlike the Pilbara further south, where small-scale mining and prospecting for tin, gold, asbestos and precious metals had developed virtually hand-in-hand with the pastoral industry, and the iron ore boom of the 1960s had transformed the region, mining had not played a big part in the history of the Kimberley up until the 1970s.

Between 1976 and 1978 hopes were building amongst many people in government and industry circles that this would change. Oil, the cornerstone of modern society, and diamonds, the most romantic of minerals, were the two resources that drew the attention of geologists and their employers from around the globe to the Kimberley.

Oil exploration in the area had a long but unsuccessful history. Hydrocarbons, the basic indicator for oil or gas deposits, had been identified as far back as 1919. In geological terms the relevant area was the Canning Basin, which stretches from the edge of the King Leopold Ranges, south into the Great Sandy Desert. Theory held that ancient coral reefs, similar to those that form the existing outcrops of the Leopolds and Oscars, but now buried deep below the ground, could hold deposits.

A number of wells had been drilled in the 1950s and 60s – including one in the St George Range in 1965/66 – by companies such as West Australian Petroleum (WAPET) and Continental Oil, an American company. Some had produced 'shows', but never enough to establish a viable field, or even the likelihood of one.

Industry opinion was mixed as to the prospects of success of further exploration. In articles in the *West Australian* newspaper early in 1978 the Mines Department's Bureau of Mineral Resources was somewhat gloomy in outlook, on the basis of available geological data and the lack of success of previous work, but an industry geologist responding claimed that improved techniques and re-interpretation of the data gave cause for optimism.

A geologist associated with the Amax joint venture gave a balanced view when he suggested:

> ...at present the evaluation of the Devonian reef play in the Canning Basin is considered in the industry as one of the most promising onshore plays in Australia. However, there are drawbacks...there [have] been quite a lot of wells sunk with relatively poor results. Although some early wells may have been poorly located, there has been sufficient activity to show that the area is not 'dripping with oil'.[7]

Interest within the industry was sufficiently keen to see virtually the whole of the West Kimberley south of the range country – including all of Noonkanbah and Millijidee Stations – and large parts of the adjoining desert taken up in the form of oil exploration permits by late 1977.

Each of these permits contained enormous areas, much larger than the pastoral leases which they covered. Companies or consortiums bid for them by submitting work programs and expenditure commitments for a five-year period which stated what they would undertake in the way of seismic work and drilling of wells. Once a bid was accepted, the permit holder was bound to the terms of its program unless permission to vary it was received from the Mines Department.

The seismic work involved bulldozing a number of straight lines, each many kilometres long, normally in a grid pattern. Sensors would then be laid out along these lines, and a vibrator – in effect an enormous hammer – would send shock waves deep into the earth. The sensors laid out on the grid lines would read these vibrations, and then by a highly complex laboratory procedure the results would be interpreted to give an impression of the underlying geological formations. The hope was to identify the underground 'domes' of the ancient reefs in which hydrocarbons may have accumulated.

The noticeable result for the station owners, black and white, and for people flying over the country, was the complex of grid lines appearing all over the countryside. In some cases these brought some advantages, opening up access roads to country that might have previously been difficult to penetrate, be it for fishing or mustering. But most regarded the seismic crews as an unwelcome intrusion of privacy. The lines also cut fences, and often became erosion points. From the Aboriginal perspective, where there was not proper consultation, there was the prospect of damage to sites and places of importance.

There had been some exploration for diamonds in the Kimberley in the 1960s and early 70s, including on Noonkanbah. The Stockdale employees who had stolen sacred boards from Tatju Hill in 1970 were looking for diamonds. But it was in 1977/78 that the boom, led by CRA, took off in a major way.

In diamond exploration, interest centred on kimberlite pipes, which took their name from the Kimberley diamond province in South Africa. These pipes, or plugs, were the remnants of the cores of ancient volcanoes, which had provided the extreme conditions necessary to form diamonds from the original carbon material. It was a chancy business, first to find the pipes, and then only a small percentage of them were diamondiferous.

There were two methods of exploration, apart from blind hope and faith, which also played its part in the boom. Pipes, or potential pipes, could be identified in some cases by satellite imagery or aeromagnetic surveys, subject to confirmation by ground sampling. Or sampling of alluvial gravels in stream beds might identify potential material washed down from a source pipe.

Often the tips of the pipes were located in small remnant hills. Pea Hill and others on Noonkanbah were classic examples of this. It so happened that these features, being relatively prominent in the landscape, were also nearly always Dreaming sites of importance to Aboriginal people.

CRA was in the forefront of both the geological theory and the on-ground pegging of the diamond boom. Their first significant find was at Ellendale, not far north of Noonkanbah, in 1977. Word circulated in the industry, and soon the race to peg ground was on. CRA held ninety-eight claims on Noonkanbah, and more on Calwynyardah, a small station between Noonkanbah and Ellendale, and large tracts of claims in the north and east Kimberley, where by 1978 their attention was focusing on the Argyle deposit.

The Premier of Western Australia, Sir Charles Court, must have responded with excitement to this exploration boom. There was no doubting his enthusiasm for industrial development in general and mining development in particular:

> Economic development had been Court's ticket to political prominence and power and it also formed his personal faith. Indeed, he spoke of development with a zeal which betrayed an almost religious conviction about the future direction of Western Australia.[8]

His greatest achievement in this field had been the establishment of the iron ore industry in the Pilbara in the 1960s, which had seen six major mines and seven associated new towns come into being. As Deputy Premier and Minister for Industrial Development and the North West at the time, Court had identified himself closely with the companies and the projects involved. With the North West Shelf gas project about to enter the construction phase, the development of the Pilbara looked set to continue.

On the other hand the Kimberley, as the second region covered by his North West portfolio, had been more of a disappointment. He had little or no input into planning for the dramatic social changes that affected the area in the late 1960s. His major project, the Ord River Dam, which he had promoted and trumpeted, was widely seen as something of an extravagant white elephant. A string of disastrous cropping experiments had failed to come up with a viable use for the vast reserves of water held by the dam. It is only in recent years, as the big schemes of the Court era have been replaced by smaller scale fruit and vegetable crops, that it has begun to look remotely worth the huge investment poured into it.

Now there was the prospect of a new era for the Kimberley. Court's earlier dreams and visions would probably have been re-ignited, and perhaps he thought in terms of another great surge of frontier industrial development to mark the closing years of his premiership.

His commitment to industrial development was combined with an explicit faith in an idealised vision of the virtues of free enterprise. In a 1976 speech extolling resource abundance and development as the path to a better world he made the statement, 'Only in the hard trading of the open market are the realities decided with devastating impartiality'.[9] The use of the word devastating in this context is an interesting clue to the hardness of Court's approach.

The trouble was, he appeared to take great exception to the free operation of forces in the community other than those of the profit oriented market. In fact his term was marked by a range of government actions designed to smother any alternative forces, and make the social equations anything but impartial. People, organisations and movements with a different vision were seen as evil, misguided, or both:

> Interviewed in 1977...he remarked that before any development project could begin, three things had to happen: first, the site would be deemed sacred or of historical significance to some group; secondly, the trade union movement would place it under a black ban; and thirdly, conservationists would declare it the last remaining location of some rare species of flora or fauna. In early 1978 he also mounted an attack on 'drop-outs' who were threatening the very fabric of society with their alternative lifestyle settlements...Challenged on his basic beliefs, his reflex action was to portray opposition as left-wing conspiracy or anarchistic dementia.[10]

As the Noonkanbah dispute developed Court and his Liberal-Country Party Government were often accused of being racist, especially after they began their attempts to denigrate and discredit the Community. If the label can be used correctly, in the pre-Noonkanbah days it was perhaps the form of latent, paternalistic racism common to most Australians.

Until the mid-1970s Aboriginal Affairs was not a high profile political issue in Western Australia. Sir Charles Court, and most other politicians, were genuinely pleased to lend assistance where they could, usually in a spirit of benevolence rather than through any sense of justice. It was this spirit that lay behind Alan Ridge's early support for community development work in the Kimberley, and the purchase of Noonkanbah; no one objected to efforts to ameliorate the most obvious hardships and iniquities suffered by Aboriginal people.

But underlying this attitude was a basic, usually unspoken belief in the inferiority of blacks. In one sense this was to be expected given the values of the education system of their time and of their elders and peers. Hence Ridge's use of terms such as 'ill-informed people who can be used like pawns', and his anger that Aborigines 'should have the right or power to determine the future of our State'.

Hence, also, the assumption that has dogged Aboriginal people in one form or another through all of Australian history, that because of their innate inferiority, measures to assist them will stop at the point where 'more important' interests are impinged upon; or the other side of the coin, an adverse impact upon Aboriginal people is never reason enough to stop an activity of benefit to the 'more important' interests. It is never stated in these terms, but an endless string of justifications and rationales has been trotted out over the years that hides this basic belief held by so many white Australians.

As Aboriginal activism became more public and more determined, and especially when it appeared to threaten the dream of industrial development, this unspoken belief in Aboriginal inferiority affected the Government's response. It could not accept that the activism was self-motivated or genuine, however obvious the root causes might be; it always looked for conspiracy theories, sinister motives, and behind the scenes manipulators, and any European working with and supportive of the Aboriginal position became a target for this thinking.

Premier Court and his Government became increasingly and openly hostile to the demands and interests of the Aboriginal people. Legislative action and policy statements in the period 1977 to 1979 reflected this changing Government attitude, with the first battleground being the Electoral Act, as the Government attempted to minimise the impact of the Aboriginal vote.

In the same letter that revealed his distaste for campaigning in Aboriginal communities, Alan Ridge said:

> I believe that we now have enough evidence to try and convince people of the necessity for amending the Electoral Act in relation to illiterate voters. If this is not done...by the next election there could be in the order of 3000 to 4000 Aborigines on the roll* and under such circumstances the Liberal Party would be doomed to failure...it is going to be difficult to get through any legislation which smacks of discrimination but I believe that we have an obligation to try.[11]

Before the Court of Disputed Returns had brought in its findings the Government introduced amendments to the Act. These were designed to prevent the practice common amongst illiterate Aborigines of handing a How to Vote card of the party of their choice to polling booth officials as evidence of their voting intentions. When this was done the booth officials would ascertain that this was how the person wished to vote, and then fill in ballot papers for them. If the practice were banned it would have effectively disenfranchised possibly thousands of Aboriginal voters certain of their voting preferences, but unable to fill in ballot papers on their own.

In the event, Ridge's forecast of the difficulties involved proved correct. In the Legislative Assembly some Government members crossed the floor or abstained, and the tied vote was defeated by the casting vote of the Liberal Party speaker of the house.

---

* At this time is was not compulsory for Aboriginal people to be on the electoral roll, as it was for others in the community.

98

Following the re-run election, the 1978 Inquiry into the Electoral Act conducted by Judge Kay recommended greater, not lesser, assistance to illiterate Aboriginal voters. But the Government's response when amendments to the Act were eventually made in 1979 went the other way.

Two major changes were made. The procedure for enrolment was altered so that applications had to be witnessed by a police officer, a Justice of the Peace, a Clerk of Courts or an Electoral Officer, whereas previously any other elector could act as a witness. This was seen to be aimed at reducing the number of Aboriginal people enrolling, as the eligible witnesses were not always available in remote areas and were generally seen as hostile authority figures by Aboriginal people; and it made the practice of Labor Party and/or Aboriginal sympathisers going out into communities on enrolment drives illegal unless accompanied by an eligible witness.

Also, it became an offence 'to persuade or induce...an elector to make application for a postal vote'. This was aimed at limiting the number of enrolled voters able to exercise their vote; postal voting was often the most convenient way for people in remote communities, distant from polling booths, to vote, and given that elections were normally held in the northern wet season when roads could be closed, it was sometimes the only way of voting.

This time the legislation was pushed through despite widespread protest from Aboriginal groups and criticism from political commentators.

There were two other legislative actions in 1978 hostile to Aboriginal interests.

After the AAPA Commissioner exercised his powers, at the request of the Oombulgurrie Community, to deny entry permits to the Forrest River Reserve to two diamond exploration companies, the Government responded immediately by amending the AAPA Act to vest the power over entry permits in the Minister for Community Welfare instead of his Commissioner.

In the same session of the Parliament the Government pushed through a long awaited overhaul of the Mining Act. This new Act aroused opposition in many quarters, including some Government members, and small prospectors throughout the State, as it was seen to favour the interests of the large mining houses and vest enormous discretionary powers in the Minister for Mines. It also contained a clause enabling the Minister to authorise the holder of a miner's right to enter an Aboriginal Reserve without an entry permit. The only obligation on the Minister before exercising this power was to 'consult' with his colleague, the Minister for Community Welfare; he did not even require his colleague's agreement in the unlikely event that this might be withheld. Effectively the Act meant that the full range of mining activity from exploration to extraction could go ahead on Aboriginal land without any consultation with, let alone approval from, the people concerned.

Premier Court's public posture, as well as his parliamentary actions, were becoming more hard-nosed. During 1978 he increasingly aligned himself with sections of the Liberal Party and the mining industry who were publicly attacking the Land Rights legislation introduced to the Northern Territory; describing it as racially divisive, apartheid in reverse, and economically harmful to mining development.

In the same year he wrote to the Australian Prime Minister, Malcolm Fraser, to complain about Ian Viner's handling of the Aboriginal Affairs portfolio, saying that he was out of touch, and that the Federal approach posed a threat to 'co-operative federalism'. This followed a public criticism of the State Government's approach to Land Rights by Viner.[12]

It was later publicly announced that Court and Viner had 'moved to settle their differences over Aboriginal policy'.[13] What was not revealed was that this settlement involved a gentlemen's agreement that there would be no further purchases of pastoral leases for Aboriginal groups in Western Australia by the ALFC; this agreement was never stated explicitly in any direction from Viner to the ALFC, but was effectively implemented by DAA vetoing any ALFC proposals for purchases in the State.[14] When the ALFC and others started to question what was going on, Viner spoke in terms of consolidation of existing properties such as Noonkanbah before considering any expansion. The State's Minister for Lands, June Craig, 'declared that she would not agree to transferring any more pastoral properties to Aboriginal communities, until they demonstrated that they could administer and run them economically'.[15]

Such disputes with the Federal Government were characteristic of Court's term in office, despite the fact that he and Fraser belonged to the same party. Court was an ardent 'state's rights' advocate, with an instinctive dislike and distrust of Canberra, whether the incumbent government be Labor or Liberal. He consistently opposed any Federal Government activity that he saw as an intrusion on the State's responsibilities or sphere of influence.

This inherent suspicion of Canberra was magnified in the Aboriginal affairs arena by personality and faction clashes within the Western Australian Liberal Party. Viner, and his successor Senator Fred Chaney, were both Western Australians, but did not belong to the conservative faction that dominated the party organisation and the State Government. Chaney in particular was a 'small l liberal' on many social issues; Fraser had once described him as 'the conscience of the Liberal Party'. He was sympathetic to the Aboriginal cause, and had been associated with the Aboriginal Legal Service. He appeared to have many enemies within the Liberal hierarchy of Perth.

During Viner's and Chaney's ministries, the Fraser Government had proceeded with an amended but substantially similar Land Rights package for the Northern Territory, as originally proposed by the Labor Government of Gough Whitlam. It had also supported the South Australian Government's Pitjanjatjarra Land Rights legislation, and continued funding organisations such as the Aboriginal Legal Service, much to the chagrin of Premier Court, and Premier Bjelke-Petersen in Queensland. Despite differences over emphasis and detail, there was still an essentially progressive and bipartisan approach to Aboriginal affairs at a Federal level, with an increasingly vocal opposition spearheaded by Court and Bjelke-Petersen, the Northern Territory administration, and the mining industry.

B y 1978 this mixture of tensions and conflicting interests involving Aboriginal communities, mining interests, and the State and Federal Governments was becoming too volatile to be contained for very much longer.

6

THE SECOND INVASION

The dislike and mistrust of the Gadiya, born of long years of bitter experience is nowhere better expressed than in the contempt for the 'mineral mob'.

Kingsley Palmer, anthropologist, in a written Report on Noonkanbah, August 1978.

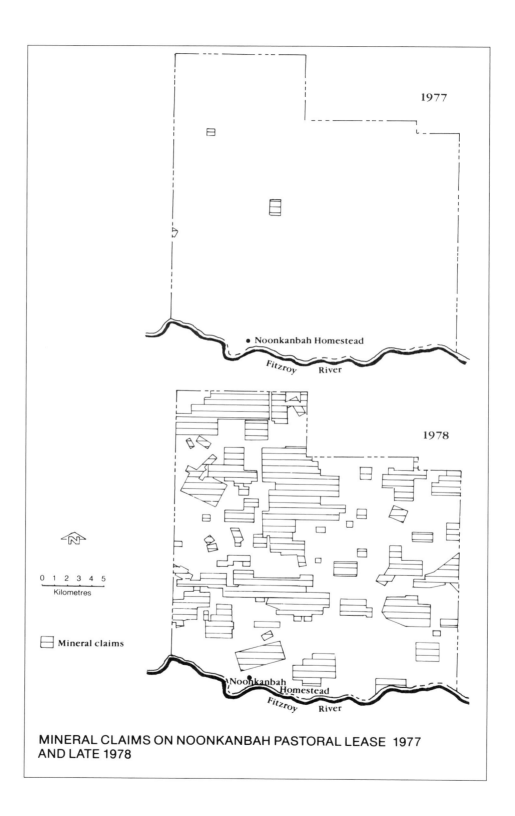

1977

● Noonkanbah Homestead

Fitzroy River

1978

N

0 1 2 3 4 5
Kilometres

Mineral claims

● Noonkanbah Homestead

Fitzroy River

MINERAL CLAIMS ON NOONKANBAH PASTORAL LEASE 1977
AND LATE 1978

The Noonkanbah Community was experiencing the full impact of both the oil and diamond exploration activities affecting the Kimberley region.

By May 1978, four hundred and ninety-seven mineral claims had been pegged on Noonkanbah Station – that is the new Noonkanbah, north of the Fitzroy River only. The claims were held by about thirty different groups ranging from the largest mining houses in the world to small-time prospectors hoping to get lucky and cash in on the boom. These claims of one hundred and twenty hectares each covered a total of just under sixty thousand hectares, or thirty-five percent of the station, including all of the main topographical features so rich in meaning to the Noonkanbah people.

As a pastoral lease Noonkanbah did not even have the limited protection the entry permit system had provided up to then on Aboriginal Reserve land. In the rush to peg claims miners either did not know or did not care about the provisions of the State's Aboriginal Heritage Act that was supposed to give protection to sacred sites.

The secrecy and frenetic pace associated with the boom meant that the people were never consulted before claims were pegged. Sometimes they were officially notified afterwards, often they were not. All they saw were strange vehicles running around, and pegs appearing in the ground all over the station.

In a feature article on the diamond boom in September of 1978, the *West Australian* reported:

> Rumours about diamonds abound in Derby amid stories of security that border on the comic and the 3500 residents are waiting for the boom to happen...
>
> Derby has shown no sign of an impending boom beyond talk, unavailability of accommodation, increased air movements, strange faces in town and reports of the latest unfriendly tactics of people in the middle of nowhere. One local resident who did not want to be named learnt that he was near a sensitive site when he was buzzed by a helicopter, which landed ahead of him.
>
> Tourists report a brusque reaction from men who suddenly appear from nowhere in the bush...
>
> There are unconfirmed reports of claim-jumping among small operators and pegging teams.
>
> Unscrupulous peggers have torn down fences on the Aboriginal-run Noonkanbah Station near Fitzroy Crossing, where there have been reports of bulldozing of sacred sites...
>
> At Noonkanbah, one Derby resident came across a man stranded in a

four-wheel-drive vehicle bogged in a pool of water. Such situations are common, but in this case the driver was wearing a suit and tie.[1]

It was this sort of activity that led the Community, early in 1978, to instruct the Aboriginal Legal Service to begin lodging objections to mining claims pegged on the station. The Community's reaction to the invasion is recorded in the report compiled by Kingsley Palmer for the hearing of the objections to CRA's claims in Broome that November:

> Feeling against, 'What tha Gadiya bin dun early days' runs strongly through Noonkanbah experience. Opposition to European-Australians and especially against mining personnel is strongly expressed. Children are taught that the Gadiya is a bogeyman, and the peggers of mineral claims are the new settlers who will steal the land yet again...[2]

> The climate of opinion, expressed through oral tradition reveals this resistance to the Gadiya quite clearly. Years of ill-treatment, murder, rape, exploitation and alienation of land have left their mark. The Biiyirn (Aborigine) is now in a position to make some show of fighting back. For the first time in many men's lives, outsiders, and particularly Gadiya must take notice of what the Aborigine is saying. The dislike and mistrust of the Gadiya, born of long years of bitter experience is nowhere better expressed than in the contempt for the 'mineral mob'.[3]

The legal attempt to control the frenzy of the diamond seekers had come to nought, and there were still the oil explorers to come to terms with. Nineteen seventy-eight was also the year in which serious problems began to emerge on this front.

Exploration Permit (EP) 97 had been granted to a consortium led by Whitestone Australia Ltd on 17 September 1976. This was exactly one week before the official transfer of the Noonkanbah and Waratea pastoral leases to the new company headed by the Aboriginal Lands Trust, and just a couple of weeks after the people had actually moved back onto the station and begun mustering.

The permit conditions set out by the Mines Department were of a standard nature. They made no mention of the requirements of the State's Aboriginal Heritage Act relating to the protection of Aboriginal sites.

Whitestone Australia was a subsidiary of the American based Whitestone Petroleum, a relatively small company that had been involved in oil exploration in countries including Libya, Kenya, Ethiopia and Irian Jaya. A senior executive of the American company had worked in the Kimberley with Continental Oil in the 1960s:

> He was not completely happy with the exploration carried out at that time, because he thought there were better prospects than the one drilled. In particular, he took a strong personal interest in one particular location in the St George Range, and maintained an interest in returning to the area.[4]

It was this link that led Whitestone to be the first company to move back into this part of the Canning Basin since WAPET's and Continental's work of the mid-1960s. Like most of the smaller players in the industry, Whitestone did not have the financial capacity to carry out an exploration program on its own. So it 'farmed out' interests in the EP in return for financial support.

Whitestone carried out the first seismic survey of the five-year program approved by the Mines Department between 24 September and 22 November 1976. As was normal practice, they directed where the seismic lines should be located, but the actual field-work was carried out by a contractor specialising in this work. The 1976 survey covered a total of three hundred and seventy-eight kilometres, two thirds of which were on Noonkanbah and Millijidee. It was concentrated on two areas at the western end of the St George Range.

Whitestone's exploration manager later stated:

> Prior to the commencement of any work [on the 1976 survey] the Company manager, accompanied by a representative of the Aboriginal Sites Department from Derby met with about twenty Community Elders led by Friday Muller and Charlie Rangie. After the location of the survey lines was explained, the community asked that one of the lines be moved to avoid an area considered 'important ground' by some of the Elders. This line was moved and there were no complaints during or after the survey.[5]

Enquiries with the then staff of the Aboriginal Sites Department have failed to find any member who participated in such a meeting. This is not to say that consultations did not occur, but perhaps Whitestone went out with an officer of the AAPA or some such body, less qualified in the specialised field of Aboriginal site surveys than the Sites Department staff.

Certainly the people of Noonkanbah were able to show damage that had occurred. An overflow channel of the Fitzroy River, upstream from the homestead, that had been used in former times as a fish trap, and had associations with stories of the Dreaming, embodied in trees at either side of the channel, was bulldozed.

Shortly after the completion of the 1976 survey a further farm out of interests in EP97 occurred. The Amax Iron Ore Corporation became a partner with a twenty-seven and a half percent share on 16 December. Amax took over from Whitestone as the operating partner, responsible for the actual conduct of work and field operations on the permit.

The parent company of Amax Iron Ore was the American giant Amax Incorporated, one of the larger mining companies on the world scene. Its interests in Australia were extensive, but until it became associated with Noonkanbah it had a deliberately cultivated low public profile.

Amax had started as a miner of the rare metal molybdenum, and expanded into coal, aluminium, uranium, oil and gas in North America. In the 1960s it had turned away from heavy investments in Africa to what it saw as the more stable political and economic climate of Australia.

With the Australian companies Broken Hill Proprietary Limited (BHP) and Colonial Sugar Refineries (CSR), it became a partner in the Mount Newman iron ore mine in the Pilbara, with control over overseas marketing of production. It acquired substantial interests in coal mines in New South Wales and Queensland. Its aluminium division, Alumax, was a partner in the joint venture in control of the huge bauxite deposits at the Mitchell Plateau in the North Kimberley. It held a one-third share in Australian Consolidated Minerals, a company with a wide range of mining and exploration projects throughout the country. Amax Australian Ventures, a wholly owned subsidiary, held the brief to look for investment opportunities in mining projects already under way or under development. Amax Exploration (Australia), another subsidiary, initiated exploration programs in many parts of the country, including participation in the new Kimberley diamond rush.

Through joint ventures and mutual shareholdings in various second tier companies,

Amax was linked to all the major mining houses of America, Britain and Australia, and some of Japan's industrial giants. It was, and still is, a major player in the big league. The head office in Houston, Texas, exercised a tight control over the planning and activities of its various interests and subsidiary companies. Senior American executives had been on first name terms with Premier Court since their involvement in the Pilbara iron ore industry dating back to the early 1960s.

In America where its public profile is much higher, the company was no stranger to controversy. The main battlefields were environmental; the company had been subject to a number of legal actions on pollution and environmental degradation grounds, though it had also been praised for reclamation work on some open cut coal mines.

More relevant to its Australian experience, Amax was a defendant in four separate legal actions initiated by American Indian groups. These actions were associated with mining on or near Indian lands.

The decision to become involved in oil exploration in the Kimberley was a deliberate investment, a risk similar to that involved in all mineral exploration. It could not be described as a highly likely, or exciting prospect, and in the overall Amax scheme of things it was very small; much larger investments were terminated regularly, for commercial or political reasons, with hardly an eye blinked. One former Amax employee who worked about that time in a different section of the Perth office has suggested that in fact the local office was under instructions that no new projects – including the proven Mitchell Plateau bauxite deposits – were to be developed; and that the exploration activities in oil and other fields were primarily for tax relief purposes, though this cannot be confirmed.[6]

No ground work was done on the permit during 1977. The time was spent analysing the data from the 1976 survey, and planning future work, including the expansion of the exploration program. In June 1977 the partners in EP97 took up new permits, EPs 101 and 102, adjoining 97 in the north and east, and Whitestone took a ninety-five percent interest in the new EP103, to the west.

The 1978 seismic program, the first to be done by Amax, was planned to include a total of over three hundred kilometres of cut lines, with eighty-three kilometres on Noonkanbah.

Early in February, Amax wrote a form letter to the relevant pastoralists advising them of the planned work 'to obtain an acknowledgement from the property manager that he is aware of our intention to conduct seismic activities on your lease...and ascertain whether any particular operational conditions may apply on your lease holdings'. Noonkanbah's letter was addressed to the manager of the Aboriginal Lands Trust in Perth, and appears to have taken some weeks to reach the station.

From this point the various versions of what happened during the conduct of the survey are somewhat confusing and conflicting. Rather than trying to combine the different accounts it is simpler to present the history compiled from Amax, Whitestone and Government records, and then the Aboriginal response.

The companies and Government record:[7]

> In April of 1978 Tom Lyon, the Amax field representative, visited Noonkanbah to explain the forthcoming seismic program, including the location of seismic lines, and obtained a signed acknowledgement from Ginger Nganawilla, who made no mention of the work intruding on any sites.
>
> On the 12th May, just before the commencement of work, an Amax geophysicist and a surveyor from the seismic contractor again met with Nganawilla, and no objections were raised to the location of the lines.

Bulldozing of the lines commenced, then on the 18th May an unnamed 'advisor' visited the base camp to say that 'the community were dissatisfied with earthmoving activities, in particular, that one line had passed across a used car dump which is a traditional visitor's area'.

At a meeting at Noonkanbah the next day this problem, and a community allegation of disturbance to cattle were discussed, but all matters were amicably resolved, and the program continued as planned.

Work in the vicinity of the homestead was completed on the 2nd June, and the lines south of the river were started. On the 8th June a letter was received from the Derby office of the Aboriginal Legal Service, much to the company's surprise, advising that 'your exploration operations to date has already entailed the violation of some sacred areas on the Station, including burial grounds and ceremonial areas', and asking them to refrain from any further work south of the river until a proposed site survey had been completed.

Amax replied by apologising if there had been any transgressions, but stressing that they would not have done so knowingly, and referred to the consultations with Nganawilla. They agreed not to continue with any further work until a survey had been arranged and completed. Unseasonal rains had made the river impassable and the ground too heavy, so work could not proceed in any event. The full seismic program approved by the Mines Department was never completed.

On the 22nd July Tom Lyon returned to the station and obtained an acknowledgement signed by Friday Muller that any damage to station property such as roads and fences had been satisfactorily repaired.

The Aboriginal version is quite different. In the opening chapter Muller described some of the effects of the seismic work; speaking first at Diadju Hill a few kilometres south of the river crossing:

> They went across there that mob. They brought a bulldozer down...They cut all the way around those old dead bodies, all around that place where we took those old people. That's nearly all sacred ground through there...[8]

and then at the river crossing:

> Two times the surveyor went across. He cut the road here and made it bad for us. And...just across at here where I was born. I am talking where I was born. I belong to here. This is where that mob put a bulldozer across my place, our sacred ground. This is a place we people don't want to get messed up, here, right in the middle of the tribal area that's been used from the early days by the old people.[9]

The seismic line that caused most of the trouble ran through the car-dump and the adjacent visitors' area, through a ceremonial ground and Muller's place, on down to the river, where it was continued down the river bank just one hundred and forty metres upstream from the river crossing. While the bulldozer was there the driver attempted to improve the crossing, as the contractors had to use it for their work on the south side; but in fact they made a terrible mess of the work, and the approach became a steep and slippery slope.

This was all happening right at the time of the cultural festival and inaugural Kimberley Land Council meeting. The visitors' area was damaged the day before the gathering started, just as the guests were starting to come in and it was about to be used. The desecration of Muller's birthplace and spirit tree, and the cut in the river bank, actually occurred during the meeting. The minutes for the second day, 20 May, record an anthropologist who had been filling in time down at the river as the meeting went on, interrupting proceedings:

> Tells meeting that he has just found that a bulldozer from mining mob has, for no reason, just dug up the sandy floor of swimming area...(A party of men departed to investigate this.)[10]

The delegation found the bulldozer coming back from the river. The driver was called down and sat against a tree. One of the men, a visitor from Arnhem Land, was so incensed that he grabbed hold of the dozer driver, knocking off his sunglasses, and told him that if such a thing had happened in his country, the transgressor would have been speared. The driver was told off in no uncertain terms, and sent back to the Amax camp.

It is interesting that this incident at the river does not appear in any of the company or Government records. Either the bulldozer driver decided discretion was the better part of valour, and did not report what had happened to his superiors, or Amax felt it was better off not mentioning the incident.

As for the signed acknowledgement of Ginger Nganawilla, his recollection when I questioned him the next year – after the letter had become an issue during a meeting with a Mines Department representative – was this:

The bulldozer driver that damaged sites is confronted by a delegation from the Land Council meeting. Left to right: The bulldozer driver's assistant, Mick Michael, Galawurry Yunupingu of the Northern Land Council, Charlie Rangi, the bulldozer driver, Yawarrin of Yuhalla, Northern Territory, and Nipper Tabagee. *(Courtesy Kim Akerman.)*

Two men came and asked me about Kalyeeda. Well I said, 'Kalyeeda, that's a different place, that's a different area. This Noonkanbah area is this side around here.' He asked me for my name. And he put it down.

Hawke: Did he tell you that when you put your name down there you were saying that it was all right to put the cut lines in?

No, he only put my name, he just write my name.

Hawke: He didn't tell you why to write it, he just asked you to write your name?

No no no no. He only just asked me, 'Who owns the station, you? What's your name?' He held my name, he wrote it down.

Hawke: At that meeting the Mines Department man said that when you wrote your name you said it was all right to put in those lines with the bulldozer.

No, he lies. He only asked me who owned this station, and what's your name. I called my name and they wrote it down. He didn't tell me [that] I wanted to put down cut lines. I didn't say cut for this place near the river. This is a good place; this is a kid place where we make him a man. [A ground for initiation ceremonies.] We put that kid there along the river, and we take him and play there all night. We play all night there, right through to the light, and take him along to another creek and make him a man.[11]

When the issue came up, the Mines Department officer gave a verbal assurance that copies of the letters allegedly signed by Nganawilla and Muller would be made available; but two subsequent written requests from the Community to forward the copies were not even acknowledged. Nor do the letters, or copies, appear in the Mines Department files viewed during research, even though one letter in the files, from Amax's exploration manager, Max Reynolds, to the Minister, refers to them, and says 'Copies of these and other relevant correspondence have been sent to the Mines Department'.[12]

What is revealed in all this is a classic case of poor communication. If one assumes that the Amax representatives were acting with integrity, they obviously did not convey their integrity, or the relevant information, to the Noonkanbah people.

During this period the Noonkanbah people came to intensely dislike Tom Lyon – Amax's main front man – for his manner as much as his message. He became almost a personal embodiment of the 'mineral mob' that were held in such contempt.

It would seem foolish for Amax to have assumed that a field operative like Lyon, with no previous experience, would be able to communicate effectively with the Community at Noonkanbah. It was considered by the Community to be extremely discourteous to conduct negotiations over the survey by arriving at the Community unannounced, as Lyon and others regularly did. It was also considered inappropriate to speak to only one old man. Written permission should have been sought for discussions with the Management Committee. It was ridiculous to have thought that sitting down with an old man and discussing lines on a map that he did not even begin to comprehend would provide the company with an accurate picture of the many sites of importance that had to be avoided.

At this time models were being developed in other parts of the country, especially in Central Australia, specificly for oil exploration, to ensure proper lines of communication, and proper identification and protection of places of importance to Aboriginal people.

These procedures did involve some time, effort and expense on the part of the companies concerned, but also safeguarded them against the sort of difficulties in which Amax embroiled themselves.

The whole issue of consultation with the Noonkanbah Community was obviously not regarded as difficult or important by the company. A superficial attempt was made to observe the niceties, as was done with other station owners, but apparently it was felt that this was enough. Even when obvious difficulties began to arise on the station, matters were left in Lyon's hands, and head office seemed to believe that all was okay.

All was far from okay. Friday Muller felt personally affronted, both by the damage to his own special place, and the offence given during the festival he had hosted. He dictated a letter to one of the young people at the station, and sent it to the Aboriginal Legal Service asking for their assistance. This led to the ALS's letter of 8 June to Amax which, along with the weather problems, brought an end to the seismic survey.

The next month Muller led his people in complaining about the damage to Ian Viner, then Federal Minister for Aboriginal Affairs, and to their local member of State Parliament Alan Ridge, by this time the Minister for Community Welfare with State responsibility for Aboriginal Affairs, when they visited Fitzroy Crossing. This was reported in the press, and subsequently raised in the State Parliament by a Labor Party Member; and Viner and Ridge both wrote to the Minister for Mines expressing their concern, and seeking assurances of better behaviour by Amax and other companies in the future.

Amax claims that these matters were never even referred to it by the Mines Department for query or explanation. The poor communications and ill-feeling were left unresolved as Amax started to make plans for its drilling operation.

Amax records show that on 24 July, two days after Tom Lyon had acquired Muller's clearance for damage repair, he visited again and met with Dicky Skinner and other unnamed members of the Community.

Tom Lyon.

Lyon indicated that further exploration including drilling was probable. All sites of possible significance to the aboriginal people and which were to be avoided were indicated and plotted.[13]

Despite the previous disaster, reinforced by an official letter of complaint from the ALS on the Community's instructions, Lyon was still regarded as competent to negotiate with the Community and conduct Aboriginal site surveys.

By October Amax had chosen the locality for the drill hole to be named Fitzroy River Number One. Lyon went out to Noonkanbah again. According to the Mines Department:

> Muller and other members of the Noonkanbah Community gave permission...to inspect possible locations for the drill. Locations were shown to the Community on a map and it was noted that they were not near any areas of special sacred significance.[14]

Amax's correspondence is not so clear, but also implies that Lyon went to the locations with a man from Richter, the company contracted to carry out the drilling, and afterwards spoke to Community members.

Again, it seems a totally inappropriate procedure had been adopted, with discussion about sites based on a brief conference over a map. Besides, the Community was so hostile to Lyon by this time, it is highly unlikely that a sensible discussion could have taken place. From the records it is also interesting that every time Lyon visits he seems to speak to a different Community member; there was no clear line of communication, but this did not seem to disturb him.

At this point Amax did make their first correct move, but received a confusing response. They approached the Aboriginal Sites section of the Western Australian Museum, requesting a site survey to 'confirm' Lyon's map. The Museum was unable to do this because no staff were available. But as a result Amax received a map showing sites plotted during the work done by Kingsley Palmer, in preparation for the CRA case. This showed major sites that did correspond fairly closely to Lyon's map.

What they did not appreciate was that Palmer had been asked by the ALS to prepare a general report on the situation of the Community, and to record all sites of significance on the station. This was an impossibility in the two weeks that Palmer had to work in, so the site-work was concentrated mainly on the areas in which CRA held claims, with other major sites recorded in passing. Amax did not receive the written report that explained the maps and the background, which contained the introductory statement, '...during a two week visit only a cursory investigation is possible. This report should be read with this limitation in mind'.[15] Magistrate David McCann had accepted and commented on this. But Amax, relying on Lyon and the Palmer map, were confident that they were all clear.

In December they finalised a drilling contract with Richter Drilling for a wildcat well to be sunk on Noonkanbah Station. On 2 March 1979 Max Reynolds, Amax's exploration manager, wrote to the Community Welfare adviser working with the Community, advising of the company's drilling plans, and stating that site-works would commence in May or June.

Amax, in its ignorance, assumed that the drilling locality it had chosen would not infringe upon sacred land, and would be acceptable to the Community. The opening paragraph of Reynolds' letter referred to the inspections done by Lyon the previous October, and stated 'it was gratifying...to note that there would not be any danger of interfering with areas of importance to the Aboriginal people'.[16]

This question of the religiosity of the land and the sites within it became the central issue in the whole affair; but the requirements of secrecy, government obfuscation, media simplification, and the basic difficulty of strangers coming to grips with the complexities of Aboriginal religious thought meant that this central issue was never very well understood by the public at large.

7

WHEN THE PEOPLE GO DREAM

I think about what my father was telling me before. He was telling me the stories that we call Ngarranggani, which means a long time ago. Stories like the emu who was a man, and the turkey who was a man, and those little birds around here that were men...And they turned into spirits. This was a long time ago. They travelled around like human beings. Everything can change, but the spirit for the people, it stays that way.

Dicky Skinner, Noonkanbah, November 1978.

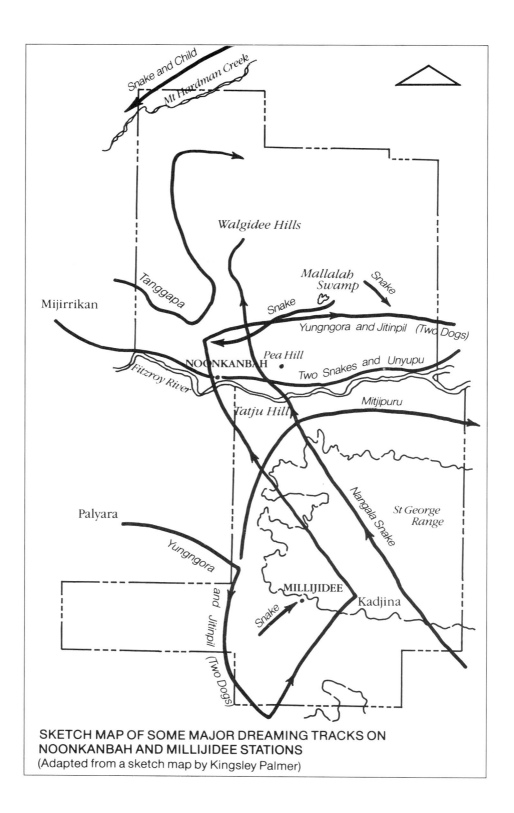

SKETCH MAP OF SOME MAJOR DREAMING TRACKS ON NOONKANBAH AND MILLIJIDEE STATIONS
(Adapted from a sketch map by Kingsley Palmer)

Aboriginal religion and the philosophy surrounding it has a complexity and richness that very few outsiders have been able to grasp and appreciate. It is not enshrined and codified in sacred texts; it is held in oral traditions in languages that few Europeans have mastered; it relies on a framework of thought and belief completely foreign to westerners; and it is guarded by layers of secrecy. In my years in the Kimberley I have received only glimpses and nuances.

Anthropologists, at Noonkanbah and elsewhere, have delved into the mysteries, and there are any number of treatises describing the practice of religion, and some which explore the underlying philosophies.[1] But one suspects that even the best of the anthropologists in their writings miss the kernel of meaning that Aboriginal believers derive from their religion, as they remain outsiders and observers, never participants in the fullest sense. Nevertheless a very basic attempt at description of the main features is necessary to provide an understanding of what motivated the Noonkanbah people.

The Noonkanbah people call the time before the land took its current form Ngarranggani. The heroes of this time are the primary figures in Aboriginal religion. The anthropologist Erich Kolig described them this way:

> Mighty heroes – most of them physically ambiguous, being simultaneously man and animal, or plant, some perpetually changing their shape – roamed the countryside, hunting and gathering, loving and fighting, fornicating and defending morality. Gallant or cowardly, wise or stupid, immoral or moral...these heroes...laid down a social and cultural maze of patterns; by good example as well as bad example they demonstrated viable social modes, instituted ritual, manufactured sacred objects and tools and introduced survival techniques.[2]

In the stories that tell of the Ngarranggani are found the principles of the Law that traditionally cover all aspects of Aboriginal life, ceremony and social relationships. But the mighty heroes, collectively known as the Ngarranggani, did more than provide a guide to life and religion, they transformed the empty land into the shape it has today, with all its physical features, and all the life within it. Each place, plant and animal is related to, and a part of, the Ngarranggani, and its particular Ngarranggani figure or figures.

Land features are the creations of the Ngarranggani: the hill formed by the digging of the blue tongue lizard woman; or the trees which are the spears of Mangunampi, a creator of springs and waterholes. Other places are the points where the Ngarranggani themselves emerged from or entered the ground, and still reside. These are places of great power and spirituality, and often of great danger as well.

Some places, known to the anthropologists as 'increase sites', and to the Noonkanbah people as malaji, were given fertility powers for various animals or plants, and other basics of life such as water. People with the correct associations and powers could tap the spiritual essence of these places through Dreams or rituals used to summon forth supplies of the plant to be harvested or the animal to be hunted. With the correct procedures the food source could even be directed to appear in particular localities at particular times.

In other places could be found the raii – the essence of human life – which also had their origin in the Ngarranggani. Raii would come from a particular place, and be part of a particular animal and totem. A woman would be impregnated with raii – in a Dream, or from an animal killed by her husband, or a fish she caught – and the child that grew from the raii belonged to that place, called his/her murrunggur, and was kin to the animal. On death and burial the raii would return to the land.

The spirituality in the land, the animals and the people was one and the same, eternally manifesting itself. Hence the people were quite literally a part of their environment. Their essential spirit was the same spirit that lay in the ground.

Before the tremendous disruptions brought on by the invasion of their land, small clans would hold the primary responsibility for their particular piece of country, and the Law and ceremony relating to it. Some of the Ngarranggani were local figures, whose deeds were confined to the land of just a few clans. Others travelled along Dreaming tracks that spanned great stretches of the continent. Thus the Law was both local and specific, but related to a larger whole that tied clans and tribes together through the land and its story and ceremony.

The doings of the various Ngarranggani were celebrated in great song cycles. A particular group would hold one section that related to their country. But this would be part of a larger cycle involving a chain of such groups. These songs and associated stories formed a key part of the ritual that governed the great ceremonies in which the clans would gather, and men and women would progress through stages of knowledge and initiation.

Sacred boards and stones called darrugu, which were used in some ceremonies, contained some of the great powers of the Ngarranggani and the country. These boards and stones upon which representational images were carved were normally stored in caves, and the localities of these repositories were in turn invested with some of that power. Smaller versions of these vessels of power were held by particular individuals and groups. They were a form of map and title to the country, and had their own powers and applications, vested in the holders.

Whilst still surrounded by various sanctions, these smaller darrugu were carried and used more freely. Men would take them to distant ceremonies and Law meetings. They were sometimes buried with their owners. New ones could be created with the consent of all the relevant people, and the appropriate ritual to accompany the carving.

Whilst the creation aspect of the Ngarranggani was before time, its heroes and its power, and the Ngarranggani itself, still live in the land. This power is tapped in all sorts of ways, from ceremony to the personal Dreaming of raii and malaji, to dreams inspired by the Ngarranggani which would manifest as new dances and corroborees. The Ngarranggani is both Dreamtime and Dreaming; past, present and future bound together to provide a framework for understanding and living in the world.

The complex interweaving of song and ceremony, dreams and daily activity, personal and inter-group relationships, was all governed by procedures which not only bore witness to the power of the Ngarranggani in all its manifestations, but were designed to renew and harness this power. One of the basic elements in all this was the belief in the land, the ground itself, as the most enduring and most powerful aspect of Ngarranggani.

Nipper Tabagee dancing.

In turn, the appropriate respect for and care of the land, and the particular sites within it, was a central part of the Aboriginal creed.

The strict practices and interpretation of Law and religion did not survive the European invasion wholly intact. The detailed knowledge of some parts of the country was lost with the deaths of the owners of that country. The fertility power of some malaji places could no longer be tapped.

Most seriously affected were the normal lines of inheritance to clan estates and sites within those estates. This was an unavoidable consequence of the sudden deaths of individuals, families and whole clans. In some instances second and third best options in traditional terms, such as inheritance through the mother's line instead of the father's, were adopted. This would often be possible because a woman would have married into a group living outside her own country, and if her own people did not survive the invasion, her children instead of her brothers' would take up responsibility for the country of her Dreaming.

The primary role of the clan structure of earlier times was also reduced as people became settled in larger, more diverse communities on the stations. And as people from different country and religious traditions that did not normally mix closely were thrown together in these station communities, so did elements of their Law become intermingled, as in the case of the Walmatjari and the Nyigina discussed previously.

Also, there is no question that some elements of the new world of experience, from the pastoral industry to Christianity, were incorporated into the interpretation and practice of the Law; just as the timing of ritual and ceremonial activity had to be adapted to the work requirements of the stations.

Many anthropologists have focused their studies and their writings on these changes and adaptations that Aboriginal people have made and continue to make in their religious and everyday lives, as they have come to terms with the white world. In the latter stages of the Noonkanbah dispute the State Government was to selectively use the work of some anthropologists in an attempt to discredit the standing of the Noonkanbah people and their Law. The most extreme example was an official Government pamphlet titled 'Noonkanbah, The Facts' published in 1980, which claimed that:

> The dominant cult in the southern Kimberley is now a mixture from the Northern Territory, the eastern and southern desert areas, Christianity, Melanesian cargo cults and a dash of racial-political activism.[3]

The very anthropologists who wrote the material from which this assertion was drawn reject its validity. The point is that in spite of the changes wrought upon them the people maintained the essential structures and beliefs. The complex of religion, Law and custom, land, sites and spirits, described so sketchily above, was maintained as a legitimate whole, and as the vital part of the people's lives. It is this body of belief and practice that Dicky Skinner is referring to when he speaks, so often in the next two years, of 'my Law'.

Over the years of white contact some of this vast store of information and knowledge about the land was revealed to some Europeans, including station managers and anthropologists – though many a manager and stockman perceived as hostile by the people spent years in the country and learnt nothing. But apart from the very few who delved deeply, and were deemed trustworthy, most knew only of the very major sites, and in some cases the ceremony grounds and the darrugu repositories.

From this limited knowledge the notion of the Aboriginal sacred site emerged. In the changing political climate of the early 1970s the Tonkin Labor Government passed the Aboriginal Heritage Act through the Western Australian Parliament in 1972. The Act was designed to provide protection for Aboriginal sites, and control the trade that had developed in darrugu boards and other sacred objects. This trade was fed by theft (as in the Tatju Hill case described previously), collection by unscrupulous individuals for museum collections, and in some cases the sale of material by Aboriginal people who had lost their faith in the Law, or accommodated the ancient trading practices to the notion of sale and replacement.

Under the Act the definition of a site that would merit registration, and in most cases protection, was 'any place, including any sacred, ritual or ceremonial site, which is of importance or of special significance to persons of Aboriginal descent'. Most of the legislators, though not necessarily the anthropological advisers who helped in the drafting, would have had a rather limited notion of this as it related to specific features, dance grounds, etc. But as Kingsley Palmer described:

> Although certain places...were recognised as being of particular importance for one reason or another, the whole land was recognised as being endowed with spiritual essence... In this sense the term Aboriginal site, as a defined location is redundant. Aboriginal thought admits that some places are more important than others, but cannot easily accommodate the notion that one place is a site and another is not.[4]

In the 1970s, as the anthropological profession was being pushed further from the academic world of written scientific inquiry towards such practical work as Aboriginal site surveys and protection in the face of mining development, it was having difficulties reconciling the Aboriginal perspective on land with the preconceptions of industry and government of narrowly defined sites.

Palmer, in his evidence to the Mining Warden at Broome, had used the term 'sphere of influence' to describe the emanation of power from a specific site to the surrounding country. Others had advocated the concept of 'buffer zones' extending outwards from a site's geographic centre.

At the time the Noonkanbah dispute erupted, the State's most eminent anthropologist, Professor Ronald Berndt, was preparing a discussion paper for the Aboriginal Cultural Materials Committee (ACMC), of which he was a member. This committee was constituted under the Heritage Act as the expert body to assess the reports of Museum field staff, and make recommendations, amongst other things, as to the protection of sites. This paper was to be addressed to the question of spheres and buffer zones, and especially to the problem of complexes of associated sites, where the land between specific neighbouring sites was part of a whole.

In the Northern Territory the Land Councils and the Pitjanjatjarra people were developing another model which turned the Western Australian equation on its head. They advocated a system whereby no specific information on sites was given to mining companies, but rather they were advised of exclusion zones, and free areas in which they could operate without fear of desecrating important land.

To the Aboriginal people this was all esoteric; they knew their land and what it meant. Amax, however unwittingly, brought the issue of the definition of sacred sites in the white man's law to a flaming head.

Peter Bindon, from the Aboriginal Sites Department of the Western Australian Museum, conducted two extensive investigations of the land in question at Noonkanbah. When he arrived the first time in May 1979, after meeting with the Community Council, explaining his task, and being briefed by the people on their version of the dispute they had with

Pea Hill.

Amax, he was set to work with a team of the relevant Elders for the country, and Dicky Skinner as assistant and translator. In the general vicinity of the proposed drill site he was shown a whole complex of sites, and told of the related stories, ceremonies and Law of the Ngarranggani.

The basic information can be revealed without compromising the secret sacred aspects any further than they were in the unfolding of the dispute.

The central feature was Umpampurru, known to non-Aborigines as Pea Hill, which was derived from its first naming as P Hill, a trig point in one of the earliest surveys of the Kimberley.

Umpampurru/Pea Hill was one of the major sites, relatively well-known to Europeans. Its importance derived from a combination of attributes, all of which are traced back to the activities of various Ngarranggani.

There was the great hero Unyupu, and the two snakes he had speared. In their great struggle they had carved out the Fitzroy River, starting from the west downstream from Noonkanbah, and passing just south of Pea Hill as they travelled east and then north.

Their track was crossed by that of Nangala, the pregnant wife of the great Jangalajarra snake, in her travels from Kalijidi (St George Range), north to the Walgidee Hills where she came to rest. According to Erich Kolig, she rested briefly at Umpampurru (Pea Hill).

And then there was Looma, the blue tongue lizard woman, who emerged from a site on Christmas Creek Station to the south-east, and passed through Noonkanbah, stopping at Pea Hill, and two other smaller hills to the west, before finally coming to rest on a hill overlooking the Community which bears her name, eighty kilometres to the north-west.

Through these associations Pea Hill had become a powerful malaji centre, and the home of a great woman spirit. One feature on the hill provides access through which kangaroos, turkeys, snakes and other reptiles can be summoned. A second feature provides access to goannas.

At various locations around Pea Hill, as far as ten kilometres west, to the north of the homestead and Community, are less powerful, associated malaji sites, and a separate fish malaji associated with the Unyupu story.

The way the malaji sites worked, and the means by which the people of Noonkanbah utilised them are important to an understanding of the area as a whole. Peter Bindon in his report described it thus:

> At one part of this site goannas are summoned from the surrounding area and 'locked up' within the hill. At a certain appropriate time these goannas are 'dreamed' out of the hill which is the repository of their body and spirit. They are then sent out underground beyond the tree-line which surrounds the hill. Goannas emanating from this site are thus made widely available as a Community food source.[5]

Kolig put it this way:

> The expert responsible for the relevant rites can open the hill in his dreams and enter it – providing the female spirit custodian, who lives in it, is willing to admit him. Once inside he meets with her and, when properly approached, she will see to the propagation of snakes, frogs and goannas.[6]

Ivan McPhee, the young Community secretary, standing one day at the proposed drill site, spoke of the area as a whole:

> Aboriginal people go Dream. They find animals in different places. They call these places malaji. It's just like a burial ground inside. And the Aborigines go Dream and try to get meat from there in the Dream.
>
> Not far, just where all the trees are, they wanted to put the hole before. [They are] trying to drill here now. But malaji are spread all over the place. This is kakaji here. Kakaji is goanna.
>
> Raii are looking after all these murrungurr, looking after all these malaji. Right up to Pea Hill, right across the plain there. All this is the malaji round here, underground.
>
> Pea Hill is the place for frogs and snakes. The woman is in the hill there. When the people go Dream, they go and meet that lady in the Dream, and tell her that we want some sort of meat, like kangaroo or goanna or frog.
>
> The animals are all over the place underground. Not to be touched this place; not only one main spot, but spread all around underground.[7]

Where McPhee was standing, at the drill site, roughly halfway between Pea Hill and the Community, was an area known as Bundarra Goodun. In this area were numerous rock outcrops of a particular type. These outcrops, and nearby clusters of trees, were regarded as emanation sites, where the goannas summoned from Pea Hill and the lesser malaji sites actually came out of the ground. Other small spherical rocks in the vicinity were believed to be goanna eggs.

Tommy Butler with goanna eggs.

These fertility aspects of the area were primarily linked to Pea Hill, with the power spreading out under the ground into the surrounding country.

In addition to this, the major initiation ritual used by the Noonkanbah people, known as the Wallangarri, was closely linked to Unyupu and the snakes. To quote Bindon:

> In the past, Aborigines visiting Noonkanbah to take part in initiation rituals would leave the sacred objects that they had brought with them at Pea Hill. Aborigines come from Christmas Creek, Go Go, Cherrabun, Jubilee and further afield for these rituals. Women and children would not then venture near the hill, being afraid of the power contained within such objects...A series of 'dancing' or 'corroboree' grounds along the creek feature to the south of Pea Hill and extending west almost to the Noonkanbah homestead were used during several stages of initiation rituals.[8]

The dance grounds damaged by Amax bulldozers in 1978 had been at the western end of this chain of ceremonial grounds stretching towards Pea Hill.

Most of this information about the country was gathered by Bindon during his first survey, without revealing to the Noonkanbah people the specific location of the proposed Amax drill site. Towards the end of this first survey Tom Lyon of Amax came to Noonkanbah, and took Bindon on his own to the site, which he pegged.

After Lyon had left, Bindon returned with the Elders to the spot, which was right in the middle of this complex of malaji and ceremonial sites, and very close to the intersection of the Unyupu and Jangalajarra Dreaming tracks:

> The informants all stated that the peg was within the sphere of influence of both sites [Pea Hill and Bundarra Goodun] and actually on a site used when preparing initiates who will participate in the Wallangarri rituals.[9]

B indon's first report in late May 1979 advised that the preferred Amax drill site was not acceptable, either to the Noonkanbah people, or in terms of the Aboriginal Heritage Act. But due to the political machinations which are described in the next chapter, he was sent back to Noonkanbah a week later. This time he had been asked to go over the ground again to discover whether there was an acceptable drilling site within a larger zone defined by Amax as being the limits of the geological formation it was targeting in the depths of the earth.

By this time the political heat had risen, and the people of Noonkanbah were getting angry. But it was not only the politics that angered them. The information they had already given to Bindon was highly religious, and some of it of a secret nature. It was serious business. They felt that in sending Bindon back the Government was challenging their word in matters that they would not dream of distorting or treating in any sense lightly.

So on the first day of his second spell of field-work, the Elders went a step further, to deliver what in their terms was conclusive proof of their earlier information.

In a secluded place Bindon was surrounded by a huddle of old and middle-aged men. An old man from Looma lectured him on how the Aboriginal people and the land had arisen through the Ngarranggani. Two of the smaller Noonkanbah darrugu, and one from Looma were produced, the relevant portions of the song cycles were sung, and the stories told.

It was a solemn occasion. The darrugu were powerful objects, not to be abused by use in the wrong context. It was acceptable for them to be produced in a serious discussion about Law and country as proof of the holders' position and authority –

Ivan McPhee.

Nipper Tabagee described them as the Aboriginal map, and in a sense they were a form of title deed. In their own terms, by showing them to Bindon the people were not only demonstrating the truth of the evidence they had given, but were placing him and the Museum under an obligation to respect them, and the reasons for which they had been produced.

The carvings on one board in particular showed a representation of Pea Hill and its association with the river story and the rest of the Noonkanbah area. It was explained that this was associated with another darrugu, now secured with the bones of its owner in a cave on another hill near Noonkanbah. This man had been the custodian of Pea Hill and Tatju Hill, and the country in between, and his darrugu related to that very particular piece of country, including the proposed drilling zone.

The people also insisted that Bindon corroborate their evidence by talking to the Elders of Looma Community, who held the associated Law. Bindon did this, and was also able to confirm the consistency of the information with other material and songs he had gathered from the Elders at Christmas Creek the previous year.

In terms of the specifics of the land, Bindon's task this time was to attempt to define as precisely as possible the extent of the country affected by Pea Hill, Bundarra Goodun, and the associated malaji sites, in order to determine whether there was any locality that Amax could drill without impinging upon it.

To do this he went over the stories, the sites, and the ground again, and asked to be taken to every surface manifestation of the goanna malajis. Whilst doing this he continually asked his informants as they were traversing the country whether or not they were still 'on top of the goanna'. In this way he defined the zone which became known as the 'area of influence', encompassing Pea Hill, with all the associated surface manifestations within the zone. (See map, p.128.) He also noticed that each of the surface sites he was shown were distinguished by the same type of limestone outcrop seen in the Bundarra Goodun area, thus lending a consistency, and a geological theme to the information he was given.

The important part of the equation was the underground aspect. The goanna essence lay beneath the surface of the ground in all of this area. The woman in Pea Hill would send the goannas out under the ground to emerge at various points. Thus, in Aboriginal terms, there is no question that the whole of the area was linked as one, that entering the land with a drill in between the specific surface sites did not avoid the problem, and that the very nature of the planned activity – a huge drill into the bowels of the earth – was particularly threatening.

This also explains why the various surface improvements and developments such as the homestead and associated facilities, roads, fences and the airstrip were not in themselves a problem, as long as they didn't impinge on the surface sites. It must also be noted that most of these had been constructed in the days when the people were in no position to object anyway: the building of the airstrip during the Second World War had in fact destroyed one location used for the storage of darrugu.

Erich Kolig, speaking in a general sense, rather than with specific application to the land in question, throws some light on this power hidden underneath the surface:

> Only 'the ground' has magnitude enough to harbour the idea of the beginning and ending of all things. Here is the source, mysteriously active and unceasingly productive, from which everything springs forth. And if we probe this crucial concept of 'the ground' even more, we find that what is really meant is not the loose sprinkle of sand and soil on top, but the stuff of the underground, the stratum not visible and only rarely accessible: the rock bed.
>
> An Aboriginal man of my acquaintance compared the concept of the

ground with a huge battery. The rocky nucleus emits the spiritual power that maintains life and human existence and in turn is recharged, in a never ending process, by ritual activity and above all, by living beings dying and decaying and thus returning their spirituality to the earth's womb...While most of the battery is hidden and operates cryptically, in certain places there are visible signs of the underground powers on the surface...

The grave danger posed by large-scale mining is that it breaks up and removes large chunks of the matrix of all life; and by so doing it does irreparable damage to the huge subterranean battery from which all life is generated...As progressively more and more of the power source is taken away, the land generally becomes weakened and with it all life, plant, beast and man. All fertility is critically and catastrophically affected, but Aboriginal man will suffer a twofold loss: not only his physical survival appears to be at risk, but much more significantly, his spiritual component, inextricably bound to the subterranean power source, is acutely endangered.[10]

Bindon also investigated the economic and nutritional importance of goanna as a food source for the Community, and found that it was an essential part of the diet, as well as the culture, particularly during the wet season.

He also attempted to find out what sort of threat the people felt was posed by the drilling. This really had four levels. Firstly there was the hurt, and the possible danger posed by any act which upset the balance of the Ngarranggani, the fabric of life. Secondly, there was the specific danger to the spirits of Pea Hill and the associated malaji, and the raii that looked after them. This in turn led to the third fear that the supply of goannas would be endangered: the people of the Fitzroy Valley attributed the virtual disappearance of kangaroos, which had once been their major food source, to similar interference with the kangaroo Dreaming about fifteen years previously.

Finally, there was the fear that Bob Mululby, the man who was the custodian for the Pea Hill malaji, and perhaps his family as well, would fall ill or even die, as a result of the displeasure of the powers. To quote Bindon:

> It is felt by some of the Noonkanbah Aboriginal Community that this man's life is threatened by the proposed oil well...People generally believe that a spiritual emanation from the site will certainly make this custodian ill and probably cause his death. Some folk believe that this 'sickness' will extend to the custodian's family and perhaps to the whole clan. This feeling has generated a certain amount of fear within the Community.[11]

And Ivan McPhee:

> If he Dreams, the raii will tell him, 'Why did you let this thing happen?' And he'll get sick in the Tribal Law.[12]

Peter Bindon's final report, June 14, 1979, contained three conclusions:

> 1. The whole area within which any drill hole could be located by the Company falls under the influence of the special sites shown to me by the Aborigines of the clan descent group for that area.
> 2. The site complex is significant in both a religious and economic context. Mythological connections are both authentic and ancient and are intimately linked to the economic present.
> 3. It is currently the opinion of the Aboriginal Community that any utilisation

Bob Mululby. *(Courtesy of Lyn McLeavy.)*

of the drill zone, particularly the substrate, by the Company, would be deleterious to the site complex.[13]

Of course, when Amax's Max Reynolds wrote to the Community in March 1979, the company was not privy to this information. Indeed, not all of the leaders of the Noonkanbah Community were aware of the full story at that point. Peter Bindon's investigations were undertaken as the dispute between the Noonkanbah people, Amax, and the State Government was beginning to unfold.

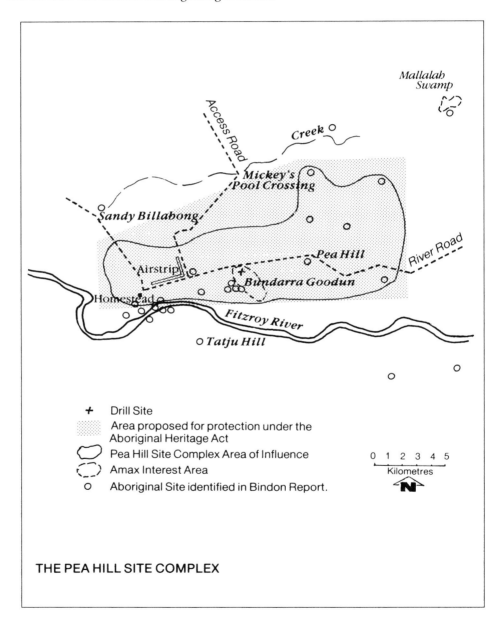

+ Drill Site

Area proposed for protection under the Aboriginal Heritage Act

Pea Hill Site Complex Area of Influence

Amax Interest Area

o Aboriginal Site identified in Bindon Report.

0 1 2 3 4 5
Kilometres

THE PEA HILL SITE COMPLEX

8

TO THEM, THE LAND IS JUST MONEY

We are sending this letter to you important people who can speak and who are now sitting down, talking in the big house.

We Aboriginal people of Noonkanbah Station are sending this letter. We truthfully beg you important people that you stop these people, namely C.R.A. and Amax, who are going into our land, which is at Noonkanbah.

These people have already made the place no good with their bulldozers. Our sacred places they have made no good. They mess up our land. They expose our sacred objects. This breaks our spirit. We lose ourselves as a people. What will we as a people do if these people continue to make our land no good?

Today we beg you that you will truly stop them.

The English translation of the Walmatjari text of a petition to the Parliament of Western Australia from the Yungngora Community of Noonkanbah. Tabled by Ron Davies, Leader of the Opposition, 17 May 1979.

Six weeks elapsed before a formal reply was sent to the letter from Max Reynolds of Amax that had told the Community of the company's plan for an oil well near Pea Hill. It is difficult in retrospect to reconstruct exactly what happened within the Community during that critical period.

The Amax drilling proposal was the first specific mining issue to be faced after the unsuccessful challenge to CRA's mining tenements the previous November, 1978. As such it presented a litmus test for the anti-mining position the people were taking. But it came just at the time when they were gearing up after the wet season for a new year of cattle work, and there was a lot of other business to attend to. And as with any important decision, there were many factors to be weighed and discussed in the Council and in the privacy of the camps.

Whilst there was total support in principle for the anti-mining stand, now that the crunch had come, there were some within the Community who felt that it had been taken as far as possible, and that in practice it would be futile to oppose the company. This was not due to any belief that the drilling was acceptable, but to a fear of the consequences of opposition.

For all the strength in the Community, there was still a large residue of fear of the power of the white man: typified by the recollection of the old man who had been beaten by his parents to indoctrinate him with the message that 'when the gudia told him to do rough work', he 'gave no cheek, just did it'.

So there was some sentiment within the Community that they should compromise themselves; rationalise the damage to the land and the Law as best they could – as had been done by necessity on previous occasions – and get on with the work of building the Community.

At the meeting in mid-March, when the Department for Community Welfare adviser brought Reynolds' letter out and the issue was first discussed at length, this feeling prevailed. The adviser drafted a letter to the Aboriginal Legal Service which made clear that Amax's presence was not wanted, but that if it were inevitable certain listed conditions should be observed in order to provide the maximum possible social protection to the Community.

But as is so often the case in Aboriginal communities, after the adviser had left, and the formal meeting was over, the real discussion took off within the Community. 'The old men changed their minds. They said we can't let them drill in that place', was how one Community member later described it.

In fact, what the old men did was educate some of the younger men as to the full meaning of the land and the stories that went with it, and persuade the few waverers amongst their own number.

With all the relevant people in the Community aware of the religious importance of the land, the element that made this situation different from earlier desecrations of sacred land – by pastoralists, by the diamond exploration of the 1960s, and by the explorers of recent years – was that the people were being advised in advance, and asked to acquiesce. Even the most recent desecrations by Amax had occurred in a situation where they had happened before the people were able to do anything to prevent them; thanks to the poor communication that existed between the company and the Community.

There were other factors in addition to the basic opposition to mining activity, and the obligation to defend the country of the Pea Hill site complex. There is no doubt that the traditionalists in the Community saw in the dilemma a means of asserting pride in the Law and the strength of the Law by attempting to manifest its authority in this situation. It could be seen as another step towards their vision of a truly traditionally oriented, independent Community.

Then there was a question of the magnitude of the Amax operation compared to the pegging, sampling and seismic work that had gone on so far. An oil drill was a much larger creature than any of the water drills and other machinery the people had experienced. There would be a camp of the despised miners just a few kilometres from the Community for a period of months. And if they struck oil, who knew what would happen?

There is no doubt that the people of Noonkanbah felt threatened by the drilling proposal, and their previous experience with miners in general, and Amax in particular, meant that the assurances of co-operation and good behaviour given by Max Reynolds were treated very sceptically.

Finally, to add to this sense of threat, while the Amax letter was under consideration, CRA representatives also visited the station, seeking to discuss their plans for work on their tenements in the central and northern parts of the station, thus increasing the pressure felt by the Community. The people declined to discuss the matter with CRA.

The old men decided that they would face their fear. This time they would not acquiesce, they would fight for the country and the Law.

The first response drafted by the DCW adviser was left unsent. By the time Tom Lyon of Amax went to Noonkanbah on 5 April to survey the road and airstrip, the Community had made up its mind as shown by Reynold's description of events a few days later:

> He was informed that the Aboriginal Community was opposed to our continued exploration and that a reply to our letter had been sent to the Aboriginal Legal Service with an instruction to indicate to Amax the Community's feelings.[1]

Amax had continued with its drilling plans on the basis of Lyon's advice that the drill site was clear of any sacred areas. In fact, while Lyon was at Noonkanbah the company knocked back an offer from the Museum, which now had staff available, to do a site survey, saying that in the light of Lyon's enquiries and Kingsley Palmer's research of the previous year, they felt that a further survey of the area was 'unwarranted'.[2] So Lyon's report on his 5 April visit must have come as something of a bombshell to head office in Perth.

Reynolds needed to know what was going on, as he had to brief his head office in America for a meeting of the partners in the EP97 Joint Venture, due to be held in Houston, Texas. On 12 April he telephoned the ALS to seek clarification. The same day, in accordance with the Community's instructions, the Derby office of the ALS telexed him to confirm the advice given to Lyon.

Reynolds was advised of the Community's opposition to mining in general, and to the Amax proposal in particular. He was told that the place the company intended to drill was a sacred area. (Though the telex did give the wrong name to the site, a fact that caused much suspicion and cynicism in the company and the Government.) He was asked to reconsider the proposal to drill, and not to enter the land. And the company was denied permission to use the road and the airstrip.

Amax could obviously proceed no further without consulting with the Government. Five days later Reynolds wrote to Andrew Mensaros, the Minister for Mines, explaining Amax's position, and giving a version of events and a chronology painting the company as the injured and innocent party. Whilst all the right sentiments about wishing to respect and co-operate with the Community were included, the relevant statement was a request for governmental support:

> I should like to emphasize that our Joint Venture would like to continue to proceed under the provisions of the Petroleum Act...we would like to ensure that we have your full support in our exploration programme. An indication of such support before our [Joint Venturers'] meetings on April 26, where we will discuss how best to proceed, would be appreciated.[3]

Mensaros and his department were already aware of the strong opposition to mining on Noonkanbah. They had followed the progress of the Community's objections through the Broome Warden's Court, and had received the letters of concern that Alan Ridge and Ian Viner had written when Friday Muller had complained of Amax's activities in June of the previous year. And in February, the ALS had written on behalf of the Community, asking Mensaros to refuse to register mineral claims on the station.

Nevertheless, Amax's version of events was apparently accepted without question. The day after receiving Reynolds' letter, Mensaros advised him that the company had the Government's full support. Reynolds advised his American superiors accordingly, and the company assumed that the Government would handle the opposition, and it would be able to proceed according to plan.[4] On 3 May Amax made formal application to Mensaros for permission to drill Fitzroy River Number One Well at the specified location on Noonkanbah.

Although Amax was becoming anxious about getting the drilling rig in on schedule and avoiding the penalty payments contained in its drilling contract with Richter, at this point the issue had not yet become an urgent priority within the Government. It was seen as an irritant, but it was assumed to be of manageable proportions.

On 10 May Mensaros met with his colleague Ray Young, the Minister for Community Welfare, with senior officers from the Mines Department, the Aboriginal Affairs Planning Authority and the Western Australian Museum also in attendance. The Noonkanbah-Amax dispute was one of a number of specific cases of mining activity on Aboriginal land discussed, and records of the meeting indicate that it was not especially high on the agenda. Young indicated that he had no objections to the proposed drilling. The Museum officers pointed out that a complete site survey had not yet been undertaken, and recommended that this be done. A Mines Department officer asked that the survey be done as quickly as possible to enable drilling to proceed that dry season. It was agreed to commence the survey within two weeks.[5] This agreement led to Peter Bindon's first investigation at Noonkanbah.

Back at Noonkanbah the Community was getting on with life as they waited to see what response the ALS's telex would draw. The school was well into the first term of its second year and the stockcamp was out mustering. But they were not waiting passively for the company's next move.

The people were aware, from their own experience and the warnings of the DCW and ALS staff, that the course they had chosen would not be an easy one. For a remote Aboriginal community they were already relatively experienced, and relatively successful, in the direct lobbying of Government Ministers and the higher levels of the bureaucracy. They had also taken the first step towards using the media to publicise their position and their views when, during the previous year, they had arranged with the help of the Kimberley Land Council to bring me to Broome and then out to the Community. They decided to continue and enlarge upon this strategy. And they enlisted the willing support of the other communities in the Fitzroy Crossing area, the KLC, and the local member of the National Aboriginal Conference, Jimmy Bieunderry.

On 12 April, the same day the ALS telexed Amax, the Marra Worra Worra organisation in Fitzroy Crossing, representing the combined communities of the Fitzroy Crossing area, telegrammed the Federal Minister for Aboriginal Affairs, Senator Fred Chaney:

> Leaders from Bayulu, Junjuwa, Kadjina, Kurnangki, Kroonull, Warringari* and Fitzroy Homemakers all worried for Noonkanbah people. They stand behind Noonkanbah to keep out all mining from their country. Miners break fences, bulldoze sacred places, disturb people who just starting new way of life. We ask your help to keep mining companies out of Noonkanbah country.

On 9 May, Marra Worra Worra wrote to Mensaros in a similar vein.

At Noonkanbah Bieunderry's wife, Olive, who was literate in Walmatjari, and a qualified translator, helped the people to prepare the petition to the State Parliament that appears in translation at the beginning of this chapter. The petition was mounted on a board, and the Community put in the money to send Dicky Skinner to Perth to present it to the Leader of the State Opposition, Ron Davies.

This trip to Perth generated the first media coverage of the Amax dispute. The unusual nature and presentation of the petition, Skinner's quiet authority and determination, and his obvious tribal and traditional background gave the event a dignified and positive impact. Television and newspaper coverage was favourable. Ron Davies was reported as saying:

> The wording of the petition is probably the simplest, yet the most moving, that I have read for many years. I hope that this petition will be given more than the cursory attention which petitions presented in the Legislative Assembly usually receive.[6]

The Aboriginal people were clearly gearing themselves up to make a stand at Noonkanbah, and had taken the first public points in what was to become as much as anything else a battle in the media to gain enough public support to force an unwilling Government to accede to their demands.

At this stage, with CRA also waiting in the wings, the people were representing their position primarily in terms of a blanket ban on mining activity on the station – a continuation of the legal action taken the previous year; because they felt that this was their right, because of the damage already caused by exploration activity, because of the fear of the spiritual, physical and social consequences of continued exploration and possible development, and because this was what they truly wanted, to be left in peace on their land.

---

* Aboriginal communities in the Fitzroy Crossing area affiliated to the Marra Worra Worra Aboriginal Corporation.

Dicky Skinner with the petition to the Western Australian Parliament. *(Courtesy West Australian Newspapers Ltd.)*

Dicky Skinner returned from Perth at the same time Peter Bindon and his assistant arrived to conduct their first survey. To the people it seemed that the arrival of a Museum anthropologist was an appropriate response to their position. They were confident that he would be able to convey their message about the land, and assisted willingly.

The very fact that the custodians of the country spent three days immersed in travelling over it and recalling the stories and ceremony that belonged to it must have increased their concern to defend it.

It was also at this time that the drill site was physically pegged by Tom Lyon, and Bindon explained exactly how the Amax camp and facilities would be laid out. The reality of the project became much clearer.

On completion of his investigations Bindon advised his superiors in Perth that there was a definite conflict between the proposed drilling location and the need for protection of the site complex. It was clear that Amax's drilling program would involve a breach of the Aboriginal Heritage Act. Though the advice was still unofficial, with Bindon yet to complete a written report, on 22 May the Director of the Museum, John Bannister, advised Amax and the Mines Department of the situation.

It seems that the Government had anticipated that the Museum's investigations would confirm the information it had been given by Amax, clearing the way for drilling to proceed. On 16 May – before Bindon had even arrived in the field – Max Reynolds was told by the Mines Department that the Museum had advised that the drill location was 'away from any sites of aboriginal significance'.[7]

Now the Government had a dilemma. It had lent its support to Amax, and this support had been conveyed to Amax headquarters in America. But it now had advice from its own expert agency that the drill site was not acceptable, and would be in breach of State legislation.

The Mines Department suggested to Reynolds that the company consider moving the drill site a few hundred metres south, the other side of a small creek that the Department advised formed the southern perimeter of the area associated with the site complex identified by Bindon.

On 23 May, Reynolds went to the Museum to discuss the possibility of alternative drill sites with senior Museum officers and Bindon, who had been rushed back to Perth to prepare a report. Reynolds advised that there was some flexibility, but the company was constrained by the geological formation being targeted. The meeting could not reach a final conclusion, though it appeared unlikely that a mutually acceptable location could be found. It was agreed that Bindon would return to Noonkanbah with a map to be supplied by Amax accurately defining the limits of their drilling zone.

Bannister wrote to Reynolds after the meeting to officially advise him that the drill location was on a site as defined in the Aboriginal Heritage Act, which was therefore protected, and any disturbance of the land would constitute an infringement of the Act.

By this time however, it was not just a matter of comparing geologically and religiously defined areas of land. Other elements had come into play which threatened to send the issue spinning out of control.

After showing Peter Bindon the drill site during his first survey, Tom Lyon had spoken to Dicky Skinner on his way out. In response to Skinner's enquiries he said it was possible that a water drill could be at the site within a week to begin site preparations. He claimed that he was then threatened by Skinner with being detained and punished under Tribal Law. Within a week he had been discredited, with a Mines Department officer concluding that he had misinterpreted what Skinner had said, and the Derby Sergeant of Police commenting that Lyon was 'excitable, to say the least'.[8]

The pressure was perhaps beginning to tell on Lyon. Skinner had no doubt spoken to him of Aboriginal Law, and his belief that it was time that it was given due recognition, and that desecration of the site would have consequences in the Law. He had spoken this way previously, and would continue to do so. To Skinner in particular, and the Community in general, this issue was a major theme. Given his dislike of Lyon, and quite possibly, the fear he sensed in the man, not to mention the pressure that was building, it is likely he spoke in particularly strong terms; but he emphatically denied that any physical threats were made.

Lyon possibly had images of spears in his leg or isolation in the desert running through his head. He laid complaints with the police and DCW in Derby. He must also have reported to his head office in Perth. On 23 May, before Reynolds went to the Museum, there was an acrimonious exchange of letters with the ALS. The Amax lawyer, who had been brought in from Sydney, wrote to the ALS advising that it intended to commence operations with the drilling of a water well the next week, and that:

> Mr. Skinner's statements gives us no option but to take steps to protect personnel on site, and to this end we are requesting an assurance from the Government of Western Australia that we may carry out our legal rights free of threats of this nature. In addition we reserve the right to take such legal action as we may be advised to protect our interests and to restrain your clients from carrying out the detention of any of our personnel or those of our contractors.[9]

The ALS replied the same day by pointing out that Amax's stated intention to conform to the Aboriginal Heritage Act was in conflict with its other statement of intent to commence drilling, and that it should refrain from any action that could put it in breach of the legislation.

The next day Premier Court received an angry telex from Lloyd Parks, the Amax Vice-President in Houston heading the petroleum and iron ore division of the company. Parks' telex raised the alleged threats to Lyon, and the expense the company faced if there were any further delays, and stated:

> We urgently request your immediate assistance...Please advise us of what steps you will take to insure safe entry and operation and to insure us of our rights granted by our exploration permit.[10]

The affair had now gone beyond the province of a minor problem to be handled by the Mines Department alone. The Government's first response was to set in train the organisation of a meeting at Noonkanbah. It proposed to send a relatively senior Mines Department official, Amax and Museum personnel, and the police.

Before the meeting took place the pressure continued to mount. The Community released Amax's letter of 23 May to the press, along with a statement saying that it had instructed the ALS 'to take all possible steps to prevent Amax from drilling on the station, as the proposed site is in a sacred area', and quoting Skinner as saying, 'The Elders and all the communities around here are working on ways in Tribal Law which will stop Amax coming and drilling on our land'.

This was carried in the *West Australian* under the headline 'Trouble Brewing Over Drilling Plan', along with rumours about the Community planning to lock the station gates to keep Amax out.

As a State Government public servant, the DCW adviser working with the Community knew that his role was bound to come under scrutiny, given the course the dispute was taking. He therefore told the Community that he would not be able to continue with his advisory role in relation to the mining matters.

It was at this point that the Community contacted me in Melbourne. I had left Noonkanbah six months earlier, promising the Community that I would do what I could to press their cause, and to find an outlet to publish the stories they had told me, and saying that I would try to come back at some point to see how they were progressing. They now asked if I could return immediately to help them in the looming battle. I arrived at Noonkanbah within a few days, and was given the responsibility from then on of handling the media and publicity side of the dispute, and of helping to build links with supporters outside the Community.

Amax provided the required map showing its drilling limitations to the Western Australian Museum. They also gave the first sign of having a fallback position. They asked the Museum to survey a site on Ellendale Station, north of Noonkanbah, but still within EP97, as an alternative drilling location.

The affair was discussed by Cabinet on 28 May 1979. No records of the meeting are available, but clearly a decision was made, despite the Museum's findings, to back Amax to the hilt, and force the issue as far as necessary. Presumably it was hoped that the forthcoming meeting at Noonkanbah would break the deadlock that had developed; but it was made clear that only one outcome – drilling by Amax – was acceptable.

It seems likely that Cabinet decided, in the light of the pressures that had been building in recent years, and especially in the Kimberley, to establish a benchmark – to discourage Noonkanbah and other similarly restless communities from believing that political agitation would be allowed to divert the Government, or impede the mining boom.

The Community was not officially advised of the meeting that had been arranged until two days beforehand, when an officer of DAA in Derby, Ian Hooper, came to tell them of the arrangements made by the Government. The people agreed to meet with the Mines Department, but said that they were not prepared to have either Amax personnel or the police present.

A specially chartered jet brought Max Reynolds, Murray Johnstone, who was the Supervising Geologist of the Sedimentary and Oil division of the Mines Department, and Peter Randolph, the Acting Registrar of the Aboriginal Sites Department at the Museum, into Derby on 29 May.

They were advised by Hooper that unless they were prepared to meet the Community's conditions there would be no meeting. A series of conferences continued until well into the night, with Johnstone speaking to his department head and his Minister, the local police sergeant consulting his Commissioner, and Dick Old, the acting Minister in charge of the Museum, unsuccessfully trying to contact Randolph. Eventually it was agreed that the police would remain in Derby, Tom Lyon would be kept well away, and Reynolds would fly out to Noonkanbah with Johnstone, but remain in the plane, to be called into the meeting if required.

At Noonkanbah the people gathered the next morning in determined mood and high spirits, feeling that whatever the day might bring, a meeting with a Government representative was a step forward. They had been joined by leaders from most of the surrounding communities.

The location for the meeting was a large bough-shade of posts and spinifex outside the old homestead, which now served as the office and operations centre for the Community. From early morning people waited with an air of expectation, sitting in small groups under the shade, and on the homestead verandah, quietly speculating as to what might eventuate.

Ian Hooper had driven out with Peter Randolph in advance of the plane carrying

Murray Johnstone and Max Reynolds. He reported on the negotiations of the previous evening, and delivered the message from the police that had been their condition for not attending. The people were warned, 'if there's any threat to people or to property the police will take normal action that they're required to by the law'.[11]

The Noonkanbah people and the other community leaders were joined by Jimmy Bieunderry of the National Aboriginal Council and the ALS lawyer, Phil Vincent, who had both travelled out from Derby. Peter Bindon had returned, independently of Randolph, to begin his second survey. And I had arrived at Noonkanbah the day before.

Jimmy Bieunderry and Dicky Skinner went to meet the plane when it was heard approaching. Bieunderry came back from the strip a few minutes in advance of Skinner. He told the people in language to be polite, and to not laugh or act surprised when Skinner arrived with Johnstone, as the man was remarkably short, well under five feet tall.

So began the first direct discussions between the people of Noonkanbah and the Government. With Reynolds stranded in the plane, the police back in Derby, and the Museum staff and Hooper seated opposite him amongst the people, Johnstone was very much on his own. By setting their own terms for the meeting, the people had effectively destroyed the Government's original intention of presenting a united front of Government and company officers to bring the Community to its senses. Instead Johnstone in isolation was very much on the defensive.

Nevertheless, he spoke for almost an hour, and was able to convey very clearly the realities of the situation from the Government's perspective, whilst simultaneously providing the Community with some ammunition it would use in the months to come.

In his opening sentence he made it clear that he was at Noonkanbah as a representative of the Minister for Mines. He described the Mines Department as 'one of the more powerful departments in the Government in Western Australia' because of the State revenue that was generated from royalties. He then explained how the Government promoted the search for oil by advertising exploration permits, and then enforcing the work done on them:

> [The companies] have to complete that work each year, or they forfeit that lease, we make them lose the lease. So we in the Mines Department are forcing the companies to do this work.
>   There's a company here that wants to drill a well to look for petroleum. Now they could drill it some other time, but the Mines Department wants them to drill it now, because this is when we said they should drill the well. So if there is any opposition to the drilling of the well, the Mines Department are the people that are forcing this drilling; and it's opposition not to a company, but it's opposition to the Government.

Having clarified that point once and for all, he then took a tack that missed the point altogether, by trying to persuade the people that it would all be over and done with quickly, and could then be forgotten. He spoke of the poor history of oil exploration in the Kimberley before saying:

> So looking at it scientifically, the chances of a well here finding oil or gas are probably ten to one, or maybe even fifty to one against them finding oil or gas. Very, very slim chances. But it's a chance the Government wants these people to take, and these people are willing to spend two million dollars to take this chance and probably find nothing.

Next he started the Government's campaign of trying to redefine the Aboriginal Heritage

Act to suit its perceived priorities.

> Now there's another Act under which companies looking for oil or looking for minerals must also work. And that's the Aboriginal Heritage Act. And that states quite definitely that the companies must not knowingly in any of their surveys or any of their activity violate any sacred sites.
> By this we mean areas where you perform your rituals, or any areas which contain sacred objects, or burials, or any areas that you consider to be specifically sacred. This does not, under the terms of the Petroleum Act, cover the whole land. It does not cover the whole area, it covers specific sites.

He seemed to assume that the Community's participation in Bindon's first survey, and the findings of the survey, were irrelevant, when he asked:

> But we need your co-operation to indicate which are the sacred areas...If you know there is something out there say, 'Please keep away from this hill, please keep away from this place'. And they will do it, because we have the power of the law on our side to force them to do it. We have the power of the law to force them to keep away.

After describing the specific nature of the work Amax intended to carry out, and the safeguards they were promising to answer the Community's concerns about social intrusion, and promising that the drill site would be cleaned up afterwards, he concluded his opening speech with an attempt at reassurance:

> I personally think that the well will not find any oil or gas, and therefore there will be nothing left for people to see; just a little plate saying this is the Fitzroy River Number One Well. That's to identify it for history.

Nipper Tabagee responded for the Community by describing the damage already done to sites, roads and fences on the station by Amax.

Johnstone replied with a statement of commitment. If honoured it would have seen the affair resolved in favour of the Community within two weeks:

> The Minister for Mines will not sign the paper authorising the company to come onto this land to drill the well until he gets a document from the Museum people to say that they have consulted with you, and that the area they want to put the well and the area they want to put the camp are not sacred sites. He will not sign that paper until he gets that document.

After some further fruitless debate in which Skinner and others tried to explain their perspective, Johnstone asked if it was possible to go out to the area in question, 'and have a look around and see if we can find some site'.

The meeting was adjourned for about an hour to enable the people to discuss privately Johnstone's request for a visit to the site. Peter Bindon told the people exactly what he had written in his first report, and explained that now instead of one particular spot, the company and the Government wanted them to look at a larger area around that site as a possible drilling zone.

The people were offended at the fact that they had taken the step of divulging the religious information, but now were being told, in effect, that this was not good enough, they had to go through the process again.

Murray Johnstone's strategy of downplaying the prospects of the well and emphasising the Government's enforcer role also backfired. The natural reaction of the people was to say, 'why should we be made to pay for something that this man says is not going to be worth anything anyway?'

The second session of the meeting had a much sharper edge to it. Johnstone was told that a visit to the area that day was out of the question, that all the appropriate people had to be consulted, which could take some time, and that such decisions could not be rushed. In this the people were quite definite. Serious discussions affecting the framework of the Law and the use of the land would be done their way, using their processes. The idea of walking over the land with a stranger to bargain over it was an anathema to them.

The debate continued:

> *Johnstone*: I don't think the Government could wait a week, couldn't wait as long as a week. Maybe tomorrow. There's too much money involved, too much money involved which is being wasted. We're dealing with big money. We're looking at millions of dollars, about two million dollars to drill this well. It's a lot of money, and once the material arrives they start paying for it. They just need to get going on it.
>
> The Government doesn't feel like letting them off the hook. The Government is saying, no, we want to drill the well.
>
> *Skinner*: We just had no time; too quick. Just can't say that, get in a rush and do what is important to us. It sometimes takes long while.
>
> *Johnstone*: No, it couldn't take a week or a month. The Government wouldn't allow it...I don't necessarily like the position I'm in. I'm a Government servant and I have to say what the Government tells me to say, and that is the situation.

When challenged again as to why there was this incredible urgency for an immediate decision, he could only reply:

> Well I've been in the oil business for twenty-five years, and this is the oil business unfortunately. You have to make decisions within twenty-four hours. This is the way it always works because big money is involved and it has to work this way.
>
> *Randolph*: I can't agree with you, the area must have been known for some time.
>
> *Johnstone*: It takes six to eight months for seismic data to be processed. You can be looking at up to ten months between shooting the survey and when you can make a decision on the site as a result of the survey. It's not the company's fault.
>
> *Randolph*: Given what you're saying it seems quite unreasonable that the Government should be pushing the Community to go ahead so fast.
>
> *Johnstone*: The alternative you're facing is another year's delay, which is unacceptable for the Mines Department, because the company might decide to go away.
>
> *Randolph*: I don't think the people have said a whole year. Dicky inferred a week or a month. I would suggest the rush is something that can be overcome by giving some consideration to the people's wishes.

Johnstone: I understand that myself, but I haven't been given that latitude by the Government...I can say this officially; the Government does not want to extend the conditions on Amax. They want Amax to drill.

Vincent: Does that mean the Government is not going to allow the people sufficient time to instruct the Museum for the preparation of a report on the Aboriginal Heritage Act?

Johnstone: The Government would like a decision to be made this afternoon.

From this point the meeting continued for another half hour or so, with each side refusing to concede any ground. Eventually Jimmy Bieunderry brought the meeting to a close:

> In many times in many places the Aboriginal people have been pushed from every angle to make a decision in twenty-four hours. I reckon this time we have to consider and have time to make the decision, rather than the mining company just coming in and saying, 'We're going to bulldoze across here and there'.
>
> We understand the Government has the power, but at the same time the Government has to understand the people in the Community...to have a consultation between the people and the Government rather than just pushing it in one day. This is the first time you from the Mines Department have come to talk to us.
>
> It would be a funny thing for the Government to force the Community to make a decision this afternoon. Crazy. We have to listen to one another, and then we can get along in the future. If we're not going to listen to one another then this conflict will be going on all the time. But if we sit down and look at each other and talk to one another properly and sort it out, then we'll know one another; the people, the mining company and the Community.

Johnstone returned to Derby to propose to his superiors that a period of one week be allowed for Bindon to make more detailed investigations into the possibility of finding an acceptable site within Amax's defined zone. He returned the following day, a Thursday, to say that the Government was far from happy with the delay, and wanted advice as to the availability of a site by the next Tuesday morning.

It was immediately after Johnstone had left Noonkanbah for the second time that Bindon was shown the darrugu from Noonkanbah and Looma, and then commenced the second round of his investigations.

After completing the Noonkanbah survey Bindon also visited the alternative Ellendale location nominated by Amax with the relevant Elders. This site was quickly cleared as being perfectly acceptable for drilling.

But whilst Bindon was still in the field, the Government in Perth was becoming impatient, and the pressure was building. The Government had already determined that it was prepared to brush aside the opposition of the Noonkanbah people, but it was becoming aware that the Aboriginal Heritage Act was looming as an obstacle to this intention.

Until this time the Act had operated fairly satisfactorily for all parties. Information relating to sites was gathered by the staff of the Aboriginal Sites Department of the Western Australian Museum, where Peter Bindon worked, or could be lodged with them by any member of the public. From this information a register of sites was compiled, and these locations were given a general protection by the Act, in that it was an offence to knowingly disturb or damage a site.

Where a site was deemed to be of particular importance, or seen to be in some way threatened by development, it could be specifically protected by declaration of Protected Area status. Such a declaration could be either permanent, or temporary, of up to six months' duration, to enable further investigation or consideration.

Such a declaration would be made by the Governor in Council, which is effectively the State Cabinet. Normally a declaration would follow recommendation by the Aboriginal Cultural Materials Committee, the expert body constituted under the Act, which would assess reports from the Sites Department staff. The ACMC included Professor Ronald Berndt, as previously mentioned, other anthropologists, Ken Colbung – the head of the Aboriginal Lands Trust – as an Aboriginal representative, and ex-officio members from the Museum, the Aboriginal Affairs Planning Authority and the Lands Department.

The Trustees of the Museum had the final authority to make recommendations to the Governor in Council, but normally delegated this function to the ACMC.

There was also a process whereby proposals to declare Protected Areas were normally circulated to interested Government departments, including the Mines Department, for their consideration and comment. The Mines Department had a record of opposing any proposals relating to land where there was even the faintest prospect of mineralisation.

The Act provided various avenues of action for a party wishing to use land affected by its provisions. In the case of a registered site, 'the owner of any land on which an Aboriginal site is located' could give written notice to the Trustees that he required to use the land; in which case the Trustees could either give consent to such use, or recommend declaration of the site as a Protected Area or a Temporarily Protected Area, in which case the Governor in Council would make a final decision. If the Trustees failed to act on such a request the 'owner' could force the issue through action in the Local Court.

A person aggrieved by any proposed or actual declaration of Protected Area status could make representations to the Minister, who could then direct the Trustees to consider such representations, and then report to the Cabinet.

The obvious intention of the Act was to ensure that the Trustees should take into account the relative importance of a site, and the effect on other parties, when assessing the expert advice of the ACMC; but if they decided that protection was warranted, the onus was on the politicians in Cabinet to take the responsibility of a final decision as to whether it would be protected by declaration or not.

The Aboriginal Cultural Materials Committee held its regular quarterly meeting on 1 June 1979 with Bindon still in the field, completing his second investigation. They had the report of his first survey before them, and they were briefed by the Museum Director, John Bannister, and Peter Randolph of the Sites Department on the political situation and the pressures that were being applied. The difficulties of the varying concepts of the sacred site that Berndt and others had anticipated had arrived, in particularly awkward circumstances.

The ACMC after lengthy discussion of the information available resolved:

> that temporary protected area status be sought for the four sites of the Bundarra Goodun complex [the sites closest to the nominated drilling location] and Pea Hill itself to allow further investigations of their significance.[12]

An ACMC sub-committee was also appointed to consider Bindon's final report, and:

assess the possibility of reaching a compromise over the location of the area of the Company's interest in respect to the Pea Hill complex. If such a compromise is not possible at least that area designated by the mining Company, within the Pea Hill complex, should be recommended for protected area status, as a matter of urgency, recognising that it may be necessary to seek such status for a wider area, to include the area of influence of Pea Hill, subsequently.[13]

Thus the Government was given notice that the duly constituted experts endorsed Bindon's work to date, and that it was facing a possible defeat unless the Trustees rejected the ACMC's advice, or Cabinet was prepared to overrule the Trustees.

It was Sunday 3 June before Randolph could contact Bindon, who advised that the survey was not yet complete, but the information to hand strongly indicated that the whole of the possible drilling zone was effectively out of bounds. Bindon was told to finish as quickly as possible and make haste to Perth.

Bannister passed Randolph's report to his acting Minister, Dick Old, and a meeting was arranged for the following day, causing Old and Andrew Mensaros, the Minister for Mines, to interrupt their long weekend holiday plans. The two Ministers refused to accept the definition of a site being adopted by Bindon and the ACMC, arguing that a site had to be a defined feature.

At this meeting the powers of the Minister to direct the Trustees under Section 11 of the Heritage Act were also raised by Mensaros and Old. The Museum staff had not previously considered this. The relevant section came under the administrative part of the Act, and bore no obvious relationship to the procedures outlined for registration and protection of sites.

In fact this section had first been brought to the attention of the Government in a Mines Department briefing paper prepared for Mensaros before the Cabinet meeting of the previous week. The paper examined the Heritage Act, quoting and underlining Section 11(2) which stated that 'The Minister, after consultation with the body concerned, may give to the Trustees, or to the [ACMC], directions of a general or specific character as to the exercise of any function under this Act and that body shall give effect to any such direction'. This was followed with the comment that 'if it becomes very necessary the Minister could direct the Trustees to consent to the Amax drilling'.[14]

On the same day that Old and Mensaros were increasing the pressure on the Museum, Premier Court received another telex from Amax. This one was from another vice-president, Arthur Reef. The Reefs and Courts were old acquaintances dating back to Amax's early involvement in Pilbara iron ore when Court held the relevant portfolio. Reef warned Court that the issue was beginning to attract widespread attention, and could endanger the State's reputation as a safe locality for international investors.

Court's concern for his reputation amongst the multinationals is revealed in his minute to his Under Secretary on the matter:

I do not want either the local or the overseas people in Amax to feel I have personally not followed this matter through. The delay is serious and will impair our reputation overseas. In other words, we will start to look like the Commonwealth Government if we are not careful.[15]

He replied to Reef apologising for the fact that the issue had become public, but put some of the blame for this on Amax personnel in Perth, and asked for Amax to refrain from public comment whilst his Government resolved the matter.

A couple of days later he telexed Reef again, expanding on this criticism, and revealing – if only to Reef – exactly what his Government's motivation was.

We were somewhat embarrassed when your man told the museum people Amax might be able to drill on Ellendale instead of Noonkanbah, and this at a time when we were preparing to take a stand about Noonkanbah.[16]

Cabinet was to meet again on Tuesday 5 June. John Bannister, the Museum Director, was contacted at home that morning and summonsed to appear before the Premier. Bannister's file notes record that Court was in no mood for what he regarded as nonsense:

Discussion in the Premier's office began with him explaining that while I might be offended by what he had to say I should realise that his Government had to govern. It could not allow instrumentalities to put obstacles in the way, when he, the Premier, knew that such obstacles were the result of political pressures being applied. From his own knowledge of the Noonkanbah situation...it was obvious to him that the presence of sites and their significance in the area in question was a 'trumped up job' and had probably been engineered by political advisers to the Community. If these kind of problems were going to continue, and he could only see the situation worsening, then the Act would have to be changed.[17]

Bannister explained the work that had been done and was continuing, and attempted to defend the integrity of the procedures, and the ACMC and his staff, who had in effect been accused by Court of being either dupes or liars. But:

The Premier made it quite clear that in his view this sequence of events was typical of the methods now being employed by the advisers to Aboriginal communities to advance their own political ends. He wanted to make it quite clear to me that the Museum would be increasingly used in this way for those ends and that his view of the Museum's activities would be coloured by that knowledge.[18]

Things were warming up. Particularly from the Museum's point of view.
The same day Bannister formally advised Dick Old that:

Mr Bindon has, despite considerable effort expended in searching the zone and discussing its significance with the relevant Aboriginal people, been unable to discover any part of the zone which can be disturbed without giving offence to the local community.[19]

The same memo advised that in accordance with the earlier ACMC resolution a submission would be made for Protected Area status to be applied, as soon as Bindon had completed a written report.

An aggressive briefing prepared for Andrew Mensaros prior to the Cabinet meeting gave the Mines Department's own interpretation on the validity of the site complex, before recommending that Cabinet instruct Old to direct the Trustees to authorise the Amax drilling. But the Crown Law Department had already advised the Museum and Old that there may have been technical problems under the Heritage Act with such a direction. Cabinet directed Mensaros to seek urgent legal opinion on the options available.

Whilst all this was going on Dicky Skinner was back in Perth with Frank Chulung, the Kununurra based Chairman of the Kimberley Land Council, raising public

Frank Chulung.

support for the Community. The issue had taken off in the Perth and eastern states media, with almost daily coverage of the various developments at Noonkanbah and in Perth that were publicly known.

Skinner appeared on television and talkback radio, and in the papers. Picking up on Murray Johnstone's talk at Noonkanbah, he was quoted in Perth's *West Australian* as saying, 'To them the land is just money. All they are looking for is money. To my people the land is part of us. We don't want drilling.'[20]

To the Melbourne *Age*:

> Mr Skinner said he was unimpressed by white man's law. 'When we sing out for help the government doesn't listen. We went to court last year to stop CRA and all the others coming on our land...But we couldn't stop them. Now we go to the newspapers and television, to ask the whites for help.'[21]

He addressed a meeting of the Western Australian Trades and Labor Council (TLC), drawing an enthusiastic response from the delegates, representing nearly all trade unions in the State. Motions of support were carried unanimously, and letters sent to Amax and CRA.

On 7 June the Government made its move, beginning the process that would lead to Dick Old directing the Museum Trustees. Andrew Mensaros formally advised the Trustees that the Crown as owner of the land required the use of a specified two hectares of land in order for the well to be drilled by Amax, and asked for their consent to such use. Old wrote also, stating that he believed the consent should be given, and requesting them to submit their views to him by five that evening.

These were the niceties of notification and consultation that had to be observed before a specific direction could be made. There were conflicting legal opinions as to whether Amax had status as an 'owner' under the Act, and alternatively, whether the Crown could request consent for the use of the site on behalf of another party; but the Government was confident it could force the issue one way or another.

The Trustees were mostly Perth establishment figures; some businessmen, a prominent lawyer, a scientist and so forth. Only Frank Gare, former head of the Western Australian Department of Native Welfare (predecessor of the Department for Community Welfare) and the AAPA, had any expertise or experience in Aboriginal affairs. They were clearly under enormous pressure in the special meeting they had that day. On the one hand were the clear desire of the Government, and its not so thinly veiled threats to the Act and the Museum itself. On the other were their responsibility for the due processes of the legislation, their relationship with the Aboriginal Cultural Materials Committee and the Museum staff, their status amongst Aboriginal people as the body vested with the responsibility of protection of sacred things, and not least, their sense of integrity in the face of the political pressure they were facing.

They met at lunchtime, before the Mensaros and Old letters had been officially received, but they had been advised that the letters were on the way, and what the contents would be. As well as considering the evidence, the ACMC resolutions, and the requests from the Ministers, they interviewed Peter Bindon at some length about his investigations and his report.

They resolved to endorse the ACMC recommendation for Protected Area status for at least the defined drilling zone.

They also resolved that the Director should reply to Mensaros' request that they were not willing to give their consent, and that on the basis of their legal advice it was inappropriate for the Crown to seek consent.

Bindon's report was still being drafted, so an actual application for a Protected Area declaration could not be made. Bannister wrote to Old late that afternoon saying that the Trustees believed that Mensaros' request for consent was not properly based, and that if they did receive an appropriate request, they would still not consent, and would continue to recommend a Protected Area declaration.

The Museum Director, John Bannister, apparently in the vain hope that the Government might yet be persuaded to back away from confrontation, wrote to Old again on 8 June. He enclosed the text of Bindon's three conclusions, and reiterated the Trustees' endorsement of the ACMC's decision to seek protection of the area, and then officially advised Old that the Ellendale site would present no problems whatsoever. But by now, as far as the Government was concerned, the die was cast, and it was only a matter of adopting the appropriate legal and political strategies to bring the opposition to a halt.

Crown Law was advising both the Museum and the Mines Department that neither Amax nor the Crown could be classed as an 'owner' under the definitions in the Heritage Act, able to request permission to use the site. An independent opinion commissioned by the Mines Department suggested the Crown possibly could be. But both sets of advice agreed that now that Mensaros had made the request, whether legal or not, and Old had 'consulted' with the Trustees, they could be directed. On 8 June Mensaros circulated a memorandum suggesting that the Cabinet meeting on the 12th should authorise Old to issue the direction.

The Trustees met again on the 11th. The Crown Law advice that Old now had the power to direct them under Section 11 was conveyed. Crunch time had come for the Trustees. They knew the direction to provide consent would come at any time. They had the choice to follow their legal advice and comply, or to stand by their previous decision to seek protection, and call the Government's bluff by refusing to issue such a consent.

They resolved that if the Minister's direction arrived, they would comply, and Bannister should reply to him accordingly.

On 14 June, the same day that the Bindon report was officially distributed, the order from Old arrived at the Museum. That afternoon Bannister wrote to Mensaros, 'In view of this direction and of their obligation under Section 11(2) of the Aboriginal Heritage Act, the Trustees now give their consent...'

The public and the media, unaware of all the previous manoeuverings, and the complexities of the Act, were unaware of the irony behind the bland statement released by Mensaros:

> that following consultation with the Museum Trustees, the Acting Minister
> for Cultural Affairs, Mr Old, had directed that no objection be raised to
> a two hectare site being made available to allow drilling to go ahead.

Why had the Government forced the Trustees to issue a consent, when they could have waited for the Protected Area recommendation to be officially submitted, as it would have been within a day or two, and then rejected it in Cabinet as the Act allowed? There was Murray Johnstone's promise at Noonkanbah that drilling would not be approved without a document from the Museum; perhaps they felt honour bound to obtain such a document by one means or another. There was the question of urgency from Amax's perspective; but if this was so important, what was another few days, when a special Cabinet meeting could have been convened on the 8th, instead of waiting for the regular meeting of the 12th?

It would seem that the primary reason was that they were trying to put up a smokescreen with this dubious consent, and avoid the political odium that would be associated with overriding a clear recommendation of the Museum Trustees endorsing the stand taken by the Noonkanbah people.

It is interesting to think what course the following weeks might have taken if the Trustees had refused to issue the consent. Their own positions may have been endangered. The veiled threats to the Museum may have been implemented in some form. But the Government would have been forced to either abandon their railroading of the Noonkanbah people and the Heritage Act, or else would have had to have been honest that that was what they were doing, and faced the political consequences.

9

AT THE BOUNDARY GATE

We been learn lately what we can do. We've been blind in the first place; soon as I been born I didn't understand the way I was. Now when I'm a full grown man today, the same as those governments making their rules, well we're making ours too. We can't be little with the gudia. So we got to fight for our own country and our own citizens...They can go back from here.

Nipper Tabagee, at the Noonkanbah boundary gate, 15 June 1979.

News of the Government's activities in Perth got to Fitroy Crossing on the afternoon of 14 June. The Mines Department had written to Amax the previous day, issuing the authority to drill, and advising that the Minister, Dick Old, was going to direct the Museum Trustees to release two hectares around the drilling site. Amax in turn had contacted the Department for Community Welfare office in Fitzroy to advise that they would be entering the station on the morning of the 15th.

Dicky Skinner was in town when the word came, followed shortly by a telexed copy of the Andrew Mensaros statement. He stayed in long enough to dictate an angry public reply·to the Mensaros press statement, rejecting the various justifications given for the Government decision, and to send a telegram to Prime Minister Malcolm Fraser, asking him to intervene:

> We appeal to you to protect our country. W.A. Government is breaking its own laws in letting Amax dig up our sacred sites. Mines Department claimed only 50 to 1 chance that oil will be found on site. For this vague chance the Government encourages destruction of our site and their own Heritage Act.

He then made the long drive back to Noonkanbah to inform his people, and discuss what to do next.

One of the mixed blessings at Noonkanbah at this time was its extreme isolation. The old river road that Skinner took was about three hours of bumpy meandering dirt, passing through a dozen or more gates in varying stages of disrepair on the neighbouring properties. The alternative access was ninety kilometres of bitumen from Fitzroy Crossing, and then another seventy-five of dirt, and took about the same time. There was no phone, and news bulletins came in on short-wave radio of dubious and unreliable reception. Only the Flying Doctor radio provided a limited and very public means of communication with the outside world.

This isolation often meant long delays in getting vital information in and out of Noonkanbah. (Not to mention many a long night-time drive for Skinner and I in times of crisis.) But it also meant – apart from the times later on when the place was inundated with journalists and other visitors – that the people were able to sit and discuss issues, developments and plans at their own pace, relatively free from external pressures.

This was particularly important given the normal style of dealing with major issues such as the one that now confronted the people. People would gather, usually under the bough-shade outside the homestead, or sometimes in the shade of the huge shearing shed that now served as a school. Skinner and I would brief the people on what had

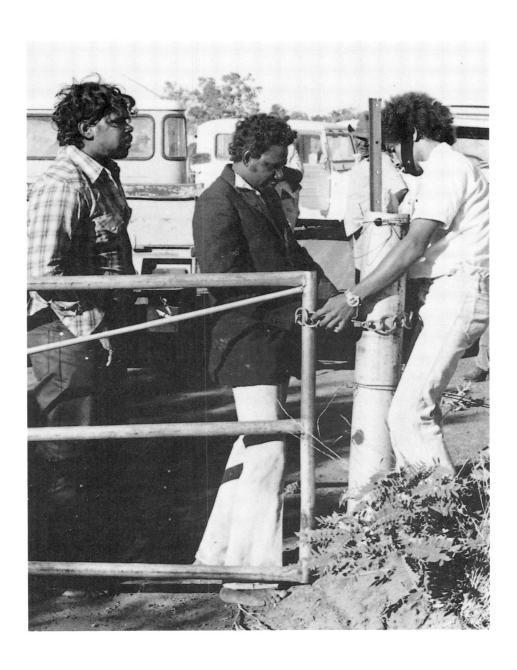

Locking the boundary gate. *(Courtesy Steve Hawke.)*

happened, and run through some of the alternative courses of action and response. The gathering would then break up, and the talk would go on in the camps, where the old people would quiz Skinner further and talk amongst themselves, before delivering the verdict as to what was to be done, at which point I would be told.

On this occasion, at daybreak the next morning a convoy was organised, and most of the men in the Community headed for the boundary gate, about twenty kilometres in from the bitumen, a good hour's drive from the Community.

A padlock was placed on the gate, cars parked on the road, and a camp set up in the midst of a desolate stretch of pindan plain and low scrub, with the nearest decent shade a large boab tree a few hundred metres back down the road. Wood was gathered and billies boiled, and the people settled down to await developments.

Over a cup of tea Nipper Tabagee spoke:

> Righto, we're here in the boundary gate today, and we're waiting for those people to come and have a meeting with us. We said three or four times, no. We got to try them again today. We understand what they're coming for; and they should understand us, what we're talking about. But they don't.
>
> We are looking forward. We are our own citizens, it's as simple as that. It's not a fight, or it's not an argument; but they should understand, more than us.
>
> We been learn lately what we can do. We've been blind in the first place; soon as I been born I didn't understand the way I was. Now when I'm a full grown man today, the same as those governments making their rules, well we're making ours too. We can't be little with the gudia. So we got to fight for our own country and our own citizens.
>
> *Hawke*: If they come today and say they want to go on the station, what are all these people here going to do?
>
> *Tabagee*: No, we don't.
>
> *Hawke*: You don't let them come on?
>
> *Tabagee*: No. They can go back from here.
>
> *Hawke*: So you're not going to shift these cars or unlock this gate?
>
> *Tabagee*: No, we don't want to. We don't want to do that.[1]

The people had been at the gate nearly two hours when the dust of a vehicle was seen approaching. The Toyota slowed to a crawl when it saw the cars blocking the road. The doors were rather slow to open when it stopped, but eventually out climbed Max Reynolds, Murray Johnstone, and an Amax geophysicist by the name of Barnes. For Reynolds, it was his first visit to Noonkanbah, apart from his long wait in the plane during the 31 May meeting.

They climbed through the gate to be met by Nipper Tabagee. His words, as always, were friendly enough; but facing each other on the lonely road, in the long morning shadows, the scene had the bizarre appearance of a Wild West cowboy showdown.

Dicky Skinner and the others came out from the shade of the cars as Johnstone began to talk:

> Yes, well we've got this copy of the letter the Government sent to Amax, to Mr Reynolds here...It says that the Government has approved the drilling of the well provided that Amax takes all reasonable precautions to keep the disturbance of the area to the absolute minimum and not to disturb

At the boundary gate, Noonkanbah, 1979. *(Courtesy Steve Hawke.)*

your community in any way...and that everything be put back just the way it was. So this gives the company the official Government approval to drill the well.

Skinner: Well, as far as we know we not really agree on that, because we said we don't want no mining company drilling on our tribal area.

Johnstone: Well this is not a reserve, this is a pastoral lease.

Skinner: Yes I know, but in the background people looking at the land. We told you people the first time, and I think we not listening to a Government no more.

Johnstone: Then you're going against the law, and you know what that means. You're going against the law of the land.

Skinner: Well the Government wants to go down there and drill a hole in there. That means you break my Law.

Johnstone: No, there's only one law; that's the law of the official Government of the country.

Skinner: You're looking at your own law.

Johnstone: That's right, and that's the only law we can look at as a Government.

Confrontation with Murray Johnstone and Max Reynolds. Left: Nipper Tabagee meeting Johnstone (foreground right) and Reynolds (centre right). *(Courtesy Steve Hawke.)* Right: Dicky Skinner arguing with Johnstone and Reynolds.

This thing has gone right to the top of the Government; the Cabinet had a meeting on Tuesday, and this is the result of that. We came here as quickly as possible...to tell you that it's right from the top Government. The Premier and all the Cabinet made this decision.

Skinner: Well as far as we know we want our land not to be cut up, and we told you people. Who put the minerals underground? This Government?

Johnstone: No. That's not a point in our law. The people who own the land, or who lease the land, only lease the top of the land. You don't lease anything underneath the land.

Skinner: You know that we told you our Tribal [Law] is brought underground. You look at your map, right?

Johnstone: That's right.

Tabagee: But you don't know our map. We're looking at our map.

Reynolds: We've been operating here for nearly three years now, and this is the first time this has been said to us.

Skinner: That's three years you people have been running around in this

154

Kimberley area, drilling, without getting permission from the Aboriginal people on the tribal side. You were just walking over our old people's bodies. The Government's looking at the money. We're looking at the land. The ground is very important.

Reynolds: It's very important to everybody. It's very important to me where I live.

Skinner: Where were you born anyhow?

Reynolds: I was born in this country.

Skinner: Whereabouts?

Reynolds: In Adelaide.

Skinner: Adelaide? That's overseas?

Reynolds: No, no. Just next door here.

The debate continued with Skinner unflappable, shooting back answers to every tack that Johnstone and Reynolds tried. When Skinner asked why they thought the oil had Amax's name on it, and Reynolds answered that they didn't even know it was there, Skinner fired back, 'Well why are you going to go down and mine?' When he again criticised the Government's greed for money, Johnstone countered with, 'What do you run your vehicles on?' Skinner's riposte: 'I was never born with a vehicle, I was born with my own foot!'

It was not exactly a logical debate, because the two sides were arguing from completely different starting premises; that their own law was paramount. Skinner's determination, and his refusal to accept their terms of debate by continually restating his own position, began to frustrate them. After a long technical explanation from Reynolds, complete with diagrams sketched in the dirt, as to why they had to drill in that particular spot, Johnstone came to the point of his presence:

We have to move. This is the Government direction, that we have to move onto this property. We want to visit that site now.

Skinner: No, you can't.

Johnstone: The idea was for me as the Government representative to see the site, to see it and photograph it to make sure there is no damage done to the area. That was my reason for coming up here; first of all to talk to you and to give you a copy of this letter, and also to see the site so that the Government could be sure the company, when it moves on, carries out that thing that the area is completely tidied up and made to look just as it was before.

Skinner (to Reynolds): You're looking at it just like the Government. You are working for the Government telling people to make a decision in twenty-four hours, and things like this. But the tribal people are different from the Government.

I would say that I'm sorry, we told you people that we're not going to listen to the Government. The Government won't listen to us. What can we say? Because we won't let the mining companies come in our area and drill.

Johnstone: But if you break our law, that's a problem; for you people. You are breaking our law by not letting us come in. We have the right to do it under our law.

Skinner: Well we got the right to say this land should not be touched.

Reynolds: What you're saying, Dicky, is that you are setting up your law on this land, which is in opposition to the law of this country.

Skinner: Not [just] for Noonkanbah, but all round the area we're looking at it. We got a number of people from different communities, coming in from the different areas. You're looking at this boundary on the map between Calwynyardah and Noonkanbah. We look at it in our own map, right through.

Reynolds: So what you're saying is that if we proceed beyond here you'll punish us for trespassing. Is that what you're saying?

Skinner: That punishing business, well I don't mention this sort of thing. In the Aboriginal tribal side, I been get punished by my own people. That's in my own culture. Our fight is coming from our tongue. We just fighting with...

Tabagee: ...our own tongues. Not punishing people. We only been tell that one man [Tom Lyon].

Skinner: But one day if we are going to do that, that's being very hard. That's up to the old people, what they want to say.

Reynolds: Is there any way that we can get any sort of agreement with you that we can come in and drill that well?

Skinner: I don't think so. You'll have to go through these tribal people, and they told me that you're not to come drilling in our land, in our tribal area. That's it.

Reynolds: The important thing is, and this is very important, we have to drill now.

Skinner: You can't. If you drill, you're breaking my Law. Well, that's all. Thank you. Sorry that we can't do anything better than that.

Reynolds: Nice to meet you people at last. It's nice to meet fellow Australians.

For the first time the people of Noonkanbah had repelled the company from their land. They left the gate locked, and returned to the Community feeling rather pleased with themselves.

The next day the police paid a visit. Following talks with Johnstone and Reynolds on their return from the gate, the senior officer in the Kimberley, Superintendent Styants, and the Derby Sergeant went to Noonkanbah, forced their way through the locked gate, and arrived unannounced at dusk on the Saturday evening.

According to Skinner, Styants claimed that he had been sent by the Premier, and spent some time trying to convince them to change their minds and allow the drilling to proceed.

Styants told Johnstone on his return to Derby 'that with about three months of discussions, they may be able to break down the resistance to the drilling'.[2]

The irony of his statement reflects his dismay at the strength he encountered in the people of Noonkanbah. Diana Plater, a journalist who spent a few days on the station at this time, reported on the daily scenes she witnessed, and the spirit of the Community. In the midst of the turmoil, the life of the Community rolled on:

The gate to Noonkanbah was chained and locked. Across it was spread a black, yellow and red Aboriginal flag...so we boiled a billy and waited. Before the tea was cold along the road came a truck delivering some water tanks for the stock camp. The driver, Hanson Boxer, drove us back to the homestead to get the key from Dicky Skinner...We drove to the stockyard and watched as the men on horseback separated the bullocks ready to be loaded on the cattle train next morning.

When Dicky saw us coming, he climbed over the fence and grinned a greeting. 'Sorry about the gate, we've been stopping those Amax people coming in.'[3]

Plater described the people working in the school, the kids eating their lunches prepared by a group of women at the homestead kitchen, the old people singing the old songs to the kids round the fires at night; and a demonstration of how the Dreaming for the Pea Hill country wound through the everyday lives of the people:

On the way back from a fishing trip to a beautiful spot on the Fitzroy River, the car loaded with children and women bumped past Pea Hill, close to Bundarra where Amax has set its site for its exploratory well.

'This is the song for this country,' Lucy Cubby said. And they all joined in singing of the time when the goannas were on Pea Hill...It is a male ceremonial ground and no women can go there, she explains.[4]

The article concluded with an insight into the pride the Community took in its defence of this Dreaming and this land, and a warning to the Government:

The walls of the homestead now have a new addition. Ivan McPhee, the Community's secretary, each day pins up newspaper clippings and photographs about the proposed mining and drilling.

One of the men has written a story about it, illustrated by Polaroid photos.

If a decision is made to allow Amax to come onto Noonkanbah Station, Dicky Skinner said the company's representatives would be met at the gate. And the gate would be locked and chained.[5]

The Saturday papers on 16 June carried reports of the confrontation at the gate. For the first time public question marks were raised as to what was contained in the Bindon report, and how it had been handled by the Government. The Opposition was highly critical, calling the Government's actions 'secretive and devious', but it had not yet been able to find out exactly what had happened.

The State Government was still trying to work out its next move when Amax was hit with an injunction. On the Saturday morning Graham McDonald of the Aboriginal Legal Service and barrister Ian Temby appeared for the Community before Justice Howard Smith of the Western Australian Supreme Court, and were able to obtain the injunction, valid until noon the following Tuesday, after submitting that they believed the appropriate procedures had not been followed under the Aboriginal Heritage Act, and that their clients would suffer irreparable damage if Amax could not be restrained until the question had been resolved. Amax and its 'servants or agents' were restrained from doing anything within a radius of three kilometres of Pea Hill.

Whilst the lawyers prepared to do battle, controversy raged around the Bindon report and the Government's treatment of it and the Museum. The media were seeking information and clarification from the Museum. Many of the staff and some of the ACMC members were angry at the way Mensaros' press release implied their endorsement of the Government's actions. Professor Berndt was demanding a public clarification, and the Trustees asked Old to issue a statement distancing them from what had happened. At the direction of the Government, the Museum staff were specifically banned from making any public comment on the affair.

When Old's statement came on the Monday afternoon he did 'confirm that he had overruled the museum's recommendations', and that 'the museum had recommended against drilling'.[6] But in the same interview he claimed that the Museum report conflicted with Kingsley Palmer's of the previous year. This claim was rejected by unnamed 'experts in the field', and subsequently drew an angry letter from Palmer, who said:

> I must protest at what I regard as a blatant misrepresentation of the facts to the press. My report and that of the WA Museum are mutually compatible, and are in no way in conflict.[7]

Tuesday's *West Australian* extensively quoted a letter from Berndt, and on the Wednesday the dispute reached the editorial columns, with the *West Australian* concluding that:

> There is one aspect on which the Government could and should have been more open. When it originally announced approval of the Noonkanbah drilling, it failed to disclose that it was overriding opposition by the museum – this from a government that denounces what it claims are half-truths in another current field of controversy. If the Government had told the whole story, the public might be more inclined to accept its assurances.[8]

When the legal argument over the injunction resumed the ALS successfully applied to have Dick Old and the State of Western Australia, and the Museum Trustees, listed as defendants along with Amax and the Joint Venture partners, on the grounds that it was their combined actions that led to the alleged improper use of the Heritage Act, and the subsequent threat to the Community.

The ALS argument was based on three grounds: firstly, that Amax, not the Crown, should have been the party to apply to use the site; secondly, that the Minister's directive powers applied only to administrative procedures, not to the extent that the Trustees could be directed in a situation such as this; thirdly, that as the Trustees had already recommended in favour of declaring that the land in question should be protected, they could not then, by the accepted meaning of the word, 'consent' to its use.

On 19 June Justice Brinsden extended Justice Smith's injunction. Amax immediately applied for a further hearing on the 22nd to lift the injunction. Max Reynolds' affidavit in support of this application cited the cost caused to his company by the delays. At that stage the costs were one thousand three hundred dollars per day, and there would be another three thousand six hundred to five thousand four hundred dollars a day due to Richter from 15 July if the site, which would take four weeks to prepare, was not ready for them. He stated:

> The likely damages which will be suffered by the Joint Venture are very large. I am concerned as to whether the plaintiffs have the resources to meet a claim for damages if the injunction is continued for any length of time.[9]

The Government's lawyer of course supported the Amax application to discharge the injunction.

Further legal argument on the ALS submission was heard on the 22nd. The Trustees angered the Government by obtaining separate representation from the Ministers and the Crown. They conceded that consent had been given, but did

> not necessarily accept that the consent issued by them in the circumstances...is effective...[and] have no objection to the Court being asked to rule on the matter. If the consent is invalid or withdrawn then the Trustees would persist with their recommendation that the area in question be declared a protected area.[10]

Justice Brinsden reserved judgement, with his decision to be delivered on the 27th. The next day, despite the possibility of a final green light from the court within four days, Reynolds wrote to Mensaros requesting permission to defer Fitzroy River Number One and drill at Ellendale instead. It appears that the court was not advised of this development.

Justice Brinsden's interpretation of the technicalities of the Act went against the ALS on the first two grounds, and on the issue of the consent of the Trustees, he said there was no argument as the formal application for declaration had not been made, and the mere indication of intent to do so was not relevant. He concluded:

> I have reached the fairly confident view therefore that the consent of the 14th June 1979 given by the Trustees to the Crown through the Minister of Mines is a consent within the meaning of [the Act]...And I should take into account that degree of confidence in determining whether the relief sought [by Amax] should be granted. There is no doubt in my view that the continuance of the injunction would cause to the first defendant serious financial loss and would effectively deny to it the ability to drill this...year...In these circumstances therefore it seems to me that I should...discharge the order I made on the 19th instant.[11]

Noonkanbah had been preparing for such a decision. Again leaders of the neighbouring communities had come in to lend their support. Early on 28 June another convoy headed north up the road to the boundary gate. Eighty people settled down again in the makeshift shade of their cars. The high spirits that had prevailed since their earlier victory here were somewhat dampened, as it seemed that this time the opposition was unlikely to be just three men in a Toyota, and there was no certainty as to whether it would come today, tonight, or next week.

Morning turned to afternoon, the mood became more apprehensive. Many of the group had retreated to the shade of the boab tree down the road. Discussion was starting as to what should be done if nothing happened by nightfall: should some people stay overnight, will we send a car back for swags?

Then a triumphant cry rang out from a group huddled round a radio. As the mob converged word spread; Mensaros had announced that drilling had been deferred, Amax would go to Ellendale!! In the joy of the moment no attention was paid to the word deferred. It was victory, and the joy and pride there at the Noonkanbah boundary gate were a sight to behold.

10

OPPORTUNITIES LOST

We now have the rest of this year and some of next year to see if we can
arrive at a solution which protects all parties.

Senator Fred Chaney, Federal Minister for Aboriginal Affairs, 6 July 1979.

It is interesting to speculate on why a decision was made to abandon the drilling plans the day after the legal obstacles had been cleared, and the company was free to move. Just six days earlier Amax had been pleading the urgency of its case in the Supreme Court.

One newspaper report claimed that the Federal Minister, Senator Fred Chaney, had 'engineered the compromise at last minute talks in his Perth office'.[1] This was angrily denied the next day by Andrew Mensaros, who was also at pains to point out that the decision was definitely not a compromise, merely a postponement.

Senator Chaney, despite his ministerial responsibilities in a matter that was obviously highly sensitive, had not been involved in, or even informed about, the previous actions of his State colleagues. Two weeks earlier, he had only found out about the direction of the Museum Trustees and the Government's approval for drilling when a journalist had rung him to ask for comment.

However, Chaney is known to have had discussions with Amax, and then with Mensaros, only two hours before Mensaros announced the postponement.

Whilst Chaney was never prepared to come out in opposition to drilling within the zone defined by the Museum, he was less than happy with the Court Government's approach to this issue, as well as others affecting his portfolio. In his meetings with Amax and Mensaros that week one presumes that he must have advocated a course other than full speed ahead; perhaps it was he that persuaded Amax to ask the Government for permission to postpone, and he chose not to claim the credit so as not to anger the State Government. His public response was to 'congratulate Amax for having put forward a proposal which gives all parties the chance to reconsider the confrontation situation which had developed'.[2]

One must also speculate as to whether his talks with Mensaros or others led to an understanding in the State Government that he would play a role in persuading the Community by some means to accept drilling in 1980. If this were the case, and in their eyes he failed to deliver, it would help to explain what has been widely seen as the vindictive attitude that Premier Court and others displayed towards him later.

Amax would have had its own reasons for being happy to withdraw, at least temporarily. The profit motive and its corporate image were much more important considerations than the political game that was now being played. Its previously low public profile in Australia had disappeared in a most unpleasant manner. The prospect of returning to face another blockade at the gate, and being subjected to a blaze of further public scrutiny, would not have been a pleasant one for the company.

If the Joint Venturers had not been bound by the terms of their lease on EP97, Amax would probably have been happy to slide quietly away at this point and concentrate its efforts on those parts of the permit outside Noonkanbah, and on the other permits in which it was involved. It would certainly have hoped that Chaney and/or the State Government would be able to reach an agreement of some form with the Community to enable it to proceed quietly the next year.

The State Government too must have had some concerns. Court and his Ministers were not averse to confrontation, but like any government, if there was to be one, it preferred to dictate the terms. Thus far, all their attempts to do so to the Noonkanbah people had been unsuccessful. The initiative and the public successes had gone to the Community. The Government needed time to develop a strategy, and time was a commodity in short supply if drilling was to proceed. There was also an election due by March of the next year, and perhaps there was some fear of what the consequences of an unmanaged confrontation might be in this regard.

For whatever reasons, the decision was made. The issue disappeared from the pages of the newspapers for almost nine months. But in this period, affairs did not stand still for any of the parties involved. There were behind the scenes developments, and events on other fronts, that all contributed to a heightening of the tensions that were to cause the Noonkanbah dispute to explode again in spectacular style.

At first there was still the question of the legal action to be resolved. Justice Brinsden had merely discharged the temporary injunction granted in favour of Noonkanbah, not finally settled the matter at law. The Government used this to place further pressure on the Museum. Peter Jones had returned from the overseas trip that had kept him away during the critical period at the Museum, and resumed this responsibility from Dick Old. John Bannister, the Museum Director, was away on leave when Jones spoke to his deputy, Ian Crawford, early in July. Notes of the conversation have Jones suggesting that Amax might be seeking compensation of up to seven hundred thousand dollars, and 'that the Museum might be in an exposed position [and] he hoped the Museum Trustees had looked into the matter of compensation'.[3] In the same phone call, Jones made it clear that he would be looking at amendments to the Heritage Act in the near future.

As it turned out the ALS was advised that on the basis of Justice Brinsden's findings to date, it had virtually no chance of successfully prosecuting the action for a permanent injunction, and it eventually withdrew the proceedings. The question of costs or compensation against any of the parties never arose.

In the meantime Senator Chaney had visited Noonkanbah within a week of the postponement. He told the press that his 'one request was that they take part in more talks on this issue...We now have the rest of this year and some of next year to see if we can arrive at a solution which protects all parties.'[4] The Community felt that he saw such a solution in terms of finding an acceptable means of allowing drilling in the area they had rejected, and were less than happy. In the wake of their recent success, they were looking for something better than this.

John Tozer, the Liberal Member for the State Upper House seat of North Province, who accompanied Chaney, wrote to Premier Court soon afterwards to report on their visit. He confirmed the Community's view by making it clear to his leader that Chaney had essentially supported the State's position that drilling must proceed, but he also echoed Chaney's call for moderation, and urged talks between Government Ministers and the Community.

The State Government did not respond to Chaney's and Tozer's suggestions, and did not initiate any further discussions with the Community following the postponement. Ray Young, the Minister for Community Welfare, wanted no part of such talks. Other Ministers were prepared to consider them, but not to make the first move.

Senator Fred Chaney meeting with the Noonkanbah Community in the Station woolshed, 1980.

The one serious meeting that had taken place, when Murray Johnstone visited, had not been a negotiation in the real sense of the word, but the delivery of an ultimatum that had backfired.

This was to be a continuing disappointment to the Community in its many meetings with State and Federal Government representatives. The initial pleasantries and the friendly appeasing noises would always be followed by the line that they must acquiesce to drilling within the Amax zone, which they continued to tell everybody was not acceptable. From their point of view, no one in power was prepared to listen properly, and understand that this was their starting point for negotiations.

The State Government, by committing itself to total support of Amax from the day in April that Max Reynolds first wrote to Andrew Mensaros, locked itself into a course from which it would not deviate. To a commercial operator all things are flexible and negotiable, depending on the priorities of the time. But it seemed that to Premier Court the reputations of himself and his Government as allies of big business and sound avenues of investment and development were absolutely paramount; with his Minister for Mines and himself having provided guarantees to the company – before the Museum investigations were completed – he felt these reputations were at stake.

Furthermore, the Government now saw Noonkanbah as a test case, symbolic not only of its commitment to development, but of the challenge raised by the growing tide of Aboriginal activism centred in the Kimberley. Dicky Skinner and the Noonkanbah mob had crystallised this into an assertion of the rights of Aboriginal Law and the defence of Aboriginal land.

Perth's *Daily News* had described it as 'the first time in WA an organised group of Aborigines is determined to keep outsiders off what they consider is their land'.[5] And the Melbourne *Age* had said:

It is seen by many as a crucial test case in the Aboriginal land rights issue, until now an insignificant political factor in Western Australia. Noonkanbah is the first place where a group of Aboriginals has banded together in a concerted effort to resist white intrusion since the days of early settlement.[6]

The Court Government was determined not to be seen as the loser in such a showdown.

At Noonkanbah there was no longer any hesitation about the opposition to Amax. The people had tasted victory, they had sensed the power they held, not only on their own land at Noonkanbah, but in the wider community. They had seen the press coverage they had generated, and now knew that they had a network of supporters.

The State Labor Party saw Ernie Bridge as an almost certain winner against Alan Ridge in the forthcoming election, and had continued its enrolment drive in Aboriginal communities, and broadly allied itself with the emerging Aboriginal movement in the Kimberley, and the Noonkanbah people in particular.

The trade union movement at a State level had already indicated its support, though the extent of its commitment was yet to be tested. Activist groups in Perth such as the Black Action Group and the Campaign Against Racial Exploitation were providing moral and organisational support. The Catholic Commission for Justice and Peace and the Uniting Church had publicly supported the Community. And the Kimberley Land Council was becoming a prominent voice, largely through its backing of the Noonkanbah people, though it was also acting on a range of other Kimberley issues.

The people also encouraged and solicited the support of other Aboriginal communities, at first in the immediate locality, and then on a wider basis. The concept that Dicky Skinner used to describe this phenomenon was that of 'shareholders': he would describe these people as shareholders in Noonkanbah, with a legitimate interest, and a role to play in the Community's decision making. This allegory was used to describe their shareholding in the wider Law and the song cycles, common to all the people, of which the Pea Hill story formed one link in a chain.

This was consistent with the Noonkanbah perspective on the dispute as being one between two laws. It was normal practice for senior Lawmen from a wide area to be involved in important meetings and decisions on matters of Aboriginal Law. Noonkanbah was extending this practice to involvement in decisions of a political nature on a matter impacting on the Law.

But the Community did not concentrate only on building support and alliances for a confrontation. It was also developing strategies and proposals to seek a way round the impasse, responding in its own way to Senator Chaney's call for further talks in search of a solution.

Back in May the DCW officers in Fitzroy Crossing had put forward a suggestion to their superiors advocating a three year moratorium on further oil and mineral exploration on Noonkanbah. Their case was argued on social grounds:

> We would re-emphasise the newness of this community's experience in handling its own affairs, in working towards self-reliance and independence. It is not possible to expect a broken community to have been able to adequately rehabilitate its families and workforce in a period of two and a half years to be able to cope with the pressures of a mining company impact.
>
> The mining intrusion will result in the destruction of the present basis of the community's religious life and disrupt its newly acquired social authority structures. The resulting purposelessness and disillusion is likely to add members of this community to the numbers of anti-social people we

have been attempting to re-establish as useful citizens.[7]

When Amax contacted the ALS, presumably at Chaney's urging, to raise the possibility of further talks, the Noonkanbah people decided to use this opportunity to press the moratorium idea. They met with Amax in Derby late in August, and at the same time wrote to CRA. Their proposal was that the companies jointly agree to a three year moratorium without prejudice on either side, during which time the Community would prepare a complete inventory of sacred land on Noonkanbah and Millijidee Stations, as well as consolidating their social and economic development. At the end of this period negotiations over access for miners would be resumed on a basis of knowledge and understanding of the relevant factors.

The hope was that if the two companies with the greatest interests in the stations could be persuaded to join the Community in an approach to the Government, Premier Court would have the ground cut from under his feet. CRA was crucial in this strategy, because it carried more clout in the Australian industry and with the Government than Amax. It had recently had a bad press on its relations with Aboriginal communities following the leaking of an internal document targeting a number of Aboriginal Reserves for exploration. Its interest was in diamonds, and it had already identified commercial deposits at Ellendale, and Argyle in the East Kimberley. It was thought that its commitment to these developments and work on its extensive claims elsewhere might mean that it would be prepared to delay work on Noonkanbah.

Amax seemed to be trying to play both sides against the middle. Without advising the Community, it had informed the Mines Department of the meeting, and requested that Murray Johnstone attend.

When the Community delegation arrived at the meeting venue in Derby with Phil Vincent and Graham McDonald of the ALS and the DCW adviser, they were surprised to find not only Max Reynolds and the Amax lawyer there, but Murray Johnstone, and representatives of DAA and the AAPA. Dicky Skinner insisted that the Community had agreed only to a private meeting with Amax, and that Johnstone and the DAA and AAPA officers would have to leave before the meeting could proceed.

When the meeting had finished, Reynolds and his lawyer emerged to tell Johnstone that they had promised to keep the content of the talks confidential until they had consulted with their Joint Venture partners. The Mines Department was infuriated. Internal memos immediately speculated that the Noonkanbah proposition had revolved around a financial deal to gain equity in the project in return for agreeing to access, on the basis of 'rumours' of similar proposals in the Pilbara.

Within a week of the meeting Amax wrote to the ALS rejecting the moratorium proposal, and CRA responded in a similarly negative vein to the Community's letter. Both companies stated that they intended to proceed with their respective exploration programs on the station. Reading between the lines, it seems clear that both companies discussed the Community's proposal with the State Government, and were left in no doubt as to the Government's strong opposition. But that was not the end of the contact between the Community and the companies.

At the Derby meeting Amax had produced a map which the Community, their lawyers and the DCW adviser all understood to represent an enlarged area for its possible drilling zone, partly outside the zone recommended for protection by the Museum. The Community leaders said they would discuss this with their people.

There was no further development on this until Chaney arranged an informal meeting on 17 November of Amax representatives and the ALS's principal legal officer, Graham McDonald. Reynolds reported confidentially on this meeting two days later to the Mines Department. He claimed that the ALS had misunderstood Amax's position at the Derby meeting, and that in fact the company's area of interest had not altered at all. He also passed on the information that the ALS had informed him that drilling on the proposed site in 1980 would be challenged in the courts.

An exchange of letters and maps between Amax and the ALS followed: Amax asked the Community again 'to indicate to us a site within the area of interest which is acceptable to them as the site of an oil well'[8]; the ALS advised that this was not possible; and Amax finally offered to fund a further survey by 'an anthropologist acceptable to all parties'[9], and suggested a meeting with the American head of Amax Petroleum, Lloyd Parks, at Camballin in January. At this point the negotiations broke down, with the ALS and the Community concluding that nothing new was being offered, and that there was no point in either further anthropological investigation of the same area of land, or further discussion about it.

Mines Department records of these developments give an indication of the State Government's uncompromising attitude to the attempts at negotiation. A briefing for the Minister, Andrew Mensaros, notes that:

> It is disappointing that Senator Chaney did not oppose Mr McDonald's threat of further litigation despite the Senator's firm stand at Noonkanbah in July last as reported by the Hon. John Tozer.

The Minister's hand-written note at the foot of the brief records:

> I spoke to Mr Pierre Gouselant* the chairman of Amax in Perth...and stressed the government's determination to start drilling with the risk of loosing permit.[10]

The ALS did write to Premier Court in December, after the talks with Amax finally broke down, to seek a meeting with him and Mensaros. Court offered to meet Community delegations in Perth, and then in Derby during a scheduled election campaign trip in February; but the Community would only meet at Noonkanbah, and nothing eventuated.

While the fruitless negotiations with Amax continued, CRA re-entered the scene. At the beginning of October they advised that they were about to start work on their claims in the middle and northern parts of the station. After a flurry of talks, and some heartache, the Community entered into an agreement with the company to allow them to proceed.

The work involved very small-scale sampling of features identified as possible diamondiferous kimberlite pipes, and was well clear of any major sites and Dreaming tracks. No camp was established on Noonkanbah, with CRA staff returning to their Calwynyardah base camp each night. The agreement covered the employment of two younger Community members in the work crew, and an older man familiar with the relevant Ngarranggani knowledge as a permanent guide-cum-scout to ensure that there was no infringement on sacred land.

The Community was not particularly happy about the agreement, representing as it did the first specific backdown from their general anti-mining position. But the timing, the nature and location of the work, the advice of their lawyers and the DCW adviser, and their uncertainty at the implications of opposition all contributed to the decision to permit the work.

They made it clear that the agreement was limited to the specific work program for that year only, and should not be interpreted as a commitment to any future agreements. They also released details of the agreement publicly, stating:

---

* Pierre Gousselant, the Chairman at the head of the Amax conglomerate, senior to Vice-Presidents Reef and Parks.

The Community hopes that the Western Australian Government will take note of what has happened, and see that they are reasonable people. But they made it clear that they will continue to fight to protect their sacred lands.[11]

It turned out that CRA worked beyond the agreed six week limit without notifying the Community of its intention to do so, thus further exacerbating the Community's distrust of the miners.

Whilst Noonkanbah had faded from the news, apart from a very limited coverage of the CRA agreement, a number of other issues in the Fitzroy Crossing area flared up, with two in particular attracting media attention.

Throughout most of the second half of 1979 the Aboriginal communities in and around Fitzroy Crossing waged a campaign for the removal of Sergeant Mal Cole, the officer in charge of the local police station. His nicknames were 'The Town Tamer', and a new one bestowed by the white drinkers at the local hotel, 'Knockemdown'. He had a history of taking on the roughest postings in the force, and years earlier had been the subject of controversy in Broome.

The Aboriginal leaders alleged that he was responsible for a series of assaults and unduly rough treatment of Aboriginal prisoners. During his term in the town the meal money allowance for the provision of meals to prisoners, which was paid direct to him as the local officer in charge, had increased by a factor of more than four; proving that if nothing else, the rate of arrests had risen dramatically.

Over a period of months there was an internal police investigation that made no findings against Cole but recommended his transfer; a public meeting with the Commissioner of Police in Fitzroy Crossing that was dominated by Cole's white supporters, and led to the transfer decision being revoked; and finally an investigation of complaints of racial discrimination by a Deputy Commissioner from the Commission for Community Relations that resulted in Cole and one of his constables being issued with certificates of discrimination. The whole affair drew much media coverage, with headlines such as 'Race Riots' and 'Police Brutality'.

Eventually Sergeant Cole requested a transfer. But in what was widely interpreted as a quick reprisal, Stan Davey, the main architect of the DCW community development programs in the local Aboriginal communities, was ordered against his will to transfer to Kalgoorlie. Letters protesting the compulsory transfer from all the Aboriginal communities in the area were ignored. Davey resigned from the Department.

In the midst of the Cole affair the people of the Wangkatjunka Community at Christmas Creek Station walked off in protest, after they alleged that half a dozen of their number working as stockmen had been beaten up without provocation by the manager and the white head stockman. Their complaints to the police in Fitzroy Crossing were not pursued, so they used the ALS to launch private criminal prosecutions for assault. Their prosecution was not successful, but the squatters camp they had set up at Pinnacles after the walk off, a dozen kilometres from the station homestead, remained.

The Noonkanbah leaders, and Dicky Skinner in particular, became drawn into these disputes through their involvement with Marra Worra Worra, the communities' umbrella organisation in Fitzroy Crossing. All in all, it was a year of unrelenting pressure.

The Noonkanbah Community had managed to keep the cattle enterprise going well, turning off nearly five hundred head of cattle – double their pre-season target – with the surplus income put into a capital improvement program. The school also continued to thrive in this, its second year. But the pressure was having an effect. There had just not been enough time and energy left for some of the little things important to Community

The stockmen from Christmas Creek Station - left to right: Dulip Tighe, Hitler Pamba, Edgar Pike, Wilfred Steele, Ned Cox and Walter Rose.

life. For the first time since they had moved back to the station the rubbish collection and firewood delivery for the camps was not working properly. The Community meetings were so much consumed with the external pressures that things such as this were not getting sorted out as they used to.

The end of the year report from the DCW adviser was positive in most of its detail, but commented that 'the Yungngora Community at Noonkanbah have, I feel, slipped backwards socially...the mining and economic push have probably caused this.'[12] The adviser sensed the first danger signs of the internal stress being imposed by the Community's strong public stand; the energy that previously had been concentrated inwardly on the Community's own development with such success was now being diffused in directions beyond its own control.

At the end of this tumultuous year, many of the Noonkanbah people made preparations for a trip to Hooker's Creek in the Northern Territory. It was for Law business; they were taking their ceremonies further afield than ever before. Picking up people from Fitzroy Crossing, Pinnacles, Billiluna and Lake Gregory as the great initiation ceremony headed east, they raced the wet season. They got stranded for a week at a flooded creek just short of their destination, and left a couple of the convoy of vehicles bogged beyond redemption, before they eventually arrived.

The Hooker's Creek trip, despite the difficulties caused by the season, was a successful celebration of the Aboriginal Law and Noonkanbah's special place in it. Coming as it did after the Community's year of struggle, as they were steeling themselves for yet more, it was a morale and prestige booster for the Lawmen and their place in the Community, and a reaffirmation of the central role of the Law in the lives of the people.

The delays caused by the rains meant that the ceremony makers were still over the border in the Northern Territory as the State Election of February 1980 approached. The prospect of them missing out on a vote caused enough concern at Noonkanbah for the Community to ask Ernie Bridge to lay on a plane to send two young Community members and myself on two flights from Fitzroy Crossing to Hooker's Creek; the first with postal vote application forms, and the second with the ballot papers.

In the event the flights were not necessary. Bridge won easily, and a former ALS lawyer, Peter Dowding, took the North Province seat from John Tozer. The Aboriginal voice had spoken at the ballot box, despite the attempts to silence it. At the Noonkanbah booth the figures were seventy-six votes to Bridge and none to Ridge, and this was not the only booth in the Kimberley with such a result.

In the rest of the State though, the Liberals held sway as expected. The Government was returned easily, with the two northern seats being the Labor Party's only gains, emphasising even further the growing distance between the Government and the Aboriginal population.

Premier Sir Charles Court's first task, once the electoral dust had settled, was to reorganise his Cabinet. The looming confrontation at Noonkanbah must have played some role in his deliberations on the allocation of jobs.

Peter Jones, the hard-nosed farmer from Narrogin, was promoted from his previous portfolio of Education and Cultural Affairs, where he had been in charge of the Museum, to become the Minister for Resources Development, Mines and Fuel and Energy, thus ensuring that he would continue to play a central role in the Noonkanbah affair.

Jones was replaced in his former portfolio by Bill Grayden. Grayden was a rather different character to the rest of the Cabinet. He had entered the Parliament in 1947 as a twenty-seven-year-old independent. He joined the Liberal Party soon afterwards, but retained an independent streak. He was regarded by many as sympathetic to Aboriginal people, based largely on his involvement in the 1950s with expeditions that brought many of the Western Desert people into Warburton when the British nuclear testing at Maralinga was imminent, and a subsequent book he had written titled 'Adam and the Atom'. Any sympathies he did have were of a very old-fashioned and outdated kind, and he had not displayed any particular interest in Aboriginal affairs for a number of years.

The most significant addition to the Cabinet was Bill Hassell, just thirty-five at the time, but seen as a rising star in the right wing of the Liberal Party. His first entry on the public stage had been in 1963 as a twenty-year-old law student and President of the Liberal Club at The University of Western Australia, where he had carried on a running debate on defence issues with the Minister for the Navy in the Menzies Liberal-Country Party Government, Fred Chaney senior, father of the Minister for Aboriginal Affairs in the Fraser Government.

In an odd combination of responsibilities, Hassell became the Minister for Community Welfare responsible for Aboriginal affairs in the State, as well as the Minister for Police, with a number of other lesser responsibilities thrown into the portfolio.

By early March 1980 this team, with Court at the helm, was ready to face the Noonkanbah people again.

11

FEELING SICK FOR MY COUNTRY

It was exactly the same like the old days with all the police lined up. It was like having a gun pointed at us and saying make up your mind straight away.

From a statement by the Elders of the Yungngora Community describing the events of Tuesday 18 March.

Sir Charles Court's election victory was on 23 February 1980. Just six days later Amax was in touch with his office to advise him of their plans to move onto Noonkanbah. The drilling rig was available from 6 March, and as soon as the roads were dry enough they would start the site preparation, with the intention of moving the drill onto the station at the earliest possible date. Vice-President Lloyd Parks of Amax was coming to Perth, and hoped to meet with Premier Court and the Minister for Mines, Peter Jones.[1]

By Thursday 6 March, word of Amax's plans had reached the ears of both Senator Chaney and the Aboriginal Legal Service, and was quickly passed on to the Community at Noonkanbah. It was believed that the company would be backed by a police presence. Amax would not talk to the ALS when it sought confirmation of the rumours; Max Reynolds insisted that any questions should be referred to the State Government.

The Community immediately issued a defiant press release, with Dicky Skinner calling the people of the Kimberley to battle stations:

> Last year a lot of people were worrying about this same place, Pea Hill, a sacred site. Tribal Elders say that we can't let miners on that sacred site. We told them, but they didn't really care about us. Amax are only listening to what the Government is saying...
>
> Way back the white man just took this land from the Aboriginal people. From that day the same thing is happening, till today, 1980.
>
> We want to live peacefully in the land. Why do these mining people come around drilling, looking for oil and minerals? We brand hundreds of calves every year, that means we are building the station up. But they just get the oil from one place and that oil doesn't fill up again the way the cattle do. When they get that oil, finish, and they just leave the land cut up.
>
> The Government says they own the land. We say the Government is not owning any land. This land belongs to Aboriginal people.
>
> Well, we don't think we'll let the mining in. We'll fight for our land. We'll stick to that word.
>
> We are sending word to every community in the Kimberley to come to Noonkanbah and stand with us; and to all the Aboriginal people in Australia to support us. If Amax push their way onto our station they will be walking over all Aborigines.[2]

True to Skinner's word, the Community and the Kimberley Land Council immediately sent people and radio messages winging around the Kimberley, and letters and telegrams to more distant parts of Australia. A mobilisation was underway.

Back in Perth, the same weekend saw the politicians busy behind the scenes as well. Chaney spoke to staff of the Museum, and to the three State Ministers involved, Peter Jones, Bill Grayden and Bill Hassell. He urged the Ministers to take a cautious approach, and sought clarification on the matter of site protection, but to little avail it seems. When Jones prepared a memo for the Premier on the Monday, it included the advice that 'Senator Chaney be asked to refrain from talking to Amax personnel and to officers of the WA Museum on this issue as this is a State Government matter'.[3]

Jones' memo also indicated that Amax's plans had firmed up, with March 17 set as the date that a water driller and earth-moving contractor would enter Noonkanbah to begin works. However the first hint of the company's reluctance also appears here, with Jones commenting that:

> ...resolution may be complicated by a sensitivity on the part of Amax, as that company feels it is in a difficult situation, not unlike similar situations it has experienced with Red Indian Reservations in North America.[4]

Reynolds did nothing to dispel this impression when, speaking to a reporter, he 'admitted that the Government had asked Amax to begin exploration "as soon as possible this year"'.[5]

The main result to come from these discussions with Chaney was a consensus amongst the politicians that it was time for a delegation of Government Ministers to go to Noonkanbah for talks with the Community.

In preparation for these talks Grayden, Jones and Hassell met with Museum staff and Trustees on Tuesday 11 March. Discussion at this meeting centred around the possibility of moving the drill location as far south as possible within the Amax target zone, to the point where it met the southern boundary of the area recommended for protection the previous year. Murray Johnstone of the Mines Department rang Reynolds during the meeting, and gained his tentative approval for the proposal.

The next day the Museum's Director contacted Grayden's office to confirm the Museum's willingness to assist in investigating this possibility, and offering to send Peter Bindon with the Ministers to Noonkanbah. But the Director was told, for reasons left unexplained, that 'the matter had proceeded too far for any assistance from us [Museum] to be useful and we were therefore not required to accompany the Ministerial party to Noonkanbah'.[6] Given the approach the Ministers would take at Noonkanbah at the end of the week, it is interesting that they did not want Museum staff to be present.

By this time 'the shareholders' had indeed gathered at Noonkanbah, and there were more than seventy people camped once again at the boundary gate. Within three days of the Community's call going out people from over a dozen communities, from Strelley and La Grange in the south to Wyndham in the north, had come in. They sent a message down to Perth that they were willing to meet with the State Government Ministers, and Senator Chaney if he was available. But they set their own terms. The meeting was to be on Friday 14 March, otherwise the shareholders would have to go home, and the meeting be postponed until they could return; unless there was a guarantee that Amax would not enter the station whilst any negotiations proceeded, the meeting would have to be at the gate; and 'the Museum has already done a report with all the old people about the Pea Hill area, and they know it is a genuine sacred site, so we will not talk about changing that'.[7]

Ken Colbung, the Chairman of the Aboriginal Lands Trust, was called in by the Government as the intermediary to arrange the meeting. He flew into Noonkanbah on the Thursday with Phil Vincent, who had moved from Derby to Perth over the wet season and now was the senior lawyer in the ALS. The people came in from the gate, and the meeting was confirmed for the next day.

The pace at Noonkanbah that week had been hectic; the initial effort to organise the Kimberley-wide mobilisation, the move to the gate, and the series of talks with the shareholders who came in. The roads were still wet enough to get a number of cars bogged, making the logistics all the more difficult. The Thursday had seen a full day of talks, first with the new Labor Members of Parliament, Ernie Bridge and Peter Dowding, then with Colbung and Vincent. On the Friday, the people waited.

That morning I came across four of the old men of Noonkanbah sitting in the shade of the workshed, talking earnestly to Eirlys Richards, the linguist who co-ordinated the Walmatjari language program in the Community school. She was frantically writing on a notepad on her lap. The old men had decided that on this occasion they wanted to give their message to these senior members of the Government in their own words. They had asked the linguist to transcribe and translate from the Walmatjari.

Their message was about the Law; its truth, its power, and the danger it could hold. Old Paddy Yamera's words are a good example:

> We're protecting this country underneath which has been here since long ago. It was buried there long ago. The important one in the West [Premier Court] has been talking. He didn't bury those things underneath the ground. They are there from long ago. If anyone should drill in this place, any sort of savage wind or rain could come. They won't believe it, they still want

Paddy Yamera, Ginger Nganawilla and Barney Barnes, Noonkanbah, 1980.

The arrival of the three Ministers, Peter Jones, Bill Hassell and Bill Grayden, Noonkanbah, 14 March 1980. Top left: Grayden introduces himself to Charlie Rangi. Ken Colbung is at left (back to camera) speaking to Ivan McPhee. Jones is in the left foreground and Hassell behind Grayden. Top right: Dicky Skinner, Grayden and Hassell begin negotiating the meeting arrangements. Centre left: Nipper Tabagee, Colbung, Hassell, Grayden, Jones, Skinner and Rangi continue negotiations. Bottom left: Dorothy Snell joins the discussion.

to come in. This (under the ground) is here from long ago. It was covered over then – not in the present. The father put it there long ago. What are they (mining people) looking for?

Are they going to keep bothering us, treating us as young men who don't know what we're talking about? We will protect our land. We say NO![8]

Unfortunately, Eirlys Richards did not have time to prepare the translations for the meeting, as the Ministers arrived shortly after the old men had finished dictating their words to her.

The Ministers, Grayden, Jones and Hassell, were met at the airstrip by Colbung and Skinner, with Colbung doing the introductions in front of the TV cameras that had arrived that morning. On arrival at the old shearing shed where the meeting was to be held there was immediate conflict about the procedure. The Ministers had obviously arrived with a pre-planned strategy; they asked for an initial meeting with three Community representatives before meeting with the whole assembly.

The people agreed reluctantly, ever suspicious of the divide and rule tactics that had brought them trouble so often before, and the group of six adjourned to a huddle on the raised shearing platform as the mob of seventy-odd men from Noonkanbah and the other communities waited tensely below, along with Phil Vincent and I, and Don McLeod from Strelley. This session did not last long, as Skinner and Tabagee insisted that they must do any real business in the presence of all the people. So the six turned their chairs towards the body of people in the lower part of the shed, looking rather like a motley group of politicians addressing the party faithful from the stage of a town hall.

Bill Grayden was the main spokesman for the Government, starting off with the soft sell, praising the Community and the progress it had made, and stating that the Government wanted to see more Aboriginal people on pastoral leases doing this sort of thing. His understanding of Aboriginal culture was shown when describing himself as 'the Minister for, among other things, Culture', he said:

...under the protection of Culture we have things like Aboriginal culture, which we want to see developed, such as drawings you have in various caves and in other places. They are of tremendous importance, and we've seen the designs, you have the dresses the women wear, you have the patterns

The Noonkanbah men and their supporters wait whilst the Ministers meet with three Community members.

176

The three Ministers meet with the Community and its supporters at the bough-shade. Don McLeod (squatting centre left) addresses the Ministers. Phil Vincent, the ALS lawyer is squatting at centre right in a white shirt.

on the curtains and other materials, and they are very popular throughout the world.[9]

He was also quite emphatic in saying that the drill would not go down in a place where the people did not want it.

But the gap between words and reality did not take long to emerge. Grayden concluded his opening address with a request for the people to take the Ministers down to the site, so they could sort out the problem there and then by marking a spot. It became clear that as far as the Ministers were concerned this was the crux of the matter, and the purpose of their visit.

Dicky Skinner referred this request to the floor, saying, 'These people are the shareholders of the land, and they are the ones who must say'. And after a short discussion in language he turned back to Grayden to announce, 'They say no mining on that important area'.

From that point the meeting degenerated. The Ministers insisted that they did not want to inspect any sacred sites, merely point out the drill site, and how far it was from any Aboriginal site. 'We want to show you where we want to put the hole because we know it's not on the area. We want you to say "Yes, I'm sorry, we're wrong, it's in a different area".' As Murray Johnstone had the year before, they kept referring to the Community's alleged agreement to the drill site in 1978. And as with Johnstone, they could not name the persons who had agreed when challenged.

When Nipper Tabagee asked if they believed the people had lied to the Museum, Peter Jones could only reply, 'No we don't believe you lied, that's why we've come to ask where the company can drill...We want to make really sure, we will show you on the map.' Jones brought out a map and started pointing out the drill site and the distances from the specific surface sites recorded by the Museum.

In response Tabagee produced the Aboriginal map, an ancient stone carved darrugu. There was a murmur of excited comment from those on the floor as it was brought out. Tabagee tried to explain its significance and relationship to the country, as Skinner aggressively asked the politicians if they understood it. Naturally, they had no idea.

The meeting broke up for a while, and the Community considered its position. The people were far from happy. The attitude taken by the three politicians reinforced the resentment felt by the Elders, best expressed in Paddy Yamera's statement that morning; 'Are they going to keep...treating us as young men who don't know what we're talking about?' The meeting then reconvened at the bough-shade in front of the homestead to repeat to the Ministers that they would not take them down to the proposed drilling zone, stressing that the full and proper story had been given to the Museum the previous year.

A futile debate followed, with Grayden's earlier statement reversed to say that there would be no more Aboriginal pastoral leases granted whilst the Community took this stance. As the five-hour meeting was finishing Jones asked Skinner for the first time whether the Community was now saying no to mining anywhere on Noonkanbah, and Skinner replied, 'Yes, that is what the people think'.

The Ministers emerged to hold a mini press conference for the reporters and cameramen who had waited outside for the duration. They were clearly angry, but unsure as to what their next move would be. They emphasised that the Community was now saying no mining on Noonkanbah Station, and claimed that the issue had nothing to do with

Olive Bieunderry talking with Bill Grayden.

sacred sites. The conference ended with Bill Hassell punching his fist into the palm of his hand, saying in fervent tones, 'This Government is dedicated to getting some exploration and finding some oil...This is an oil hungry world.'

Olive Bieunderry approached Grayden as the Ministers were making to leave, and made a last, fruitless attempt to explain the people's feelings to him.

As the first meeting between the protagonists in the Government and the Community, and the first skirmish of the new year, it was a disappointing encounter for both parties, and typical of what was to come. There was no real communication established, no common ground on which to set foot.

The Community had entered the meeting with every intent of trying to express their feelings to the Government; especially the Elders, through their prepared statements and the significant decision to produce the darrugu. But they had no real negotiating position except a refusal to accept mining in the Amax zone, merely a hope that something new would emerge, and a willingness to stall and seek time. The Ministers came with an equal determination that drilling would proceed as planned, and an ill-conceived belief that they could somehow convince the people of Noonkanbah that what they, the custodians, were saying about the land and the sites was incorrect.

The Community had no warning that a visit to the site by the Ministers would be on the agenda, and their response was interesting. They felt that their honesty was being challenged, and they refused to go out to the site. A comment of Kingsley Palmer's in a site survey he did in another part of the Kimberley is informative in this context:

> Constructive anthropological investigations are both exacting and time-consuming. They generally involve the collecting, sifting and accumulation of substantive data about how people relate to one another, both inside and outside their own community. More than anything else, this involves 'getting to know' how people behave in social interchanges, and having time to gain helpers' co-operation. In Aboriginal Australia, there is an additional consideration. Aboriginal thought does not work like a data bank that can spill out information just when the right stimulus is applied. Aboriginal people utilize their knowledge collectively, and it is generated through shared experiences, rather than expressed in individual pronouncements. The conveying of information, and particularly the sort of knowledge that concerns religious matters, is bound up with many complex rules and obligations. It may take a long period of time before all who have the right to comment on, say, a particular site, agree that it is necessary to impart that information to a stranger. This method of conveying and utilizing information is largely foreign to our own understanding, but it represents a complex and highly structured system that must be understood for what it is, rather than misinterpreted as some form of post facto rationalization.[10]

From the Aboriginal perspective the Ministers' demand, abruptly announced out of the blue, was rude and presumptuous. But it was also inappropriate; they could not talk about the Law, about sites, in this way. But the Ministers had no understanding of this, and their ignorance made them suspicious. Their strategy had failed, their day had been wasted; they had not delivered the goods for their leader in the first assignment he had set them in their new portfolios.

Most of the supporters from the other communities headed home after the Ministers had flown out late on the Friday afternoon. Over the next three days there was a series of Community meetings to try to determine what should be done.

The next move was really up to the Government and Amax, but the people's fears were calmed to some extent by Premier Court's public statement over the weekend, confirmed in a letter hand-delivered by DCW staff from Derby on the Sunday, that Amax would be expected to have talks at Noonkanbah 'to ensure that the drilling programme will not interfere with the known sacred sites which have been established on Noonkanbah'.[11] The problem lay in the Government's continuing refusal to accept the Aboriginal and Museum definition of the sacred.

On Monday 17 March the Community authorised the ALS to release the Bindon report and recommendations of June 1979, with the secret sacred information edited out, in an effort to combat the Government's continuing campaign of confusion on the sites issue. On the Tuesday morning the people prepared to make a statement that contained a request and an offer, in the form of an open letter to the Premier:

> We have had a lot of meetings here at Noonkanbah, a lot of people coming in who don't really love Aborigines, just trying to push the mining through. We have heard too much humbug. People won't believe when we talk about sacred sites.
>
> When the Museum mob came up last year they only looked at one area, around Pea Hill, where the goanna is. This Noonkanbah is a big country with sacred places all over. We are worried for the whole station.
>
> If that drill moves away from the goanna place, we have another Maladji, for fire, nearby. If the drill goes in that area a big fire will come up and kill everything. This happened before one time, a long time ago.
>
> The Government promised no drilling in sacred places. But they don't know all our places.
>
> We want at least four months so the Museum and the Kimberley Land Council can work full-time with the old people to put all the places on the map. This takes a long time because there are many stories, many places, and we have to talk slowly in our own way to old people from all over the Kimberley.
>
> We don't want any mining or any more meetings until this four months is up, or until we've finished putting all the places on the map.
>
> If the Government won't let us do this how are we going to look after all this country properly, and make sure it doesn't get damaged.[12]

Essentially this was a response to the Government having seized on Skinner's answer to Jones at the end of Friday's meeting, and claiming that the issue was now Community opposition to mining anywhere on the station, and to Court's promise of further talks about the drill site. Implicit in the statement was a recognition that once all the sites were mapped – 'slowly in our own way', as Palmer described – they would have to negotiate access for Amax to an acceptable area.

Of course the Community's preferred position was a complete ban on mining on Noonkanbah, but since the Museum investigation of the previous year had focused the Amax dispute on sacred sites there had been a tension between the preferred position and the site protection argument. A concession had already been made for CRA the previous year. Now in its own way, the Community was indicating that it would extend this concession if the Government would truly respect its Law, land and dignity.

But the letter was never sent. At the bough-shade in front of the homestead on Tuesday morning as Ivan McPhee was preparing to read it to yet another TV reporter, Murray Johnstone and Tom Lyon arrived. The presence of the TV crew made Johnstone sure that the Community had been tipped off about his impending arrival. In fact it was purely coincidence. The crew had come to do a general feature on the dispute, and

Ginger Nganawilla signing the letter to the State Government, 18 March 1980. Nipper Tabagee is seated beside him.

Joe Wunmah signing the letter to the State Government.

they were the only media present.

Johnstone and Lyon were made to wait as the letter was read and signed by a number of Elders, then Johnstone stated that the Amax contractors were on the property, and were about to head for the drill site to set up camp and start their work. The people closed in around the two men with the TV cameras still rolling. They were outraged because they felt that Court's assurance of talks before any action was being broken. An extremely nervous Lyon and Johnstone and an angry McPhee argued the point, with myself and some Community members chipping in.[13]

McPhee: So where those trucks now?

Johnstone: They're way back the other side of the airport.

McPhee: Why didn't you let us know yesterday?

Johnstone: We didn't know when we were coming. It depended on when everything was ready.

Hawke: You said you were going to tell the Community when they were coming in.

Johnstone: Yes, I'm telling you right now.

Hawke: What, on an hour's notice?

Johnstone: This is the twentieth century my friend. They are coming in. There will be a bulldozer coming in later today, and there will be three more loads of bulldozers coming in the next couple of days to do this work. What we're concerned about is with any of the work out there we may accidentally disturb a sacred site that you haven't told us about. If there are sites, we can move a hundred yards here, a hundred yards there. That's the only latitude we are given by the Government. If we accidentally disturb a sacred site and you don't tell us about it, we won't be responsible.

McPhee: They are all around. We're thinking to get the Museum to walk around, but it's too late now.

Johnstone: The Museum is not coming.

McPhee: You're pushing the Aboriginal around. We know you don't like Aboriginal.

Johnstone: I like Aborigines. It's the Government

McPhee: You should tell the Government, we don't want to do that to Aboriginal...You should tell the equipment to wait.

Lyon: It is important we get the equipment moving quickly.

McPhee: Well that land is important to us.

Tabagee: You telling lie old bloke.

McPhee: You feel sorry for the Aboriginal or you thinking about that oil?

Lyon: The Aboriginals have no injustice done to them.

McPhee: Aboriginal people, when you go like this you are destroying their home and you never bring it back again.

Lyon: We are not destroying.

McPhee: You are. You are killing Aboriginal mind. That's what you are doing

Murray Johnstone and Tom Lyon arrive at Nookanbah to announce the arrival of the Amax contractors. Top left: Ivan McPhee argues with Lyon and Johnstone. Top right: Joe Wunmah, Alec Buck, McPhee and Lyon.

now. You not listening to Aboriginal.

Lyon: We have been listening to Aboriginals for a long time.

McPhee: No not really. That been started way back two hundred years ago. It's still happening today to the Aboriginal people. Do you know that? It's still happening to Aboriginals. Nothing changed. European never change, or give Aboriginal a fair go. It's still happening right now.

This confrontation was broken up by the arrival of two policemen in plainclothes and an unmarked car, much to Johnstone and Lyon's relief. Unknown to the Community, this was the leading edge of a convoy; 'a mini-exercise of what was to follow', to quote Jeremy O'Driscoll, one of the contractors involved.[14] Lyon and Johnstone, the contractors and the police had gathered at the turn off from the bitumen road, ninety kilometres north, at six in the morning.

Jeremy O'Driscoll was the owner of Clan Contracting, which had the contract to do the earthworks to prepare the drill site and sludge dam. He describes what happened:

I was running late. I flew out to Calwynyardah and had someone organised to pick me up at Calwynyardah airstrip. I flew over and the cops thought it was the enemy, so to speak, and they would have advance notice. All these cars hit the scrub, and of course all the cops disappeared. They thought I'd sprung the whole military operation and we'd been caught before we got in the front gate.

...We were all told to assemble. There were cops everywhere. There were cops in gravel pits. They had a lot of cops that never presented themselves, never showed themselves ...they didn't want to be seen as being inflammatory, as hitting them with a sledgehammer. So six or seven accompanied this convoy, and ostensibly that's all there was. Amax were expecting to be forcibly evicted, and they were going to go through regardless.

...It was very regimented, almost like the army. We had to take our place. There was no 'How you going mate', it was 'Right, you shall proceed'. So off we went down there, and we pulled up at the airstrip. We had to wait there for about an hour while Murray and the others went down.

My next recollection is of seeing this Range Rover coming down the road at about a million miles an hour and doing this erratic three point turn as it crunched gears. [The police and Johnstone and Lyon returning from the homestead.] All crazy, big deal over-reactive stuff. 'You will follow us. You will not break the convoy. You will not stop under any circumstances.'...and all this sort of nonsense. So we got to the site.[15]

With the Community's initiative of the morning killed as it was being announced, and the miners on the site for the first time, there was the smell of defeat in the air, and no immediately apparent options. Following out to the site, the people watched from the nearby river road as Lyon located two pegs which marked the drill site chosen by the company in 1978, and the location cleared by the Supreme Court in 1979.

As they watched, another nine police officers in three cars, including a four-wheel-drive vehicle with a large canvas covered mesh cage used for holding prisoners, pulled in and parked between the people and the miners. The police said nothing, but their very presence was ominous. To the old men in particular, it brought echoes of the old days when the police were used as the enforcers for the station managers.

Negotiations at the drill site. Top: Tom Lyon explains the choice of drill sites. Bottom left: Nipper Tabagee and Lyon. Bottom right: Joe Wunmah and Ginger Nganawilla.

The TV crew was still there, the DCW adviser had raced out from Fitzroy Crossing on hearing of the crisis, and Terry Long, the AAPA Commissioner who answered to both Bill Hassell and Senator Chaney, had come back for the second day in a row with the senior DAA officer from Derby. It was the middle of the day, and extremely hot on this barren plain that had become the focus of national attention.

Over the next two tension-charged hours a series of discussions took place under the blazing sun, with various players moving in and out. First Skinner demanded to know of Lyon why the police were there and asked that they leave:

> We don't want no fight...but we want to know why police come down here...Aboriginal people they got weapon? What sort of weapon they use?...We

Discussions continue. Top: Steve Hawke, Dicky Skinner and Charlie Rangi. Bottom left: Police awaiting the outcome. Bottom right: Dicky Skinner exchanging words with Superintendent Bowers.

talk today because we not so silly to use anything like spear or boomerang or anything like that. I told you this last year.[16]

There was no way Lyon was going to agree to this, and he kept referring back to the time he believed Skinner had threatened him the previous year. The officer in charge of the police force was called in a couple of times. He insisted that the argument between the parties over the drill site was not his business, but nor would he withdraw, he was merely there to make sure there was no breach of the peace. Apart from this the police took no direct part in proceedings, but they certainly added to the atmosphere.

Lyon was pressing his advantage.

Skinner: I think what you're saying you want the police here because you don't trust us. But now we can say that is no fight and so we can say that the police can leave.

Lyon: Okay, if we say that there is no fight you acknowledge that we have a right to drill here. No matter where we drill, we will do it. Is that right?

Skinner: These old people they don't want you to drill here.

Johnstone: We're only going to go through all this again and again and again. I'm getting a little fed up.

Skinner: Police leave and we would like to talk to you, with these old people.

Johnstone: But what is there to talk about?

Skinner: Move your camp and where you're going to drill.

Lyon: So you acknowledge that we are going to drill.

Skinner: We will talk about that a bit later.

Lyon: There is no point in any talk if you don't acknowledge that we will drill whether it be here or whether it be there.

Skinner: Let us point it out where you drill.

Lyon: But if it's not within an area that we can drill that will not be acceptable.

Eventually Johnstone produced a map which he handed to Terry Long before retiring to a vehicle, overcome by the heat. The people sat in a circle around Long, Lyon and Nipper Tabagee, with Skinner facing them across the map that Long spread out on the ground. Lyon said they had a choice. The drill would go down in one of two spots marked on the map; either where they were sitting, or about a kilometre to the north. If they did not make a decision there and then, the company would start work where they were now.

Crunch point had come. Even Skinner could find nothing to say. The DCW officer, sensing the despair, asked Lyon to withdraw and give the people a chance to talk amongst themselves. This he did.

There was no advice that could be offered in the circumstances. The old men had one last try, still believing, it seemed, that if only they could make these white men open their eyes to the truth the situation could be saved. The younger men and I were sent away. One man went to a car and returned with a canvas bag. Some darrugu were brought out, different to the one Tabagee had produced the previous Friday. These were shown to Long, and the old men spoke to him.

I do not know exactly what passed between them, but watching from a distance, it left a bitter taste. It seemed almost demeaning that they felt forced to bare their soul in this fashion in these circumstances. I do not know if they did truly believe that the darrugu could turn back Lyon, the contractors and the police at this point, but I felt a poignant sadness. On the Friday, however fruitless the exercise had been, there was a certain dignity as in Aboriginal terms information was exchanged between senior Lawmen. This was a travesty.

Maps are the story of the land. The Aboriginal people invest their maps with religious significance and layers of meaning, because of what the land means to them. As on Friday, the two maps were side by side; the eternal stone and the ephemeral paper, each symbolising a greater power. Two powers that could not accommodate each other, could not, it seemed, even communicate with each other. On this day the power of the paper was greater.

Ginger Nganawilla - 'Feeling sick for my country'.

Heads were shaken, and old men's shoulders visibly drooped. Lyon returned, blithely unaware as always of what was really happening, and demanded to know which site. The choice seemed irrelevant. I still believe the people named the second site only to make Lyon and his contractors go to the trouble of moving from where they were.

I had to go to Fitzroy Crossing immediately after this to convey the news to the Aboriginal Legal Service and the network of supporters, but it must have been a terrible night at Noonkanbah. One of my most vivid memories of the whole two years is talking to Ginger Nganawilla the next day on my return. When I asked how he was feeling he replied in an unusually low and dispirited voice, 'Little bit all right, but feeling sick for my country'.

To the old men especially it was not only the violation of the land and the Dreaming that had now commenced. In their halting attempts to speak to the politicians and the bureaucrats, and in their testimony with the darrugu, they had staked their Law and their prestige as Lawmen, and been found wanting. They must have pondered on whether the old methods of stoic acceptance of the intrusions of the white man were less painful.

The Premier was the first to reach the press that Tuesday, in time for the evening news bulletins. He had obviously been monitoring progress closely:

> Communications to the area are poor but, from messages received I understand that representatives of Amax, the Mines Department and the Departments of Aboriginal Afairs and Community Welfare went to Noonkanbah early this morning, ahead of the arrival of the first equipment, to talk to the local Aboriginal community about the proposed drill and camp site.
>
> This was in accordance with the undertaking we gave.
>
> Subsequently, I was advised that the first of the equipment had moved on to the agreed location and commenced preparation of the site.
>
> Later messages advised that, as a result of the meeting at Noonkanbah, Amax had been given approval to proceed.
>
> To meet a community request, Amax has agreed to use No. 2 drilling site instead of their preferred site which had previously been referred to as No. 1 site.
>
> It was also agreed that the camp site would be near the drill site. This was preferred by the community.
>
> The community has agreed that contractors can upgrade the roads.
>
> There has been an assurance from the community that there will be no further difficulties.
>
> Naturally, I will have to wait until we get more detailed information, which no doubt will be available when someone returns to Derby, where there are better communications. But it would appear that things have proceeded largely as we predicted.[17]

Court didn't revise his story on receipt of more detailed information. He never retracted this myth of the Number Two site being the free choice of the Community.

That evening Phil Vincent of the ALS was on the ABC's Nationwide television program rejecting the Court version, detailing the police presence that Court had declined to mention, and the nature of the choice given to the Community.

Noonkanbah had already been the major media story in Western Australia for two weeks, but now, as the bulldozers began their work of turning the earth of Noonkanbah into a sludge dam for the drilling mud, the coverage reached saturation point, and developments became hard to keep up with.

The papers the next morning carried maps and excerpts from the Bindon report and my rebuttal of the Government version of events at Noonkanbah. And it emerged that in fact the total police force on Noonkanbah on the Tuesday had been thirty-four officers in ten vehicles.

The public and the media were starting to question the Government's actions and its version of events in the Kimberley. By Thursday the *West Australian* was moved to editorialise:

> Now that we have a WA Museum assessment of what is at stake at Noonkanbah, plans to drill there should be called off, for the time being at least. There is a heavy obligation on the State Government and Amax to give reasons why the museum's findings were set aside.
>
> ...Even more disturbing is the Government's apparent change of face in the past two days. Till Friday, the Government was pursuing consultation and compromise to the point of having three ministers on site. Suddenly, with policemen present, Friday's deadlock became Tuesday's agreement and the public is left to wonder why the Aborigines yielded so much ground so quickly.
>
> Without a full explanation the world at large is entitled to believe that Western Australia has trampled on Aborigines.[18]

In Perth Ron Davies, the Labor Leader of the Opposition, was accusing Premier Court of disgraceful behaviour and calling for his resignation. In Canberra Labor members were calling in Federal Parliament for Commonwealth intervention. Senator Jim Keeffe, speaking on behalf of a group of six Senators, demanded:

> Senator Chaney must now take full control on behalf of the Commonwealth Government of the dispute at Noonkanbah Station, following Sir Charles Court's rejection of Aboriginal rights there. The pastoral lease at Noonkanbah was acquired with Commonwealth funds...The land must now be acquired by the Commonwealth.[19]

Chaney had no intention of heeding this advice, but he was feeling the pressure. On the morning of Wednesday 19 March he telexed Court:

> ...As you would know, parliamentary and press interest is intense...It appears that there was very early entry of equipment onto the property and it is said that the Amax camp has been established on land claimed to be sacred. I understand also the police did go to the property although there was no suggestion of any breach of the peace. I am concerned that the spirit if not the letter of your statements re consultation with the community will be regarded as breached if work commences before there has been a reasonable opportunity for community consultation.[20]

The rest of the telex related to the relationship of the drill site to sacred sites and the Museum report, concluding:

> This appears to me to be the critical point and I would appreciate confirmation that sites identified by the Museum have been and will be respected, in time for questions and debate today.[21]

Court was not impressed; his reply the same day, with a copy to the Prime Minister, was terse with a none too subtle warning:

> I suggest with respect you do not overreact to the information which will be fed to you, or queries raised with you. My guess is that much of it will be completely biased against the State Government and will not reflect the genuine views of the Aborigines...
>
> I have said that all genuine identified sacred sites will be respected. This is the position. If, however, you are referring to some of the so-called areas 'of influence' that are being peddled then it is another matter because this is part of the current attempt to blanket the whole of Kimberley and other places in due course. I think our information on this objective – with Noonkanbah as a starting point – is reliable...
>
> I sincerely hope the Commonwealth will not seek to intervene because I would have to react very strongly.[22]

The most significant new development was the decision of the union movement to upgrade its support to a practical level. A meeting on the Wednesday of the relevant unions recommended the imposition of bans on all work for the Noonkanbah drilling. The key unions in this regard were the Transport Workers Union whose members would have to transport the rig from Broome where it was now waiting in a trucking company yard, and the Australian Workers Union, which covered the drilling crew. And on the same day the President of the Australian Council of Trade Unions, Bob Hawke, revealed that he had contacted Max Reynolds of Amax asking the company to pull back.

This added an extra dimension to the dispute. To the Community, it meant that they had some real muscle on their side; they did not have to carry the struggle on their own. Maybe there was real hope that Amax could be frustrated.

On the Friday there was a well-attended rally in the grounds of St George's Cathedral in the centre of Perth, and a protest petition began circulating in the Perth Aboriginal Community.

Premier Court issued a five page press release detailing and defending the Government's position, and attacking the 'area of influence' concept, the Community's request for four months to map sites, and the involvement of advisers and the union movement. This enabled him to recover some ground with the editorial writers of the *West Australian*:

> The Premier's long statement to the news media on Thursday threw some fresh light on the controversy over drilling at Noonkanbah Station. It does not amount to a total defence of what is happening there, nor will it sweep away all public doubt...
>
> Like so many other complex issues with which a concerned public has to grapple in this age of social conscience, Noonkanbah called for the frankest possible presentation of the facts. Yet the Government, despite its battery of public relations officers, has not kept the public properly informed. On the contrary, it has again shown its penchant for concealment and telling half the truth.[23]

12

WE HUNTED THEM OUT

If we are to allow Amax to return to Noonkanbah they must show us Law, not paper law. Paper is nothing. Paper can be washed away. Our Law, Aboriginal Law will last forever. If Amax has this Law then they must show us.

Ginger Nganawilla, translation from the Walmatjari, quoted in *Minyarti Wangki Kulkarriyajangka*, the Kulkarriya Community School newsletter, April 1980.

In directing Amax to move operations to the Number Two drill site the Community had unwittingly gained a strategic advantage. In the court proceedings of 1979 Justice Brinsden had accepted that the land identified by the Museum report warranted protection under the Aboriginal Heritage Act, whilst also accepting the legality of the Government's direction of the Museum Trustees to approve the use of a particular part of that land for drilling. Amax had now moved away from the specific site that had been so approved, and its operations were now in breach of the Act.

As soon as this became apparent the ALS issued a writ to restrain Amax on the grounds that the land they were working on had not been approved, and was still a site within the meaning of the Heritage Act. On 21 March, just three days after work had commenced, Justice Wallace issued an injunction valid for ten days restraining any work within five kilometres of Pea Hill. The Amax contractors were forced to withdraw, though only to a camp at the northern end of the station. From there they continued work on upgrading the access road.

From Tuesday's low point, the morale of the Community began to lift again, as they watched this withdrawal, and received the news of the union bans and the controversy raging in Perth and the eastern states. But already, they saw the desecration of the land taking its toll. Bob Mululby, the man who was the primary custodian of the Pea Hill complex, became ill. To outsiders this could well be a coincidence, or the effects of stress, but to the Community it was evidence that the spirits of the land had been disturbed, and the warnings they had given were starting to come true.

They decided to keep fighting, and to send Ivan McPhee and Nipper Tabagee to Perth to try to rally further support for their cause. In two statements that week they made their feelings and their position clear:

> We are very cross and upset about the police coming in to Noonkanbah on Tuesday. From that first day in 1829 when the white people came to this country and put out their flag the police and the soldiers were against the Aborigines. They said this is their land. Aborigines were sitting here, but they didn't really worry about it. That's the police way from the first day, they were using that white weapon to shoot Aboriginal people.
>
> Right from Captain Cook's time police and other Gudia were shooting Aboriginal people. From King Edward's time they've been shooting Aboriginal people here in the Kimberley.
>
> It was the same at that meeting on Tuesday. We had no weapons, but the police came in with that mining company against this little group of people. We were talking with simple words for our country. Amax brought

those police in to frighten us.

We didn't do anything. Those policemen came in and didn't say any word, they were just waiting. It was exactly the same like the old days with all the police lined up. It was just like having a gun pointed at us and saying make up your mind straight away.

Amax are the ones causing trouble all the time. Aborigines have got more sense than the white men. We know what we are doing, and we don't think the whitefeller is going to take all this country from us and leave us behind...

If Aborigines give up their sites and their special places there will be no more Law, no more storytelling, no more initiation ceremonies. It will be like it's all gone out into space.[1]

...[Amax] were only on the station three days before we got an injunction to force them off. But already they have messed up the roads, and made a big mess in the Maladji place for the goanna. They are making the old people upset. One old man who has to look after that place is already sick, the spirits from that place are getting him. The Government and the miners didn't listen to our word. We told them this would happen, but they didn't care.

We are doing our best up there on Noonkanbah. We ask for help from all our friends down here, the Trade Unions, the Churches, and all other people who agree with what we are doing. For now the main thing is to stop Amax drilling. We are asking for the Trade Unions to keep the bans on Amax and the companies working with them...We are calling for the Canberra Government to use their power to step in to stop the State Government forcing drilling on our sacred land. We ask all people, specially the Churches and the unions, to put pressure on Amax at their headquarters in America, to tell them what their company is doing to us here.

That was no proper agreement on Tuesday. We are still going to fight for our country. Not with guns or spears, only with our own voice and our own bodies.

So we are very pleased that all these people are coming out to help us, all the Trade Union mob trying to stop Amax, and all the other people. That never happened in the first place. If we all stand together like this we can be friends and have respect for each other.[2]

In Perth McPhee and Tabagee took this message to a meeting of the Trades and Labor Council, a gathering of the heads of the Uniting, Anglican and Catholic Churches, and a public meeting in the Perth Town Hall attended by over four hundred people.

Following addresses from Peter Dowding and Ivan McPhee, a full meeting of one hundred and twenty delegates of the TLC formally supported an earlier decision of a meeting of key unions, resolving that:

In these circumstances, we believe that we should respond to the request for support from the Noonkanbah community by:

Requesting the ACTU to ask the Federal Government to use its constitutional power to take the matter out of the hands of the Court Government and protect the sacred areas as defined in the Museum Study as a matter of urgency.

Requesting the ACTU to object direct to AMAX's Head Office in Australia and through the International Confederation of Free Trade Unions to its International Head Office.

Imposing a TLC sponsored ban on the movement of equipment needed for the project and the activities of AMAX in Western Australia, to be lifted when advised by the Noonkanbah community that discussions have concluded to their satisfaction.[3]

Any bans, to be effective, would have had to be ratified and supported by the workers concerned, but the scene was set for the possibility of a major industrial confrontation, particularly given Amax's involvement in the Mount Newman iron ore mine in the Pilbara. The following day the Australian Workers Union was suggesting that all nine oil rigs operating in the State could be closed down if drilling started at Noonkanbah.

The three Church leaders, following their meeting with the Community representatives, in a joint public statement expressed their 'deep concern about the situation that has developed...This concern is based first of all upon what appears to be an insensitive disregard of Aboriginal spirituality in favour of the materialistic values of western society.'

Adopting the role of conciliators, they also stated their 'hope that the State Government will give full support to the Minister for Aboriginal Affairs, Senator Chaney, who has stressed that there is a dividing line between the sacred site deserving of protection and the generality of Aboriginal land with its legends and stories and religious significance'.[4]

Chaney was pursuing a line of trying to find shades of meaning that did not exist for the Community or the State Government. He had two long meetings that week with Museum staff and Trustees and anthropologists, discussing 'gradations' in the definition of sites, and distinctions between sites and protected areas. He was urging that the Museum 'should be a possible source of advice leading to solutions'.[5]

A rational discussion of a redefinition of the concept of sacred sites hardly seemed likely in the atmosphere that prevailed. Nor was it realistic to think that the Museum could take any sort of leading role given the hostility it faced from the State Government. Less than a week before, in separate memos to the Premier commenting on Chaney's telex of 19 March, Peter Jones had said, 'It would be a completely fruitless exercise to approach the Museum on any further matter related to Noonkanbah'; and Bill Hassell had commented, after an attack on the Museum, 'In dealing with Chaney on these issues, I think you should seek to keep him out of the Noonkanbah conflict which cannot be resolved to his satisfaction now and seek to work on future arrangements which will be acceptable to us'.[6]

In fact, as Chaney was meeting with Museum personnel, the Trustees were being pressured just as they had been the previous year. The day Amax had entered the station Max Reynolds had provided Jones with a hasty hand-written letter seeking approval from the Mines Department and the Museum Trustees for the use of two hectares of ground at the new site.

On the 21st, the day the injunction was granted, letters from Jones and Bill Grayden respectively gave notice of the requirement to use the land, and sought the consent of the Trustees by midday of Monday 24 March. On the 24th, after meeting with Chaney, the Trustees agonised once again. After asking for an extension of time, they eventually had a letter delivered to Grayden in a Cabinet meeting at five o'clock, stating that they could not give their consent to the new site without further evaluation. By six o'clock they had received a typed reply from Grayden directing them to provide their written consent by ten o'clock the following morning. The consent was duly delivered.

On 27 March McPhee and Tabagee were in the Supreme Court to witness the lifting of the injunction. The initiative now returned to the company and the Government. The Federal Liberal Member for the seat of Kalgoorlie, Mick Cotter, spoke in Parliament that day supporting the Chaney line, and going one step further. He called on the State Government to withdraw from the dispute, saying that he was sure that the matter could be settled given time, and direct talks between the company and the Community in a calmer atmosphere. His comments were endorsed by Chaney's ministerial predecessor, Ian Viner.

But Premier Court made it perfectly clear that he would set his own course. Immediately after the lifting of the injunction was announced he issued a press release:

> So far as the State Government is concerned, petroleum exploration will now commence on the Noonkanbah pastoral lease without further delay. There is no legal barrier, and both the Government and Amax have fulfilled their responsibility to consult with the Noonkanbah Aboriginal Community at length concerning the protection of sacred sites...Further delay would only provide more opportunity to those interlopers whose real objectives have nothing to do with preserving sacred sites to cause more disharmony, both within the Noonkanbah Community and between Aboriginal and white people.[7]

Court's statement also criticised the Church leaders for their statement of support for the Community, and Cotter and Viner for their interference. Mines Department files reveal that on the same day Court had been putting the pressure on Amax to take a stronger stance. Max Reynolds telexed Lloyd Parks of Amax in Houston to say: 'Sir Charles Court has suggested that the time may be appropriate for an Amax statement on the facts of the Noonkanbah situation to be made as an advertisement in the Australian press. The following draft is for your consideration.'[8] (The draft advertisement was not in the Mines Department file, and it is not clear whether the draft was prepared by Amax or Government staff. It was never published.)

At the drill site, 28 March 1980.

Top left: Edward Yamera, Joe Wunmah and David Mowaljarli. Right: Watching Brian McGaffin's drill. Bottom left: Dicky Skinner.

That evening in Derby Tom Lyon went to see Brian McGaffin, the contracted water driller. He asked McGaffin to begin work urgently, assuring him that he would have no problems. By mid-morning of the 28th McGaffin and his offsider were on site and setting the drill up.

About thirty men from the Community watched the drillers from some distance away as they worked. The people were waiting for Lyon to turn up. Some of them knew McGaffin from his days as a shire works foreman, and they accepted that their argument was not really with him. Nevertheless, when no one else turned up they eventually approached him and made it clear that he should leave, and after some discussion he agreed to do so, packing up and withdrawing to Jeremy O'Driscoll's camp back up the access road.

I witnessed this discussion, as did Michael Gallagher, Les Mack – the Principal of the Community school – and a reporter from the Melbourne *Age*. We stood at the back of the group of Noonkanbah people, and to all of us it had seemed to be a calm, almost friendly discussion despite the difference of opinion. In fact McGaffin's offsider was so relaxed he lay in the shade of the drilling rig reading a book, not paying much attention to proceedings. For a while Les Mack sat next to him in the shade, and there was no animosity.

According to McGaffin though, at one point after he had said that he was obliged by his contract to continue with the work, one of the Noonkanbah men said to him,

M. Thirkall: We heard it on the wireless news.

Lyon: Do you want me to talk? So be quiet and let me talk.

M. Thirkall: Go on, talk.

Lyon: What came from Amax was that a group of Aboriginals approached the drilling contractor and they were apprehensive of their safety and thought it better to retreat from the location.

Skinner: Can you put that in some sort of word that people can understand you?

Lyon: They were frightened of what might happen to them if they stayed.

And a bit later:

Lyon: We are going to do that [drill]. It appears that you are not going to allow this or you are going to try to stop us.

Skinner: And what will happen?

Lyon: That's for you to decide.

Skinner: All right. What we say is that we don't want any drilling. We said this before.

Lyon: But what is going to happen?

Skinner: Well, you have got to find out a bit later. I won't tell you.

Lyon: So this is another threat you are issuing?

Skinner: Well, this I am just putting to you. Why do you never listen?

Lyon: But this is what you are saying. You're threatening aren't you?

Skinner: What do you mean threatening? Same as you people.

M. Thirkall: You are threatening us.

Lyon: We are not going to do anything to you individually.

Skinner: If you're not going to do anything why have you got that rig?

Lyon: To carry out our lawful work.

Skinner: That's the same thing.

Lyon: You are going to stop us from doing our work.

M. Thirkall: But this has got nothing to do with the police.

Lyon: You are stopping us from doing our work.

M. Thirkall: That's right. You wouldn't let us go barging into your property and drilling like this.

Lyon: You're breaking the law.

M. Thirkall: You are.

Wadgie Thirkall: You are breaking my Law. This is my Law here.

M. Thirkall: You're wrecking this country you know. We are poor people. What would you think if we went to your home and cut down your trees? You white people just don't listen to us. You mob bring trouble here.

Skinner: They reckon *we* are causing trouble.

Alec Buck: White man causing a *lot* of trouble.

George Bell: I reckon black man got better brains, white man got no brains.

Buck: He got no fucking brains you know.

M. Thirkall: White man can't listen. He can't understand English.

Buck: If I go to your place and if I get in your house and burn it, what will you do?

Lyon: But you wouldn't because that would be –

Buck: Or dig the ground alongside your house, what would you do?

Lyon: Well if you had a Miner's Right I could not stop you.

Skinner: What Miner's Right?

Lyon: Any Miner's Right.

Skinner: That's your law that you brought from overseas.

Buck: That's your law. That's not my Law, that's your law.

W. Thirkall: Can I ask you – if you can't understand my Law you are welcome to pass my certificate from this Law.

Lyon: Do I understand you right when you say you are inviting me to learn your Law?

W. Thirkall: Yes, to pass my certificate.

Amax returns, 29 March 1980. Tom Lyon talks with members of the Community.

Confrontation and discussion at the drill site. Top: Wadgie and Michael Thirkall facing Tom Lyon. Centre: Dicky Skinner emphasising a point. Right: Michael Thirkall speaking. Bottom left: Superintendent Bowers speaks to the members of the Community.

David Mowaljarli.

Lyon: And how long would that take? That doesn't have a bearing on it at the present moment does it? That has nothing to do with the situation we are in now.

Skinner: I think that's looking at it from two laws. You said that Aboriginal people break the law and stopping you from drilling. We are breaking white man's law. I think you people are breaking Aborigines' Law.

A police officer came in and out of the discussion. Lyon walked off at one point and then returned.

David Mowaljarli attempted in his own way to explain the Aboriginal reality to Lyon:

Every Aboriginal man, woman and kid has a name from a tree or rocks or grass. That's their name, their own name. The white man name came later. But the real Aboriginal name is from this land here, this land. These Aborigines can tell which is the oldest tree that belongs to Australia, and they know it. They know what happened at every sacred place. We all know. We didn't sow or reap, we didn't plant any food because our Great Spirit put all the food here for us and we have to look after it. And that means until death, we have to die that way. That's the Aborigine. This is an increase place where we go to take prayer and get our food. We go to the right places. We know, and that's why we are deeply concerned.

Dicky Skinner addresses Tom Lyon.

When anything is ripped, it's cutting Aborigines, cutting his stomach, everything. In the same way, boring something bores a hole through a human being. This hurts. Because we have the name of every animal; it's our relation, and when we kill it we have to eat it and finish it all up – we have to eat our own flesh, every liver, kidney, everything. We eat our own flesh and we drink our own blood, and that's the way we live, every Aborigine. It's a deep concern. We are not concerned about how beautiful vehicle we have, whatever plane we have. We aren't concerned about that. We are not interested in money. We are concerned about the life of human beings.

Shortly after listening to this speech Lyon responded by giving the order to start work. The machines took up where they had left off a week earlier, ignoring the people still there, watching. And this time the police stayed with them. The *West Australian* carried a report of Skinner's parting words to Lyon:

'We want to say to your wife and children that you did not listen to us,' Mr Skinner said.

Mr Lyon: 'What has it to do with my wife and children? Are you trying more threats?'

Mr Skinner: 'Looks like it. (You) Have not listened and you make it very hard. I don't want to fight you but you are not listening. We are trying to save you. You should be careful. Whether you will see another sunrise or sunset – the law will decide.

...Mr Skinner later explained that Mr Lyon was in no physical danger from the Aborigines. 'The people on top of the land won't hurt him. The law under the land will hurt him.'[13]

In Perth the controversy had become one of the biggest media stories for years. The *West Australian* was carrying up to five or six stories a day about various aspects of the dispute.

On 28 March, Premier Court and Police Commissioner Owen Leitch made controversial speeches to a passing out parade of graduating police trainees. Court told the new policemen that the greatest enemy they would face would be political and social activists, whom he described as evil. Leitch spoke of entering a dangerous era of strikes, protests and demonstrations. Their remarks generated an outcry, and were seen by many to be particularly threatening in the context of the ongoing Noonkanbah dispute.

Just the week before, Leitch had made an astonishing entry into the political arena when he claimed that it was likely a re-election for the seat of Kimberley would be needed. This had followed the arrest and charging of me and three other people with offences under the amended Electoral Act. I had been raised from my bed in Fitzroy Crossing just before midnight by fraud squad detectives from Perth, and charged with forty-four counts, relating to the people who had made postal votes from Hooker's Creek. To all except the Government it seemed a clear case of political revenge and intimidation. (All charges were subsequently dropped, some months later, after the hearing of the first charge in the East Kimberley was thrown out of court.)

Also on the 28th, Jimmy Bieunderry, in Canberra for a meeting of the National Aboriginal Conference, called at a press conference for the Federal Government to intervene, and spoke of the possibility of the issue going to the High Court. And reports were leaked from a meeting of the staff of the Museum; the staff were demanding that the Trustees and the Director clearly distance the Museum from the Government, and defend their integrity against attacks from Bill Grayden, their Minister. A feature article in that afternoon's *Daily*

News quoted an unnamed 'Senior Liberal' as saying, ' The fight for the north has begun. If we don't hold on the blacks could take over right through the Territory and Queensland.'[14]

The next day thirty of the Swan Valley fringedwellers led by Bob Bropho briefly occupied Perth's main cemetery at Karrakatta in support of the Noonkanbah people, saying that Aboriginal sites and burial grounds deserved the same respect as that shown by Aborigines and whites to cemeteries.

After visiting the Karrakatta camp Ivan McPhee and Nipper Tabagee went to a meeting of the Aboriginal Lands Trust. This meeting of the Government's official advisory body prepared a letter to the State Governor, Sir Wallace Kyle, asking him to proclaim the pastoral lease as an Aboriginal Reserve, and give exclusive use to Aboriginal people, effectively banning miners. When members took the letter to Government House they were told that the Governor was in the shower, and unable to receive them.

On Sunday 30 March Premier Court met with Senator Chaney and NAC members Cedric Jacobs and Bieunderry. No progress was made in the meeting, but Court accepted an invitation from Bieunderry to meet with the Noonkanbah Communiuty at an unspecified date in the future.

On 1 April the Federal Opposition spokesman on Aboriginal Affairs, Stewart West, and the Member for Fremantle, John Dawkins, headed for Noonkanbah. That evening Professor Ronald Berndt issued a statement that was the lead story in the *West Australian* on the morning of 2 April. He demanded a halt to drilling on the station, and criticised the Government's repeated direction of the Museum Trustees. He also called for the appointment of a specialist group to assist Amax in negotiating with the Community, and for a Royal Commission to 'look into all matters relating to Aboriginal land rights'.[15] The Western Australian Anthropological Society supported his call and attacked Grayden and the Government.

On 2 April a city demonstration of over five hundred people heard attacks on the actions of the Government by a number of speakers, including Cedric Jacobs who was known as by far the most moderate of Aboriginal leaders. He went so far as to say he was considering resigning from his membership of the Liberal Party over the issue.

No sooner had McPhee and Tabagee returned from Perth at the beginning of April than Dicky Skinner and David Mowaljarli were on their way there; flown down by a television station for a debate with Grayden. There were any amount of background and colour stories in the press and on the airwaves, numerous letters to the editor, and plenty of speculation as to the motives and likely moves of the various parties.

Despite the raging controversy, the Government was confident that there was little more the Community could do but protest; the drilling program would proceed as long as the union bans could be circumvented.

On the morning of Monday 31 March, Mines Department officers met with Amax to plan the logistics of moving the drill from its yard in Broome. It was thought that the move, which would require fifty-two semi-trailer loads for the rig alone, plus casing, supplies and miscellaneous equipment, would begin on the coming weekend.

But there was one big cloud on the Government's horizon. During the meeting 'Mr Reynolds indicated that the President of Amax Petroleum Division, Mr Lloyd Parks, had indicated in a phone call early today that if the affair was not settled within a day or two at most, he would abandon the attempt to drill the well'.[16]

Having gone this far the Government could not afford such a possibility. The well had to be sunk. An options paper was immediately prepared by the Mines Department. Four options were presented. The first two concentrated on removing the financial burden on the company: the Government could pay the standby costs of up to fifteen thousand dollars per day being incurred by Amax; or it could enter an agreement to pay a proportion of the overall drilling costs and effectively become a partner in the operation. Alternatively, either Amax could be prevailed upon to surrender all or part of its permit, or the Government could cancel the permit, and 'the State could then drill the well'. In this case the State Energy Commission, supported by Mines Department personnel, would be the driller.[17]

As the paper noted, 'If the Energy Commission were involved there is the risk of industrial action and consequent blackouts. Further it would have to recruit or hire expertise causing additional expensive delays...Accordingly if it becomes necessary to overcome reluctance by the Amax group to continue with the Noonkanbah drilling' the financial compensation option was preferred.[18]

And the same morning this options paper was drafted, under the headline 'Chief of Amax Fed Up', Lloyd Parks was quoted in the *West Australian* as having told its reporter that the State Government was telling the company what to do.

> Any time your Premier Sir Charles Court, tells us to stop we will get out and take our rig to where we can make money instead of losing it. I run an oil business and we have never had these problems before – not with Indians. We treat people fairly and expect to be treated fairly by them. The press and socialist workers in government jobs and other areas have caused these problems, not us. We are sick of being given hell by the press and communists over there.[19]

It was not the Aboriginal Lands Trust or Professor Berndt, nor Amax, or the Labor Party or the demonstrators that threw the next spanner in the Government's works. As they had said at the meeting on the morning of the 29th, the old Lawmen of Noonkanbah had taken matters into their own hands.

They had called in their colleagues from many of the West Kimberley communities and made their own plans. As the presses ran to print the story of Parks' frustration, and the demonstrators met in Perth, the people were weaving their spell around the drill site in the process of winning a dramatic victory.

At the time I knew very little about just what the old men were doing. I was frantically busy with the press, politicians and others, driving in and out of Fitzroy Crossing almost every day or night. My main relationship was with Dicky Skinner and Ivan McPhee, who were mouthpieces for the old men, and I in turn passed on what they told me. But when the Elders took over they were operating at a different level. I am not much the wiser today.

It began on Sunday 30 March, the day after the Amax contractors had restarted their work. I remember Skinner telling me a little about one of the Lawmen who came in; he was a lightning man, he had special stones that could talk to the lightning. There was a rainmaker there from Looma too.

Notes of a report I phoned in to the Kimberley Land Council from Fitzroy Crossing that day say: 'They hope the magic will start working this afternoon. The Elders in good spirits – have confidence in their Law.' That evening when I returned a gusty, angry, squalling wind blew up. Everyone huddled in the shearing shed for shelter as it blew in from the east, the direction of the Amax camp. There was an air of tension and expectation disproportionate to the response one would expect for a late seasonal storm. The rain began, but petered out before developing into a real downpour.

It appeared that the first attempt had been only partially successful. Those of us who knew a little said nothing to the media and other outsiders who knew nothing, as we had not been officially told anything, let alone given authority to speak of it.

Yet we wondered what might be still to come if this had developed in less than a day. We were left wondering, as the Monday and Tuesday morning were quiet. McPhee and Tabagee returned, and gave a heartening report of the reception they had received in Perth, though McPhee complained of having a 'big [sore] throat' from too much talking.

On the Tuesday afternoon, 1 April, the Labor Party delegation, led by Stewart West and John Dawkins, arrived, and this signalled the next move. I could not say whether the Elders had been waiting for them to arrive or whether it was mere coincidence.

In the late afternoon, after a short Community meeting, the politicians were taken out to the drill site. No one from the Community had been on the site since the Saturday, and by now the siteworks were almost complete. The sludge dam looked huge; a great square scar in the ground, with built-up walls. The people moved round inspecting the works.

There was some discussion with Tom Lyon and the police. Lyon would not answer the questions from Stewart West and John Dawkins. But there was none of the hard edge or anger of the Saturday.

We returned to the Community. I was expecting an evening of talks with the politicians, but I was summoned, and told to bring my tape recorder. The Lawmen's plan was swinging into action. The politicians were left to camp in the shearing shed.

It seemed that every man in the Community, and many from other places, were moving to the drill site, with cars going backwards and forwards. When we were all there the vehicles were parked across the access road the company had made. It would have been easy enough to skirt around them through the spinifex. But the message was clear; the drillers, and the police guarding them, were being closed in.

Firewood had been brought in the vehicles. A camp was set up on the edge of the cleared area, less than a hundred metres from the campfires of the contractors and the police.

At first I just watched the scene unfold. It was about nine o'clock as two singers began their night's work. The circles of dancers formed around them. And then a small group of old men sat to one side, with the dancers between them and Amax, and they began their own songs.

I was asked to record the men singing for the large group of dancers. But I was also told that I was not allowed under any circumstances to let the songs of the old Lawmen, who were sitting outside the circle of dancers, be recorded. So I was placed next to the two singers in the middle of the dancers, where the Lawmen's songs were drowned out.

In the dances of Noonkanbah each song is fairly short, not more than a minute

Discussions at the drill site – the evening of 1 April 1980.

or two. The singers beat time with clapping boomerangs, as the dancers move in a circle around them. At the end of each song the dancers lean inwards towards the singers, stamp, and shout a short sharp 'Yoo', and as this dies the song fades to a rapid rattling of the singers' boomerangs.

Most of the night there were three circles around the singers; the inner one moving in one direction, the middle ring going the other way, and the outer circle in the same direction as the first. At times there were a hundred men dancing to the strong voices with more vigour than I had ever seen, and every couple of minutes stamping and chanting in unison, followed by the eerie rattle of the boomerangs.

It was an awesome experience to sit in the centre of this circle of human energy.

The old men were singing the secret songs of the Law and the land. They sang to lend power to the voices and the feet of the larger circle, and probably for other purposes as well.

The dancing was for the benefit of the Amax camp. They had no choice but to listen, and most of them could not help but watch. Not a word was said to them, hardly a look cast in their direction. But the dancing continued with hardly a pause for more than six hours, until after three o'clock, into the witching hour before dawn. It was a masterly piece of psychological warfare.

Jeremy O'Driscoll recalls:

> The afternoon of this fateful, dancing-all-night evening you could tell the waters were getting a bit troubled. I'd never seen so many Toyotas coming and going, people were walking around. There was clearly a strengthening of numbers, for whatever reasons. I got a bit nervous just on dusk about my plane. I went up and flew it down [from the airstrip, just a kilometre and a half away] and landed it in the dark on the grassy plain, and put it on the location.
>
> I just got an uneasy feeling. Put it this way, I thought that if there was a bulldozer there, it might have got a tank full of sugar or something. I had that feeling. So I flew this thing down, and nearly ran through a policeman's tent in the dark.
>
> So I was there on site for that night. People just came and came and came. I can still see it. It was a frightening night, you asked me if it was scary, and yes it was. I would have said there was a hundred and fifty people there, and they were silhouetted everywhere. There was a time when they were on the cab of the dozer, and I wasn't game to tell them to get off.
>
> They had four or five cops there in this tent. And they didn't know quite what to do. They didn't know what they were going to do, if they were going to get overrun. I don't think they had any reinforcements.
>
> It went on to the wee small hours. Whatever bravado you may have in your body at nine o'clock at night, it does get to you at three o'clock in the morning.
>
> Clearly there must have been enough discipline, because they didn't do anything provocative. I'm sure there would have had to have been a couple of young blokes that would have loved to have done something provocative, because it was exciting. So they must have been quite well disciplined, upon reflection.
>
> It was a bit spooky. In my young days my pride and joy was my plane. I can remember getting in the plane, and having the throttle back, and the thing right to go, so all it needed was the key. It would have started up running, with the wheels rolling. But it never came to that. Morning came.
>
> ...That's where they had the psychological advantage on us. I all of a

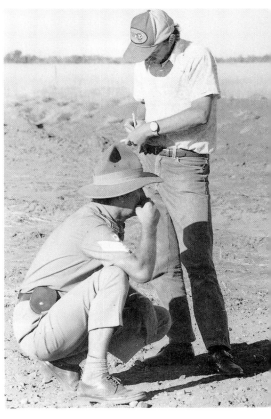

The morning of 2 April. Top left: Ivan McPhee talks with the police sergeant. Centre left: Jimmy James in discussion. Top right: Tom Lyon and the police sergeant. Bottom: Ivan McPhee and Tom Lyon.

Brian McGaffin and Ivan McPhee.

sudden went from being this great nationalistic Aussie, saying this was bad, Aussies being precluded from going about their business, to in the morning the standpoint of saying, this is Amax's problem, not mine.[20]

The seeds of doubt and confusion had been well and truly sown. But when the dawn came on 2 April, still nothing happened. Billies were boiled, tall bundles of spear grass were thrown on the fires for warmth against the early morning chill. As I went back to collect the politicians, O'Driscoll and company put on a brave face and began their work, as if the noise of their machines could dispel the aura of the singing.

The police made the first move. A sergeant came over and pointed out that the Community vehicles were still blocking the access road, and that if they were not moved if the company so requested, arrests would have to follow. But he spoke gently, very careful not to provoke the situation at all. I'm sure he would have preferred to be anywhere but Noonkanbah. Ivan McPhee made it clear that the vehicles were not going to be moved, they had every intention of stopping Amax from working.

At the mention of arrests, there were suggestions from a couple of young blokes that any such action might be countered by the arrest of Tom Lyon under Tribal Law. The sergeant advised against such a move, but again in the most reasonable tones.

The machines stopped, and Tom Lyon approached the people, looking somewhat the worse for wear, and much less sure of himself than usual. McPhee told him that it was time to go. He should pack up the camp, and move off. Lyon departed for further talks with his contractors and the police.

It was still only eight o'clock. But the site had a midday stillness about it, and the air was heavy with expectation. One side was going to suffer a humiliating retreat.

The Lawmen gathered again, excluding all the younger people and the hovering media. Intermittently, singing would come from where they sat, as they talked over yet again the intricacies of the Law of this land. After almost an hour of this they called the politicians in to their meeting, and once again brought out the darrugu:

> The spokesman for the old men attempted to explain Aboriginal individual relationships to this land and the responsibility invested in each tribal elder for various sections in it. They advised us that great personal misfortune would befall the Elders, the local Aborigines, Amax representatives, WA Police, Sir Charles Court and all concerned with the violation of the site.[21]

With the leaders having explained their position, it was time to break the stalemate. McPhee was the spokesman. At the head of the assembled people, with the media hovering, he strode over to the Amax camp. When Lyon emerged McPhee announced, 'We don't want any more talking. We want you to leave now.'[22] Lyon was still reluctant. This time he was the one stalling; the balance of power had been subtly reversed. It was a stunning inversion of the day two weeks earlier when he had demanded a reply from the people on a choice of drill site. There were suggestions from the mob that his tent should be pulled down, as theirs had been on the Saturday.

Leaving Lyon, McPhee approached Jeremy O'Driscoll, and then Brian McGaffin. They were given the same message. O'Driscoll was ready to go, he said he would leave that afternoon. McGaffin said it would take time to pull the rig out. McPhee said, 'We will give you to two o'clock. You fellers have to listen to us.' When McGaffin asked for time to talk to the others, he was warned that he had better go, or 'we will pull everything down. You tell him [Lyon] that you want to leave now. You tell him it is your gear.'[23] McGaffin was convinced.

Lyon had no choice. His contractors had deserted him. The police wanted only to defuse the situation as quietly as possible. He was beaten. Just before eleven he met McPhee and the mob in the middle of the cleared ground. 'Because of the pressure which has been put on us and the possibility that damage will occur to the equipment, we have decided to pull out temporarily.'[24]

Ivan McPhee, in total control of the situation, was not satisfied. He pointed to his watch, and said that everyone was to be gone from the site by two o'clock. Everyone except Lyon laughed. He tried to retain his dignity by saying that the evacuation would be done when the gear and the camp had been pulled down and packed away.

As the people celebrated, the contractors, Lyon and the police set about their task, trying to ignore the triumphant crowd. By one-thirty they were gone.

The Lawmen had won through. The Law itself was vindicated, as Ginger Nganawilla said:

> We had a meeting with all the Elders from Looma, the Pinnacles and Noonkanbah, and we showed the politicians the Aboriginal Law.
>
> The group then told the Amax people to pack up their rig and go. We told them that we did not want to continue arguing. We then went to the Police and told them to leave.
>
> If we are to allow Amax to return to Noonkanbah they must show us Law, not paper law. Paper is nothing. Paper can be washed away. Our Law, Aboriginal Law will last forever. If Amax has this Law then they must show us.[25]

These events were soon recorded in the annals of Noonkanbah folklore in the format of a song composed by George Manyanji Bell. The chapter closes with this song: the Walmatjari original, and an adaptation of the translation by the school linguist, Eirlys Richards.

NGUNYIPINYA MARNALUNYA

Manyanjirlu yutukaniny minyarti juju

Karajarri Nyikina, Mangala Walmajarri, tamarrapinyangurra,
Karajarri Nyikina, Mangala Walmajarri, tamarrapinyangurra.

Kayilungu parla jurtu pakarrkarrinya,
Kayilungu parla jurtu pakarrkarrinya.

Kuniyanti Yulparija tamarrapinyangurra,
Kuniyanti Yulparija tamarrapinyangurra.

Japirrmani parlipanya, 'Nyapartukarra?'
Japirrmani parlipanya, 'Nyapartukarra?'

Pingayirlu manya japirrmani,

'Purrkuwarnti, wirriya ngantarla nguniny minyartiwu wangki?
Purrkuwarnti, wirriya ngantarla nguniny minyartiwu wangki?'

Purrkuwarnti palu marni, 'Ngajirta, tikirryanku',
Purrkuwarnti palu marni, 'Ngajirta, tikirryanku'.

Kayirrampalu parla jurtu pakarrkarrinya,
Kayirrampalu parla jurtu pakarrkarrinya.

Kakarrara parla jurtu pakarrkarrinya,
Kakarrara parla jurtu pakarrkarrinya.

Ngajirta manya japirrmantarla purrkuwarnti,
Ngajirta manya japirrmantarla purrkuwarnti.

Murtarni pa jaatlani malajirla,
Murtarni pa jaatlani malajirla.

Karlangurlu palu parlipinya karrinyangurra,
Karlangurlu palu parlipinya karrinyangurra.

Murtarni palu karlarnimarrangu pirriyani,
Murtarni palu karlarnimarrangu pirriyani.

Marni palurla, 'Nganapirri manu minyawurla jaatlani?'
Marni palurla, 'Nganapirri manu minyawurla jaatlani?'

'Purrkuwarnti japirrmani ngankunya?
Purrkuwarnti japirrmani ngankunya?'

Pingkayirlu layingu parla marni,
Pingkayirlu layingu parla marni,

'Warra marnantalu nyaku kumanta,
Warra marnantalu nyaku kumanta.'

Tikiyani palu pajanyangu ngurtiwarntijarti,
Tikiyani palu pajanyangu ngurtiwarntijarti.

Ngurra palu juntumani,
Ngurra palu juntumani.

Pukanyjajarrinya jujula palu yinparni Warlungarri,
Pukanyjajarrinya jujula palu yinparni Warlungarri,

WE HUNTED THEM OUT

George Bell made this song[26]

People from the Garadjeri, Nyigina, Mangala and Walmatjari tribes had gathered together.

They saw the dust rising in the north from the trucks bringing the water drilling rig.

Gunian and Yulbaridja people had also gathered.

The white men asked us, 'What about it?'

The young Aboriginal man asked the old men,
'Old men, are you happy about this decision?'

The old men said, 'No, the drill can go back'.

Around the north the dust was rising.

Around the east the dust was rising.

The white man did not ask the old men.

Without asking he drilled that sacred site.

They came from the west and found the site standing there.

They came from the west without asking.

The Aborigines said to them, 'Why have you drilled here?'

'Did you ask the old men?'

The young Aboriginal man said to them,

'We will discuss this with you tomorrow'.

They all went back in their cars.

They made camp.

When night came they sang the Walungarri corroboree

Munganga warurrurla kaparnkaparnta,
Munganga warurrurla kaparnkaparnta.

Ngajirta palu yukanyjarla manyan limpawarntijaa wajpalwarnti,
Ngajirta palu yukanyjarla manyan limpawarntijaa wajpalwarnti.

Wangkila palurlanyanu kumantajarti yiparni limpawarntirlu,
Wangkila palurlanyanu kumantajarti yiparni limpawarntirlu.

Pajanyangurla palu piyirn karrinyangurra kumantjarti,
Pajanyangurla palu piyirn karrinyangurra kumantjarti.

Limpa ngajirta palu rayin nyakarla,
Limpa ngajirta palu rayin nyakarla.

Marni palurla ngiljarti nyanarti, 'Kumantajarti mana man nyanarti kurtajmanku',
Marni palurla ngiljarti nyanarti, 'Kumantajarti mana man nyanarti kurtajmanku'.

'Jarranyaku marnantalu kitangarni man kurtajmanku,
Jarranyaku marnantalu kitangarni man kurtajmanku.'

Limpawarnti mapirri palu karrinyangurra,
Limpawarnti mapirri palu karrinyangurra.

Piyirnwarnti ngajirta palu rayinkarrirla,
Piyirnwarnti ngajirta palu rayinkarrirla.

Kumantajarti layi limpa pirriyani,
Kumantajarti layi limpa pirriyani.

Marni parla pingkayiwu,

'Ngurti nyanarti manta rirripkujiwu,
Ngurti nyanarti manta rirripkujiwu.'

'Ngiljawurlu palu warrkammalku,
Ngiljawurlu palu warrkammalku.'

Pingkayirlu parla marni,

'Ngajirta, ngurti minyarti wali pa karrilany,
            Ngurti minyarti wali pa karrilany.'

'Nyanarti ngurti marnalu nyaku, rirripkujiwu palu,
Nyanarti ngurti marnalu nyaku, rirripkujiwu palu.'

'Jininyarajarti marnalu jarranyaku.
Jininyarajarti marnalu jarranyaku.'

Piyirnwarnti palu yani, pingkayi nyanarti layi palu kanya piyirnwarntilu,
Piyirnwarnti palu yani, pingkayi nyanarti layi palu kanya piyirnwarntilu.

Marni palurla nyanartiwu ngurtikarrajiwu ngiljartiwu,
Marni palurla nyanartiwu ngurtikarrajiwu ngiljartiwu,

'Nyanarti ngurti nyuntu ngangu?
Nyanarti ngurti nyuntu ngangu?'

Marnila manyanangu, 'Yu, ngajukura paji nyanarti ngurti'.
Marnila manyanangu, 'Yu, ngajukura paji nyanarti ngurti'.

'Wal jalarra manu kurtajpanku,
      jalarra manu kurtajpanku.'

Right through the middle of the night.

The police and white men didn't sleep.

In the morning the police sent radio messages to other police.

In the morning there was a crowd of Aborigines standing there.

They weren't afraid of the policemen.

The young Aboriginal man said, 'This morning you must take this drill away'.

'We will stay here till you take it.'

The police were standing there too.

The Aborigines were not afraid.

Then a policeman came.

He said to the young man,
'Shift that car blocking the road'.

'These men have to work.'

The young man said,
'No, the car will stay here'.

'We are waiting for you to shift that drill.'

'We'll stay here right through the afternoon.'

The Aboriginal men and the young man moved off.

They said to the driver of the drilling truck,

'Is that your vehicle?'

He said to them, 'Yes, that's mine'.

'Then shift it right now.'

'Yuwayi', marni manyanangu nyanartirlu ngiljartirlu.
'Yuwayi', marni manyanangu nyanartirlu ngiljartirlu.

Yani palunyanangu limpawarntijarti jurrupirni,
Yani palunyanangu limpawarntijarti jurrupirni,

Marni palunyanangu, 'Pujurni manta turtangkarra kangku'.
Marni palunyanangu, 'Pujurni manta turtangkarra kangku'.

Marnila palu, 'Yu mapunparni jalarra marnalu minyarti turtangkarra kangku.
                    Jalarra marnalu minyarti turtangkarra kangku.'

Yarripulayinpiliny marnalu nyanya turtangkarra kanya,
Yarripulayinpiliny marnalu nyanya turtangkarra kanya.

Nyanartijangka ngurti pa purlka karlarnimarrangu pirriyani,

Warntarnkarra kanya katipila,
Warntarnkarra kanya katipila.

Purlkala tayingkajaa tiyi turtangkarra kanya,
Purlkala tayingkajaa tiyi turtangkarra kanya.

Nyantila palu ngurrkujirni,
Nyantila palu ngurrkujirni.

Limpawarnti palu kajalu laparningurra,
Limpawarnti palu kajalu laparningurra.

Nyantirni ngiljarti pa kaparn laparni ngurtijarti,
Nyantirni ngiljarti pa kaparn laparni ngurtijarti.

Wartangurnula pa jurrupi lani piyirnwarntikura ngurti,
Wartangurnula pa jurrupi lani piyirnwarntikura ngurti.

'Yes', that white man said to them.

They went in a line to the policemen.

The Aboriginal men said to them, 'Take all of this equipment and vehicles away'.

They answered, 'Yes truly, we will take them all away'.

First we saw the aeroplane go.

Then a big truck came from the west side,
And loaded on the bulldozer.

Then the truck with the tank of diesel began to move.

They all had their engines running ready to go.

The police went first.

The white men went next in their vehicles.

Then the Aborigines followed behind in a line in their vehicles, escorting them off.

George Bell centre with (left to right) Harry Yamalulu, Edward Yamera and Neville George.

13

NO MIDDLE GROUND

Everything was focused in on Noonkanbah.

Pat Dodson, Director of the Central Land Council, 1988.

The Community's eviction of Amax and the police on 2 April 1980 attracted headlines around the nation. Never in the modern era had the country seen such a dramatic assertion of Aboriginal power and resolve.

The State Government was infuriated, but there was very little it could do in terms of an immediate response. Even if the union bans could be circumvented by force or by stealth to get the rig to Noonkanbah, it could not be erected or operated until the site-works and the water bore were complete. There was no way Jeremy O'Driscoll and Brian McGaffin would return, and the probability of finding alternative contractors in the atmosphere that prevailed was minimal.

In the absence of any real options the Premier's first reaction was outrage, and a message to the wider Aboriginal community:

> Today's incident at Noonkanbah deserves the strongest condemnation. It will have a devastating effect on the reputation and standing of Aborigines in the Western Australian community.
>
> ...In the future, responsible Aborigines will look back with very deep regret on what has happened today and on the way they have been misled by outsiders to follow such a disastrous course. As far as the Government is concerned – drilling will proceed, whether by Amax or someone else.
>
> Speaking for the Government, I can say that we hope wiser counsel will prevail and that Aborigines will soon learn how seriously they have been subverted. Aborigines have placed at risk the rights responsible Aborigines have wanted, to express their independence and self-reliance in the operation of pastoral stations under their own management. In a climate like that which prevails at the present time, it would be impossible to get approval for a pastoral station for another Aboriginal group.
>
> ...To avoid placing in jeopardy all they have gained in goodwill and in very material terms, responsible Aborigines throughout the State should be taking a special interest in persuading the group at Noonkanbah to come to their senses and get rid of the stirrers who have so changed their normal behaviour.
>
> The Government will do what it has to do in this matter – let there be no mistake about that...As always, we stand ready to talk to responsible Aborigines, but we will have no truck with the stirrers, and those who would subvert not only the Aborigines but the nation.[1]

Premier Court had misread the mood of Aboriginal people. The Noonkanbah

Community was riding high, and carrying Aboriginal Australia with it on a wave of hope and optimism. By defying the precedents of almost two hundred years, by demonstrating the power of Aboriginal culture, by driving out the seemingly irresistible forces of government and industry, Noonkanbah had become a symbol.

In the eyes of the Perth Aboriginal poet and playwright Jack Davis it brought new meaning to Aboriginality for urban blacks:

> I think every caring person both black and white realised what the Noonkanbah incident was about. Especially blacks in the south and in the cities. For years we had been demonstrating for Land Rights. I think to most blacks the call for Land Rights was slightly nebulous. They knew it was an important black issue but had difficulty in defining it. But what happened at Noonkanbah seemed to solidify their feelings.[2]

Pat Dodson, who later became the Director of the Central Land Council, and the Deputy Chairman of the Aboriginal Development Commission, was at Monash University in Melbourne at the time. His recollections show something of the impact events were having on Aboriginal activists, and the communities around the country facing encroachment on their land by developers.

> Everything was focused in on Noonkanbah. The emotional struggle of these people standing up against the mining company, and the Government and its blatant use of force to break down the resistance of the people. Up to that point it was considered that there was no way of dealing with mining companies. Noonkanbah was a watershed situation in terms of standing up to the companies and trying to think of ways to influence them, and to protect Aboriginal interests in land and in particular sacred sites, instead of subordinating Aboriginal spirituality to financial gain.[3]

The day after the withdrawal Premier Court was denying that Amax had asked to be released from their obligation to drill, and saying, 'If they want to go on tomorrow, we will make it possible for them to go on tomorrow'.[4] But both parties must have decided on reflection that such a course was neither practical or advisable. On 6 April, Easter Saturday, Court announced that the company had been given an extension of time. The rig was immediately moved over a thousand kilometres south, from Broome to a site near Eneabba to drill a hole for Strata Oil. This meant that it would not become available for at least two months. Noonkanbah had won another reprieve.

Court tried to minimise the significance of this backdown by an attack on those who had frustrated him. The announcement specified that the company was still obliged to complete the drilling that year, and spoke of 'temporary relief out of consideration for the ordeal of intimidation and standover...the State Government's sympathy and regret at the extreme and unwarranted harrassment...Federal Labor Members having desecrated their public trust.'[5] He also threatened, 'We are preparing to serve on the Aboriginal people at Noonkanbah an explicit and simply expressed form of notice', and spoke of 'a major appraisal of the grave issues that have grown out of Aboriginal, union and activist behaviour related to Noonkanbah'.[6]

And so, each side took stock of the situation, and girded its loins for the next round.

There appeared to be two basic factors driving Sir Charles Court and his Government on their course of 'drill at any cost'. There was the sheer anger at the way they were being frustrated at every turn by the Community, be it in meetings, in the courts, or by direct action. They were not accustomed to such a situation, and were determined to emerge ultimately victorious. Then there was Court's political analysis of the realities behind the dispute, best summarised in a sentence from a letter he wrote to Prime Minister Fraser early in April:

> It is the most blatant case to date of Aborigines being used as a front to undermine elected Government and, in my opinion, being expertly manipulated to destroy confidence in our nation as a place to invest, live and work.[7]

Crushing the opposition at Noonkanbah seemed to be part of a personal crusade to save the nation, or at least ensure that it was not diverted from the vision he held for it. Like any crusader, he could not afford to admit anything good or positive in those who stood in his way.

It is one of the peculiarities of Aboriginal Affairs that most whites assume themselves to be experts, and think it is legitimate to ignore the actual voices and expressed opinions of the Aboriginal people themselves. They create their own versions of what they think should be, and assert these as the 'real' feelings of the 'genuine' Aborigines.

Earlier mention has been made of the paternalistic type of racism that is rooted in a latent belief that blacks are inherently inferior. This causes a blind spot which cannot see the actions of Aboriginal people as being of their own initiative, and must extol or blame, as the case may be, an external party. When the guard is not up, this blind spot is sometimes revealed; as in two examples of Court's correspondence with supportive members of the public during the Noonkanbah episode.

One was a telegram of congratulations from a pastoralist near Meekatharra. Before replying Court asked his Under Secretary to make enquiries about the sender, and check if the reply he had drafted was suitable. The telegram and draft reply were shown to the local Liberal Member, Norman Moore, and the advice came back:

> Moore knows Mr. ... very well, and describes him as a typical pastoralist of the area, with a known dislike for the Aborigines. Moore advised that the intended letter is quite satisfactory, and the sentiments would be well received by Mr. ... .[8]

With this curious endorsement, Court's reply was duly sent.

The other came later, a hand-written letter from Tasmania. It began, 'We want *oil*, not nigger witchcraft'; quoted the bible lines about destroying idols of false gods; told of the writer's grandfather in India having 'to put down with the sword' the Sikhs who buried live virgins with their chiefs; had an exposition about why nobody could object to the use of the term 'nigger', because it was a corruption of negro, which was a corruption of negri, which meant black; and spoke of the 'Australian niggers delivered from Demonism into Christianity'.[9]

To this Court replied – and it was not a form letter:

> It was refreshing to find somebody who took the time and the trouble to write as you did. I wish more people could appreciate the Noonkanbah situation in its proper perspective, as you have done in your letter.[10]

Admittedly, these examples are extreme, but they illustrate the very basic problem. Court either could not see, or would not oppose, racism when it stared him in the face. His sense of the order of human and political affairs was challenged by the events of Noonkanbah.

The Government tried to create a picture of events at Noonkanbah that was consistent with its interpretations and would justify its actions to the wider community. Whether this was done by deliberate design, or gradually by default, is open to debate. The process had begun back in 1979, but reached its fullest extent during the media blitz of March and April 1980.

The Government scenario had four main elements. First: Noonkanbah had been a community of reasonable and simple people when left to its own devices, and in this state had co-operated on a friendly basis with Amax, until it came under the influence of outside agitators. Second: The old men of Noonkanbah did not oppose drilling, but their leadership, personified in Friday Muller, had been usurped by young radicals led by Dicky Skinner, with the assistance of the agitators. Third: The agitators, personified by me and the Aboriginal Legal Service, and the unions when they became involved, had no regard for the Noonkanbah people, and were driven by a subversive anti-government, anti-development agenda. Fourth: Though there were some 'genuine' sacred sites in the general vicinity, additional sites and the area of influence concept had been manufactured by the agitators and their dupes in the Community, to further their subversive agenda and promote other causes such as Land Rights and royalties.

In trying to sell these views to the public, Court and some of his Ministers used language that can only be described as extreme. Some examples can be seen in the press releases quoted above; a few others amongst many included: 'Raw racial hatred on the part of some Aboriginals [as] the result of ideological penetration and manipulation'[11]; 'The Noonkanbah insurrection'[12], and 'An insurrection against legitimate authority'[13]; 'The aim [of the unions] has been to destroy the authority of the Government and the law'.[14]

In addition the Government produced a series of diversionary allegations that served to confuse the issues, and force the Community into denials and explanations.

First came Bill Grayden's attack on the Aboriginal Heritage Act, which he described as shocking legislation in need of a major overhaul. He wanted it 'tightened to ensure that it protected only the genuine sites of initiated tribal Aborigines. The culture of such Aborigines was the only one worth preserving, not some watered down version.'[15] Grayden had placed Noonkanbah in the latter category on the advice of his neighbour, Duncan Beaton, the former manager of Noonkanbah. Beaton had advised him that in all his time on the station he had never been told of these sites, and therefore Grayden concluded that it was a 'beat up'.[16]

A public debate with the anthropological community ensued, with alternative definitions of 'secret' and 'sacred' and 'site' being discussed in the media. At the same time Grayden had the Museum staff working nights and weekends supplying him with answers to a list of queries about its overall site mapping program, and various aspects of Peter Bindon's 1979 report.

This debate took off in another direction following a call to Grayden from Professor Ronald Berndt. Berndt, in a search for a compromise solution, had promoted the idea of a gradation of importance of sacred land. Part of this theory was the concept that parts of the land that made up site complexes, such as the Pea Hill zone, were traditionally used for economic purposes, that is for hunting and food exploitation. From this he suggested that economic exploitation of a different kind, such as oil drilling, may be acceptable if appropriate compensation was paid.

Berndt had met with Ivan McPhee and Nipper Tabagee in Perth on 25 March, just before the court injunction was about to be lifted. He discussed the gradation and compensation concept with them at length, urging them to consider it as a way out of an impossible situation, and of creating a precedent for other communities. He and McPhee and Tabagee, and other observers at the meeting, all confirmed later that the concept was not approved or supported, there was merely an agreement that it could be talked about at the Community level. Nevertheless Berndt rang Grayden and asked him to see if a further stay of proceedings could be arranged to enable time to talk about the idea.

The Government seized on this, going public and saying that an 'unnamed intermediary' had approached them to say that the problem could be solved by compensation payments. 'So called' sites were now up for sale, the Community now had no credibility and so forth. Berndt's name emerged as the intermediary; there were denials from him and the Community of the Government's claims. But for days, as the on-site drama continued at Noonkanbah, the Government continued to pursue this line.

They said that the Community had asked for royalties at the meeting with the three Ministers, and released a transcript allegedly proving their case. All it showed was Jimmy Bieunderry discussing in very general terms the question of a reasonable return in the form of royalties for mining on Aboriginal land, in response to a dissertation by Grayden about the enormous benefits to the general community from mining revenue.

In the same period the Government tried to ridicule the Noonkanbah Community's position by revealing that a number of small shot-holes for diamond exploration had been drilled on and around Pea Hill in the late 1960s, with no objections from the Community. The diamond holes had been drilled by the same crews that stole the darrugu boards from Tatju Hill, causing such heartache. Skinner rebutted this red herring:

> Mining people came secretly and did not talk to the Aborigines. Later people were going around mustering and they found samples and told the old people. When the Aboriginal people found out about the holes, they wondered why the mining people didn't come and talk to them. After one year all the kangaroos disappeared and the people knew they had gone back to the spirit hole because of the mining.[17]

The Government also continually pointed out the extensive network of roads, fences, a water bore and the homestead complex within the Museum defined area of influence. As the Community said:

> Charlie Court talks about all the roads and fences and bores on this sacred land. How did that road come on here? And that fence? And that bore? The white man put it there. He never asked the Aboriginal people. He never bought this land. He just took it. Aboriginal people never agreed on that before. We didn't want all these things on our sacred land. Now they are trying to do the same thing today. We've got the land back now, and we don't want that to happen.[18]

The nett effect of this plethora of stories and rebuttals, of the radically differing accounts emerging of events at Noonkanbah, and of the entry into the debate of all manner of interested parties and experts, was to confuse most of the media and those members of the public who were not committed by inclination to one side or the other. This in turn made it more difficult for the Community to get across the real message of what it was about.

At Noonkanbah there was almost an air of disbelief at what had happened at the drill site. I suspect that almost everyone, except perhaps the inner circle of old men, was surprised at the victory that had come their way. All believed in the power of the Law; but never had the power been manifested in this manner before.

What had driven the old men to take this course, to channel the power of the Law in such a way? The obvious answer is that there were no alternatives; they had said, 'we will ask them to leave one more time, and then hand it over to us'. But so often before, in so many places, Aboriginal people had withdrawn from conflict when faced with seemingly lesser odds. Why was it different this time?

In some part it was due to the 'stirrers and subversives', as they were called by the Government. By creating networks of support in the Aboriginal and the wider communities, the KLC and the ALS, the Churches and unions, I and many others had made the people feel less alone than they so often had been in the past, and thus more willing to give expression to their true feelings.

More than anything else though, it was a dynamic of pride and anger that had built up. There was pride in the stand the Community had taken; and the struggle itself was both a manifestation of the pride in the culture and the Law the people held, and a process of building such pride.

The old men in particular felt anger and insult at the failure to take their words and the darrugu seriously, at 'being treated as young men'. If words were not enough, then action was the only recourse left. And the whole Community was angry, as well as fearful, at the presence of the police, and the conduct of the Government and the company, and especially at Tom Lyon.

The tension between Lyon and the Community was a very significant factor. The mutual antagonism and suspicion had become intense. It seemed that Lyon looked for and found threats in almost everything that was said to him. The Community in its anger fed his fear with its talk of the Law, and the danger he faced from it.

The relationship had never been good, and in this period it became disastrous. This was clear to all of the local contractors and workers associated with the company, many of whom also disliked Lyon for what they saw as his 'pommy' officiousness. Some of these people who were involved on the company side have commented subsequently on how Lyon was unable to go near anyone from the Community without an argument developing. One of them went so far as to contact Max Reynolds at the Amax office in Perth and plead with him to remove Lyon in the interests of establishing some sort of dialogue with the Community. Yet Tom Lyon remained the main channel of communication and source of information and advice to the company and the Government up to the time of his eviction by the Community on 2 April. Although he remained with Amax, Lyon did not reappear at Noonkanbah after this.

From the pride and anger dynamic came the strength and purpose of that long night and day of April 1st and 2nd. If the victory had not come then, it probably would have been all over, for the tensions and pressures upon and within the Community were becoming severe.

The rate and weight and number of matters coming up for decision and action were becoming too much for the Community to handle through its normal processes of internal consultation. The number of politicians, bureaucrats, media people and various others that had been through Noonkanbah in the space of a month was almost unbelievable. All made demands for meetings, information, time, decisions.

The very basic function of control over entry which had been an important manifestation of the Community's independence and control came under threat from this deluge. Yet the Community could not afford to say no, or slow down, as they needed most of these people in one way or another for their campaign.

And as the Noonkanbah Community became a symbol for Aboriginal Australia, so they began to be caught up in the internal politics of the wider Aboriginal community, being pulled different ways by different factions. Their two main avenues of support were the KLC, and the Nomads organisation and people of Strelley.

The Nomads had been linked to Noonkanbah since the establishment of the Community school in 1978. Nomads provided the administrative backup for the school, and their organisation also supplied the Community store. More importantly, from the time of the first call for help early in March, key Elders from Strelley had spent a lot of time at Noonkanbah. These men were veterans of the great Aboriginal strike of the 1940s. They were senior Lawmen in their own right, they were strong, and they knew all about struggle with authority.

They provided great moral support to the Noonkanbah Lawmen, and after one had spent a week being inducted into the Noonkanbah Law, he became a part of the inner circle of the Elders in their councils.

The KLC provided invaluable organisational support, liaison with other Kimberley communities, and practical assistance in terms of disseminating information to the press and others as the pace of events hotted up. It was also the main link into the Australia-wide network of Aboriginal activists and organisations that was mobilising in support of the Community. Jimmy Bieunderry of the KLC was particularly close to Dicky Skinner, and a valuable adviser to him.

All of these people were working towards the same end, and most of the time at Noonkanbah they were acting in unison. But as the pressure mounted, thorough communication was not always possible; and at times the different perspectives and spheres of operation of the old men and the younger generation, personified in the spokesman Skinner, created a tension.

The eviction of Amax had seen this tension between the way of the Law and the way of political activism produce a stunningly positive result. But with the differing allegiances and agendas of some of the supporting actors there was also the potential for conflict, as was to be seen within a couple of weeks.

In the euphoria of early April these potential problems were not a concern. The Community had two priorities. The first was to enjoy the reprieve given by the Amax withdrawal to get on with some of the more mundane Community activities, particularly that season's mustering program. Skinner was supposed to be a station manager as well as a Community spokesman, and he had found little time for that role so far that year. The other priority was to continue building on their strength and their support to make ready for the next round of hostilities when it eventuated, and to see if there might be any ways around the seemingly impossible impasse.

Dicky Skinner and David Mowaljarli had returned from Perth on Easter Saturday, 5 April. On that day Skinner met in Derby with a two-man delegation from the Trades and Labor Council. These two did the rounds of the wharves and trucking yards and contractors in Broome and Derby to assess options and the level of support for the union initiatives amongst local workers, and flew the flag out at Noonkanbah. The labour force in the Kimberley was largely ununionised and anti-Aboriginal, and it became clear that the muscle would have to be applied at higher levels to be successful.

The stance the unions had taken was quite remarkable in terms of the lengths they were prepared to go on a non-industrial issue, and the principle of their stand. The Government was very quick to use the fact that I was the son of the high-profile ACTU President, Bob Hawke, to promote claims of conspiracy. Obviously we were in contact about the issues and developments, though not nearly as much as most people believed.

The real drive for the union stance came from Peter Cook, the Secretary of the TLC in Perth. He had a long-standing interest in Aboriginal issues, and had been converted to the Noonkanbah cause primarily by meetings with the Noonkanbah delegations to Perth in 1979 and 1980. The addresses of Skinner and McPhee to the full assemblies of TLC delegates on these occasions had made a very positive impact on all concerned, and made the union movement well aware at senior levels of the Community's feelings and position.

Cook was able to use this basis of genuine support to get the numbers over the minority of unions that were reluctant to become involved. The position taken was very significant, in that the criterion they set was the needs of the Community. Their resolution of 25 March, passed in the presence of Ivan McPhee and Nipper Tabagee, had been to impose bans 'to be lifted when advised by the Noonkanbah Community that discussions have concluded to their satisfaction'.

To date their muscle had not been needed, but it was very much a factor in everyone's minds. The extent of the commitment shown by the Community in the weeks immediately following the announcement of union bans did much to solidify the union support. And of course the escalating profile of the dispute and the rhetoric of Sir Charles Court made it less likely the unions would back out, and did nothing to lessen their enthusiasm for the battle they had become involved in. The union movement had some scores to settle with Sir Charles Court, and for some elements this was part of their motivation.

The Pro-Noonkanbah forces gathered in numbers for a KLC sponsored meeting at the station on 18 and 19 April. This was to be a great show of strength, but also an occasion for some of the tensions to spill over.

People came from communities all over the Kimberley, with some from the Northern Territory. The Strelley mob were there, along with their leader and spokesman, Don McLeod. Stewart West of the ALP was back with Peter Cook, and a few representatives of the Churches. Cedric Jacobs had come, as had Brian Wyatt and Rob Riley of Perth to represent the ALS and Aboriginal groups in Perth. A Film Australia documentary team had joined a sizeable contingent of media representatives.

The first activity was a piece of theatre dreamed up by Jimmy Bieunderry and Dicky Skinner. They organised a march from the homestead to the airstrip and back, complete with banners and chanting. Many of the whites present found it hard to see the point of the march up the dusty road with no audience; but it was fun to watch, with all except the old people participating, kids charging out the front, everyone in high spirits

Nipper Tabagee, Peter Yu, KLC field officer, and Kim Akerman, KLC anthropologist, before the KLC meeting.

Kimberley Land Council March, Noonkanbah Station, 18 April 1980.

at this novel activity, and the stockmen with a mob of horses out on the plain forming a wonderful backdrop.

This march was followed by an open session at the bough-shade in front of the homestead. This had been intended as a forum for the visitors to speak their minds before the real business of the meeting commenced the next day. However an acrimonious debate ensued.

Don McLeod and the Strelley mob had a very particular and individual political line, dating back to the days of the Pilbara strike. McLeod, supported by the mob, claimed the leadership of all the traditional people, emanating from his appointment as a Lawman and spokesman in the 1940s. His main platform was a continuing campaign against the illegal and retrospective removal, during the struggle between the colonists and the British Crown for control of 'native affairs' in the 1890s, of Section 70 of the State's

The meeting held in the bough-shade in front of the Noonkanbah homestead. Top: Don McLeod speaking. Bottom left: Jacob Oberdoo of Strelley Station addresses the meeting. Bottom right: Nipper Tabagee speaking to the meeting.

colonial Constitution Act and its reservation of one percent of State revenue for the benefit of Aboriginal people.

But he also made an unyielding distinction between traditional Aborigines who held the Law, and 'the rest'. This included opposition to virtually all representative organisations such as the NAC and the KLC, which he saw as illegitimate and not representative of the authority of the Lawmen; and dismissal of the 'half-castes', whom he saw as a separate group of people.

These attitudes, to say the least, were out of tune with the sentiments and activities that had driven the Aboriginal political renaissance in the Kimberley for the previous few years. When he made his pitch he was opposed by Bieunderry and other Kimberley

231

Jimmy Bieunderry.

spokesmen as well as some of the southern blacks who had come. It became clear that he did not have the numbers or the support in that forum.

After this session West, Cook, and the Churchmen addressed the meeting to underline their support, and explain in what ways they might be able to assist the Noonkanbah mob in their struggle.

The next day the serious meetings got underway down at the riverside. The differences of the previous day were easily forgotten. It was an impressive display of Aboriginal organisation and purpose. The talks continued all day, with a number of issues canvassed both in full session and smaller meetings of the various language groupings.

By the end of the day two major resolutions had been passed. The first repeated the earlier call of the Community for a three year moratorium on any mining activity on any part of Noonkanbah. The second, even more ominous to the Government and the mining industry, reflected the growing mood of strength and solidarity:

> This meeting strongly supports the Noonkanbah Community in its opposition to mining on sacred sites and resolves that we be ready to give the same determined support by sending Community representatives, and in other ways, to other communities whose sacred sites are threatened by mining companies, the Court Government, or other groups bent on desecrating sacred sites.

KLC meeting on the riverside, 19 April 1980. Bottom: Nipper Tabagee speaking.

The dance held after the KLC meeting.

The main thrust of this motion was directed towards the looming prospect of CRA's diamond deposit at Argyle in the East Kimberley. By now the source kimberlite pipe had been identified as potentially one of the world's richest diamond mines. The pipe came to the surface at Barramundi Gap, a site of the Barramundi Dreaming.

John Toby, the leader of the Mandangala, a group within the community at Turkey Creek that hoped to establish an outstation in the vicinity, was emerging as an articulate spokesman and a strong opponent of the proposed mine.

Just before the Noonkanbah meeting Bill Grayden had 'asserted that the Mandangala people are detribalised to such an extent that they regard Turkey Creek as civilisation...and that the barramundi dreaming is no longer sacred to the Turkey Creek people'.[19]

The media at the Noonkanbah meeting took great delight in reporting Toby's angry denials of Grayden's comments, and the spectacular and enthusiastic dancing of the Turkey Creek and Mandangala people at the corroborees on the intervening night.

The possibilities seemed horrendous. Could there be an immediate repeat of the Noonkanbah dramas, only this time with a billion dollar mine at stake instead of a wildcat oil well? The speculation was intense, and many observers began to interpret Noonkanbah as a test case on the Government's part to establish the necessary climate and precedents for Argyle.

Despite the arguments on the first day the meeting was an enormous success as a display of Aboriginal determination and the breadth of support for the Community. The Strelley mob and the KLC both continued to be involved and supportive. Noonkanbah, the Community and the issue, was proving big enough to accommodate the differences.

One feature of the Noonkanbah controversy was that there was almost no middle ground, at least in public. Some members of the State Government were privately aghast at the extreme position of the leadership and the tone of its rhetoric, but they kept their reservations very much to themselves. The editorialists of the *West Australian* were openly confused and inconsistent; along with other media commentators they made pleas for moderation and reason, but without being able to offer any realistic alternatives except the vague proposal of expert committees or inquiries. Some supporters of the Aboriginal side felt that perhaps the Noonkanbah people had gone too far, or that the case for the sacred site was not absolutely sound, or that previous gains might be lost in the fallout, but few said so in public.

Almost the only occupant of the middle ground was Senator Chaney on behalf of the Federal Government, and he was finding the position increasingly uncomfortable as attitudes hardened and stakes were raised. In his public statements he tended to be mildly critical of both sides while stressing his understanding of their respective positions and the complexities of the dispute. Behind the scenes he made many fruitless attempts to build bridges across the ever-widening chasm.

Over the second half of 1979 and early 1980 Chaney had a number of discussions with Max Reynolds of the Amax Perth office. Unlike Tom Lyon, Reynolds was well regarded by nearly all who dealt with him in this period; more than one person has described him since as a gentleman. There is little doubt that personally he would have been prepared to explore alternative solutions to the impasse, but the State Government never allowed him the option.

Chaney had also talked at length with Professor Berndt, and was attracted to Berndt's concept of the gradation of importance of sites and land, and the subsequent argument of compensation for economic exploitation. Back at the beginning of March when he had first contacted the ALS about the rumours of Amax's imminent entry, he had 'suggested that Amax would be willing to pay compensation and provide other benefits for the Community in recognition of their claims but that this aspect would have to be dealt with delicately'.[20] The circumstances indicated that the question must have been discussed with Reynolds without being rejected out of hand.

When Dicky Skinner and David Mowaljarli had been in Perth Chaney had spent many hours talking with them at his home on the Good Friday. He claims that this conversation reinforced his belief that the area was not inviolable as claimed by the Community and the Museum, and that there was room for discussion.[21]

But the two Community spokesmen never raised this on their return from Perth; and if they had given Chaney grounds for any such belief, it was certainly not consistent with the repeated and unchanging position of the senior Lawmen on the matter. Anyhow, by that time, the public wrangle over the concept and the associated issue of royalties/compensation between Professor Berndt and the Government, and the subsequent denials by the Community, had made the possibility of realistic or fruitful discussions of the concept unlikely.

(Senator Chaney tells an interesting story of the Good Friday meeting. Explaining to Skinner and Mowaljarli that Good Friday was the one day of the year he always tried to keep aside for religious rather than political activity, he expressed his regret that the circumstances meant that he could not observe this practice. He referred to the biblical allegory of the ox and the pit. Mowaljarli, who had had a mission education, immediately responded, 'Yes, and Noonkanbah is the pit'.

The relevant bible verses are in The Gospel According to St Luke:

> And it came to pass, as he went into the house of one of the chief Pharisees to eat bread on the sabbath day, that they watched him. And, behold, there was a certain man before him which had the dropsy. And Jesus answering spake unto the lawyers and Pharisees, saying, 'Is it lawful to heal on the sabbath day'. And they held their peace. And he took him, and healed him, and let him go: And answered them, saying, 'Which of you shall have an

ass or an ox fallen into a pit, and will not straightaway pull him out on the sabbath day?' And they could not answer him again to these things.

Chaney clearly saw the parallel in terms of the obligation to perform his work despite the nature of the day. Mowaljarli's response, however, seems to indicate that he had a more down to earth view, and perhaps saw Chaney as the unfortunate ox.)[22]

Chaney did support strongly and publicly the notion of the protection of Aboriginal sites. And he also supported the notion of controls on the company to protect the Community against the potential social impact of drilling operations. But he did not seem to appreciate or accept the Community view of the integrated and interrelated nature of the complex of surface sites and the land between them, or the importance of the subsurface that would be violated by the oil drill. His theory of gradation lay somewhere between this and the narrow 'genuine sites only' line of the State Government.

Early in April he rejected an approach from Members of the Federal Opposition Stewart West and John Dawkins, on their return from Noonkanbah, to support a proposal that could have explored these theories. They suggested a new investigation and mapping of sites under the leadership of an independent authority, provided that the State Government and the company would commit themselves in advance to acceptance of its findings. Chaney knew this would not be acceptable to the State.

He also stubbornly resisted acknowledging the wider interpretations that both sides were placing on the dispute: the State's claims of a political agenda of Land Rights, royalties and subversion of the Government; the Community's demands for acceptance of the validity of its Law. He seemed to recognise that his only hope was to narrow the focus to the specific question of the sites at Noonkanbah, and seek compromise there. But with the emergence of Argyle as a factor, with the knowledge that a vast source of diamonds lay underneath an acknowledged site, even the question of guaranteed protection for the 'genuine' sites was becoming problematic.

He was constrained by the political realities: of his position as a Western Australian Liberal out of tune with the dominant forces in the State Party; of the hard heads within the Federal Government; and of the State Government's unyielding position and threats of a vehement response to any Federal wavering. And all this was in the context of a Federal Election due before the end of the year in which no one on his side of politics was willing to risk an open confrontation between State and Federal Liberal Governments.

Immediately after the eviction of Amax early in April Chaney had indicated his willingness to act as a mediator if all parties would accept him, and he could be of any use. This had been rejected out of hand by Premier Court in a pointed press release:

> We can see no useful purpose in taking up Senator Chaney's offer...We do not question his sincerity, but he must surely know that talk has got us nowhere and the time for talking has gone. As Federal Minister there is nothing to stop him, at any time, from telling the Noonkanbah Aborigines that their confrontation is unjustified, unlawful and dishonours the terms under which they accepted the responsibilities of their pastoral lease.
>
> There is also no reason why, as Minister, he cannot remind them that it is taxpayers' money that made it possible for them to occupy Noonkanbah as pastoralists...Senator Chaney must know that, if the Commonwealth were doing its job by the Aboriginal population generally, and by the taxpayers of this country, it would make it clear without any delay that if Aboriginal groups are not prepared to act responsibly in accordance with their commitments, Commonwealth funds will be withdrawn from them.[23]

Chaney summarised his attitude in the conclusion of a long letter to the *West Australian* on 9 April:

> Let my own position be clear. For eight months I have sought community acceptance of drilling on Noonkanbah subject only to clearly defined rules protecting both sacred sites and this living community. The Commonwealth will continue to work for an agreed solution. I do not deal with the solution here but I do ask for patience and tolerance in our approach to the current dispute and to others which may develop in the future.[24]

When it boiled down though, his position was much closer to the State's than the Community's for two reasons. Firstly, his failure to take any action was effectively a tacit acceptance of the State's actions. Secondly, his attempts to gain 'community acceptance of drilling' were predicated on the Community abandoning its position of exclusion of Amax from the sacred area, rather than exploring the option of Amax moving away from its designated zone.

The Community was demanding acceptance not only of its Law, but of its perspective on land and community life, as a legitimate starting point for any discussions; whereas Chaney insisted that the Aboriginal reality must be squeezed and reshaped to accommodate the foreign, external, 'rational' perspective of a measurable gradation of sanctity and accessibility of land.

In one sense Premier Court was correct. The Community and its supporters were challenging the authority of the Government and its law. But he had completely misread the intention behind this challenge. It was not a matter of destroying the Government. As Dicky Skinner had said eighteen months earlier, it was a question of making the two laws equal, finding a means to respect the Aboriginal way in its broadest sense. The Pea Hill complex had become a very concrete symbol of this way and all it meant to the people. Senator Chaney it seems mistakenly believed that it was possible to reconcile the two sides without addressing this broader aspect.

From the Community's perspective there were four possible courses that could lead to a satisfactory outcome of the dispute.

Despite the State having dismissed the possibility, there remained the hope that either a moratorium for a fixed period, or a move by the company to an acceptable area, could somehow be negotiated.

There was the possibility that effective union bans could eventually force Amax and the contracting companies to withdraw altogether, or force the State to the negotiating table.

There was the belief that sufficient pressure may eventually force the Federal Government to intervene in some form, using either political persuasion or its constitutional powers. Its constitutional power to intervene arose from the 1967 referendum, granting the Federal Government the power to make laws for Aboriginal people. In turn this opened the way for the use of Section 51 of the Constitution, which enabled it to compulsorily acquire land to which its laws applied. To date this power had never been used in the context of Aboriginal Affairs, but the acquisition and protection of Noonkanbah was undoubtedly an option.

And there remained the wildcard of the Lawmen and their powers, but any plans they might have had were shrouded in the mysteries and secrecy of the Law.

14

WE ARE YOUR FRIENDS

Can't these people just be left alone? Isn't...the rest of Australia enough?

Olive Bieunderry to Sir Charles Court at Noonkanbah, 30 May 1980.

Whilst the drilling rig was busy at Eneabba, the State Government was quietly preparing for the next phase, to try to ensure that there would be no further unforeseen setbacks. It also had to keep the pressure on the Federal Government and on Amax to ensure that they held the line. The Community and its supporters were kept in the dark in term of specific plans, and on the defensive through a continuing media campaign of confusion and intimidation.

After the initial media blitz early in April the pressure on the Community was maintained by claims such as those of Bill Grayden of an Aboriginal agenda 'spearheaded' by Noonkanbah, of 'Aboriginal territorial advancement' through land claims for over a third of northern Australia.[1] This was followed by announcement of a State Cabinet decision late in the month specifically confirming that there would be no more pastoral leases approved for transfer to Aboriginal communities until the Noonkanbah dispute was resolved. This confirmation of earlier threats was a serious blow to Aboriginal aspirations, as it jeopardised negotiations that the Federal Government was pursuing through the Aboriginal Land Fund Commission for groups outside the Kimberley that had no involvement whatsoever with events at Noonkanbah.

Sir Charles Court worked on the Federal Government in long letters to Senator Chaney and Prime Minister Fraser early in April. These were almost as strongly worded as his press releases, full of justifications of the State Government position and dire warnings of the consequences of allowing his steadfast wall to be breached at Noonkanbah. In his letter to Fraser, Court raised the need for Federal co-operation in countering the unions, saying, 'Because of federal registration of key Unions involved, our new deregistration procedures are of limited immediate use in the present situation'. He sought, and presumably obtained, an early meeting with Fraser to discuss the situation.[2]

It seemed the State's biggest problem might lie with Amax. There had already been suggestions earlier that it was becoming an increasingly reluctant partner in Court's crusade. Then late in April the press carried reports of an address by company Vice-President Arthur Reef in Tokyo under the headline 'Amax Threatens Pullout Over Land Rights'. Reef had complained about the company's search for oil in Australia being held up by Land Rights disputes, and followed this by suggesting that the company was 'turning to mineral and energy exploration in Brazil where there are also good prospects'.[3]

Court wrote to Max Reynolds early in May to say:

> On your visit to Houston I would like you to convey to Mr. Lloyd Parks and others to whom you are reporting, the Western Australian Government's appreciation of Amax's consistent support of sound principle over the Noonkanbah issue...In the case of Amax, the position remains that...[it]...is

required by the Government to complete its drilling plan on Noonkanbah under the terms of your exploration permit…[and]…That the State in imposing this requirement, is correctly exercising its powers in support of mineral exploration.[4]

During May the Government also began to lay the groundwork for overcoming any obstacles that might be put in its path. On the 13th, the Museum Trustees were given maps showing an enlarged area at the drilling site, and the access road from the Great Northern Highway into Noonkanbah. The Trustees were requested by the acting Minister for Mines, Andrew Mensaros, to once again give their consent to the use of this land.[5] And a former executive of a major trucking company was engaged to investigate means of getting the rig transported from Eneabba up to Noonkanbah.

The 'explicit and simply expressed form of notice' that the Premier had promised on 6 April was delivered to the Community three weeks later, on the 27th. It came in the form of a tape recorded message from Bill Grayden.

Grayden read the message as if reading a book to a kindergarten class: extremely slowly, with exaggerated emphasis, and in what was considered by those who heard it a condescending and patronising tone. The full text was as follows:

I am speaking for the Government of Western Australia.
I am Minister for Cultural Affairs.
I bring you a message from the Government.
It is important to all of you.

I am trying to help you.
I want to talk about the trouble over drilling on Noonkanbah.
It was wrong to stop the drilling.
It was bad for the people of Noonkanbah.
It was bad for all of us.

We need oil to make petrol for cars and trucks.
It was wrong to stop the drilling.
We need to find oil.
Oil is a mineral.
We need to find other minerals too.

To help find minerals we have a law.
The law says people who obey the law can look for minerals.
They can look on Noonkanbah and any other stations.
And it is wrong to stop them.
Let me tell you why.

Noonkanbah is a cattle station.
People who use it make an agreement with the Government.
When white people use it they make an agreement.
The agreement says they can use it for cattle.
The agreement lets people look for minerals on Noonkanbah.
The agreement is part of our law.
And the law has always been obeyed.
The law is for everyone – we are all the same.
The law cannot be different for Aboriginal people.
We are all Australians.
We are all Australians together.

If Aborigines or white men break the law it means trouble.
Other Australians will say, 'Why should Aborigines have a different law. It is
    not right. The law must be the same for everyone.'

We want you to stay on Noonkanbah.
When you got the station we made an agreement.
The agreement lets you use the land as a place to live and run your cattle.
The agreement also lets anyone who obeys the law look for minerals on
    Noonkanbah.
But you have broken the agreement.

Some of your people have locked the gate to stop people looking for
    minerals.
Some of your people have tried to stop trucks going in and stop drilling.
They came together in big numbers and frightened the drilling people away.
This is wrong.
You should keep the agreement.
You should let the mineral people in.

If you are worried about sacred sites, please remember our law says proper
    sacred sites must not be damaged.
They will be looked after.
We will look after them because we respect them.

Aboriginal people have lived at Noonkanbah for many years.
They have seen many things built there; houses, yards, fences, roads,
    airstrips and many other things.
Many mineral people have been through the land.
We got along together without any trouble all those years.
We can still get along without any trouble if we help each other now.

The mineral people must be allowed on Noonkanbah.
The people who came to drill, and went away, must be allowed to come
    back.
When they come back there will be no harm to your people or your sacred
    sites.
The camp and the work area for the drillers will be fenced off, so your cattle
    will not be hurt.
The drilling people will live inside the fence.
They will not be allowed to have alcohol.
They will not be allowed to have guns.
Only one of them will be allowed to meet with you.
That man and your people will be able to talk about what is happening, so
    there will be no problems.

The Government will make sure that any drilling or mining will not hurt
    your way of life.
These are the things we promise you, to help you and protect you.
But we must also protect the drillers.
You must leave them alone and let them get on with their work.
You must respect their rights, and they must respect your rights.

I ask your Elders to talk to all your people about this message.
Let them hear this message with their own ears.
Let them talk to you with their own voices.
Let the outside voices be quiet.

242

Your Elders can tell us what you feel.
We trust your Elders.
We believe they trust us.

Soon, Premier Court will come to Noonkanbah.
He will sit down with your Elders and listen to them.
He has been wanting to come for a long time.
He has been wanting private talks, just him and you.

But private talks cannot be held when some of your people ask strangers to
      join in.
The Premier will come at the right time when it is agreed the talks will be
      private, just him and you.
I ask the Elders to make this happen.

We want this to be a new start, so there will be no more trouble for anyone.
This is the way we can all live happily together.
We are your friends.

We helped you get Noonkanbah, because we want you to live there.
We want you to be happy at Noonkanbah, and that is why we want you to
      obey the law like everyone else.
Help us to help you to make a wonderful cattle station at Noonkanbah.

Please remember, the Government must go with the law.
We can help you if you go with the law.
The law says you must not make trouble for the mineral people, and the
      mineral people must not make trouble for you.

You can use Noonkanbah as long as you wish, if you go with the law.
Please go with the law and help us help you.

We are your friends.

We want to help you.

Thank you for listening.

The tape was far from explicit in terms of notice as to what was going to happen, though there seemed to be an implied threat that the Government would move to evict the people from the station if they continued to oppose drilling. As for simplicity, the Government made a big mistake. The message was not straightforward, and it was seen by the Community as insulting.

The impact of the Grayden tape is hard to convey properly; suffice to say that years later when I spoke to one of the Noonkanbah people of those times, his first recollection and comment was of this tape, and the bitter reaction it produced. The Film Australia team in their documentary, 'On Sacred Ground', captured the stony hard faces of the Elders as they listened to it. To listen to Grayden saying, and repeating, 'We are your friends', after all that had happened, created a deep anger in the hearts of the people.

Bill Grayden has since denied authorship of the message. He says it was written by W.W. 'Bill' Mitchell, a public relations consultant and confidant of Court's. 'He wrote it, and they couldn't find anyone to read it. Because they couldn't get anyone else to read the damn thing they asked me to.'[6]

Mitchell was to play an increasingly important behind-the-scenes role in the Noonkanbah dispute in coming months. He became Court's principal adviser and strategist, the editor of much of Court's correspondence on the affair, and later a key organiser in the final stages of the drama.

Mitchell was vehemently opposed to Land Rights. He had been a vocal critic at the time the South Australian Government, with the support of the Commonwealth, had introduced the Pitjanjatjarra Land Rights legislation in 1978. The nature of his attitude towards Aboriginal people, sites and culture can be gauged from one of his many letters to the editor published in the *West Australian*:

> In 40,000 years, Aborigines gave the land nothing; took what they could find; wandered from one eaten-out place to another, leaving nature to repair the damage; created no arable culture; discovered no minerals and created no durable structures.[7]

The same letter spoke, by way of comparison, of the wonders of modern Australian achievement based on 'white sweat' and 'brilliantly applied intelligence', and complained of 'the Aboriginal holiday camp at Noonkanbah costing taxpayers $2 million a year for virtually no return'. In other letters and interviews in 1980, he used such throwaway lines as: 'the alleged spirituality of the Aborigines is a front', 'they aren't religious, they are animists', and 'sacred sites have been invented'.

The Community replied to the Mitchell/Grayden message with a tape from Dicky Skinner to Grayden. They agreed to meet with Sir Charles Court, but insisted that Phil Vincent of the ALS and Jimmy Bieunderry attend the meeting. On the basis of their experience with the Government thus far they were not prepared to trust Court without witnesses present. The tape also made it clear that they were not going to abandon their defence of their land:

> We will be friends if you go along with the Law to help us. If you don't go with the Law, with our Law, well that means we can't help you. We already told you that this is a sacred site; it's very important. Now you just don't listen.

After a bit of public sparring the meeting was set for 30 May. But before this, there was a meeting with Senator Chaney on the 18th. This followed his refusal to come at the time of the KLC meeting in mid-April, on the grounds that the forum would not be 'a good time for serious discussions with the community'[8], and the Community's subsequent refusal to meet with him a week later, because it would be busy mustering.

By the time of the meeting with Chaney the Community attitude had hardened even further as a result of the Grayden tape. There was also a growing feeling that perhaps the Government had lost the initiative in the dispute as the weeks passed. Public opinion polls had shown an equal three-way split between support for the Community, support for the Government, and the don't knows; with many of the don't knows indicating concern over the nature of the Government's campaign. The proposed talks with Court were interpreted by some of the media as a backdown by him from earlier assertions about the time for talking being over. Also, a well-publicised agreement had been reached between the oil giant Mobil and a group of Walmatjari people led by Bieunderry for oil exploration in the desert south-east of Noonkanbah that guaranteed protection of sites; this had been done without Government involvement.

One newspaper feature summarised these and other developments under the headline 'Sir Charles In Retreat', with the comment that:

> His threat to send the Amax drillers back on to Noonkanbah under police guard is now empty, because Amax does not want that and the Federal

Government in an election year, cannot afford to let it happen.[9]

In this atmosphere the Community was looking to pressure Senator Chaney. After the formalities, Chaney began by describing the range of support and assistance he and his Government had given the Community, and saying, 'I don't want one trouble to spoil all that'. Dicky Skinner replied, 'This one trouble from the mining company we're worried can spoil all this. It's happened in the past that white people did this, and we don't want it to happen again.'[10]

Chaney wanted to discuss the State's proposed conditions for social protection and limits on the company, such as a fence around the drill site. Skinner's riposte of 'Any snake can get through a fence' was followed by Ivan McPhee, 'We just want that area left alone; not the miners fenced in it'.

When Chaney tried to suggest that it was necessary to examine and talk about all the issues to find the answer that he believed was there, McPhee replied, 'Is the answer to let the company in? Is that the answer you want?' Chaney responded that it may be.

When the people asked for his response to the idea of a three-year moratorium he was at first sceptical. But they explained that they wanted to use this time to undertake a complete mapping of sites with the help of David Mowaljarli. Nipper Tabagee spoke of the Law and the fears the people had, and Skinner referred to the disappearance of the kangaroos after the drilling at Pea Hill. Chaney seemed half-convinced, and suggested that they should talk about these things to Court, saying, 'I believe he will take notice. He has said he will.'

He was asked again and again whether he would support the moratorium proposal. At first he said it wasn't his area, the request would have to go to the State, then he argued that three years was too long; eventually he agreed to pass the request on to the State Government without endorsing it.

The meeting was not as tense as some that had been held with State Government representatives, but in the end it was equally unproductive for the participants.

Unknown to the Community or the public the stakes had increased dramatically for the State Government as negotiations for the meeting with the Premier were nearing completion. At the meeting in Houston attended by Max Reynolds, the Joint Venture companies decided that they had had enough:

> Partners in the Amax Joint Venture, aggravated by the ACTU pledge of support to aborigines on Noonkanbah, advised the Government on May 21 that they would release the rig at the end of the Woodada [Strata Oil] programme, unless some agreement or reconciliation could be reached with the aborigines. The final decision was deferred until after the Premier's visit.[11]

It was on this day, 21 May, that Premier Court finally agreed to the Community's conditions and the date for the meeting. He now faced the prospect of total isolation in his crusade if he could not achieve an extraordinary breakthrough at Noonkanbah.

The media of course was intensely interested in the proceedings, but both sides had agreed that they should be excluded in the interests of a freer discussion, so they remained in Derby when the Premier flew out on Friday morning, 30 May.

Clearly Court came with no intention of changing his basic position, but he offered two new ideas in an attempt to sway the Community. The first was an offer of special twenty-one year leases direct to the Community of Pea Hill and the other five 'genuine specific sacred sites' in the area. The second was an offer that the State Energy Commission

Bob Mululby.

drill the hole instead of Amax, if this was preferable to the Community.

The meeting in the shearing shed lasted five hours, in three sessions. Court and one of his staff, Community members, Bieunderry and Vincent were the only people present. Records of the meeting come from detailed notes kept by Vincent. What they reveal more than anything else is Court's seeming inability to actually listen to and hear what the people were saying to him. For months he had claimed that the situation had been created by external forces, and that the Elders, given the chance, would see reason. Here he was sitting with them, hearing the same message from the horse's mouth, yet still believing the horse was a ventriloquist's dummy.

Nipper Tabagee opened proceedings by thanking him for coming, and immediately stating the Elders' position:

> We need that place that everybody's talking about. It's been there since the beginning of time, now we are looking after it. That word has been from the beginning. If people touch that place, then everybody get upset. There is something underneath.

Court did not try to find out what Tabagee meant, or what the Community felt. He moved to the ground from which he felt safe to argue by saying, 'We cannot put a blanket over a large area like Noonkanbah, the Kimberley or Western Australia' – which was not what Tabagee had been talking about at all – and then pulled out a map and said, 'There are five sacred sites'.

He made his offer to protect these, and gave a long rundown on the conditions that would be imposed on the company, and the benefits such as the water bore the Community would get. Tabagee tried again: 'But that's right on top of a sacred site where they want to drill'. Court replied again by saying they couldn't put a blanket over the whole of Noonkanbah. One of the old men put in: 'We know this area, kangaroos went away, now goannas. Something might get up and kill everybody.' But no impression was made. Court ignored Jimmy Bieunderry's allegations of site damage by Amax in 1978; he claimed that all the anthropologists and Aborigines he spoke to agreed that drilling was acceptable as long as the sites were protected; he rejected the three-year moratorium idea out of hand when it was raised.

After a break for lunch the meeting went back to the starting point, with Tabagee expanding upon his previous attempts to describe the importance of the land at stake, and the people's fears. This is what Chaney had urged the Community to do.

> If the drill comes that will make people upset. Bob Mululby got sick by that place. His grandfather said, 'You never protect it, that place I gave you'. His grandfather said this in a Dream and talked about this goanna place. Another place was drilled – kangaroo place – now no kangaroos anywhere. Same with this place. I know it's all right for white people, but not for us. We can't see it cut up in half...We don't want argument all the time, but just can't come in our country all the time where you find something. It's important for all our people. That's all I can say.

Court either could not or would not understand. He responded to Tabagee, 'Are you saying you are not prepared to allow anyone to drill on Noonkanbah?' Of course, Tabagee had not been talking about this at all, but with the frustration level rising, when the question was put he answered yes, and Court was away:

> Well that is not what we can sustain. Other Aborigines would not back that up. This is a breach of your pastoral lease, it is a serious situation.

Sir Charles Court, Noonkanbah woolshed, 30 May 1980. *(Courtesy Bobby Kogolo.)*

Clearly the Community's message was not getting through, so after more argument Tabagee eventually brought out the stone map, the darrugu. Court virtually ignored this, saying, 'This does not solve anything', and he started talking about the conditions and special leases, and then raised the SEC drilling option.

Eventually he asked the question, albeit with a sarcastic twist, that he should have begun with in response to Nipper's explanations: 'Where does the area of influence finish, at the boundary?'

Skinner and Bieunderry explained it just as it had been identified in the original Bindon report. They amplified on this by explaining that here were two different clans whose territory was involved. Skinner had been through this many times before, and often used the analogy of boundaries being like fences that divide the land of each clan.

A startling illustration of Court's inability to listen is seen in his description of this episode in Parliament some time later:

> I then said, 'Look, when you talk about areas of influence, how far does this influence extend around a genuine sacred site?' Then they went into a huddle to try to agree amongst themselves. I said, 'Is it a mile? Is it two miles? Is it ten miles?'
>
> They could not agree amongst themselves and they said, 'Look, there are two groups of us. Some on that side of the fence believe it is one thing;

some on the other side of the fence believe it is another.' That is the sort of situation we are in.[12]

Vincent's notes end with a poignant plea from Olive Bieunderry:

Can't these people just be left alone. Isn't Barrow Island* and the rest of Australia enough? These people are out of their minds with tension.

The meeting dragged on, but there was no progress, no change. Court's offer of the special leases and SEC drilling was formally rejected.

The next day Premier Court wrote a five-page letter to the Community repeating the details of the offer he had made and asking them to reconsider:

I am sure that most members of your Community would agree that the Western Australian Government and myself have shown a genuine desire to consider your representations over many months leading up to my personal visit yesterday...

I am sure your Community will understand that the Government must allow the drilling to proceed. I endeavoured to make this clear on Friday. The programme and conditions we proposed have full regard for your expressed views. I would hope that, now you have had time to reflect on our long discussions on Friday, you will understand that the Government has gone a long way to meet your wishes.

I sincerely hope you will now join with us in making it possible to proceed in a peaceful way. There are many benefits that can accrue to the local community under the programme we propose but these cannot be achieved to the maximum extent possible if you continue to oppose the proposals.

I have to make it clear that your three-year moratorium proposal is not an alternative. It would achieve nothing but postpone the day when drilling has to take place...

I would be failing in my duty if I did not remind you of the damage your stand on this matter could do to the Aboriginal people. There are many people in the community – including myself – who want to help you but you make it very difficult if you adopt an uncompromising attitude by demanding what you claim are your rights but refuse to acknowledge that other people might have some needs and rights also.[13]

Unless one side collapsed under the pressure it seemed that there was now no resolution short of total confrontation. It was merely a matter of the tactics each side would adopt.

The Community mulled over Court's letter and the state of play for some days before replying. When it did, in the form of a letter signed by eight of the senior Elders, there was no hint of any remorse or concession. Indeed the opening lines were perhaps stronger than anything else they had said to that time:

---

* Barrow Island is off the north-west coast of Western Australia. It is a rich oil field. The Premier had referred to it during the meeting as an example of what a producing oil field would look like.

At the meeting on the 30th May, 1980, and in your letter dated 31st May 1980, you assumed that we recognise the State Government's ownership of the Land. Instead of this you should have recognised us, the Elders who hold the law for this country, as the real owners of the Land.

You are wrong thinking that the Museum and others know everything about our Law and Sacred Areas. Already the Museum has treated the maps they made of our Sacred Areas like a comic. Do you think we would be trying so hard to stop the drilling if that area was not important to us?

We have our own Law which we must live by, and we have our own religion which we must protect. By forcing this drilling programme to go ahead you are denying us our right to religious freedom.

We do not trust the State Government or Amax or any mining company as they put money above our Sacred Areas.

Amax did not come and ask us where the Sacred Areas were when they first came. Instead, they pushed their bulldozers through our Sacred Areas and cut our fences. If they had asked us three years ago we would have shown them where it was safe to drill. The mining companies and the Government are greedy.

To expect us to tell you everything in our Law in one day is arrogant. The State Government has not given us a proper hearing and you demonstrated this on Friday. Instead of talking you should have been listening; instead of assuming you had all the knowledge, you should have been trying to learn.

At the moment there is a contract surveyor working for the Government, placing pegs in our Sacred Areas, and working in places he should not be. He is breaking our Law and the State Government's [Heritage Act]...You do not even treat us with respect.

If the drilling goes ahead, you will be placing our Community and those working on the drilling site in great danger. We do not know if we will be able to protect ourselves or the people working the rig. We are frightened...

We cannot agree to Amax mining in our Sacred Areas because we would be breaking our Law. We cannot break our Law. If you force the drilling on our Sacred Areas, we cannot help you and you will be held responsible for the consequences.

This is a rich country and the Government is living off land that belongs to the Aboriginal. It is riding on the back of the Aboriginal.[14]

15

THE PROSPECT OF
CONFRONTATION

The Government talks about one law for everybody. But it looks like they
only use the laws they have to keep us down.

Yungngora Community Press Release, 19 June 1980.

A series of incidents in the first three weeks of June, immediately after the Premier's visit, did little to improve the Community's temper.

First came an attempt by two senior officers from the Museum to do a site investigation for the access road and enlarged drilling area now required by the Government. At that stage the Community still did not know of the Government's plan to resume the road and enlarge the drill site. The Museum officers' radio telegram requesting permission to visit was received at Noonkanbah on 4 June, but it did not identify the purpose of the visit. The Community had by now become cynical about the Museum and its role in the dispute, and wanted to know more. As a subsequent press release explained:

> The Community refused to allow the Museum employees to visit the station because they had only been informed the day before, and because they felt that the Museum was now being used by the Government to push mining through. They said if the Community is given proper notice and told what the Museum employees wish to do on the station the Community will consider whether or not to see them.[1]

In the same week, two contract surveyors working for the Mines Department were discovered in the course of mapping work in the area under contention. They had re-established an old trig point on top of Pea Hill itself, and clambered over Tatju Hill, just south of the river.

When the two surveyors returned the next Monday, 9 June, to continue their work, they were asked to leave the station and come back on the Friday for a meeting to discuss what they were doing.

The third incident was more fundamentally disturbing to the Community. On the same Monday that the surveyors were turned away another man turned up uninvited and unannounced. He sought out Nipper Tabagee and Ivan McPhee, telling them that he was a film maker, and that he wanted to make a film for the ABC.

He set up camp on Noonkanbah, and when approached by Dicky Skinner the next day, said he was a surveyor, and that he wanted to survey the sacred sites. When Skinner pointed out that this had already been done by the Museum, he argued that he was independent, and did not work for the Government like the Museum.

The next day he managed to arrange a meeting with a number of the old men. The Elders' puzzled and fearful report of this meeting, as relayed later that day to Les Mack – the Principal of the Community School – and me, was along these lines: he claimed that he was there on behalf of the Government, and that he had been involved in Land Rights in South Australia, and he argued the case for drilling; he told them that if they agreed to the drilling, the company would build houses, a school, dams, bores and roads, and spoke of freehold title to the land and mining royalties.

He also told them that if they tried to stop the mining going ahead the police would come and some of them would be shot, and the rest would be forced to leave Noonkanbah. And he spoke of arranging a plane for the Elders to go to Perth to meet with Premier Court.

In an effort to discover what was going on, information was passed back through the school radio to the Nomads office in Perth. Nomads contacted the Premier's office to find out if they knew anything about it all. They said they had no knowledge of the man.

The next morning, 12 June, the film maker/surveyor radioed from Derby to say that he would be there with a plane that afternoon. When told that the Premier's office had disowned him, and that no one would be going on his plane, he insisted that he was working for the Premier, and had spoken to him the previous night.

Nomads contacted Court's office again. This time they were told that the person they had spoken to before had not been fully briefed, and had been unaware of previous developments. Though the man was independent, the Premier knew of his work, and would support any agreement he made.

The mystery of this bizarre episode was never properly unravelled, but an Amax report to the Mines Department does reveal that 'An independent surveyor volunteered in early June to visit Noonkanbah to assess Aboriginal attitudes on behalf of the Joint Venture'.[2] So it would appear that this interloper was operating with the blessing of the company and the Government.

With all this going on, the Community took steps to try to bring some semblance of order to the stream of unwelcome visitors that seemed to be besieging them. A press release on 11 June explained the refusal to see the Museum officers and the departure of the contract surveyors, and concluded with a demand that all visitors and Government departments go through the proper channels if they wished to come to Noonkanbah, as 'the Community is sick of visitors of all kinds arriving at the station with little or no warning'.[3]

The Government countered by interpreting these developments as an attempt by the Community to impose a complete ban on entry by Europeans. It used this claim as a justification in announcing the gazettal of the access road as a public road on 10 June, a month after they had made the first moves in this direction. Peter Jones, the Minister for Mines, claimed that the surveyors 'had been surrounded and virtually held prisoner for some time by about 25 or 30 Aborigines at Noonkanbah'. On the same day, Bill Grayden wrote to the Museum Trustees and formally directed them to consent to the use of the enlarged site and the road, and for third time, the Trustees complied with a ministerial direction.

The incident with the surveyors had taken place near the school, and had been witnessed by Les Mack and his wife and mother-in-law. They were all astounded by Jones' claim. The discussion had not been a friendly one, but at no stage was there the remotest suggestion that the surveyors had been or were likely to be detained against their will.

The surveyors eventually came back on the 17th with a police escort. A long meeting failed to reach any agreement. It had been reasonably amicable until one of the surveyors claimed that the people made up sacred sites as they went along, and therefore refused to guarantee to abide by the directions of guides the Community offered to supply. They went ahead and did their work of mapping mining claims, and presumably the newly excised drill site, with a permanent police escort, prompting another Community press release:

Sir Charles Court and his Ministers have been telling lies about we people for a long time now, trying to say we are wild people who break our word and threaten other people all the time.

But what is he doing to us? He is trying to threaten and scare us, and he breaks his word to us. He told us when he came to Noonkanbah that he would protect our sacred sites... Only two days after Sir Charles was here, offering us a lease to protect Pea Hill, two surveyors were climbing all over it and putting a peg in there. Now they have got the police here with those same surveyors, going all round the area where our old people are buried. And there are four more police hiding in the bush near the station. What are they here for? We never hurt anybody. We never used any violence. And those surveyors are breaking the government's own law, the Aboriginal Heritage Act.

The government talks about one law for everybody. But it looks like they only use the laws they have to keep us down, not the law they made that was meant to protect our sacred places.[4]

Behind the scenes, the Government had some problems to work out. At the Woodada well near Eneabba, the drill had struck gas. On 4 June, Strata Oil advised that it needed to drill a second hole to ascertain the worth of its find. If this were allowed it would make the timetable for a drilling operation at Noonkanbah before the possible onset of the wet season very tight indeed. Yet the Government could hardly justify pulling the rig out of a successful program when it was not yet in a position to guarantee its movement to Noonkanbah. Jones gave his approval for drilling of the second well.

In one way this was perhaps a blessing for the Government. Amax had advised that it would release the rig at the end of the Woodada program if Court's meeting at Noonkanbah had not produced results. At least the Government now had some time to persuade Amax.

Jones was given the job, and reading between the lines, it seems it was no easy matter. Some hint of the resistance he found is given in a report lodged with his department a few days later by Amax.

Meetings have continued with both State and Federal Government on the Noonkanbah problem culminating in meetings in Honolulu on June 11 and 12 between the Minister for Mines and Joint Venture representatives. The Joint Venture agreed finally to make one more attempt to drill the well in view of the Government's intention to resume the access road and area of 4 hectares around the drilling location, and having been assured of adequate protection.[5]

Jones' quick trip to Honolulu was anything but a pleasure jaunt. One is left to wonder whether perhaps there were any threats made to EP97 and the other nearby permits, along with the promises of support.

Within days of Jones' return to Perth, either as part of the deal with Amax, or as insurance against any decision by the company to withdraw, the Government quietly organised the incorporation of a company named Omen.[6] This two dollar company, with a pair of Perth solicitors as shareholders, was to play a crucial role in the months to come. A senior partner in the law firm that employed the two solicitors was Ian Warner, the State President of the Liberal Party, and a close colleague of Court's.

Omen remained a secret for the time being, but in Perth word had leaked out about the former trucking company executive engaged to prepare a report for Cabinet on options for transporting the rig north. When Opposition parliamentarian Peter Dowding suggested that the Government had developed contingency plans to use the police and the State Emergency Service to escort a convoy of trucks to carry the rig to Noonkanbah, Court 'described such reports as "romancing or mischief making"'.[7]

Federal Cabinet had discussed Noonkanbah and its ramifications on 3 June. It saw little hope of positive resolution, and was already concentrating on damage control. On the 6th, Prime Minister Malcolm Fraser wrote to Court:

> We are now faced with the prospect of confrontation...It is important that both governments should be as one on the issues and jointly we are in the best possible position to demonstrate both in Australia and overseas that despite the Aboriginal community's opposition to drilling, Aboriginal interests are being protected. For this reason I should be grateful if you could keep me informed.[8]

Fraser went on to say that he had asked a group of six Ministers to examine the issues, and that two of them, Senator Chaney and Attorney-General Peter Durack, another Western Australian Senator, would be available for talks with the State. But his diplomatic expressions of concern apparently cut no ice with Sir Charles Court, who replied the same day:

> [I am] rather concerned that you are now suggesting that we have to further demonstrate both in Australia and overseas that the Aboriginal interests are being protected...I think we now have to work on the basis that it is confrontation between the Community and the Western Australian Government ...
>
> We are only too pleased to keep you informed of the events, but I am rather disturbed that you seem to be marshalling a Ministerial team with very serious prospects of not only having a confrontation between the Aboriginal community and the Western Australian Government, but also between the Commonwealth Government and the Government of Western Australia. I hope this is not the intention because our position is very clear in the matter...
>
> If the Commonwealth Government has any intention of claiming to have some constitutional power to intervene in the matter I should like to hear from you as a matter of urgency.[9]

Fraser and Chaney were most uncomfortable with Court's hard-nosed attitude; but there was little they could do in the face of his determination. They were not privy to the preparations the State was making. Perhaps if they had been, they might have considered some sort of preventive action more seriously.

Chaney, to his credit, continued to act and argue at a general level for his more enlightened approach. He answered some of the more rabid letters to the papers in fine style. He appointed Jimmy Bieunderry as one of the Commissioners of the new Aboriginal Development Commission, which he established as a largely Aboriginal-controlled land and enterprise agency. This happened less than a week after Bill Grayden had launched a public attack on Bieunderry for going to the Netherlands for a World Council of Churches conference on racism. Bieunderry's trip was the first significant move to internationalise the Noonkanbah dispute.

Chaney went back to Federal Cabinet on 20 June with an options paper on the Noonkanbah dispute. Presumably Federal intervention was one of the options discussed, but Chaney insists it was never a realistic one. It seemed that there was nothing they could do but sit on the fence and await developments.

This fence sitting produced some curious statements from Fraser and Chaney. Fraser embarked on a week-long tour of the north-west that was seen by the pundits as a trial campaign run for the coming election. In Derby on 1 July he met with a gathering of Aboriginal people, and inevitably Noonkanbah was the major issue raised. Fraser commented:

> On the question of sacred sites as I understand it I don't know of any difference between the Aboriginal people – the people of Noonkanbah – the West Australian Government or the Commonwealth Government. There has been an absolute commitment on the part of the Premier Sir Charles Court that sacred sites will be protected, and that of course is the view of the Commonwealth, and the view I am quite certain he would want us to adopt.[10]

Premier Court and the Noonkanbah Elders would have been quite surprised to find they shared the same views. Fraser followed this with an assertion of the national importance of the oil search, and an appeal to the Community 'to look to its Elders, those with great experience and wisdom'[11], – an implied backing for Court's assertions of manipulation. Court must have been pleased with the newspaper headlines: 'Fraser Warns Aborigines', and 'Fraser Backs WA On Noonkanbah'.

The Labor Opposition at State and Federal levels were strident in their criticisms, but making little headway. The State Party was unsuccessfully probing for details of the Government's plans and preparations, and proposing changes to the Aboriginal Heritage Act to remove Ministerial control and place disputes in the hands of a judicial tribunal.

The Federal Party was making repeated calls for Fraser and Chaney to intervene. And late in June Stewart West released a new Aboriginal Affairs policy, which amongst other things promised to use Section 51 of the Constitution to intervene at Noonkanbah, and similar situations that might arise elsewhere. This promised another faint hope for Noonkanbah; if Amax could be frustrated beyond the wet season deadline, and if Federal Opposition Leader Bill Hayden could lead Labor to victory against Fraser, Court could be overridden.

From the north-west Fraser went to Perth to attend the annual conference of the State branch of the Liberal Party, where he said:

> At Derby I made it plain that on the Commonwealth's part, we stood as one with the State, in firmly believing and supporting the State in a State commitment to preserve sacred sites. Also I indicated that the support of the State and its determination in the national interest, that drilling must, at the appropriate time proceed.[12]

Senator Chaney's isolation in his home State Party became clear when the *West Australian* reported his speech to the conference under the headline 'Don't Exclude Me, Says Chaney':

> It has interested me that over the 16 months or so that I have held this portfolio, I have not had, that I can recall, any invitation to speak to a Liberal Party group on Aboriginal affairs. It has interested me that in a field in which there is a great deal of debate within the Liberal Party, you are totally uninterested in my taking part in the debate.[13]

But Fraser's speech had also contained the first indirect hint of behind the scenes negotiations. He suggested that as a result of discussions with Chaney and Acting Western Australian Premier Ray O'Connor (Court had departed for a three-week overseas trip), negotiations between the State Government and the Community were likely to take place.

After the State's move to resume the road and drill site the union movement realised that Court was prepared to go to extraordinary lengths to defeat their bans and the Community opposition. A group of union and Labor Party figures got Peter Cook to write to Bob Hawke of the ACTU and ask him to arrange a meeting between the ACTU and the Federal Government.

This led to a meeting in Melbourne between Hawke and Chaney on 2 July. Both men made it clear that they were seeking a negotiated settlement, but Hawke also insisted that the union movement would continue to support the Community with bans unless an acceptable agreement could be reached.

Chaney indicated that he 'felt sure the WA Government was anxious to find a positive settlement and would be likely to be responsive to any gesture from the aboriginal community'.[14] They agreed that the most appropriate 'gestures' might be a shortening of the moratorium period from three years, and a clear acceptance of the possibility of drilling in alternative areas. It was agreed that the content of their discussions would remain confidential, except that Chaney said he would report to Court.

At about the same time Ernie Bridge, the State Member of Parliament representing the Kimberley area, had had a private meeting with Court, before the Premier's departure overseas, following separate discussions Bridge had held with the Community. Bridge believed that he had come away from his meeting with Court with an undertaking that the Government would seriously consider any new proposals from the Community, and that the Government would make no further moves until it had received and considered such a proposal.

When these developments were reported back to Noonkanbah, there was a feeling that a breakthrough might have finally been made; perhaps the use of these intermediaries could succeed where direct discussions had continually foundered in the chasm of poor communication.

The Community leaders sat down with Bridge, and worked up a proposal that contained the two key elements that Chaney and Hawke had identified, yet maintained their strong stand on the defence of sacred lands in general, and the Pea Hill complex in particular.

On 17 July, they put this framework as their terms of settlement:

Sir Charles Court,

We have asked Mr Ernie Bridge to deliver this letter to you for your consideration. We want to put these proposals to you as a way of reaching agreement on the question of mining on Noonkanbah. We hope you will accept this as being made in good faith in a real effort to resolve these difficult questions. The main thing is that we must know that all our sacred places will be safe from mining and that you will believe our word about these places.

We have asked Ernie Bridge to take this word to you, and now we wait for your answer.

Proposed Agreement Between State Government and Yungngora Community.

1. The community agrees to carry out a program of mapping of sacred areas on the station in conjunction with Museum and community anthropologists by stages as follows:

(a) The area along the Fitzroy River from Paradise to Quanbun boundaries and ten miles north of the river, by the end of this year.

(b) Balance of the station done within eighteen months.

2. Such mapping to be done on the following conditions:

(a) The Government is to accept any future recommendations of the Museum.

(b) The mapping to be carried out with the present Aboriginal Heritage Act to apply.

(c) No mineral exploration to be carried out on the station until the mapping is done, then such exploration to be done through negotiations between the parties involved.

3. To that end the community undertakes to negotiate with the Government towards terms and conditions for such mining explorations and development on those areas of the station which are not Aboriginal sites within the meaning of the Heritage Act.

4. No drilling on protected areas or mineral explorations of any kind within such areas.

5. A promise from the Government that it will accept any further recommendations from the Museum about the protection of sacred areas.

6. A promise that there will at no time be mining or drilling in the area delineated by the Museum Report of 1979 and recommended for protection.

7. The cancellation of all mineral leases held in the area mentioned in 6 above.

8. This agreement to be properly drafted by government and community solicitors and signed by both parties.

Signed by Joe Wunmah, Bob Mululby, Mick Michael and George Bell.

In effect the Community was saying that it would accept the law of the Parliament, the Aboriginal Heritage Act, as the determinant of the dispute; but only if the Government undertook to accept the spirit of the Act, and the judgement of the experts; and if the Government would give them the time to ensure that its provisions could apply before mining activity proceeded. They had to add the proviso of the Heritage Act in its current form, because on 13 July the Government had announced its intention to make amendments to the Act as a matter of priority once the Parliament resumed sittings.

Bridge was to say later that when he first relayed the proposal to O'Connor, in his capacity as Acting Premier, the response had been reasonably positive, although no promises were given. But while the Community was waiting on an answer there were other developments that they saw as a breach of the understanding that the Government would take no new initiatives whilst the proposal was under consideration.

On 17 July it was revealed by the press that a water drilling rig owned by the Mines Department had been hired out to Amax, and had left Perth bound for Noonkanbah to complete the job Brian McGaffin had left undone in April. The next day Peter Dowding said that this action had been taken to sabotage sensitive negotiations. The cat was out of the bag.

By the 19th the *West Australian* had revealed the nature of the Community's proposal, but could get no comment from O'Connor. The same day an advertisement appeared under the auspices of the Government's Transport Commission calling for personal applications from truck owners for an unspecified operation that could only be the transport of the oil rig from Eneabba to Noonkanbah. Applicants had this confirmed, and were told to be on standby to move at less than twelve hours' notice.

On 20 July, a Saturday, Dicky Skinner publicly confirmed the Community's proposal to the Government, saying:

> We thought that these talks and our proposal would be secret, and we were
> told that there would be no moves to start drilling while the talks were
> going on. Now the whole lot is in the newspapers, and there is a drilling
> rig on its way to Noonkanbah.
> We have tried to do the right thing to sort this business out, and we
> hope the government will still listen to our proposal. But it is very hard
> for us to sit quiet and wait when a drilling rig is on its way here. We still
> can't let that drill go down in our sacred area, and we must try to protect
> that place.[15]

It would seem that the proposal must have received some serious consideration within
the Government as a starting point for negotiations. It cannot have been rejected out
of hand, for on 22 July, Peter Cook rang Bob Hawke at midday from Perth, after speaking
to O'Connor, to say that there was still a possibility of a negotiated settlement, but
time was running out.[16]

But the hardliners prevailed; on the same day the Government's reply was sent to
Noonkanbah by Ray O'Connor. It was an outright rejection. Point by point answers were
given to the Community proposal. There was 'surprise' that it would take eighteen months
to map sites; a rejection of the notion of giving the Museum Trustees the final say
on sites, and an expressed determination to continue with the planned Heritage Act
amendments; a refusal to 'negotiate special terms and conditions for mineral exploration
where there are no Aboriginal sacred sites'; and a guarantee to 'protect genuine identified
sacred sites', with a repeat of Court's previous offer of special leases.[17] O'Connor's letter
concluded:

> We note that you agree in principle to mining on Noonkanbah. As the permit
> holders intend to put down only one exploratory petroleum drill hole this
> year on a site that does not affect your sacred sites, we presume that you
> will have no objection to the work proceeding.[18]

Publicly the Government presented the Community proposal as an outrageous tactic
designed merely to stall for time, and suggested that acceptance would have been an
abdication of responsibility of the rule of law. O'Connor said:

> Close examination of the community's proposal reveals two fundamentally
> unacceptable principles that are the basis of their position. The first is that
> the Yungngora Community and the Noonkanbah pastoral lease are to be
> regarded as outside the normal law and administration of the State of Western
> Australia. The second is that the Government of this State must go outside
> the laws that bind it and must abandon its duty to accept responsibility
> for decisions made in the name of the people of Western Australia. No
> government can negotiate on those bases and still call itself a government.[19]

O'Connor's assertions about the processes and the rigidity of the law are difficult
to accept. The original and subsequent decisions to override the recommendations of
the Museum Trustees, and direct them to approve of use of the land for oil drilling,
were exercises of ministerial discretion that the courts had accepted were legitimate
steps within the framework of the law. Equally open to ministerial discretion within
the terms of the Mining Act was a decision to cancel or temporarily suspend the right
to work on any particular mineral claim.

As the Community had pointed out a month earlier, the Government was being selective on the grounds of political bias as to how it would apply the respective laws. It would 'only use the laws they have to keep us down, not the law they made that was supposed to protect our sacred places'.[20]

One reason for the success of the hardliners in the Government, apart from the reluctance to admit any semblance of error or defeat, was probably the developing situation in the East Kimberley with regard to the Argyle diamond find. Precedents under the Aboriginal Heritage Act were beginning to loom particularly large up there.

Two anthropological surveys had found that CRA Exploration had severely damaged one Aboriginal site in the course of their work, and that the major diamond pipe emerged from the bowels of the earth at another site, and that damage had already been done there. Back in February, after the first survey, the miners had written to the Museum seeking permission to utilise the site at the main diamond deposit, but to date had not received an official answer.

In May, John Toby, with the support of the Warmun Community at Turkey Creek, had initiated a private prosecution against CRA under the Heritage Act for the site damage. Early in July, after experiencing difficulties in proceeding with the action, because he had no powers under the Act to investigate or demand information of the company as an individual, Toby agreed to withdraw his action in favour of prosecution by the Museum.

Bill Grayden asked the Museum Trustees to defer any action, and at their meeting on 14 July the Trustees agreed to do so. Complaints by the Warmun Community and the KLC of improper political pressure received some coverage, but tended to get lost in the blanket coverage of Noonkanbah developments. In announcing the proposed changes to the Heritage Act, Grayden made no reference to the Argyle situation, where even by the Government's own standards there was no doubt that a 'genuine, identified' site had already been damaged, and was in danger of total obliteration if the mine went ahead; Noonkanbah was their justification.

So the Noonkanbah compromise was rejected out of hand and, in effect, war was declared. The Government shrugged off expressions of outrage from many quarters, and assertions from the unions that they were more determined than ever, in the face of the Government's intransigence, to uphold their bans.

On 24 July, with the Mines Department water rig camped on Calwynyardah Station, just north of the Noonkanbah boundary, objections to the road and site resumption were dismissed after the formality of a hearing at which the ALS presented the Community's opposition. The Government and the police now had formal control of the road; any further blockades would be clearly illegal.

The same day Senator Chaney again went to Noonkanbah. Four hours of talks at the homestead and the drill site produced no last minute breakthroughs. Dicky Skinner told reporters afterwards that the Community was disappointed with Chaney's approach, which was to tell them that drilling was now inevitable, and to make the best of a bad situation. He unsuccessfully sought an assurance from the Community that they would keep their protests within the bounds of the law. He once again rejected the possibility of the Federal Government intervening.

The other issue discussed with Chaney was a last ditch possibility. The failure of Amax to complete their 1978 seismic survey due to the unseasonal rain and the antagonism caused by their bulldozing of sites had come to light. The Community suggested that perhaps Amax could complete the unfinished work in an effort to find an alternative drilling site. But Peter Cook had already gone to O'Connor in Perth that morning to convey the idea, and within hours Peter Jones had telegrammed him to say that it was out of the question, purely on the grounds that it would force the deferment of drilling that year.

On the 25th Jones announced that the State Government 'had moved in as planned to take over the transport of the oil drilling rig set aside for Noonkanbah', in response to a formal request from Amax.[21] He felt constrained to add, 'I am disappointed that the private transport companies whose business it is to undertake transport have seen fit to succumb to the pressure of industrial blackmail rather than undertake work which is available'.[22]

The same day, the water rig moved on to the station, accompanied by an earth-moving crew to complete Jeremy O'Driscoll's work, contractors to erect a fence around the site, and two senior police. Tom Lyon had been replaced, and the man in charge for Amax on this occasion was a freelance drilling contractor they had engaged by the name of Keith Arnott. At the point where the newly resumed road left the Noonkanbah airstrip and headed towards the drill site, this convoy of seven vehicles was met by a blockade of about thirty people sitting in front of a Toyota parked sideways across the road.

The police failed to persuade the people to abandon the blockade. A mini-bus with seven extra officers was called up. Superintendent Bowers informed them that they were on public property, not their station; a telex with the legal details of the resumption was read out. Bowers said, 'This is law now, the Parliament has made it law. If you people don't move now, you will be breaking that law and will be liable to be arrested.

The blockade, 25 July 1980.

The drama unfolds. Top: Keith Arnott of Amax arguing with the Noonkanbah people. Bottom: Superintendent Bowers informs the people that the road and drill site are no longer part of the Station lease.

We must warn you that we will take action if you refuse to move.'[23] Four of the reinforcements were ordered to march forward and break up the protest.

The blockade started to waver. Some of the Strelley mob urged them to hold firm. But the Elders decided that it was not the time to make their stand. With the protest having been organised at the last minute, they were not buoyed up the way they had been back in April, and their fear of the police and arrest prevailed. After some discussion, they gave the word to stand back, and the convoy passed through and continued on to the site. Amax was back in occupation.

The military overtones of the occupation were reinforced by an article three days later in the *Daily News*.

The confrontation continues. Bottom left: An impasse. Bottom right: The police advance.

The police break up the blockade.

The Amax drilling site at Noonkanbah Station has all the trappings of a desert fort. Police sentries guard the entrance gate – the only gate – and a sturdy wire mesh security fence has begun to ring the perimeter of the four hectare area. The impression of a wild west 'them-and-us' stronghold is unmistakable.

When a WA Newspapers team called at the site, two policemen stepped from the shade of a tent near the gate and moved to the Press vehicle on the road outside. One of the khaki-uniformed officers asked for the driver's name...The police wanted to know who we represented and noted the registration number of the vehicle. There was no invitation to proceed into the drill area...

It was noticeable that the mesh wire of the fence did not extend to the top of the metal poles. Three holes in the top sections of the poles appeared to be for single threads of security wire.[24]

As well as their camp at the drill site, the police had established a base on Calwynyardah Station. They were making their presence well and truly felt. Nearly every vehicle that travelled the road was now being stopped, and the drivers were quizzed about licences, whether they were carrying guns, and how long they were staying or when they would be returning to Noonkanbah. This questioning included a delegation of sixty odd people that had come into Noonkanbah to give messages of solidarity after a KLC meeting downriver at Looma on the 26th and 27th.

The police insisted that the boundary gate be left open, despite the fact that this allowed cattle to wander off the property. Police cars would come at all hours, and cruise around the open plain in front of the Community camps, some kilometres off the gazetted road. In the midst of the crisis the stockcamp was still mustering, and were holding cattle at the Sandy Billabong yards and holding paddock, a few kilometres from the homestead, also well off the road. On the night of the 26th police cars were moving around there. In the middle of the night they drove right up to the sleeping stockcamp, playing their headlights over the men, and they spooked the cattle, almost causing a stampede.

On the Monday, 28 July, the Community wrote to the ALS asking them to lodge complaints with the Commissioner of Police about the behaviour of his men. The Community was feeling harrassed and beseiged.

On the 30th, Dicky Skinner and Ivan McPhee wrote to Gordon Jackson, the chairman of Colonial Sugar Refineries, the parent company of Richter Drilling, whose rig was the one to come to Noonkanbah. CSR was a large, diversified company with a reputation as one of the more reasonable and moderate players on the corporate scene, with a good relationship with the union movement. They told Jackson:

> The situation has now become desperate for us. A Mines Department water drill has forced its way through our people with a police guard. The police are running all over the station harrassing us and our visitors – yesterday the police even came and watched and took pictures of a sick old man being loaded on the flying doctor plane to go to hospital. And the Richter oil drill is said to be coming very soon.
>
> The goanna spirit under the ground must be saved, it is very important to us. We are afraid of what could happen if this drill goes down.
>
> So many people have come and heard us, but still tell us we must accept this drilling. They will not understand us.
>
> We call on you to use your power to stop the drilling rig and send it somewhere else. We have done all in our power so far to be reasonable and friendly without compromising our religion and our sacred places. Perhaps now you can help us.
>
> We invite you to come to Noonkanbah to hear straight from us about what is really going on. If you do this maybe you will be able to listen and believe, and see why it is so important...
>
> We invite you to Noonkanbah to talk with us. We call on you to make no decision on this drilling until you have done this, and can be aware of what you are doing to us if you tell the drill to go in.
>
> Please reply as soon as possible to tell us that you will call the drilling off, or that you will come to see us.[25]

The Community was also making plans for a large gathering of people in a couple of weeks' time. But no one really expected that they would be able to repeat their success of April this time, although none of us were quite prepared to dismiss the possibility if the old men swung into action again.

Aboriginal morale was dealt a blow at this time by another development. John Toby was not at the Looma KLC meeting; he was in Perth at the time with a small group of relatives.

CRA had decided that they would not allow themselves to be led down the Amax path of being directed by the Government into escalating confrontation. They decided to buy their way out of any potential trouble. Rumours had been circulating from early July that they had been having secret meetings with Toby and a small, select group amongst the wider spectrum of those with associations to the land threatened by the diamond mine. The rumours indicated that substantial sums of money were involved.

Toby had become frustrated by the lack of progress in his dispute with the company.

He also became aware that he was dealing with a billion dollar mine, not a wildcat oil well. And his Mandangala group was a new and fragile creature compared to Noonkanbah, struggling to find the funds and resources to establish themselves on the barren Glen Hill Pastoral Lease.

When the company made secret contact with him outside the channel of Warmun Community that had been used to that time, he made the judgement that he could not bear the burden he faced in continuing the struggle. It was a reasonable decision to take in the circumstances. What was not considered reasonable by many was the way he proceeded. Encouraged, aided and abetted by the company he agreed to do a secret deal.

Without informing the rest of his people, he and five of his closest family flew to Perth at the company's expense. The ALS refused an approach from the company to represent Toby at the signing of the deal, as they knew the people as a whole had not been informed of or involved in the move, and they had reservations about being brought in at such a late stage of such an important issue. Telegrams of protest to the company from Turkey Creek were ignored. The company brought in a private lawyer to allegedly represent Toby's interests.

The full details of the agreement entered into on 26 July between the company and the Toby group were never made public. But in essence the group agreed to drop all opposition to development of the mine in return for $200,000 in the first year, and $100,000 a year thereafter, to be provided in the form of capital works and equipment for the Mandangala Community and Glen Hill Pastoral Lease.[26] For the company it was a small price to pay in comparison to the anticipated profits.

The immediate reaction from the Warmun people and the KLC was bitter condemnation of Toby and the company. The divisions created amongst the people of the affected region took many years to subside, and have never been fully resolved. At the time it was the first real public departure by an Aboriginal group from the stand of principle on the Law and land that was being articulated by the KLC and typified by the Noonkanbah people; and as such it weakened this stand, at least in the eyes of some of the public.

The Government's reaction was ambiguous. In his first press conference on his return from overseas Sir Charles Court said that he welcomed the 'good neighbour arrangement'. Yet the next day he was insisting that the Government remained 'firmly opposed to direct cash payments by development enterprises to individuals or groups affected by mining exploration...to adopt any other approach would imply that land-holders had rights not granted under the law'.[27] His distinction between cash payments and payments in kind seemed rather tenuous, especially in the light of his earlier outrage at the supposed 'sites for sale' position he had accused Noonkanbah of. But then, he did not want to jeopardise the development of the Argyle prospect.

For a week and a half the uneasy stand off at Noonkanbah continued. The fence at the drill site was completed, the water bore was sunk, the police continued to roam all over the station at will. And everybody waited to see what would happen next.

During this tense interlude Senator Chaney and his predecessor as Aboriginal Affairs Minister, Ian Viner, co-authored a lengthy letter setting out their thoughts, which first appeared as an article in the *West Australian* on 4 August. There was some fine rhetoric, and some thinly veiled attacks on the State Government:

> It has been said the dispute [at Noonkanbah] is a cloak for land rights and that Western Australia does not want to introduce the evils of Northern Territory Land Rights legislation in the form of a black state and apartheid within its borders. [Grayden had said exactly this just a couple of days earlier.]

The allegation is as unfair to the Aborigines of Noonkanbah as it is false...

In WA it has become fashionable to ridicule and condemn [the] spiritual association with the land, to insult Aborigines to whom it is still of great importance, and to assert that sacred sites are found only after mineral exploration has uncovered promising finds on Aboriginal land. This attitude assumes that while the traditional culture of the Aboriginal people may be surviving in small pockets of isolated land in Central Australia and Arnhem Land, the invasion of the dominant white culture with its seductive trappings has effectively destroyed Aboriginal culture elsewhere. [Again, this echoed almost exactly recent statements of Grayden.]

Nothing could be further from the truth. Those who espouse this view are effectively cutting off all common ground for negotiating a just settlement in both social and economical terms with Australia's Aboriginal people. In simple terms it is an unwillingness to be tolerant, or to accept that all people do not have the same ways of looking at things. Importantly – and significantly for the Western Australian situation right now – it is a failure to accept the enduring qualities of Aboriginal culture which despite all odds have survived 200 years of the intrusion of western culture. The one aid to that survival has been land.

They argued the justice and benefits of the Northern Territory and South Australian Land Rights legislation, particularly the provisions these Acts made to regulate relationships between miners and Aboriginal communities on an agreed pattern, and then commented:

Other States, notably Queensland and WA, have been more hesitant and often openly hostile to the suggestion that Aborigines should have their traditional association with their land recognised in law through some form of ownership. But even Queensland moved dramatically forward by granting 50 year leases to Aurukun and Mornington Island communities with explicit recognition of traditional interests and the right to negotiate with mining companies.

The only solution that they could propose, though, was one that was unacceptable to both sides in the dispute:

One hears it said that financial compensation is discriminatory. Indeed it is the position taken by some over Noonkanbah. However, this is not the case. Under State mining laws, owners of private land around Australia have various rights including in some cases to negotiate terms and conditions for mining to take place on their land.

It is ironic that the Noonkanbah issue, which has brought land rights into focus in Western Australia, should centre on the question of equal rights after centuries of what can only be described as unequal rights...

In Noonkanbah, cultural tradition through language, ritual and lifestyle is still strong and, despite all odds, still surviving. There are many projects which could benefit from cash flowing from compensation for mining incursion...

At Noonkanbah established Aboriginal interests of a traditional nature have been overridden in the interest of the wider community in oil exploration. Legally the Noonkanbah Community as pastoral leaseholders have no mineral rights, as the Commonwealth has already acknowledged.

But would it not be sensible to acknowledge that the people there are losing something and to provide within the law a mediating structure to work out the best solution and to provide for compensation if agreement can't be reached?... Reputation, like religion, is priceless but we pay damages for reputations taken away by defamation.

It was a persuasive argument, but hardly realistic in the prevailing circumstances. One is forced to the conclusion that Chaney was attracted so persistently to the notion of compensation because it was the only way of reconciling his conscience to what he saw as the inevitability of the triumph of mining interests and the State.

Court made a detailed rebuttal of the Chaney-Viner case in the same forum four days later. This included his most detailed exposition thus far of a theme that had been emerging in some of his statements – an attack on the legitimacy of the Noonkanbah case in terms of Aboriginal Law and tradition:

> Despite the efforts of some romantics to argue that aborigines can find their identity only in the land and in the mythology of the past, the fact remains that the majority of them seek to establish themselves in the broader community and there can be little doubt about the inevitability of this trend for the future...
>
> [Aboriginal pastoral leases] should not be seen as a permanent retreat to the dreamtime nor the beginning and the end of the options for present and future generations...And perhaps most of all, from the Aboriginal viewpoint, they must not be regarded as land being occupied by some sort of divine right because of an attachment to the land through sacred sites or vague traditional links...
>
> The fact is that most of the people at Noonkanbah have no direct spiritual or traditional links with that land. Big numbers of Aborigines have not been through the law and it is rare these days for young people to show interest in reversing that trend...
>
> [Chaney and Viner] had a lot to say about the Northern Territory situation and the law that prevails there, but they failed to point out that West Australian Aborigines are almost totally detribalised and have nothing like the uninterrupted occupation of land which still applies in many parts of the Territory.

Court's assertions about young people's passage through and interest in the Law were certainly not true of Noonkanbah. If only he could have seen the young men dancing in the many corroborees and ceremonies of those years.

But by the time Court's article appeared, the interlude was over. His Government had commenced on the next, and perhaps the most dramatic, phase of the whole confrontation.

16

THE CONVOY

The most disgraceful expedition any Australian government has ever launched.

Dr Charles Rowley, August 1980.

Gordon Jackson of CSR had ignored the Community's plea. On 6 August the rig was officially released by Strata Oil and made available to Amax. That morning word went out to the drivers who had answered the Transport Commission's advertisement.

Most of them were farmers, and small independent owner-drivers who operated outside the umbrella of the Transport Workers Union. Some were anti-union and attracted to the job on principle, but the lure for most was the generous payment being offered, well in excess of the standard industry tonnage rates, with the added guarantee of standby pay for any delays incurred.

They were told to observe strict secrecy, and assemble that evening at the yard of the Midland Brick Company in the outer suburbs of Perth. The Government said this was used merely as a convenient assembly point; but the owner of Midland Brick, Rick New, was a prominent member of the Liberal Party and an antagonist of the union movement who had previously been involved in strike-breaking operations. At this yard the drivers were issued with new numberplates to protect their identities and, according to one newspaper report, photographed and fingerprinted.

At one o'clock in the morning, on 7 August, the convoy of forty-five trucks and four support vehicles, including a team from the State Emergency Service, pulled out of the Midland Brick yard with a police escort, and made a four-hour dash to the Woodada site, just out of Eneabba. One of the trucks was fully loaded with forty-four gallon drums of fuel. Apparently with this fuel supply, and food supplied by the SES, the intention was to make the convoy fully self-sufficient.

A juggernaut was underway; a convoy that was described by the late Dr Charles Rowley, a respected academic, historian, and the first Chairman of the Aboriginal Land Fund Commission, as 'the most disgraceful expedition any Australian government has ever launched'.[1]

Secrecy had not been strict enough. Word had leaked out, and press teams followed the convoy on the first leg of its journey to Eneabba. Full front page coverage in the *Daily News* that afternoon described it: 'stretched for several kilometres along the Brand Highway and its lights appeared like a giant snake moving through the low hills'.[2]

At Eneabba the press were joined by a number of TV crews, and for six days, as it made its way north, the convoy received saturation coverage in Australia, and extensive reporting overseas.

There was a day's delay at Eneabba as the trucks were loaded. Seven more arrived during the day to take the total to over fifty. They were split into two groups, one with the accommodation units and the ancillary equipment, and the second with the rig itself.

Excerpts from the *Daily News* described preparations and departure of the first group of trucks on the morning of 8 August.

About 5.00 am seven police vehicles arrived at the site. It is believed that there are now more than 25 police officers working with the convoy. A police guard has been kept on the drill site gate since the convoy arrived early yesterday morning. The police were kept informed of the arrival of any trucks by officers stationed along the Brand Highway...

The action started at 8.00 am as the trucks pulled onto the unsealed road leading to the drill site. A thunderous roar could be heard as the convoy stopped behind a police car about 300 metres from the site entrance...

The drivers turned off their engines and waited. At precisely 8.30 the trucks started their engines and the convoy rolled off...

A police aircraft circled overhead as 32 semi-trailers and a fuel tanker roared out of the Strata Oil drilling site. The convoy was led by two police cars and several other police cars had earlier spread out along the road...

As the convoy left the site there were five police vehicles at the entrance with 10 policemen, and four other policemen in two vehicles were guarding the Brand Highway intersection...

The convoy was followed by a police car and a vehicle towing a trailer believed to be carrying food...

Police stopped vehicles on the Brand Highway to allow the convoy to enter. The convoy stretched out over several kilometres and was interspersed with cars slowly passing truck by truck. At some narrow sections of the highway police stopped oncoming traffic to give the convoy priority.

Peter Cook of the Trades and Labor Council was in the Pilbara, meeting with union organisers and key groups of workers. It became clear that the workers of the Pilbara were not prepared to put themselves on the line on this issue. This lack of enthusiasm, the sheer enormity of the convoy and its police support, and the uncertainty of what reaction there would be from the Noonkanbah people themselves, left the union leaders in an awkward position.

They were far from sure that a full-scale attempt to block the convoy would succeed anyway, and they did not want to be seen to be exceeding their role to date of supporting and acting at the request of the Noonkanbah Community. Cook was quoted in the press as saying that the convoy might make it to Noonkanbah despite the union bans, and that

> The union movement was playing a secondary support role in the dispute.
> If the Aborigines did not support union action against the convoy he would expect them to publicly ask to have all bans and limitations removed.[3]

Around Australia outrage at the convoy was mounting. On the 8th the Chairman of the National Aboriginal Conference, Jim Hagan, issued a statement on behalf of that organisation, plus the Central and Northern Land Councils of the Northern Territory, the Aboriginal Development Commission and the Council for Aboriginal Development, a Federal advisory body. They noted the 'growing tide of international opinion supporting the Noonkanbah Aborigines', and concluded by saying,

> In the interests of preserving any semblance of good race relations in Australia, the NAC suggests Amax and CSR refuse to be pressured by the Western Australian Government and demand a conference of all parties to reach a negotiated settlement.

In Perth, thirty-three Uniting Church ministers at a theological conference signed a letter to Premier Court calling on him to halt the convoy, and resolved to send two of their number to Noonkanbah to show their support for the Community.

In the Saturday newspapers around the country on 9 August there were a number of editorials heavily critical of the Government's actions.

At Noonkanbah news of the convoy caused fear and despair. Under Don McLeod's direction the people had been preparing for a major ceremony on Sunday the 10th, but as they met on the Saturday to discuss this drastic development there seemed to be nothing they could do in the face of such force. The presence of the police had already made the people nervous. The dire threats made by the film maker/surveyor of shootings, mass arrests and eviction were recalled. Rumours began to circulate in the Community that there would be helicopters with gunmen in them accompanying the convoy when it reached Noonkanbah. News of the planned union pickets and the support and outrage that were emerging had not got through to Noonkanbah at that stage.

After long and heartbreaking talks and deliberation, I was directed to prepare the following statement:

> For three years now we have been struggling with Amax and the West Australian Government to save our sacred land. We are a small group, but because of our faith in our Law, and the help of our people from far and wide and the supporters who have gathered round us, we have carried this fight further than anybody thought we could. We are proud of what we have done, both for ourselves and that we have made white people think about Aborigines, their land, their Law and their sacred places.
>
> However the State Government is obviously determined to push this drilling through at any cost at all. The history of this country is the same ever since the white man arrived – we the Aboriginal people sitting down on our country minding our own business, looking after the land and trying to live our own life. Then the white man comes along using the only thing he knows in the end, which is force, to push us out. They used to shoot and whip us, now they bring an army of police, and who knows, they may even do the same thing again.
>
> In the early days the old people fought for their rights, but they would return to the bush to carry on rather than wait to be shot. In the same way we will not give Charlie Court the chance to provoke violence or the satisfaction of running his trucks over us or putting us in jail. They can bring their fifty trucks and dozens of police, and the world will see what sort of a government we have.
>
> We will make our peace with the spirits in that place as best we can, they know we have done our best for them. And we will get on with our life, with educating our children and making our Community strong.
>
> Let it be known that this is not a surrender or a recognition of the Government's right, but a withdrawal in the face of overwhelming force.
>
> We realise that the West Australian Government is one that works by force, and is looking for a fight with the unions over this issue. We thank the union movement for their strong support for us over the last two years, but in this situation we ask them to lift their bans and only take action against the scabs who have broken the union law.
>
> We also thank our many other friends and supporters for their work for us, and call on them to remember what has happened, take strength like

us from the success we have had, and continue to work with us and all the other communities struggling for justice.

We trust the Government, now having notice of our intentions will withdraw all police from the station. And we expect that when Amax has done its work the gazetted road and four hectare site will be returned to us and the land will be returned as nearly as possible to its original state.

We recall the words of the Mines Department over a year ago that there is a 'very very slim chance of finding oil or gas here'. When this business is over and Amax has found nothing, let people remember what sort of a government this is that would get an army in and do all in its power to try to humiliate and destroy us for a dry hole in the ground.

It was agreed that this statement would be read the next day, before Don McLeod's ceremony. Mixed with the sorrow, and the fear of what reaction the drilling would bring from the spirits, there was for the Community a sense of relief that the draining struggles of the last two years would be over, and that they would not have to face the convoy. I was sent in to Fitzroy Crossing to convey the news to the unions and the network of supporters in advance of the public announcement the next day.

I reached Fitzroy Crossing after dark. By that time the first section of the convoy had struck camp about one hundred kilometres south of Karratha; it would run the gauntlet of union actions in the Pilbara the next day – potentially the most dangerous section of its journey north. The second section with the rig was camped near Carnarvon.

I can recall the dismal feeling, making reverse charge calls from the public phone box at the town's roadhouse – the manual exchange had closed for the day. I was unable to contact Peter Cook, who was en route from Port Hedland to Derby, or my father, who was in Darwin for an unrelated union conference. I managed to contact Peter Dowding, one of our main links in Perth, and read the statement to him over the crackling line.

The dance at the beginning of Don McLeod's ceremony, 10 August 1980.

273

Dicky Skinner raises the Aboriginal flag.

He was appalled at the news. He passed on information about the union pickets that were planned in the Pilbara, and indicated that pressure on CSR and talks planned with the drilling crew could yet frustrate the Government's plans. He told me that Cook and Stewart West would be coming to Noonkanbah the next day, and that a number of churchmen were heading for Noonkanbah to lend their support in any way they could. He conveyed a sense that a remarkable victory could still be pulled out of the fire, and asked that the Community reconsider their action.

So I turned back to Noonkanbah in a state of confusion, saying that I would take the information back to the Community, but had no idea what they would do.

At Noonkanbah the next morning there were large numbers gathered for McLeod's ceremony, plus, of course, a contingent of media. The latter were excluded for a hurried discussion about Dowding's message. There was an uncertain response from the Community. Hope was raised again, but so was the fear. It was decided that the statement of defiant resignation would be withheld for the time being, but no one was sure what would be done instead.

Don McLeod's ceremony went ahead on Sunday the 10th. It was a ceremonial proclamation echoing the first seizure of the land by Captain Stirling at the Swan River one hundred and fifty-one years earlier; reclaiming the land and rejecting the legitimacy of the State's administration of Aboriginal affairs.

After half an hour of dancing, Dicky Skinner climbed atop a vehicle in front of the Noonkanbah homestead, holding the Aboriginal flag on high. Nipper Tabagee fired a volley of three rifle shots into the air from another vehicle, and then McLeod, surrounded by the painted dancers, read his proclamation that began:

> Before the coming of the white man, there was a law for all men and all time. This Law guaranteed the undisputed tenure of the Land from generation to generation. The collective rights, titles and interests of the people were

Don McLeod reads the proclamation.

Attempting to present the proclamation to the police officer in charge at the drill site.

protected by this Law. The people lived in a state of virtue and democracy under the Law, without recourse to kings, princes or police.

Let it be known that this Law of the Land continues to guide us up to the present time. Next to the food we eat, it is the thing which keeps us alive and which we cherish most.

Let it be known that, in spite of our misery, the Land and its Law provide hope for us.

The white man has never understood our Law nor taken it seriously.

The rest of the proclamation dealt with the State's seizure of control of Aboriginal affairs in the 1890s and the subsequent illegalities and injustices to the Aboriginal people; made the symbolic reclamation of the land; and called on the Federal Government to enter into negotiations to right the injustices.

McLeod and a delegation of Strelley and Noonkanbah men attempted to deliver the proclamation to the police officer in charge at the drill site, but he refused to put his hand through the security fence to receive it. McLeod was forced to deliver it to the State Governor by post.

The historical detail and import of the proclamation appeared to go over the heads of the press and the public, but the ceremony was widely seen as a dramatic and defiant act of symbolism in the circumstances.

When Cook and West arrived later in the day, confusion still reigned as to what would follow over the next few days. Cook made it clear that the unions could not stop the convoy reaching Noonkanbah, but that he also believed that the actual drilling of the oil well may still be stopped. He insisted that it was up to the Community to decide whether to call the whole thing off, or keep fighting; but he also made it clear that the union movement would not act on its own. If the Community wanted their continued support, they would have to continue their opposition, and make some sort of protest against the convoy.

The Community was torn by the dilemma of hope and fear. The old men were talking in unspecific terms about secret action they might take using the power of the Law, but what this meant was not quite clear to those of us who were not privy to their dealings. Eventually they told Cook that they would keep going, but they could not spell out to him what they would do to oppose the convoy, for it seemed they did not know themselves.

As these events unfolded at Noonkanbah, the two arms of the convoy continued their journey. The lead arm was the one that confronted the opposition. In Roebourne forty Aboriginal people stood in protest beside the road, but made no attempt to halt the convoy.

In the end the union pickets were manned only by union officials; the rank and file stayed at home, except for those who came to watch. There had been talk that one of the massive, kilometres-long iron ore trains would be used to block the highway, but this did not eventuate, when Hamersley Iron rearranged the train schedules.

Near Karratha the picket line was easily outnumbered by the police. Six union officials were arrested. Their banners proclaiming an 'Official ACTU, TLC picket line' were torn away by the police. Attempts to park cars on the road in the path of the convoy were foiled.

In the confusion a television cameraman was knocked down by a police car. The media witnesses claimed the action was deliberate. There were numerous complaints that the police were trying to hinder news coverage of the convoy.

At Port Hedland another two union officials were arrested at a smaller picket line. But the convoy rolled on regardless.

It was first brought to a halt by the Strelley mob. The highway ran through their property, just north of Port Hedland. About one hundred and sixty of the mob occupied the bridge at Tabba Tabba Creek, and covered it with rocks and stones.

There was clearly a strategy that it was not politic to arrest Aboriginal protesters in the same manner as the union officials had been. The convoy had to stop and wait as officers on foot with paddy wagons behind them slowly forced the people back until the bridge was cleared and it could proceed. The convoy made camp for the night a few kilometres down the road.

That evening in Darwin, Bob Hawke gave the first public hint of behind-the-scenes work co-ordinated by the Australian Workers Union in Perth. Without specifying why, he stated that he believed it was unlikely that the drilling would proceed.

The next day, Monday 11 August, protesters in Perth occupied the Amax office, and amidst angry exchanges with company officials, eighteen were arrested before the office was cleared.

Late that day the convoy reached the Broome turnoff. Here, over two hundred protesters had waited since that morning. There had been speeches and singing, and an almost festive mood as people waited. When the convoy was sighted approaching, a lone protester sat in the middle of the road in a yoga position. A sergeant in the police car leading the convoy leaned out the window as he approached, yelling to the Broome officers, 'Drag him off the road, grab him by the hair'.[4] The protester was unceremoniously removed

Picket line being broken by police. *(Courtesy West Australian Newspapers.)*

to a nearby paddy wagon.

Two union officials dragged a picket line banner across the road just as the first truck approached, only just missing going under the huge wheels. The trucks were showered with stones and gravel as they passed. In all there were six arrests.

TV film of the convoy driving slowly yet inexorably through the protesters, led by police cars with sirens blaring and blue lights flashing against the orange sunset sky, made dramatic and disturbing footage.

When the convoy had passed, Tommy Edgar, a leading Elder of the Broome Community, tore off his shirt, and abused the police, shouting in his distress, 'Kill me! Why don't you kill me?'5

The Noonkanbah people had made the commitment to oppose the entry of the convoy, but translating this into action was no simple matter. The station was crawling with police. It was not known when the convoy would arrive; it seemed highly likely that it might press on through the night from Broome and arrive in the early hours of Tuesday 12 August.

At dusk on the 11th, as the convoy was passing Broome, a decision was made to attempt another blockade of the road. A few kilometres north of the Noonkanbah homestead the road passed through Mickey's Pool. At this point it came around a bend and dipped into a sandy creek crossing. There were no alternative routes or detours possible. It was relatively close to the Community, where the school and Community radios were on standby for any news or messages. Strategically it was an ideal location.

Five Church ministers had arrived during the day; four from the Uniting Church, and an Anglican from the office of the Australian Council of Churches. They had come in response to earlier calls for support from Noonkanbah, and as part of a growing concern expressed by Church organisations and councils around the country.

The churchmen were asked whether they would prefer to come to Mickey's Pool as observers, or as participants with the people in the blockade. It was felt that the symbolism of their presence at a defence of sacred land would be appropriate, and it was not as easy for men of the cloth to be dismissed as rabble rousers or subversives. And, though the blockade was planned as a purely passive resistance, it was thought that the ministers' presence may act as a restraining influence on the police, if the situation became too volatile.

All five said that the reason they had come to Noonkanbah was to show their solidarity with the people, and that they would join with them on the road.

The men of the Community returned to their camps for supper, and then reassembled outside the school at about nine that night. There was little talk, apart from the usual confusion of getting all the people and their swags into the available cars. Everyone was apprehensive. The string of cars headed out for Mickey's Pool, with headlights off, to try to avoid the attention of the police. The events that followed were reported in the school newsletter:

> Sixty men moved out on Monday night to form a blockade at the creek crossing. They had to form the blockade that night because they thought the convoy might drive through the night and come early in the morning.
>
> They parked seven vehicles on the crossing. First the Millijidee Toyota and Strelley truck, then two utes belonging to Jacob and Snowy. They left a space to sit and parked Tiepin's panel van and Monty's ute behind. The Kimberley Land Council's Toyota was parked sideways across the road.
>
> Jacob and some of the men made a yard between the vehicles with rope. When the police came the men all sat down inside the yard. They knew the police had seen them. They sat around the fires and waited.
>
> Four police cars came from the north. As soon as the men saw the lights, everyone moved from the fires and sat in the yard. Nipper was still rolling his swag when the police walked up. The police shone their torches in everyone's faces and took photographs. The police said they wanted to speak to the Community leaders. No one moved or spoke.
>
> The police walked up to Nipper, but he just walked past and sat with the rest of the mob. The police said they would have to bring a bulldozer to drag away the cars and arrest anyone who stayed on the road. Still no one moved or spoke.[6]

Waiting for the convoy at Mickey's Pool, 11 August 1980.

It was a bizarre and nerve-racking night. No one slept except in brief snatches. The blockade had separated the two police camps at the drill site and Calwynyardah Station. The first time the police were heard approaching, the people and the churchmen moved from the fires they had made in the creekbed, into a tightly packed bunch inside the stockade they had made of cars and rope. After this, most of them stayed in the stockade, curling up under blankets, or sitting and talking quietly.

Despite the darkness you could see the fear and tension in the hunched shoulders, and hear it in the tones of the low whispers. Each time the police came that night, people expected an assault of some kind. They maintained their silence, and shielded their eyes from the police headlights and torches playing over them.

The Strelley men, especially the leaders Jacob Oberdoo and Snowy Jittermurra, who were veterans of the long strike and the Pilbara gaols, were a strong and reassuring presence.

The dawn brought some relief. Limbs stiff from the long uncomfortable night were stretched. Fires were stoked and billies boiled for cups of tea. But faces were tired and tense. And there was a certainty that the police would make their move before too much longer. Soon the signs came that the opposition was marshalling its forces:

> Early the next morning the men saw a lot of dust. They knew the police were coming. Kurilji and Tiepin went up on the hill. They saw ten vehicles and thirty police waiting on the other side of the rise. The men knew they must be waiting for the bulldozer to come. Two paddy wagons were parked to the south.
>
> At this time Jimmy Bieunderry arrived and parked his car in the blockade. Jimmy read some telegrams sent by black and white people from all around Australia supporting the Yungngora Community's stand.[7]

Police waiting over the hill from Mickey's Pool, early morning, 12 August.

Bieunderry's arrival and the messages he brought helped to raise the spirits of the mob. With him had come Darryl Kickett, who had recently stepped into Bieunderry's shoes as Chairman of the KLC, and Rob Riley from the ALS in Perth. Bieunderry and Kickett joined the people in the stockade, and Riley let it be known that he would be watching the behaviour of the police closely. But the moment had come:

> *Police Superintendent*: You people are obstructing. If these vehicles and you people don't move then we have some machines up there that will move the vehicles and if we have to we might take them all the way to Fitzroy Crossing because if nobody will move them, and we have to, they are abandoned vehicles and therefore liable to be impounded, that means taken away...Now that's going to cost you plenty of time and money. Now I can't say any more than that. All I can do is give you five minutes...[8]

It was plain that the police had no brief for compromise. Nobody moved.

> The police then drove up to the crossing with a grader and front-end loader and waited. Everyone was sitting on the road. No one spoke.
> One by one the grader and front-end loader dragged the cars away. First the Millijidee Toyota was pushed off the road. Then the Strelley vehicles. No one moved or spoke while the machines dragged the cars out of the way. Finally Jimmy's, Monty's and Ivan's cars were dragged out of the way. Only the men were left sitting on the road.[9]

There was an awful and solemn relentlessness about this operation, amidst the noise of the machinery the police had commandeered, and their barked orders. Chains and ropes were swinging and stretching, wheels spinning and gears grinding, within less

Removing the vehicles from the blockade.

The final warning.

than a metre of the people on the road. Throughout the half-hour operation, nearly all of the people stared hard at the ground, seemingly trying to steel themselves and concentrate their thoughts inwards.

One reporter from the *West Australian* had been at Mickey's Pool throughout the night. But at this point some of the media contingent that had been travelling with the convoy arrived, including a couple of TV crews. They immediately zeroed in, and hovering reporters, cameramen and sound recordists and their equipment added to the sense of chaos.

The last of the vehicles was cleared away, but as Michael Gallagher recalls:

> A legal technicality had to be established. The law required that an obstruction be seen to have occurred. So everyone in the Creek was treated to a curious legal pantomime. The Superintendent instructed the driver of a Toyota belonging to one of the drilling company's contractors to attempt to use the road. The Toyota drove up to the blockade and stopped. 'We have a contractor here who wants to go across the creek. You are obstructing him.' Silence. With this the law was satisfied that 'people had been prevented from going about their lawful business.'[10]

The contractor reversed away. There was a moment's hiatus. Then Ginger Nganawilla began a slow chant-like song. Others joined in, until only the white churchmen amongst those on the road were silent.

The sight, and the sound, of these people singing for their country as they huddled together and the police began to wade in amongst them was indescribably moving. I saw more than one hard-bitten journalist biting his lips, or swallowing hard.

The faces of the police showed different emotions. Some were plainly

The police move in.

uncomfortable in what they were doing, others were simply doing their duty, understanding nothing. Only one or two seemed to take a perverse enjoyment from the task and the attention they were receiving from the large press gallery. The Aboriginal Police Aides, who were used in the front-line of the assault, had a doubly difficult task because relatives were amongst the men sitting in the creek bed.[11]

The police moved in and tried to arrest the white church people first. The police must have thought that once the Europeans were arrested then everyone else would give up and walk away. No one gave in.

Everyone held on to the church people. Sam Fuller held on to them as hard as he could and pulled the church people down as the police lifted them up. [Roger Stringer, a Uniting Church minister from Perth, looked as if he was going to be torn in half at one point, when he became the prize in a tug of war between Fuller and the police.] The police got frightened when the men kept on singing and pulling at their legs to try and make them fall.

Tiepin and Tojo were some of the first people arrested. Sam Fuller had to be carried away by two policemen because he kept on grabbing others when the police placed him under arrest. The police kicked Truman Boxer to make him walk to the paddy wagon. Joe Wunmah kept holding Kurilji's

The arrests are made. Top left: The churchmen are arrested first. Top right: Followed by Noonkanbah people. Bottom: Wadgie Thirkall is arrested as another police officer tries to persuade Mick Michael to move.

legs to stop the police carrying Kurilji away. As soon as they locked Kurilji up the police arrested Joe.

The road was cleared after twenty-two people had been arrested. The men who were left behind had broken hearts because they could not do anything but sit and wait for the convoy to come. Meanwhile the police stood along the road and watched everyone. It was a very sad time.[12]

The melee had been brief but intense. In their desire to arrest the churchmen, who were scattered through the inner ranks of the mob, the police had trampled over those on the outside. The police and the people were tripping, shoving, pulling and shouting. The old men had started the singing to control their fear, and draw strength. They continued

Waiting for the convoy.

this almost until the end of the struggle, providing an eerie counterpoint to the surrounding chaos.

By nine-thirty the road was cleared. Those arrested were crammed into the back of the two paddy wagons and taken to Fitzroy Crossing. Skinner and Bieunderry were gone, old Joe Wunmah, many of the Strelley mob, and Darryl Kickett. The five Church ministers, too. One of them asked the police, on the way into Fitzroy Crossing, why they had been targeted as the first to be arrested. He was told, 'We didn't want to be seen as being racist'.

It was indeed a sad time for those left behind. They regrouped in the creekbed downstream from the crossing. There was absolutely nothing they could do but worry about those who had been taken away, and wait for the final blow, for the convoy to carry the rig through. The media waited on the other side of the road, which was lined by police on both sides, and a larger crowd of police and various other hangers-on watched from the banks above.

The next eight hours were spent waiting. For the whole day the two lines of police remained as sentinels across fifty metres of sandy creek bed to beat off any rearguard action that might be mounted against their newly won territory. No one was permitted to stand on the road, groups were not allowed to gather near its edge and crossing was done under close scrutiny. An absurd situation arose concerning the impounded vehicles. Technically, they were now the property of the Commissioner of Police and this meant that it was illegal to touch them or get water-bottles or other personal belongings from them. If anyone even leaned on one a constable was immediately despatched to protect the Commissioner's new property.[13]

As the hours passed with still no sign of the convoy, the media became desperate to know whether the people would try anything else. People of all kinds arrived in a steady stream throughout the day in cars and by plane. Aboriginal people were making their way out from Broome and Derby and Fitzroy Crossing. Yet more police arrived, and media. A few curious spectators came all the way out, just to watch.

In the afternoon the women of the Community came up to wait with their men. The camps back at Noonkanbah were deserted.

The convoy arrives at Mickey's Pool.

As each hour passed, the atmosphere became more strained; heavy with the expectation of the convoy arriving. Some of the new arrivals were urging the mob to try to re-occupy the road when the convoy arrived. But quite apart from the impracticality of this now that the police were in control, there was no likelihood of it being attempted; the spirit of the people was almost as low as it could go.

In mid-afternoon they moved further down the creekbed, out of sight and earshot of the media and the police, purportedly to discuss the situation, but more to escape the expectations of the watchers. The talk was desultory; there was no enthusiasm for any of the ideas thrown up, but nor would they leave Mickey's Pool. I had to bluff the hovering media, saying that no decisions had been made. I did not tell them that none was likely.

Then I was summonsed by one of the reporters. He played me a recording he had just made of a news broadcast he had managed to pick up. The drilling crew had met in Perth. They had decided that they would not work the rig! It was nearly here, but it would not be able to do its job!

Borrowing the cassette player, I raced back to the mob, and it was played three or four times over as people gathered round, and gloom gave way to grins and cheers. The timing was incredible. People were still exclaiming and explaining to one another as the rumble of the convoy was heard in the distance.

The endless line of trucks and their police escort rolled one by one across the narrow crossing at Mickey's Pool between the two lines of grim-faced policemen to an exuberant

The people greet the convoy.

mixture of jeers and cheers, waves and two-finger signs.

Once the convoy had passed, there was a sense of wonderment, almost disbelief. When the immediate euphoria of the news from Perth had subsided, everyone was confused as to what they should do, even what they should feel and think. It had been too dramatic a swing of mood and circumstance for people to come to terms with easily.

The media raced back to Derby to file their stories. Most of the police returned to either Calwynyardah or the drill site, but a small contingent stayed on to guard the impounded vehicles. Eventually, the people began to drift back to the station, with the few cars still in use taking them in relays.

> Ginger Nganawilla was one of the last to leave...As he walked over to his ute to pick up his swag, two constables sprinted thirty metres to claim the ute and the swag for the Commissioner of Police, shouting as they ran, 'Get out of it, old man, get out of it'. They made him sleep without his blanket.[14]

Now the people could only wait; wait for their fellows to return from the Fitzroy Crossing lock up, and wait to see what the morrow would bring.

Yet again, the Government had been frustrated on the brink of apparent victory. The rig had finally reached its destination, and was secure behind the high fence of the compound. But no one was sure what would happen now.

The convoy at the drill site. (Courtesy West Australian Newspapers.)

17

NO TIME FOR BLEEDING HEARTS

All we can say is that the white man is mad.
From A Statement By The Yungngora Community, 30 August 1980.

The ban imposed by the drilling crew was the union movement's triumphant tactical counter to the convoy. The roughnecks, as they were known, who worked the drilling rigs were renowned as a hard-working, hard-drinking, high-living, independent-minded mob. There was a high degree of mobility in the industry, with workers moving between rigs around the world. No one had counted on them coming out on an issue like this.

However six months earlier the Australian Workers Union had succeeded in a recruitment drive to unionise the Richter drill. It had a good relationship with the crew. And Gil Barr, the State Secretary of the union, was one of those officials who had supported Peter Cook in his backing of the Noonkanbah mob.

As the convoy had begun its journey north, a telephone conference of the AWU State Executive had debated the issue, and decided to authorise Barr to convene a meeting of the Richter crew and recommend that they ban the Noonkanbah drilling.

Most of the crew were in Perth, and Barr was able to get fifteen of the twenty in for the meeting on the morning of the Mickey's Pool drama.

It was far from certain which way the meeting would go. Certainly the drillers were not 'bleeding hearts' who would come out in sympathy for the blacks, but according to Barr there were a few strong unionists amongst them who saw the convoy as an attack on union principles. Barr briefed them on the background of the dispute, and had Ernie Bridge talk to them about the position of the Noonkanbah people.

By all reports it was a finely balanced affair, until one of the more fiery crew members declared that there was no way he was going to work behind a barbed-wire fence, guarded by an army of police. They endorsed the union recommendation. But they also went to some pains to make it clear that it was not an action against their employers; they declared their availability to work on other rigs or at other locations, and said that they were prepared to go to Noonkanbah as soon as a reasonable settlement was reached.

Barr's first move was to pass the news on to Peter Cook who had gone on to Darwin from Noonkanbah to the same union conference my father was attending. Cook immediately rang the Premier's office. He told Sir Charles Court of the new development, and appealed to him to halt the convoy before it reached Noonkanbah to avoid any confrontation on the station. He was unaware of the arrests at Mickey's Pool a few hours earlier. Court consulted Peter Jones before advising Cook that the convoy would continue regardless.

Whilst the drillers were meeting, Bob Hawke was putting the pressure on CSR. Caught in a difficult position, the company declared that it would not operate the rig without the normal union crew. So as long as the crew in Perth held firm, it appeared that the Government was stalemated.

Jones was unable to move CSR from this position, which was confirmed by a telex from a senior company executive on 13 August. So the Government switched its attention to trying to change the minds of the drilling crew. The day the crew met and voted for the bans, Richter telexed the names and addresses of those who had attended the union meeting to Bill Mitchell. And the next day these men received letters from Jones telling them that they had been misled, and inviting them to a meeting with him and Bill Grayden on the 14th.

Barr gatecrashed this meeting, bluffing his way past a couple of security men posted at the doors of the conference room in the government offices where it was held. He says if anything this session worked in the union's favour, with Jones' dourness and Grayden's bumbling making little impression on the men. Certainly there was no public comment from the Ministers on the meeting subsequently, despite the fact that word of its occurrence had leaked to the media.

The union movement was doing all it could to reinforce the position of the crew. Messages of congratulation on their stand poured in to the AWU office in Perth from all quarters: Hawke as ACTU President, union offices from around the country, and shopfloor meetings. Aboriginal organisations and supporters did the same; even Neville Bonner, the Liberal Senator from Queensland, sent this telegram:

> As a former member of the AWU, an Aborigine, and now a Senator, may I thank you for your support of my fellow Aborigines of Noonkanbah. I am sure that all fair minded Australians applaud your stand and sacrifices in helping to obtain justice and good old Aussie fair go for my people. To you all, my sincere thanks.

One obvious weak point was that it was unlikely the crew would hold for long if the financial effect became too severe. Hawke took the step of guaranteeing their income for as long as they maintained the bans, and launched an appeal through the union movement for contributions to this most unusual strike fund.

At their third meeting in four days, on the 15th, back at the union offices, the men reaffirmed their decision to maintain the bans.

During the second half of August the scope of the dispute reached unprecedented proportions; but as the drama ebbed and flowed, and the various parties manoeuvered and bluffed, the Community became almost detached. Events had now moved totally out of their hands. The drill was ensconced behind wire and a police guard. The police continued to roam the station. It seemed the people could do little but wait.

Mickey's Pool was the last direct action by the Community. The events there had been particularly traumatic for the old men, and at first seemed to have drained their energy. But as those arrested returned home, and a few days passed, it became apparent that they had turned again to the realm of the Law.

The old men showed only a superficial interest in the briefings Skinner and I gave about the various external developments. But they held a number of meetings of their own, at times including Lawmen from Looma and other communities.

The *West Australian* carried a story under the headline 'Aborigines Turn To Spiritual Law':

> Old men in the community have been deeply upset by the arrests ...They are now involved in a series of meetings to decide what to do under Aboriginal law about any drilling. The meetings could take many weeks...
> The recourse to Aboriginal law was referred to by Nipper Tabagee [who]

said that the Community had tried to stop the rig in the white people's way. No one in government had listened. The community should now do things in the Aboriginal way if the drilling went ahead, he said.

A WA Newspapers team has had several discussions with Mr Tabagee and other old men. They are reluctant to elaborate on the ground that Aboriginal law is not for white people to know.[1]

I have never found out just what these meetings entailed. I presume one part of it was a process of attempting to make peace with the spirits and powers of the land. Whether it went any further than this, I was never told, and one did not trespass on their territory by enquiring.

Bob Hawke had now become closely involved in the dispute and the negotiations that were taking place. He was in the last months of his time as President of the ACTU. His reputation had been made as a master negotiator, able to craft settlements of seemingly unresolvable industrial disputes.

Of course, part of this art was having leverage with which to apply pressure, and finding the points at which to apply this pressure to force the concessions needed for a settlement. In this case the lever was the drilling crew, and it was useful only as long as they held. The first of the weak points was CSR, a late and reluctant party to the whole affair; their 'no union labour, no drilling' position had to be maintained.

Whilst these elements were in place, there was room to seek alternative solutions. The State Government refused to even come to the table. So the next point was Amax itself.

American unions and the International Confederation of Free Trade Unions were asked to lobby Amax in America. They lodged protests, but were not well enough informed, and did not have enough at stake to go beyond such formal protests.

So Hawke went direct to the company. Discussions focused on the earlier discovery of the incomplete 1978 seismic survey. It also emerged that Amax already had pencilled in a likely drill site on Go Go Station, a hundred kilometres to the east, for their 1981 drilling program.

When briefed on these developments, the Community undertook to do all it could to expedite completion of the seismic survey and selection of an alternative, acceptable drilling site on Noonkanbah. The outline of a solution emerged, revolving around the company drilling at Go Go that year, and returning to Noonkanbah in 1981.

By 19 August Hawke felt confident enough to say that all parties except the State Government were close to an agreement, and a major breakthrough was imminent.

The next day he publicly revealed the outline of the plan, saying that in three separate conversations with Amax Vice-President Arthur Reef, he had been 'assured that Amax would be happy to drill on Go Go to allow the Noonkanbah dispute to be settled'.[2]

There is some doubt as to just how practical it was to finalise and prepare an alternative site on Go Go, shift the rig, and complete a drilling program in what remained of the dry season. But there is no doubt that Amax would have liked to extricate itself from the mess; it would have been more than happy to pull out of Noonkanbah, and take things one step at a time from there.

But there was no way the Premier would let them. They were still legally obliged to drill at Noonkanbah, and they could not drill at Go Go without a permit signed by the Minister for Mines:

Sir Charles agreed last night that Mr Reef had been in touch with him to tell him of Mr Hawke's proposal.

'I reminded Mr Reef in very frank terms that the permit to drill was from the WA Government and Amax was committed to drill on Noonkanbah this year,' Sir Charles said.

Either Amax drilled on Noonkanbah this year or it forfeited its permit.[3]

And so this eleventh hour attempt fell by the wayside of the State's intransigence, degenerating into an exchange of bitter accusations between Court and Hawke.

Whilst these negotiations were proceeding the controversy continued to rage. On the day of the Mickey's Pool arrests there had been protest meetings in the streets of Melbourne and Canberra; eleven academics from the Australian National University, including some of the country's most prominent, signed a letter to Prime Minister Fraser calling on him to use the Commonwealth's 'undoubted legal powers and moral authority' to intervene.

That night in Perth, the Speaker of the State Parliament was eventually forced to clear the public gallery for the first time in many years, to remove a hundred protesters who would not stop hissing and interjecting during a long and angry urgency debate brought on by the Opposition.

The next day Police Minister Hassell overruled the supposedly independent head of the Road Traffic Authority, who had said that the names of the holders of the special numberplates issued to the convoy drivers would soon be available to anyone who paid the required search fee. Hassell said the plates would be returned, and the papers placed on the dead record file, inaccessible to the public.

A group of Uniting Church ministers led three hundred people in a prayer meeting in Forrest Place in the centre of Perth, in defiance of the Government's ban on public meetings without permits under the notorious Section 54B of the Police Act.[4]

The Opposition was pressing in the State Parliament to no avail for detailed information on the cost of the convoy: who would pay, the role of the State Emergency Service, and various other issues. Grayden's war of words with the anthropological community continued, after he claimed that on the Noonkanbah precedent, there could be up to two hundred thousand Aboriginal sites in Western Australia.

Newspaper editorials around the country were highly critical of the State Government: some for the overkill of the convoy, if nothing else; with others providing a more searching examination of some of the underlying issues, and addressing the need for a more equitable relationship between Aboriginal and white Australia.

The *West Australian* also published a series of statements collected by Bob Bropho of the Swan Valley fringedwellers from Aboriginal people and leaders all around the State strongly supporting the Noonkanbah mob. Ken Colbung of the Aboriginal Lands Trust, always the individualist, went against this tide with a statement suggesting that the affair had become a 'three ring circus' driven by political confrontation rather than the needs of the people at Noonkanbah.

Police Commissioner Leitch re-entered the fray, undaunted by previous criticism, using a defence of the role of his officers during the convoy and at Noonkanbah to take a swipe at the Churches and the union movement. The long-standing enmity between the State Government and the ALS boiled over when the Government called for the ALS to be disbanded.

Though the Noonkanbah mob had turned back inwards, their actions, the publicity generated, and particularly the international coverage of the convoy had opened the way to a whole new chapter in Aboriginal affairs. The mood was captured by the

Chairman of the National Aboriginal Conference, Jim Hagan, addressing a meeting of the Aboriginal Treaty Committee in Canberra on 21 August. His audience included a number of foreign embassy representatives:

> What is happening at Noonkanbah now is more than a local issue. It is not just one community fighting with one government over one sacred site. It is the turning point...
>
> Noonkanbah cannot be looked upon in the future as just another episode in the long series of white intrusions into what is left of Aboriginal land and Aboriginal life. Not another Mapoon, Gove, Oenpelli, Aurukun or Mornington Island. No, Noonkanbah must be the breakthrough.
>
> It must be the moment in history when the Aboriginal people know that they are recognised, that they are in control of their own destiny, that they are free...
>
> The Federal Government now faces a choice between action and talk. It can act immediately to protect the Yungngora Community from the virtual invasion organised by the Western Australian Government, or, it can continue to talk but not act...Australia is now dangerously out of step with international opinion in failing to come to terms with its indigenous inhabitants.[5]

The NAC had taken steps towards the first real internationalisation of the Aboriginal cause. It was affiliated to the World Council of Indigenous Peoples, which in turn had the status of a non-government consultative member of the Geneva based United Nations' Human Rights Commission Sub-Commission on Prevention of Discrimination and Protection of Minorities.

The NAC had announced its intention, with the support of the Yungngora Community, to take Noonkanbah's case to the next meeting of this Sub-Commission in Geneva early in September. This would be the first appearance of the Aboriginal community in a United Nations forum.

The Federal Government was becoming more uncomfortable by the day. The international attention was particularly discomforting for Prime Minister Fraser. In international, and especially Commonwealth, forums, he had developed a reputation as an advocate of human rights, and a strong anti-racist. He had played a prominent role in the 1979 negotiations that led to a settlement of the civil war in Zimbabwe/Rhodesia and the establishment there of black majority rule. Fraser had been the only white Head of government to attend the Zimbabwe independence celebrations that April, and he was on good personal terms with a number of black African Heads of State.

On 1 September Fraser was due in New York to receive a prestigious award from the international Jewish organisation B'nai Brith 'in recognition of his services to humanity'. The perception of a nation prepared to trample the rights and beliefs of its indigenous people was not one that sat comfortably with this image.

It had reached the point where Australian embassies were monitoring and reporting on international reaction, and the *West Australian's* Canberra correspondent filed this story:

> Well-placed Commonwealth informants say that Mr Fraser is privately concerned that the long-running row could seriously undermine Australia's international standing...
>
> [Fraser] is understood to have expressed private reservations this week about the WA Government's insensitive handling of the issue. And he believes that the international publicity over the oil-drilling project could lead to an African boycott of the 1982 Commonwealth Games in Brisbane...

Mr Fraser and other members of the Government are believed to have been working actively behind the scenes to put pressure on the State Government to reach a satisfactory settlement with the Aborigines...

A spokesman for the Foreign Affairs Department said that Noonkanbah could erode the credit Australia had around the world. 'This would be disastrous for Australia, not just for the Commonwealth Games but in our international wheeling and dealing. It could all be sabotaged from our international relations point of view'.[6]

But the back-room pressure was getting nowhere, and domestic political considerations were deemed to be a higher priority than diplomatic concerns, or the rights and wrongs of the issue. Moves were made to initiate general talks with mining industry organisations, and with the NAC; but nothing was done to address the real issues of Noonkanbah.

When Bob Hawke was involved in the last-ditch settlement talks, Fred Chaney refused to take any direct role, referring Hawke back to the State Government. There are indications from Hawke's diary notes of the time that Chaney was privately hoping that the drilling crew's bans would hold, thus increasing the time for, and chances of, a negotiated settlement. The situation was perhaps best summarised by a cartoon showing Fraser with his back turned, and heavily blindfolded, saying, 'Tell me someone – has Noonkanbah gone away yet?'

This knowledge that the Federal Government was in a sense a closet supporter of the Community, yet refused to use its position as the only party with the undoubted power to frustrate the State, was particularly galling to Noonkanbah's supporters. This was the real breakthrough, and turning point that Hagan and the Aboriginal movement was looking for. Such a move would have changed the face of Aboriginal affairs, and relationships between the Aboriginal community and governments irrevocably.

It must be conceded that the consequences of Federal intervention would have been enormous. The State would not have lain down quietly. There would have been court challenges, and a brawl of unprecedented proportions within the Liberal Party, with an election due within months. These were the domestic considerations that constrained Fraser and Chaney. Yet the fact remains that, however compelling the demands of Realpolitik, the Federal Government lacked the courage of its convictions. It knew Court and the State Government were wrong and excessive in their actions, but allowed them to get away with it.

Back in Perth, the drilling crew was due to meet again on 19 August. CSR senior management had given the ACTU guarantees that the men would not be victimised, and their jobs would be secure. But the lower level management and staff at Richter had been playing their own hand.

One staff member in particular, Jack Lambert, who was the on-site boss for the crew, had been putting the pressure on. He had been briefed on the earlier meetings by one of the crew who had voted to go ahead with the drilling. This fellow had a brother in the crew who had voted for the bans.

The pro-bans brother told Gil Barr that Lambert was saying that those who had voted for the bans would lose their jobs, that staff would go ahead with the drilling anyway, and that even those who had voted against the bans and kept their jobs would not get work until Christmas at earliest.

With these threats hanging over them, the meeting on the 19th was very tense. It seemed that the vote was going to tip the other way by a narrow margin. The ACTU executive was meeting in Melbourne the same day. Barr got Hawke and Cook to speak to the meeting by phone from Melbourne. They tried to convince the crew that the guarantees given would override the bluster from Lambert, and advised that the executive had endorsed the recommendation to guarantee their wages. They also briefed the crew on the negotiations that were proceeding with Amax and CSR, which at that point were still looking promising.

Barr spoke to the men once more, and then left the room, saying it was up to them. He was called back in to be told that it was a unanimous decision to maintain the bans. But there was one proviso. The crew made it clear that they wanted a resolution one way or another very soon. They resolved to meet again on the 22nd, and called on all parties to reach a definite settlement.

CSR was not enjoying its role in the affair at all. Its Richter subsidiary was contractually obliged to the drilling program, having committed itself in 1978, unaware of the trouble that lay ahead. There was division within the company; one executive told Hawke at one point, 'We want the same result as you want'.[7] The company was under intense pressure from the union movement on one hand, and the State Government on the other.

It tried to present the best face to all sides, and satisfied none. It told the ACTU that it would withdraw the rig from Noonkanbah the moment that Amax gave it permission to do so. Yet it flew in staff members to erect the rig, so it could be ready to start work as soon as the crew lifted its bans. It told the State Government that it could not risk the consequences of defying the union bans by bringing in a scab crew. Yet it initially told the unions that it could not afford to oppose any move by Amax to exercise an option in the contract to take over operation of the rig if it did not perform its work. It told both sides that if the matter was not settled by the first week of September it would have to withdraw the rig to avoid the possibility of being trapped by the wet.

By the time the drilling crew gathered for its meeting on the 22nd, the attempt to switch drilling to Go Go had fallen through. The definite settlement the crew had looked for had not materialised. It was clear to the men that a settlement would have been achieved had it not been for the State's intransigence. And Cook and Hawke still believed that such an outcome was possible if pressure could be maintained on the State Government.

Lambert's threats had been put to rest by now. And the men took exception to the Government's claims that they had been stood over by union officials and threatened with life bans; they resented the implication that they were not strong enough to take their own decisions. These factors, plus the confirmation of a secure income, led them to reaffirm the bans; this time indefinitely. They did not schedule any further meetings.

Hawke believed by this time that he had a firm commitment from CSR that it would not approve release of the rig to any other operator, and a renewed commitment not to use non-union labour. Peter Cook emerged from the meeting of the drilling crew confidently predicting that there would be no drilling at Noonkanbah that year.

Since the first announcement of the drilling bans the State Government had been relatively quiet. There had been a number of statements criticising the unions, its blunt rejection of the Go Go alternative, and a couple of outbursts from backbenchers; but it had done nothing, publicly, to seize back the initiative.

Immediately after Cook announced the result of the final meeting of the crew and made his prediction, Peter Jones made a brief statement that received only minor coverage amongst the detailed reporting of the drillers' meeting, and the dilemmas of the Federal Government. He said:

> The Government's approach to drilling will be the same as to the transport of the rig. We are preparing to do the same... We are taking steps of our own which will be announced at the appropriate time.[8]

The Federal Government had floated an idea with the State of establishing a 'summit team' with four Federal Ministers and State representatives to seek a settlement. This had been rejected by the State. Fraser's next move, apparently aimed more at damage control than anything else, was to approach mining industry councils about talks to establish guidelines to prevent similar clashes in the future. This prompted further angry responses from the State.

With Jones and Court alerted by a confidential leak from a member of the Australian Mining Industry Council, they briefed State Party President, Ian Warner, who was at a Federal Liberal Party Executive meeting in Canberra on the 22nd, to warn Fraser against talking to the mining industry in general, or Amax and CSR in particular, without consulting the State Government. And in the ensuing days Court sent a series of stern, lecturing messages to Fraser.

> There is nothing I can do to stop you talking to the mining and petroleum exploration companies, or to the Aborigines but – based on past experience – this will finish up as yet another intrusion into the erosion of a true federal system...
>
> I have to repeat what I have said previously, namely, that we would not be in the present situation at Noonkanbah had it not been for Commonwealth interference.
>
> I understand that you would want to avoid a situation where Australia is subject to criticism overseas...but my considered view is that there comes a time when we have to call a halt to appeasement...People in Australia are becoming a little tired of the 'tail wagging the dog' – and so are we.
>
> I can see no purpose in meeting your four ministerial colleagues. If I knew what they wanted to discuss maybe I could give the matter some further thought. In any case, I imagine it would only be a matter of a short time after we agreed to such a meeting that the newspapers would be running banner headlines, such as 'Federal Ministers To Lean On Court'. I would be forced to react strongly...
>
> The public patience throughout Australia, according to the best information we are able to obtain, is fast running out with the Aborigines. It only wants a degree of firmness on the part of the Commonwealth and I think the nonsense would end. It is no time for 'bleeding hearts'.[9]

When Court discovered that Fraser and some of his Ministers were to meet with an NAC delegation he felt the need to offer this advice:

> I refer to our phone discussion this morning. I felt I should reiterate my request and also my considered advice to you that the time has come when you, as Prime Minister, should say to the Aborigines from the National Aboriginal Council you are to meet tomorrow that they have had a fair go and what is currently being done to stop drilling at Noonkanbah is against the interests of Aborigines generally throughout Australia.
>
> I can assure you...that the public are heartily fed up with the Noonkanbah saga. They feel it is about time both Commonwealth and State Governments started to assert themselves and got on with the job of governing...
>
> I also confirm that we are not impressed by the threats of Aborigines going overseas to Geneva and 'pouring a bucket' over their country which is trying to do the right thing by them and has treated them in recent years with generosity and understanding. I assume the taxpayers of Australia will be paying their fares and all other expenses to allow them to denigrate

the governments and the people of Australia. If this is correct, it is rather odd. The public will not be amused...

I have a strong feeling that as soon as the Commonwealth Government shows a firm stance in the matter and backs us there will be a completely different attitude to Noonkanbah within the various Aboriginal organisations – most of which are so handsomely financed by the Commonwealth Government...

It is a sorry day if a State Government, having done all the right things in the matter, is going to be let down by a Federal Government which really, at this stage, has no position in a mining exploration project entirely under State Government control...I should like to feel that, on this occasion, instead of the Commonwealth trying to placate the Aborigines, they talk from a position of strength and get the Aborigines to understand that there is a limit to the patience of both the taxpayer and the Government.[10]

The meeting between the Federal Government and the NAC took place on 25 August. Never before or since has an Aboriginal issue produced such a demonstration of political concern. Fraser and seven senior Ministers – half of the Cabinet – attended the meeting.

Each side claimed that the other had asked for the meeting. It was commonly assumed that the Government's main concern was to persuade the NAC to withdraw from the Geneva trip, though it denied this was the case.

The meeting started in the late afternoon, and continued well into the night. There were early reports that there would be a joint statement issued, but as the meeting dragged on this prospect faded. In fact, nothing came of the meeting. Both sides emerged making soothing noises about fruitful discussions, but the NAC made it clear that the result had fallen short of its demand for Federal intervention, and that they would be proceeding with the Geneva initiative.

'Noonkanbah Deadlock' was the headline. In the next couple of days, Court went public with an angry criticism of the Commonwealth's 'meddling and interference', Fraser repeated that there would be no Federal intervention, and Peter Cook repeated claims that CSR had said it would not release its rig to any third parties.

The situation seemed so tense and finely balanced that if the balloon was pricked, it could explode in all directions.

At Fitzroy Crossing it was races time; the biggest social event of the year for black and white, when people from all the communities in the district come to town for the week for a good time. For the Noonkanbah mob the prospect was a welcome change from the tension, the waiting and the hope. After meeting to prepare and issue instructions to Phil Vincent of the ALS – who was to accompany the NAC delegation of Hagan and the two Kimberley members, Jimmy Bieunderry and Reg Birch, to Geneva – everyone except a few of the oldest people and a couple of caretakers headed to town; leaving behind the police and the drilling rig that now towered above the sacred land.

As Peter Jones had indicated, following the final decision of the drilling crew, the Government put its plan in place. It was merely a matter of timing as to when they would deliver their final blow. But they did not have much time to play with; CSR had given its deadline, and they could not afford the risk of any word of their plans leaking to any of the other players or the media.

The departure of the mob for the Fitzroy Crossing races created the right circumstances at Noonkanbah. But the excuse to move was provided, either by fortuitous coincidence, or clever engineering on the part of the Government, by Aboriginal Lands Trust Chairman, Ken Colbung.

Until his 'three ring circus' statement of mid-August, Colbung had publicly been a supporter of the Community, and had made some statements severely critical of the State Government. As a member of the Aboriginal Cultural Materials Committee of the Museum that had assessed Peter Bindon's 1979 reports and unanimously recommended protection, he was familiar with the information about the religious nature of the land in question. As Chairman of the Aboriginal Lands Trust he was nominally the senior holder of the Noonkanbah Pastoral Lease.

Colbung had always been something of a wildcard on the Aboriginal scene. He had been in and out of the chairmanship of a number of Aboriginal organisations such as the ALS. He was the most accessible and recognised Aboriginal media figure in the State, always ready to provide comment. Yet one was never sure what sort of comment would come forth; on any given issue he might take a position from the radical, to the middle of the road, to something entirely individual. He had no particular relationship with the Noonkanbah Community beyond the legal one through the ALT, and was certainly not one of their confidants.

His actions on Noonkanbah, though generally supportive, had not always been helpful. When the dispute raised its head again at the beginning of 1980 he had unsuccessfully demanded a meeting with Malcolm Fraser. A few days later he had claimed that Don McLeod was urging the Noonkanbah people to form a resistance army. In April his comments calling for a review of the royalty provisions for mining on Aboriginal land, however legitimate in principle, had contributed to the confusion created by the Government with its claims that Noonkanbah was about royalties.

The State Government had quietly cultivated him. When Colbung complained in May that the Lands Trust had not been involved in discussions about the dispute, a meeting with Court and senior Ministers was quickly arranged. And earlier, in March, there had been a curious exchange when Court phoned him to thank him for his assistance in convening the three Ministers' meeting at Noonkanbah on short notice. A subsequent memo from Court to Jones, Hassell and Grayden made these comments about the conversation:

> He seemed appreciative of the call...He said he felt the crisis had really passed and there would now be some protest but not any physical attempts to delay the entry of the company...
>
> He went on to explain that the Aborigines change their minds very often – in fact, he said their law is always changing and is inclined to reflect the current situation and the current environment, rather than be something that was permanent and stable.[11]

It is impossible to know how accurately Court had reported Colbung's comments. What is apparent is that his dealings with the Government were not always consistent with his public position. It is clear that he was attracted to the limelight, and wanted to be at the centre of things. Perhaps he was frustrated that the Community never gave him such a role.

His return to the limelight in the Noonkanbah affair was certainly sensational. On 26 August Court was able to telex Fraser with the following information:

> I thought I should let you know confidentially that Ken Colbung, the chairman of the Aboriginal Lands Trust in this state, has advised me twice today that the ALT is of the opinion that the State Government should proceed with its drilling operations at Noonkanbah Station...
>
> This is consistent with the views expressed by the Trust when they held a meeting in Broome recently and the minutes of which meeting we have

seen...

Unfortunately, Colbung is in Rockhampton on Aboriginal business at the present time, but will be back in Perth late on Wednesday night. He will be seeing me on Thursday morning [the 28th]. It is anticipated that he will make a statement on behalf of the Trust, confirming its opinion...

I do not propose to make any public statement at this stage, but we are proceeding on the basis of my discussion with Colbung this morning.[12]

This turnaround by Colbung was remarkable in a number of ways. Why did it happen at that particularly significant time, when the Lands Trust meeting he used as his justification had taken place seven weeks earlier, in the first week of July? Why did he ring Court from Rockhampton, instead of speaking to him before leaving Perth or on his return? These questions have never been satisfactorily answered.

Extracts of the minutes of the Lands Trust meeting in Broome had been released by the Government a couple of weeks earlier:

The Trust discussed the Noonkanbah situation at length, particularly those matters relating to Aboriginal lore. Opinions were expressed that the lore appeared to vary at Noonkanbah from traditional patterns.[13]

A motion had been moved by a Trust member from the South-west, and seconded by a non-traditional man from the Goldfields:

That the Minister be informed that senior loremen in the Noonkanbah area expressed grave doubts regarding the validity and authenticity of claims by the Yungngora Community on lore matters concerning the excision of land at Noonkanbah.[14]

When Bill Hassell had released this, it had been a minor story amidst the welter of information. It was only Colbung's moves that lent it any weight or credibility.

It was not possible at the time, or in enquiries made since, to get a full record of that meeting to find out who the Trust members had talked to. The Noonkanbah people denied that it was any of their number. They had not even known of the meeting.

Colbung remained coy about the source of his information. He never came to the Community to seek its opinion, nor even inform them of what he intended to do. He did not consult with other Trust members before making his move, and subsequently refused a request from member Gwen Corunna, who had disassociated herself from his actions, for an emergency meeting of the Trust.

On his way back from Rockhampton, on the Wednesday afternoon, 27 August, Colbung ran into Bob Hawke at Tullamarine airport in Melbourne. He told Hawke that the bans should be lifted, but was given short shrift. Hawke said that the unions would continue to deal directly with the Community. Colbung says that he immediately rang the ALT secretariat in Perth and dictated a message to be delivered to the ACTU and the TLC:

As the senior Aboriginal responsible for Aboriginal land matters in Western Australia I call upon you to lift the ban on drilling by Richter for Amax corporation at Noonkanbah. Aboriginal sites are not at risk. Disturbance settlement of Yungngora community is being negotiated.[15]

It would seem that the Premier's office knew what was going on. Peter Cook said that late on the Wednesday afternoon his office received a call from Telecom, asking if they had a telex number, because the Premier's Department wished to send a message.

The number of the adjacent Metal Workers Union was given. Shortly afterwards Colbung's message was telexed to the Metal Workers' number.

Back in Perth, Colbung met the next morning with Peter Cook, and apparently was convinced to hold off going public after Cook briefed him on the Go Go alternative, and he agreed to discuss this with Court. The Community had been alerted to Colbung's move by Cook, who arranged for Colbung to speak to Ivan McPhee. McPhee pleaded with Colbung to withdraw his message to the unions. Colbung claimed that in this discussion McPhee rejected the Go Go idea because the Go Go people had to be consulted, and said this decided him to go ahead.

He met with Court in the afternoon, and confirmed his advice, as Chairman of the Lands Trust, that drilling should proceed. Court was away, immediately releasing the news.

Hawke and Cook rejected Colbung's approaches, insisting that they were still advised by the Community that it wanted the bans maintained. Dicky Skinner issued a statement that night:

> This is his [Colbung's] own thing he is pushing...We still want the unions to keep their bans on drilling until Amax shifts to another place off our sacred land...Ken Colbung said he talked to Aboriginal people in the Kimberleys, but we know the people all around support us and what we are doing.
>
> The last time Ken Colbung came up here with the three Government Ministers he told us to stick up for our rights and our sacred sites. I don't know why he is saying this now. Ken is an Aboriginal and he should know why we are sticking up for our sacred sites.[16]

The next day, the 29th, the NAC delegation was to leave the country, to take the Aboriginal case to the United Nations.

The morning papers carried about five different versions of events leading to Court's announcement of Colbung's actions. Later that day Court insisted that 'There was no pressure and no collusion between the Government and the ALT on the issue'; and he claimed that 'The first the Government knew of Mr Colbung's action was when we received a copy of the telex he had already sent to the ACTU and the Trades and Labor Council'.[17] In the light of his letter to Fraser three days earlier, the most charitable description of this statement is the one used earlier in the year by the *West Australian*'s editorialist – a 'penchant for concealment and telling half the truth'.

Colbung himself was making no apologies:

> Mr Colbung said he knew that some people might try to cast him in the role of a Judas because of his action. But his conscience was clear...there was no way he would do a deal.
>
> 'I am highly conscious of the implications of my statement,' Mr Colbung said. 'But information has come to us from Noonkanbah and from Aboriginal people in the Kimberleys in general and I cannot let those views go unheard. I have evaluated the information through weeks and weeks of careful consideration and am simply stating the situation as I see it.'[18]

Noonkanbah insisted that none of their people had given such information to Colbung. None of those who spoke to him were ever named, or ever came forward in their own right. Yet Colbung claimed it was his duty to represent these unknown figures above the Community and the multitudes of Aboriginal people who had publicly supported it.

The trouble was, he had not simply stated the position as he saw it. In the name of the holder of the pastoral lease he had called for drilling to proceed, and given the Court Government the green light.

And, indeed, Court had moved with alacrity. At a press conference that afternoon, ostensibly called to take questions on the Colbung move, he answered questions for about half an hour, before closing the conference with the dramatic announcement that drilling had started that day at noon. The nation was stunned.

It took some time for the story to emerge of just how the Government had engineered this coup. Despite the CSR assurances to the unions that it would not be a party to assigning the rig, Richter staff had discussed a number of scenarios with the State, without reaching agreement on any of them.

One of these scenarios had been that Amax would invoke clause six of the drilling contract relating to unsatisfactory performance by the driller. It had been suggested that it should then assign its rights, which would include the right to take over operation of the rig itself, to the State Government.

This is in fact what was done. Exactly how and when it was done is a little less clear. According to Richter, it was on Friday 29 August. But for the drill to have been spudded on noon of the same day, one would have thought at least an informal agreement must have been reached somewhat earlier, perhaps on the Wednesday of Colbung's announcement. Gordon Jackson of CSR put it this way:

> 'This proposal [assignment to the Government] had got to an advanced stage of negotiation but we were mildly surprised to hear on Friday that, when we thought we were still settling the details, the Government had made its announcement [that the drilling had started].'
>
> Asked if his reaction was one of more than just surprise, Mr Jackson said, 'My capacity for being surprised in this situation is now diminished.'
>
> Mr Jackson said that CSR did not regard the latest development as seizure of its rig. It was simply the Government assuming the right on behalf of another party to the contract. 'There was a certain amount of jumping the gun involved,' he said. 'We still have not yet given our consent. We have not put pen to paper.'[19]

This statement cast grave doubt on the propriety of the actions of Peter Jones, who had organised the takeover and, as Minister for Mines, had become Amax's assignee. The relevant clause of the drilling contract required Amax to give written reasons of its dissatisfaction, and to allow seven days for Richter to reply, before it could take over the rig.

The matter was quickly rectified by a letter from Richter to Jones on 1 September, the day after Jackson's comments, stating that it had agreed to the assignment on the 29th, and that it had waived the seven days' notice requirement.

When pressed by the union movement as to why the company had reneged on undertakings to not agree to any assignment, and why it had not taken legal action to prevent the takeover of its rig, Deputy General Manager, Brian Kelman, was to say:

> We concluded that such action would be pointless. We had been informed that the WA government was prepared, and intended if necessary, to pass special legislation empowering it to take possession of the rig.[20]

Clearly the Government would have gone to any lengths at all to achieve its ends.

With the State having acquired the right to drill, Omen Pty Ltd, the two dollar company that had been sitting quietly on the shelf of the chambers of Party President Ian Warner, was dusted off and brought into play.

The two solicitors from Warner's office were replaced as directors. The new owners and directors became Keith Arnott, the drilling consultant engaged by Amax back in July, and Jack Lambert of Richter. An account was opened at a Perth bank to fund the operation. This was able to operate on the basis of an overdraft backed by a $750,000 guarantee provided by the State owned Rural and Industries Bank, on instructions from the Government. It is worth noting that Jones insisted that a Mines Department officer be made one of the signatories of the Omen cheque account. Bill Mitchell was one of the key figures involved in the organisation of these moves.

Lambert and Arnott already had a crew organised, including three of the men from the original crew. At the very latest they must have been given the green light sometime on Thursday 28th, to have got enough of the men up there in time to spud the drill in at midday on Friday.

It was a truly extraordinary series of events. As a feat of organisation, if nothing else, it must be admired. Rarely has a Government moved so swiftly or singlemindedly. But for what purpose?

Two editorials written before even the full facts were known asked the same question. The *West Australian* on 30 August:

> The WA Government yesterday used extreme tactics to turn a drilling rig into a symbol of white dominance...Tactics such as the Government has employed might have been understandable in circumstances of crisis, but the only emergency that exists at Noonkanbah is of the Government's own making.

And the Perth *Sunday Independent*, on the 31st August:

> Sir Charles Court has bulldozed himself into history through his Government's carefully orchestrated drilling operation at Noonkanbah. But he's more likely to achieve notoriety than fame for his action.
>
> Legal technicalities appear to have been swept aside in this latest chapter which has exposed – as never before – the current Government's dangerously dictatorial attitude...
>
> Sir Charles tries to justify his dictatorial actions by the very fact that he is in Government. He has no mandate for his current actions...What has transpired during almost the whole shameful Noonkanbah exercise is, we suggest, contrary to the fundamentals of true liberal government. But when has Sir Charles previously let those ideals interfere when he has a goal in his sights?

The news that drilling had started reached Fitzroy Crossing late in the afternoon. I was at a friend's house, with a reporter from the Melbourne *Age*, when the phone call came. The reporter accompanied me down to the rodeo grounds, and filed this story:

> Dicky Skinner, the young man who speaks for the Noonkanbah Aborigines, was walking away from the rodeo, smiling as usual.
>
> Five hours before, ninety kilometres away, oil drilling on his sacred homeland had begun, and now the community's liaison man, Mr Steve Hawke,

ran up to him with the news.

'They started drilling at Noonkanbah this afternoon Dicky', he said. 'They've come in behind your back.'

Mr Skinner's smile disappeared. It was a scene to be repeated several times as the news spread among the men of the community who were in Fitzroy Crossing for the annual racing and rodeo carnival.

Mr Skinner said just one thing: 'That's it.'

At first he appeared calm, but the news had hit him like a sledgehammer. He stood motionless for minutes as members of the community waited around for him to speak. He swallowed hard to hold back tears.

Steve Hawke advised him to get together with his people and think about what they wanted to do. Mr Skinner nodded and said that one carload of people had already left to return to the station. But it was not clear at that stage whether Mr Skinner and some of the older men would go back last night too.

As the crowd left the rodeo, creating a cloud of dust, Mr Hawke broke the news to other community members. They showed hurt and betrayal. One old man walked up to me and said: 'There's nothing we can do.'

They stood around for a long time not knowing what to do now that the great goanna had been disturbed.

Steve Hawke was asked how Mr Skinner was feeling. 'Sick,' he said. 'We all feel sick.'[21]

The next day, after a sad discussion with a few of the leaders, punctuated by long silences, the following statement was issued:

We had this fight for a long time now, for three years. Charlie Court got round us using a dirty trick. All we can say is that the white man is mad. He doesn't know what he is doing.

They might hurt that sacred maladji place. But we've still got our Law. We will live by that law. The white man can't kill the Aboriginal Law no matter how hard he tries.

We can't say any more now, but we know we are not beaten. We are still strong. And we know that we are proud, and that Charlie Court, and Senator Chaney, and the Federal Government, and Ken Colbung are the ones who are weak and shamed.[22]

18

THE AFTERMATH

The Noonkanbah Community have sought justice, and they have been given obstruction. They have sought negotiation and they have been given confrontation, they have sought peace and they have been given violence.

Jim Hagan, Chairman of the National Aboriginal Conference, Geneva, 3 September 1980.

Noonkanbah's sadness was reflected in many parts of the country. And with the sadness was coupled anger. Noonkanbah had become such a symbol that the desperate measures of the Court Government had done more than violate the Law of Noonkanbah; they had shattered hopes and modern dreams that had become entwined with the battle to protect this ancient Dreaming.

Over the weekend Dicky Skinner took phone calls from Aboriginal leaders around the country expressing their sympathy and outrage, and also conferred with Peter Cook of the TLC. Out of these calls and another round of Community talks down at the racecourse came the idea of a pan-Aboriginal meeting at Noonkanbah the following week. Skinner was still talking and acting defiantly, though the Elders were more subdued.

Sir Charles Court and Peter Jones seemed determined to rub salt into everybody's wounds by revelling in their victory. On the Sunday they flew in for a surprise visit to the site. Court reported glowingly in a press release:

> They [Court and Jones] inspected the drilling operations and met the men involved with the work. Sir Charles said he was impressed by the efficiency with which they had got the drilling underway so quickly.
>
> 'They are professional drillers and it shows in the way they go about their work,' Sir Charles said. 'Their cool efficiency is a welcome change from the hysterical attempts of some union leaders to try to stop these men earning their livelihood in their normal way.'...
>
> The Premier met media representatives at the drill site and explained the excellent progress made with drilling and cementing in the surface casing.[1]

A later report gave the lie to this rosy picture, and the earlier claims of a flood of experienced drillers volunteering their services for the project. In fact it seems Arnott and Lambert had had to cobble a crew together. For Amax was to say in a progress report on 6 November that 'Drilling progress has been slow due initially to the inexperience of some of the rig workers employed'.[2]

Whilst Court and Jones were lunching at the drilling compound an official was despatched down to the homestead in a police car with an offer from Court to meet with the Community. Naturally, this was rejected out of hand. One of Court's more offensive statements appeared in the *West Australian* the next day, when he was quoted as saying, 'I am surprised that some of the Elders did not want to see their old mates'.[3]

Over the next few days the media was full of indignant statements from many quarters about the Government's actions. A number of Aboriginal people and organisations disassociated themselves from Colbung's stand, and many called for his resignation or

Sir Charles Court and Peter Jones at the drill site, 31 August 1980.

removal from the Lands Trust.

The unions were intensely angered: that their bans had been circumvented; at what they saw as a plot hatched using Colbung as the fall guy; and at CSR, who they believed had misled them. There was talk of widespread industrial action against the Government, Amax and CSR. The executive of the Trades and Labor Council met on 1 September and drew up a plan of retaliatory action, but this plan was held in reserve pending talks with CSR, the ACTU and the Aboriginal community, and the faint hope that the Federal Government might yet act.

The Federal Government soon made it clear that it still had no intention of intervening, but the reaction of various spokesmen varied. Senator Chaney distanced himself from the State's actions; initially saying that he deeply regretted the failure to settle the matter by negotiation, and then a few days later washing his hands of the affair by admitting his failure to achieve what he wanted, and saying that there was nothing further that could be done. Then the *Australian* quoted Ian Sinclair, the Deputy Leader of the Liberals' coalition partner, the National Party, as saying he had a great deal of sympathy for the State Government – producing the headline 'Cabinet Rift Opens Over Drilling At Noonkanbah'.

Malcolm Fraser, in an airport press conference before he left for New York to receive his humanitarian award, continued the doublespeak he had employed since his visit to Derby, defending, if not endorsing, the State Government, saying 'he believed it was determined to protect the way of life of the Aboriginal people and their sites and customs'.[4]

The Canberra based Aboriginal Treaty Committee led by Nugget Coombs telegrammed B'nai Brith in New York to say that 'You should be aware that many Australians are shamed that your award should be conferred on an Australian whose record in his own country denies his suitability for it'.[5] This sour note to Fraser's international image was emphasised by a demonstration led by American Indians, chanting 'Fraser the Razor', and holding a huge banner that read 'Human Rights Begin At Home', outside the award-giving ceremony.

On the other side of the Atlantic attention was also focused on Noonkanbah, with the NAC delegation about to appear in Geneva. And at the same time Aboriginal leaders were gathering at Noonkanbah. These events made 3 September 1980 a doubly historic day for the Aboriginal movement in terms of symbolic landmarks: the first appearance in a United Nations forum in the stately diplomatic halls of Geneva; and in the bed of the Fitzroy River at Noonkanbah, the first ever joint meeting of Aboriginal land councils from throughout northern and central Australia.

The NAC delegation had a positive build-up to its formal appearance in Geneva. International Church and union organisations had assisted with contacts and publicity. Jimmy Bieunderry in particular made quite an impression; the full-blood tribal man from the Kimberley, with his slow but dignified way of speaking, striding the boulevards of Geneva in his riding boots and stockman's hat. There was plenty of scope for imagery in the stories filed home by the correspondents covering the story for Australian newspapers.

A press conference the day before the appearance at the Sub-Commission was remarkably well attended by a range of European media, and the biggest fish of all, one of the major American television networks. A collection of Michael Gallagher's photographs of the melee and arrests at Mickey's Pool added weight to the briefing given by Jim Hagan, and Bieunderry's explanations of the meaning of the land and the beliefs of the Noonkanbah people.

In real terms their presence was less than earth shattering. Geneva was host to thousands of diplomats and lobbyists, permanent and visiting, all pushing their various barrows. A committee hearing of a sub-commission of one of the United Nations' many commissions was not exactly the front line of world affairs.

But when the delegation was due to appear before the Sub-Commission, the media, including the American networks, arrived at the conference room. Jim Hagan was given the floor. Flanked by Reg Birch and Bieunderry, and speaking officially as a delegate of the World Council of Indigenous Peoples, he gave the delegates a brief and eloquent Aboriginal perspective on the history of Australian settlement, the Noonkanbah affair, and the Federal Government's failure to act, concluding in this manner:

> The Australian Federal Government has chosen to remain merely an observer to this gross injustice being perpetrated on an innocent people, and to ignore its responsibilities under the various international Human Rights Covenants to which it is a party. In a climate of despair, the Aboriginal people of Australia now turn to you, the men of International law, to assist in their struggle for equality and for freedom.
>
> The Noonkanbah Community have sought justice, and they have been given obstruction. They have sought negotiation and they have been given confrontation, they have sought peace and they have been given violence.
>
> The Australian Government's acquiescence in this continuing breach of human rights must see it stand condemned in the eyes of the world.
>
> We ask this Sub-Commission, having heard our submission, to urge the

Australian Government to take appropriate measures to protect the rights of the Noonkanbah Aboriginal people to freedom of their religion and to the enjoyment of their own culture as guaranteed by the international covenants to which Australia is party.

We also ask that this Sub-Commission undertake a study of discrimination against Aborigines in Australia and in particular the failure of the Australian Government to provide for the right of Aborigines to obtain proper title to their traditional land or compensation for the loss of that land in the States of Australia, and to make such recommendations to the Human Rights Commission arising out of that study as you see fit.[6]

The media coverage of Hagan's speech was, 'according to reports, unprecedented in the history of the Sub-Commission'.[7]

There were also separate meetings in Geneva with United Nations officials and a representative of the Organisation of African Unity, and afterwards in London with Commonwealth officials, Jamaican Government members, and supporters of the Aboriginal cause. All in all it was a highly successful debut on the international stage.

The Federal Government's response, in Geneva and at home, was to develop and repeat the theme that Noonkanbah was 'the exception to the rule', and that it was doing its utmost to put in place systems which would ensure that there were no more such aberrations.

The State Government was furious at being pilloried in this way. Premier Court made no secret of what he saw as the inadequacy of the Commonwealth's response, and he continued to bluntly reject the Commonwealth's suggestions of more acceptable guidelines for mining on Aboriginal lands.

The Sub-Commission's resolution at the end of its sittings specifically recognised the submission of the NAC without going any further. But this in itself, in diplomatic terms, was something of a victory, as it had been only one of dozens of matters heard, and reflected the impression that had been made.

The Noonkanbah meeting saw delegates come in at short notice from the three statutory land councils in the Northern Territory, the Pitjanjatjarra Council that operated out of Alice Springs, but extended its coverage into parts of South Australia and Western Australia, and the Cairns based North Queensland Land Council, plus the Strelley mob and the Kimberley Land Council. Between them, these groups represented nearly all the traditionally-oriented Aboriginal people in the country.

The resolution that came out of the meeting caused shivers in many a boardroom at first. It contained condemnations of Ken Colbung and the State and Federal Governments, and a statement of support for the Noonkanbah mob. But the contentious part was a call for all the attending councils to suspend talks with mining companies in their regions until such time as meaningful talks began about removing the drill from Noonkanbah.

In a move that took the media and the drillers by surprise, the meeting moved from the riverbank in convoy to the drill site, where Darryl Kickett of the KLC read the resolution in front of the locked gates.

In fact, the ban on negotiations was soon shown to be a hollow threat. The Territory land councils had statutory obligations through the legislation under which they operated. The Pitjanjatjarra were well into negotiations on a major exploration agreement, and specified that they would have to exempt this from the ban. And the non-statutory status of the Kimberley and North Queensland councils made it easy for the indusrty to circum-vent them. After the initial flurry caused by the announcement the concern soon passed.

Nor was the meeting a total success as an exercise in unity. The old dispute between Don McLeod and the land councils flared again. Nevertheless, it was a ground-breaking exercise, and prepared the way for the formal establishment a few months later of a Federation of Land Councils that has since become a significant voice in Aboriginal affairs.

Peter Cook and Gil Barr came to Noonkanbah for the second day of this meeting. They tried to go into the drill site, but were met at the gates by a Mines Department engineer and told that they needed written permission from the Minister for Mines to enter, and that they would be arrested if they entered otherwise.

In talks with the Community and the land council representatives they were told that the people wanted the unions to continue to bring what pressure they could to

The Joint Land Councils meeting at Noonkanbah, 3 September 1980. Top left: Mick Miller of the North Queensland Land Council speaks to the meeting. Bottom: Friday Muller.

Dicky Skinner addressing the Joint Land Councils meeting.

The Joint Land Councils meeting at the drill site.

achieve a withdrawal of the rig. But by then everybody knew that such an outcome was not likely.

It seems that on his return from overseas Prime Minister Fraser made one last abortive attempt to resolve the crisis. For his efforts he had his knuckles severely rapped, and was nearly plunged into an even deeper crisis.

On 11 September he met with the Amax Chairman, Pierre Gousselant, and his deputy, Arthur Reef, in Sydney. The two were in Australia ostensibly to examine a range of investment opportunities, but no doubt Noonkanbah was very much on their minds. No details of the meeting were ever released.

But presumably it was this meeting that gave rise to a story some months later in the *Western Mail*, written by journalist Tony Warton, who had been Court's press secretary at the time of the Noonkanbah dispute. The story was part of a piece examining the forces ranged against Fraser within the Liberal Party, and speculating on the possibility of a leadership challenge by Andrew Peacock. Court was listed as one of the Liberals less than happy with the Prime Minister, for the following reasons:

> Last year Mr Fraser made a catastrophic blunder. He gave Sir Charles a firm assurance that there would be no federal interference in the handling of the Noonkanbah confrontation.

312

Despite this, he called in a senior executive of Amax and tried to persuade him to get the company to pull out of oil exploration at Noonkanbah.

Caught in a sandwich between two governments his company had to live with, the executive reported the matter to Sir Charles – who threatened to campaign against Mr Fraser in the federal election.[8]

It would indeed be fascinating to know the substance of what passed between the two leaders. The version related by Warton may well be exaggerated. The thought of a Liberal State Premier campaigning against a Liberal Prime Minister in a Federal Election is almost beyond imagination. However, Court seemed so obsessed with securing his victory at Noonkanbah that perhaps he may have made the threat, and possibly he would even have gone so far as to carry it out if Fraser had not backed off.

The unions had been outmanoeuvred by the State Government, and their options were now very limited. Within a week of the drilling starting there was a noticeable change of mood in the media and the public. Whilst criticism of Court continued, there seemed to be a growing feeling that the worst had now been done, and there was little public appetite for the saga to drag on yet further.

The ACTU Executive met in Melbourne on 10 September. It endorsed the TLC's planned industrial action, and made some additional plans. But it also authorised, and placed emphasis on, further talks with the companies. In his press conference afterwards, Bob Hawke said:

Now the drilling is taking place our main concern is not retribution and punishment, appropriate as that is. The ACTU is seeking to bring about a situation that all parties except the State Government had previously agreed to before the Government took over the drilling operation.[9]

Hawke was in the final days of his term as ACTU President. In his last major negotiating role, he flew to Sydney on 11 September for discussions with CSR, and an evening meeting with Gousselant and Reef of Amax. The talks with CSR focused on trying to convince the company to appeal in the courts against the takeover of its drilling rig, and to seek an injunction restraining the Western Australian Government from using it. But CSR avoided any further involvement, saying:

Some of the parties to the dispute have attempted to engage CSR to act on their behalf; CSR has not done so. We respect the integrity and high motives of all that are involved; but no course of action is open to us by which we can influence events in any significant way.[10]

The discussions with Amax were equally unsuccessful.

The last hopes of forcing a halt to the drilling at Noonkanbah had disappeared.

A telephone conference of senior ACTU officials on 18 September called on the postal and telecommunications unions, and those unions with members employed in Amax and CSR owned enterprises, to call meetings of members and recommend bans to apply until the completion of drilling at Noonkanbah. But the response from the shopfloor was far from enthusiastic.

For the unions from that point on it became a matter of escaping from the situation as gracefully as possible. The original Richter drilling crew still had to be paid, and contributions to their strike fund had ceased to flow. The TLC quietly negotiated a settlement with CSR. On 3 October it was announced that they had resolved their differences, and all bans were lifted. The two keys to this were a public guarantee of future work for the crew, and an unannounced agreement from the company to make up the shortfall in the strike fund, and take on payment of the crew from that point on.

Sir Charles Court and his Ministers enjoyed the discomfiture of the unions greatly, missing no opportunity to let fly with another attack. Their interpretation was a victory for strong and determined government over union threats and anarchy. Their manner was that of the righteous vindicated.

In the first week of September, Bill Grayden introduced the long threatened amendments to the Aboriginal Heritage Act. The definition of an Aboriginal site was narrowed. The Minister's powers to direct the Museum Trustees and staff were enlarged and clarified. And a right of appeal was given to any person with an interest in land to appeal against any decision under the Act, without any similar right of appeal being given to Aboriginal people whose sites may be affected.

The conspiracy theories of those who believed Noonkanbah was an extravagant decoy created to clear the way for development of the Argyle mine were given greater credence than ever, when, two days after these amendments became law, Grayden officially gave CRA permission to utilise the Barramundi site. This was seven months after the company had first sought permission to do so.

Court did not relent in his private attack on Senator Fred Chaney. He was provoked by a letter from Chaney early in September defending the action of various churchmen in the dispute. Court's reply was stinging in its tone:

> I do not know what this is meant to prove beyond the fact that, from your statements in your letter, and statements you have been making in recent days, there is no possibility of the State Government having a sensible communication with you to achieve a practical result in respect of Aborigines, their land, and mining and petroleum operations.
>
> I must admit I am bitterly disappointed at the way you handled this matter and we have reached a point when there appears to be no way in which we can reconcile your attitude with our own.
>
> We are getting very tired of you, and others, assuming that we have no sensitivity in these matters, nor appreciation of Aboriginal aspirations and attachments.
>
> I can hardly recall a statement which you have made which does not imply some criticism of the Western Australian Government. Perhaps if you had a look at the overall situation and realised that we might have some capacity in these matters, and also some sensitivity in a deep and sensible Christian way, you might be able to reverse the situation which has developed.[11]

This letter shows the bitterness Court felt at what he believed to be the unfair perception held of him by Chaney, and large sections of the media and the public. Throughout the dispute he had gone to great lengths to explain and justify his position, and he was pained and angered when this was not accepted.

Late in September, once the threat of union bans had faded, the Government quietly re-assigned the drilling contract back to Amax. Omen continued as the driller, but its accounts went to the company, and the Government's guarantee was never called on. The Mines Department eventually recovered the cost of the convoy – a total of over two hundred and fifty thousand dollars – from Amax as well.

The only costs the Government acknowledged in the whole exercise were one hundred and seventy-three thousand dollars for the role of the State Emergency Service in the convoy, and sixty-six thousand dollars for upgrading of the Noonkanbah road after it was made public. It refused to detail the costs of the police involvement. Mines Department records do show small payments to Bill Mitchell and another unnamed consultant.

Drilling at Noonkanbah was halted in mid-November, and the hole was plugged on the 23rd. It was of course, as everyone had expected, a dry hole. The farcical nature of the whole exercise is revealed in a letter from Max Reynolds to Peter Jones early in November:

> It was realised at the time [that drilling commenced] that the prognosis at Location 2 would not be the same as for Location 1, but as this was a wildcat well, with very little stratigraphic control, there was little point in making changes at that stage. The main seismic anomalies, although deeper at Location 2, still appeared to be accessible. The difference was that the strong seismic event... is at about 4000m at location 2; this event clearly could not be reached in the time available.[12]

Citing the approaching wet, Reynolds requested permission to vary the drilling program approved by Jones, to pull out early. The drilling was stopped at three thousand one hundred and thirty-four metres. In other words, the drill never got to the real target; and it must have been known at the time Omen was sent in that it was not likely to do so in the time available.

Very weak gas shows had been found at a higher, weaker seismic anomaly, and Court was to say in a statement to the Parliament:

> Although no major discovery has been made, the well has shown the presence of hydrocarbons varying from liquid to dry gas over a section of more than 800 metres. In our opinion, this provides further encouragement for the search for those areas in the Fitzroy Basin which could provide the necessary reservoir conditions to store such hydrocarbons.
>
> The search for oil is essentially a search for information. Through the painstaking collection of information – often at great cost – petroleum discoveries are made. Most of the world's wells are dry wells. But without the information they give us there would be no oil production at all.
>
> The well drilled on Noonkanbah was an essential part of exploration for petroleum which must proceed with all the encouragement we can give it in Australia's interests.[13]

Certainly the drilling would have yielded some information. But in fact it was a half-baked exercise of no real value except the proving of a point by the Government. In industry terms it was a non-event. It is ironic to think that this was the end result of the Government's extraordinary efforts.

And the Noonkanbah people, how did they handle the aftermath of their great battle? There was a sort of withdrawal, amongst the Elders particularly, as if they needed time to absorb and reflect upon what had happened.

After the meeting of the land councils there were no more visits to the drill site. It was ignored as much as possible, but no one could pretend it wasn't there. The lights at the top of the rig could be seen from the station, and most nights the noise of the big generators could be heard on the breeze. And every time people headed into town along the river road, there it was, turning away, boring deeper into the earth.

The charges from the Mickey's Pool incident were heard in the Fitzroy Crossing court in November. The traffic related charges were dismissed after the ALS successfully argued that the police had failed to show that the actual location of the incident was consistent with the road gazetted and described on the map. The hindering and resisting charges were adjourned, and eventually convictions were recorded, but with no penalties.

Despite the turmoil of the year, the station had continued to operate successfully, with almost four hundred head of cattle turned off, and a total of nine windmills rehabilitated by the end of the year.

The Department for Community Welfare's end of year report was surprisingly optimistic:

> The community has been under extreme pressure and stress, both physically, socially and culturally. The leaders have been pushed to their limits in just coping with the huge influx of visitors. The Elders have been tested by the community and other Aboriginal groups regarding the culture and law. The workforce has been struggling to achieve their goals because of the large amount of time taken up with meetings. Yet, considering all these pressures, the community has coped very well. They are still functioning as a viable economic group, and socially they have remained very stable...
>
> The most important and surprising thing is that the community is still intact. Many times throughout the year I was worried that the community was going to split up and drift back to Fitzroy Crossing...I feel that a much stronger community has developed from this experience. The community was looking to the Elders for decisions and reasons why these things were important...
>
> The other exciting thing is that the youth, especially the young men, are still at Noonkanbah and looking proud and have a good idea of where they are heading...Noonkanbah has not had any young men in trouble the whole of this year, something I doubt any other community can say.[14]

But there was a weariness and malaise underlying that apparent resilience. Bob Mululby, the principal custodian of the affected country, was still ill. And amongst the Elders there was an air of sadness, almost mourning, for the country, for what had been lost.

The Community had been irrevocably changed by the drama it had endured. In pursuit of the Elders' vision of a truly Aboriginal community, they had become embroiled in the maelstrom of the white man's world more deeply than ever, and picking up the pieces once the storm had passed was not an easy matter.

The internal systems for controlling visitors and regulating community affairs had been weakened by taking second place for so long to the fight against drilling; and there was not the energy there for the rebuilding process.

As the quiet time of the wet season approached, all concerned looked forward to the relief it would bring. More than anything else, the Community now wanted to be left alone.

EPILOGUE

I believe the Noonkanbah confrontation highlighted and still highlights the issue of two hundred years of complete disregard for Aboriginal opinion and Aboriginal law and religion. I firmly believe that what happened at Noonkanbah has more political and racial implications for the betterment of Aborigines than most people believe.

Jack Davis, 1988.

Obviously this history of the Noonkanbah conflict has not come hot on the heels of the events described. Hopefully, the intervening years have brought a sense of perspective that would have been difficult to achieve back then.

In fact, it has been written during Australia's Bicentennial year, marking the two hundredth anniversary of the arrival of the first permanent white inhabitants at Sydney Cove. The unfolding of the Bicentenary has provided a curious counterpoint, with its parallels to the pattern of events at Noonkanbah.

Against all odds and expectations, it started as a year of hope for things positive for the Aboriginal community. Sydney on Australia Day, 26 January, saw what was probably the largest ever gathering of Aboriginal people, in an emotional and hugely successful demonstration of solidarity and unity that reminded white Australia in no uncertain terms that it had yet to come to terms with the history it was celebrating.

Using the theme 'We Have Survived', the Aboriginal community struck a near perfect balance of a strong and powerful statement of its perspective on two hundred years of invasion and suffering, without being so negative as to alienate the majority of white Australia that would have preferred to indulge in nostalgia and good times.

For the first six months, it seemed that the Bicentenary was indeed forcing Australia towards a more realistic recognition of the history, the role and the rights of the first Australians. This culminated in the Barunga Festival, near Katherine in the Northern Territory in June, when Aboriginal leaders, and the Prime Minister and Minister for Aboriginal Affairs announced the intention to explore the possibilities and requirements of a treaty that would seek to address in a concrete way these issues.

Also, the proposal emerged for a new Aboriginal and Torres Strait Islander Commission (ATSIC) to replace the Department of Aboriginal Affairs and the Aboriginal Development Commission, holding the promise of the most significant step yet towards placing real power over the administration of Aboriginal affairs in the hands of local Aboriginal assemblies instead of government bureaucrats.

Yet since the Barunga Festival, the momentum that had been created seems to have faded and dissipated. By the end of 1988 the treaty proposal had made no apparent progress. ATSIC was under severe threat from a combination of vested and political interests. The Minister was under siege from attacks that seemed motivated more by political issues than any real concern for Aboriginal people. Aboriginal deaths in custody continued to occur, and the Muirhead Inquiry established to investigate the tragedy of those deaths was under attack in Western Australia from police and prison officer unions and the State Labor Government.

And perhaps of greatest concern, the conservative parties at the Federal and Western Australian levels had adopted the 'One Australia' theme, with its ethnocentric bias and opposition to Land Rights and 'special privileges and services' for blacks. In fact, these policies seem to hark way back to the failed days of assimilation policies.

There is an unfortunate, and seemingly inevitable pattern, of white Australia's response to Aboriginal people, and the handling of Aboriginal affairs. There are occasional surges of a general sense of sympathy and concern, prompted by guilt, scandal, compassion or the initiative and demands of Aboriginal people. Noonkanbah and the Bicentenary provide examples of this.

Out of such surges grow hope, and a range of governmental policies and initiatives of varying quality. But then things are perceived as going too far, and the barriers of the inherent conservatism and racism of middle Australia, and the vested interests of the powerful land owners and users, are confronted, and the 'backlash effect' comes into play. This 'backlash effect' can be either a reality, or a convenient excuse of the politicians. Hopes are dashed, policies are abandoned or watered down, and Aboriginal affairs go on the backburner, until the cycle begins again.

The close of the Bicentennial year saw all the signs of the downward trend of the cycle beginning. The challenge at the close of the year was to see whether this time it might be different; whether the barriers could be breached at last, to open up a real and long-term change in the administration of Aboriginal affairs, and the relationship between black and white Australia.

In this context it is worth looking back at what has happened in the eight years from the completion of oil drilling at Noonkanbah to the Bicentenary; to the Yungngora Community, to the players in the drama, and to some of the contentious issues of the time.

For the Community it has not been a happy or productive time, on the whole. In the aftermath of the great dispute, it never recovered the clear focus and drive of the early years. The mental exhaustion that lingered and the bitterness of defeat were factors in this, but only two among many.

Beginning in 1981, there was a prolonged battle with the government bureaucracy over the provision of housing to the Community. The Community's preference for establishing its own co-operative to plan, supervise and run the housing project was refused. This was the first major blow to the autonomy the Community had enjoyed up until then in the management of its internal affairs.

When the State Housing Commission was eventually accepted with reluctance as the building agency, there was another losing battle over the right of the Commission's supervisor to bring alcohol onto the property. The Commission insisted that it could not find non-drinking personnel, and on the right of its people to drink in their homes on the station. Though the Community succeeded in getting strict rules banning the supply to Community members, the bureaucrats had managed to break down the most basic rule of the Community.

The provision of housing has certainly been a forward step in material terms, but the social consequences of the manner in which it was provided have been less positive.

Bob Mululby recovered from his illness; but Friday Muller passed away in 1981, marking the end of an era. Then in 1982, following the death of his daughter, Ginger Nganawilla moved out to establish an outstation at Warrimbah, still on the Noonkanbah lease, but a separate place. His dreams for Noonkanbah seemed to have fallen by the wayside, and he preferred to re-establish a smaller, more family-oriented community. He too passed away, in 1984, and the strongest, most visionary man of the old generation was gone.

These losses, and the fragmentation arising from the Warrimbah move, the departure of a couple of families to other communities, and the Kadjina mob becoming more settled on Millijidee, all contributed to the weakening of the sense of being one mob

– the Noonkanbah mob – in control of their own lives.

The original vision of the Community, the strong, yet simplistic idea of an insular community living the Aboriginal way, unfettered by whitefellers and whitefeller ideas, had become lost.

The mining fight and all that had gone with it had brought the realisation that retreat into an insular world was no longer possible. As the possibility of turning the vision into reality faded, so did the incentive to fight for and work on issues big and small that together make a community what it is. The Community began to flounder.

Clearly another factor which caused the Community to flounder was the decreasing prestige of the Law. The mining dispute itself had ultimately been a defeat for the Law and the Lawmen. The heroic battle to go one step further and demand recognition, even parity of some kind, for the Aboriginal Law had foundered. The Lawmen had not been able to halt the incursions of the miners that were perceived as such a threat. There was no rejection *per se* of the Law, but something had been lost. This was emphasised by the death of the two most senior Lawmen.

A whitefeller moved in to supervise the housing program. The number of white staff in the Community school increased. Eventually another whitefeller arrived to manage the store. The cattle mustering failed one year, and outside contractors were brought in. One of them stripped the place of much of its breeding stock, and the cattle enterprise was in dire straits. The confusion and apathy that afflict so many Aboriginal communities became more and more apparent at Noonkanbah.

In 1982 the Kimberley saw a big Christian crusade, with busloads of Christians from the goldfields and Arnhem Land sweeping through. Many at Noonkanbah joined hundreds from other communities in conversion.

The Arnhem Landers incorporated Aboriginal languages and some Aboriginal practices into their Christianity. But once they had passed through, the missionaries who had been in the area for years stepped into the breach. Their brand of religion was heavily fundamentalist. The preachers insisted that the end of the world was nigh. Only those who rejected the old ways, embraced the Lord, and gave up the grog and smoking and gambling would be saved. Their call seemed based largely on fear and negativities.

For some, conversion was a passing thing, for others it was real and lasting. Notable amongst the latter was Dicky Skinner. Through 1981 and 1982 he had remained socially and politically involved in regional issues as an active and inspiring Chairman of the Marra Worra Worra Resource Centre in Fitzroy Crossing. But he was growing weary of the fight, and the Noonkanbah Community and Station had missed his strong presence during the weeks and months he was away at meetings and Marra Worra Worra business.

He threw all this off and, rejecting the Law that he had fought so hard for, became a Christian and a committed lay preacher. In 1983 he spent most of the year quietly at nearby Looma. The next year his wife died, and he became more deeply involved than ever in the Church.

He has since moved back to Noonkanbah, resuming his position as Community Chairman, and station manager, and is not so active as a lay preacher. But he has retained his commitment to Christianity, and still rejects the Law. He supported the writing of this book, so that the story could be told. He makes no apologies for his actions at the time, but makes it clear that he now follows a different path.

Jimmy Bieunderry too went this path. He had been involved in the Church for many years before he became politically active through the NAC and the KLC. His activism had grown out of his role as a lay preacher helping the people during the difficult times of the walk-offs and the fringe camps in the early 1970s. He had managed to combine his Christianity and his Aboriginality, including his support for the Law and culture.

But within a couple of years of Noonkanbah, exhausted, he extricated himself from the political life, and returned wholly to the Christian fold. He died a tragically early death in 1985. His funeral at Christmas Creek was the largest in memory in the area, with a cortege of almost one hundred cars winding its way to the dusty bush cemetery. Hundreds of Aboriginal people, and white friends and acquaintances from both his Church involvement and his days in the Land Council and the NAC, were there to share the sadness of his loss.

The Law has not died at Noonkanbah. Young men are still initiated. It is still very much a part of the lives of most of the people. But it is not the all encompassing force and motivation it was eight and ten years ago.

Noonkanbah was not the only community in the Kimberley to go backwards in this period. There were two general problems, as well as a host of local difficulties.

First was the general political atmosphere. Just as the vision was lost at Noonkanbah, in a more general way, the activism and positiveness of the late 1970s lost direction with the setbacks at Noonkanbah and Argyle. The Kimberley Land Council remained a voice in the wilderness, with no prospect of success in the campaign for Land Rights, control over the miners, or any other issues. People became less enthusiastic about making the effort to travel long distances for meetings that were leading nowhere. Tensions and divisions that had lain submerged in the more hopeful years began to emerge with greater force.

A more fundamental problem at the community level was the proliferation of the bureaucracy during the first half of the 1980s. The preferred answer of governments of both parties in this period was an ever increasing number of programs and officers to run them. The number of public servants going into communities demanding information and decisions seemed to mushroom at an alarming rate.

Long overdue material and physical improvements had been delivered. But there was no overall sense of purpose or direction, and very little co-ordination of the various programs. Community leaders in many places became increasingly confused, and eventually apathetic. Many communities had lost control.

In 1988 there were signs in Noonkanbah and other communities in the Kimberley that the situation was beginning to improve. There was a recognition of the need to consolidate and reorganise.

A revamped council at Noonkanbah was becoming more effective, and beginning to assert itself. A rehabilitation program was well underway for the cattle enterprise. But there was still a long way to go. From the early days of no whitefellers living on the station, and then just the two schoolteachers, the numbers had crept up to well over a dozen white residents in various roles, and still an enormous number of visiting public servants, contractors and others. There was still no clear vision or direction.

The years brought changes for many of the other players in the dispute as well.

By the middle of 1981 Amax had been reluctantly replaced as the operator of EP97 and the neighbouring oil permits were operated by a new company that had bought into the consortium, the International Energy Development Corporation (IEDC). Soon afterwards Amax withdrew from any active exploration role in Australia.

IEDC, to Peter Jones' chagrin, negotiated a revision of the exploration program which temporarily abandoned further drilling plans, and concentrated on seismic work well away from Noonkanbah.

The drill site was never cleaned up, as had been promised on dozens of occasions. Attempts by the Community to have the road degazetted and the site returned to them were rejected by the Government. Jones insisted that the uncompleted drilling might yet be finished, and the site was therefore still required. It has remained in the state in which Amax left it to this day.

The hoped for oil boom in the Canning Basin never eventuated. One small oil field at Blina, north-west of Noonkanbah, has been the only positive result. Exploration has continued, but on nowhere near the same scale as earlier.

For one of the original Richter drill crew, at least, there was a happy ending. He had drifted out of touch with his family, from a coal mining town in the north of England. His family saw him on the TV news, coming out of a union meeting in far away Perth, Australia. Good unionists all, the family was proud of him. They tracked him down, and there was a happy reunion.

For Sir Charles Court, Noonkanbah was the last big battle. After a relatively quiet year in 1981, he retired at the beginning of 1982, to be succeeded by his long-time deputy, Ray O'Connor.

Although he would vehemently argue the case, Noonkanbah was described by some commentators as his swan song. Certainly it was the dominant issue of his last term as Premier. And in a very real sense it tarnished his image. For many who had previously accepted his image of a tough but fair 'can do' leader, the excesses of Noonkanbah revealed a meanness and lack of charity in his make up.

He fervently maintained that his actions had had the support of the general public. The two opinion polls taken at the time in fact showed a remarkably even split.

In October of 1980, in the immediate aftermath of the dispute, this question was posed by the pollsters: 'Should the federal government have tried to use its powers to stop oil drilling at Noonkanbah?' Forty-five percent, including an astonishing thirty-one percent of Liberal voters, had answered yes, compared to forty-seven percent who had answered no.[1]

Considering the drastic nature of the Federal Government intervening against a State, the level of support for the proposition in the conservative Australian electorate was remarkable. A large number of the negative respondents would no doubt have given less than full approval to the actions of the State Government, without actually sanctioning Federal intervention. So it is reasonable to infer that perhaps Court did not in fact have majority support.

Apart from Premier Sir Joh Bjelke-Petersen in Queensland, Court was the last of the Australian political leaders who had grown to adulthood in the pre-war era. He was an ideologist who was confident enough to govern according to what he believed in, rather than by what the opinion polls told him. But his ideology had been exposed in a harsh light by the end of his term, to the extent that his previously broad base of support had narrowed considerably.

He remained bitter at what he had seen as the failure of the Federal Government to support him; and never one to forgive and forget, he continued to make life difficult for Malcolm Fraser and Fred Chaney.

'Red Fred' Chaney, as he became known in some Liberal circles, paid a heavy price for his estrangement from the power brokers in the Western Australian party. In 1981 he was looking to fulfil a long-held ambition by transferring from the Senate to the House of Representatives. He sought preselection for the safe Liberal seat of Curtin in Western Australia.

In a humiliating defeat for a Minister, he lost the ballot to a political unknown supported by the party establishment. Bill Hassell and other members of the State Cabinet were prominent in the lobbying campaign against him.

By 1988 he had risen to the position of Opposition Leader in the Senate. In December of 1988 he announced that he would try again to enter the House of Representatives via a new seat created in a redistribution. Many pundits believe that had he not been frustrated in 1981 he would have already been the Federal Leader of the Opposition.

People who knew him have commented that he was a changed man after the Noonkanbah experience. It may have been that, or it may have been the chastening experience of 1981. He moved out of the Aboriginal Affairs portfolio in a Cabinet reshuffle late in 1980. And over the years he has gradually distanced himself from the 'small l' liberal side of the party, repositioning more towards the middle.

The union leaders and politicians who were prominent supporters of Noonkanbah prospered with the rise of the Labor Party to government at State and Federal level in 1983.

Bob Hawke, of course, is the Prime Minister, and Peter Cook is a Minister in his government. John Dawkins and Stewart West are both members of the Hawke Cabinet. Peter Dowding was the first Minister for Mines in the Brian Burke Government in Western Australia, and succeeded Burke as Premier early in 1988. Ernie Bridge became the first Aboriginal Minister in an Australian government when he was appointed Minister for Aboriginal Affairs in Burke's second ministry in 1986.

If at the close of 1980, in the light of Noonkanbah, it had been known that the Bicentennial year would mark the fifth year of Labor Governments in Perth and Canberra, with these individuals in key positions, it would have been assumed that Land Rights legislation would be in place, sacred sites would be secure, and that there would be reasonable controls on mining companies wanting to work on Aboriginal land.

Neither Government has implemented the planks in their 1983 platforms that committed them to introducing Land Rights legislation. The Federal Government has enacted site protection legislation that would strengthen its hand in any future confrontation like Noonkanbah, but this was significantly watered down from the bill that was originally proposed. The 1980 Grayden amendments to the State's Aboriginal Heritage Act still stand. And there is still no defined set of guidelines for mining companies operating on Aboriginal land.

Within weeks of becoming the Minister for Mines in 1983, Peter Dowding was dealing with the issue of mining on Noonkanbah. IEDC had come to the Community with proposals for another round of seismic work on Noonkanbah and Millijidee. The Community's first response was to write to Dowding to say that it wanted a comprehensive set of guidelines for mining on all Aboriginal land before it would deal with the company.

Dowding flew to a meeting in Fitzroy Crossing, and the outcome was an agreement to negotiate with IEDC to try to set a positive precedent, with talk about comprehensive guidelines to follow. A thorough site survey was done at the company's expense, and it agreed to all the major conditions set by the Community. The seismic work was done to everyone's satisfaction. As a model exercise, it worked beautifully. The new Government was quick to compare this to the previous debacle.

Yet the wider talks that followed never produced a result. Industry and Aboriginal groups remained too far apart, and the Government remained reluctant to make a determination favouring either side. A liaison officer was appointed within the Mines Department, but this did nothing to change the legal situation.

One of the Burke Government's early initiatives was to establish the Seaman Inquiry to prepare recommendations for Land Rights legislation. But as Paul Seaman was doing his job a concerted, and at times vicious, campaign of opposition developed, with mining industry groups amongst its leaders. Television advertisements showed anonymous black hands grasping and locking away huge portions of the State. Premier Burke quickly shied away from taking them on.

Seaman's report was received favourably by Aboriginal organisations, but the day it was publicly released the State Government announced that it would not accept many of the basic recommendations seen as favourable to Aboriginal interests. Miners and pastoralists were brought into a drafting committee to frame the legislation. Most Aboriginal groups around the State refused to participate in the drafting committee, with many of their basic positions already ruled to be out of the question by the Government. And they rejected the watered-down bill that resulted, and the Government's line that it was the best that could be achieved. The legislation was introduced, but even this was unacceptable to the Liberal Party dominated State Upper House.

Premier Brian Burke lost no time in saying that the Government had done its best, and would make no further attempts to introduce such legislation. He also very publicly warned the Federal Labor Government against trying to introduce overriding Federal Land Rights legislation, saying he would fiercely oppose any such moves.

All of this was a bitter blow to the Aboriginal community, which again had seen hopes raised, and had put a large effort into the Seaman Inquiry, only to be beaten down again. Relationships with the State Government deteriorated badly, and took years to begin to recover.

The Federal Government's proposals for national Land Rights legislation had run into similar problems, and Burke's stance signalled the final death knell of any such plans.

Perhaps things would have turned out very differently if Hawke and Burke had made an early decision in 1984, when the campaign of opposition to Land Rights had begun, to meet it head on. But Burke had no taste for such a battle, his priorities lay in other areas. And the Federal Government hesitated too long, and the 'backlash effect' had taken hold, with the 1985 election in the offing.

In 1988 hopes rose again. The effect of the Bicentenary, a new Federal Minister and a new State Premier all seemed to hold hopes of things positive. However, Land Rights legislation is still not on either Government's agenda; the possibility of a treaty, and reform of the bureaucracies and program and funding arrangements are the focus of attention. Another eight years down the track, will it be the same story of the cycle repeating itself? Or will the breakthroughs come in one or more areas?

Noonkanbah was one of the major milestones in the long struggle of the Aboriginal people to reclaim a real place in the Australian community.

The Gurindji of Daguragu fought the seminal battle for the principle of Land Rights. Their battle began when they walked off Wave Hill Station in 1966, and petitioned the Governor-General in 1967 for the return of their traditional land; it was not resolved until the Federal Government bought a part of Wave Hill for the Gurindji in 1975.

The freedom riders in outback New South Wales and the tent embassy in Canberra laid the ground for the continuing battle for racial equality and political rights.

The Yirrkala people, with their High Court battle against bauxite mining on their land, were the first to seriously challenge the great lie of white Australia, the myth of *Terra Nullius*.

In a way, Noonkanbah drew together all of these strands, around the theme of equality between the two laws. In addition, more than any of the other great public battles of the Aboriginal people, it drew attention to the role of the Law and culture in Aboriginal life, and the fact that the land derives its meaning and importance through the Law. It helped get across the message once and for all that Aboriginal culture is more than quaint corroborees and tea towel designs and bark paintings for dollar notes.

The incremental improvements in community attitudes, policy, and the situation of Aboriginal people are inextricably bound to the consciousness-raising effect of these milestones.

It is only by Aboriginal people asserting themselves that they have won ground. They cannot rely on passive acceptance of the goodwill of governments. Sometimes the frontline fighters are not those that see the benefits, and unfortunately this can be said of the Noonkanbah Community. They have gained nothing real from their two year battle, and in some ways they have suffered for it.

The causes of their loss and suffering were also key factors in the successes they had during the battle. Unlike the freedom riders, the tent embassy, and the Yirrkala people, they were fighting on their own terms, and on their own ground. They set the parameters of their struggle, but it was not on the white man's ground, or in the white man's forums. There was nowhere to withdraw to. And unlike the Gurindji, who were on the offensive, making a claim for land that was eventually won after great struggle, the Yungngora Community of Noonkanbah was in essence defending something, a particular piece of land and all it stood for. And with defeat came the violation of that land.

A hallmark of the Noonkanbah dispute was that, having established the parameters – the defence of sacred land – the Community refused to compromise its principles. It sought negotiation, accommodation and compromise, but always under terms consistent with its principles.

Under the most intense and prolonged pressure it refused to either collapse, or negotiate a face-saving defeat of the type that Senator Chaney sought that meant abandoning its beliefs and sanctioning the breaking of its Law.

Very rarely have Aboriginal people been strong enough to do this. Noonkanbah challenged many of the assumptions and values of white Australia, not the least being the common belief amongst many of the bureaucrats, the politicians and the power brokers that sooner or later the blacks can be cajoled, tricked or pressured into giving way to the perceived needs of the dominant society.

The strength and the qualities of the Noonkanbah people were clear enough to overcome the propaganda and the obfuscations of the State Government; and the spokesmen like Dicky Skinner and Jimmy Bieunderry, through their demeanour and their simple eloquence, were able to convey the essence, if not the complexity, of the Community's message. They were able to tap a responsive chord in the wider Aboriginal community and in many quarters of the white community. With the support they generated, they went within an ace of securing a quite remarkable victory.

Senator Fred Chaney has said that Noonkanbah was a very negative episode in Aboriginal affairs. He believes that it hardened attitudes, and was a major factor in the destruction of a progressive bipartisan approach to Aboriginal issues at the Federal level, making real progress much more difficult to achieve.

At one level it is hard to argue with this analysis. One cannot point to specific positive results of the Noonkanbah episode. And it did mark the end of a relatively positive cycle in Aboriginal affairs. But the low key, bipartisan approach has its limitations. It is geared to the lowest common denominator: what will the conservative State governments be prepared to accept?

It is also predicated on the assumption that Aboriginal people should accept operating within the constraints of 'political reality' and the limitations of the two party system of government. It does not allow for the principle that Aboriginal people should be free to set their own agenda, according to the priorities that arise from their own needs, culture and world view, as the Noonkanbah people did.

Noonkanbah did highlight the profound questions that are raised if we are to seriously address a resolution of the Aboriginal and European approaches to life. In a sense, it was a very concrete example of the conflicts inherent in the issue of sovereignty. The Community did not accept the sovereignty of white law as the Court Government sought to apply it, or the natural superiority of the white law.

In 1980 Senator Chaney was supporting the concept of a 'Makarrata', which was variously described as a formal reconciliation or a treaty between black and white Australia, without venturing to define the terms such an agreement might entail. This was a very similar stance to that taken by Prime Minister Hawke at the Barunga Festival in 1988. It is notable that Chaney has accepted in silence the Federal Opposition's rejection of the concept this time round.

Noonkanbah shows both the need for, and the inherent difficulties of, such a resolution of the two hundred-year-old conflict. Is it possible to negotiate any agreement that truly recognises the reality that the Aboriginal people did not cede sovereignty over their land, and that there is no legitimate basis to assume that white law is superior to Aboriginal Law? Can the two systems be accommodated? Will white Australia allow such an accommodation at anything more than a superficial level?

The greatest strength and resource of Aboriginal Australia lies in the living Law and culture, ahead even of the land that draws its meaning from this source. The Law lives, and gives meaning to Aboriginal life, even indirectly to those who do not follow it, and those in the cities and country towns who seem far removed from its influence. But each year it loses a bit more ground to whitefeller ways and influences.

Policies and programs designed to provide economic and educational opportunity, and alleviate poverty traps, are necessary. But the brutal truth is that history, geography and economic reality have condemned the majority of Aboriginal people to live as an underclass in Australia. Like the underclass in any society, they are plagued by the curses of despair and self-destruction.

When Aboriginal people organise, as they did in the Kimberley in the 1970s, when they fight as they did at Noonkanbah, the central and prominent issues are the primary ones of the Law and the land precisely because Aboriginal people recognise that these provide the source and the strength which can perhaps overcome the despair and the self-destruction. The social engineering programs will only ever be palliatives; they will not of their own accord provide the energy or the impetus for the majority of Aboriginal people to fight their way out of the underclass and define their own place in the world.

A redefinition of the place of Aboriginal people in the nation, that recognises their history and their reality, is necessary. Some believe that a treaty is the way to do this. There is no other obvious avenue that could cover the spectrum of Aboriginal Australia. As much as anything, Noonkanbah was about one community's attempt to redefine its own reality, fulfil its vision, and have this accepted by white Australia.

The events of 1979 and 1980 are variously described as the Noonkanbah dispute, the Noonkanbah episode, the Noonkanbah confrontation, and the Noonkanbah drama. The word Noonkanbah even took on a meaning beyond itself, as in the phrase 'there will never be another Noonkanbah'.

The most fitting description is 'the Noonkanbah drama'. The best theatrical drama provides profound insights into its characters by placing them in extreme situations that reveal their true natures and the forces that motivate them. On rare occasions a community or a nation will throw up, as if by chance, a set of circumstances that provides similar insights and revelations about itself.

Noonkanbah was such an occasion. Both sides took positions that were consistent with their ideologies and world views, and then gradually provoked each other to exaggerated stances beyond the normal realms of behaviour.

As in any great drama the actors became totally immersed in, and obsessed by, their roles. And the critics and the audience provided an astonishing variety of interpretations of the meaning of the performance, and the merits of the performers. The perceptions of the Noonkanbah Community ranged from noble and stalwart defenders of tradition against the ruthless power of the State, to shiftless, untrustworthy niggers manipulated by devious subversives. The State Government was seen as anything from a stern yet fair proponent of the rule of law and the march of progress, to racist and ruthless powermongers crushing a spiritual people with the might of force and technology.

Perhaps the key to the way in which the drama of Noonkanbah impinged so deeply on the consciousness of Aboriginal and European Australia lay in the echoes it contained of times past; the brutal conflict over land that is the essence of Australian history.

In its unfolding – from the initial skirmishing, through the endless and fruitless attempts at communication and dialogue, to the horrific finale of the juggernaut convoy bearing down as the police dragged away the singing band at Mickey's Pool – the dispute was a parable of the nationwide dispossession of the first custodians of the land.

It was as if the Yungngora people were the reincarnation of the Kalkadoon warriors, Yagan of Swan River, Jandamarra/Pigeon of the Leopolds. The Court Government was a throwback to the days of the righteous colonists of the Empire. The Federal Government took the role of the British Crown; disapproving of the excesses of its colonial agents, yet unwilling to exercise its authority to bring them to heel. The police were the troopers, and the convoy drivers the vengeance posses, come back to life.

The history of Australia was being replayed with only the guns and spears absent, and each side was fearful that the other may yet bring the gun or the spear to bear. In a modern context the nation confronted these realities once again. Perhaps subconsciously many recognised the parallels.

The Noonkanbah people were certainly aware of this, and pointed out the parallels again and again. More than once they claimed that nothing had really changed.

And if one accepts the validity of the parable, they were proved right. Ultimately, however hollow the victory may have been, the oil well was drilled. The white man won.

The victory was hollow. The well was dry. This too, it could be argued, is a parable of sorts. The triumph of the white man's religion of progress and material wealth – so aptly symbolised by the holy fluid oil, and the icon of the petrol bowser – has left a hollowness. For only a nation with a hollow soul could have allowed the State to perpetrate such a vengeful injustice on a small and isolated community which had demanded only respect; respect for its Law and religion, its land, and its dignity.

The hope lies in the fact that so many people were prepared to fight such an injustice, even if they were, in the end, unsuccessful.

ENDNOTES

CHAPTER ONE

1. McCann, Magistrate David, 'Mineral Claims by C.R.A. Exploration Pty Ltd, Objections by Noonkanbah Pastoral Company and Others', Broome Mining Warden's Court, 8- 9/11/78.
2. Aboriginal Lands Trust: the State Government agency in which Aboriginal lands are vested.
3. Department of Native Welfare: the State Government department responsible for Aboriginal matters until it was abolished in a legislative and bureaucratic reorganisation in 1972.
4. The first stage of oil exploration is carried out by the process of making seismic 'cut lines'. Normally in a grid pattern, these are straight lines cleared by bulldozers, stretching for kilometres. From the air patterns formed by the cut lines can be seen all over the Kimberley and the desert to the south.

CHAPTER TWO

1. Pedersen, Howard, 'Pigeon, An Aboriginal Rebel', unpublished honours thesis, Murdoch University, Perth, 1980. (Pedersen will be publishing a book in 1989 about Pigeon/Jandamarra, developed from this thesis. It will be published by Magabala Books, Broome, Western Australia.)
2. Bolton, Professor G.C., and Pedersen, Howard, 'The Emanuels of Noonkanbah and Go Go', in *The Early Days Journal*, Vol. 8, part 4, 1980, published by the Royal Western Australian Historical Society.
3. Biskup, Peter, *Not Slaves Not Citizens*, University of Queensland Press, St Lucia, Queensland, 1973, pp.24-25.
4. ibid.
5. ibid., p.37.
6. Pedersen, op. cit., p.19.
7. Western Australian State Archives, Colonial Secretary's Office, 431/87.
8. ibid.
9. Bolton and Pedersen, op. cit.
10. Western Australian Parliamentary Debates, 1893, pp. 1051-52, quoted in Pedersen, op. cit., p.38.
11. *North West Times*, 28/7/1894, quoted in Pedersen, op. cit., p.66.
12. Pedersen, op. cit., pp.78-79.
13. *North West Times*, 2/10/1894, quoted in Pedersen, op. cit., p.66.
14. These details and the following account of the uprising led by Jandamarra are taken from Pedersen, op. cit.
15. Colonial Secretary's Office, 2741/96, 'Report from the Commissioner of Police', dated 31/8/1896.
16. ibid.
17. ibid.
18. ibid.
19. Reynolds, Professor Henry, James Cook University, Townsville, personal communication.
20. Pedersen, op. cit., p.86.
21. Western Australian Aborigines Department (WAAD), Annual Report, 1906, p.8.
22. WAAD Annual Report, 1910, pp.10-11.
23. Kolig, Erich, *The Noonkanbah Story*, University of Otago Press, New Zealand, 1987, p.17.
24. Bolton, G.C., 'A Survey of the Kimberley Pastoral Industry, from 1885 to the Present', M.A. thesis, 1953, p.25 (J.S. Battye Library of Western Australian History).
25. Bolton and Pedersen, op. cit.

26. Western Australian State Archives, Department of Native Welfare, 745/38.
27. ibid.
28. Tindale, N.B., *Aboriginal Tribes of Australia*, Australian National University Press, Canberra, 1974, p.148.
29. Haynes, B.T., Barrett, G.E.B., Brennan, A., and Brennan, L., *Western Australian Aborigines, 1622-1972*, History Association of Western Australia, 1972, p.49.

CHAPTER THREE

1. Kolig, Erich, *The Noonkanbah Story*, University of Otago Press, New Zealand, 1987, p.39.
2. Transcript of interview by Steve Hawke, 1979.
3. Kolig, op. cit., p.88.
4. WAAD Annual Report, 1910, p.11-12.
5. Report of Travelling Inspector Isdell, in the WAAD Annual Report, 1909, p.9.
6. Sally Morgan's *My Place* (Fremantle Arts Centre Press, Perth, 1987) provides a fascinating account of this phenomenon.
7. Biskup, Peter, *Not Slaves Not Citizens*, University of Queensland Press, St Lucia, Queensland, 1973, p.73.
8. ibid, p.76.
9. Don McLeod's account of the strike and the history of the Strelley mob is told in his self-published book, *How The West Was Lost* (Perth, 1984.)
10. Western Australian State Archives, Department of Native Welfare, 745/38.
11. ibid.
12. ibid.
13. ibid.
14. Biskup, op. cit., p.241.
15. The Department of Native Welfare patrol reports quoted in the following passages, at the time of writing, were held in the Fitzroy Crossing office of the Western Australian Department for Community Services.

CHAPTER FOUR

1. In 1972 new State legislation abolished the former Department of Native Welfare, creating in its place the Aboriginal Affairs Planning Authority (AAPA) as a policy body and co-ordinating agency, and the Department for Community Welfare, which combined the field and welfare services of the former department with the Department for Child Welfare. A unique and curious arrangement with the Federal Government also saw the Head of the AAPA become the Head of the Western Australian branch of the Federal Department of Aboriginal Affairs; a move engineered by the State Government to ensure that they continued to effectively control Aboriginal Affairs policy in the State, despite the new Federal initiatives that had resulted from the historic 1967 referendum that had given the Federal Government the power to make laws concerning Aboriginal affairs.
2. Department for Community Services, Fitzroy Crossing office files.
3. Kolig, Erich, 'The Kadjina (Karjunna) Group's Land Claim: Barbwire Range', 1973, Department for Community Services, Fitzroy Crossing.
4. ibid.
5. Department for Community Services, Fitzroy Crossing office files.
6. ibid.
7. ibid.
8. ibid.
9. Quoted from private correspondence of Stan Davey, Department for Community Welfare, 23/7/75.
10. Department for Community Services, Fitzroy Crossing office files.
11. ibid.
12. McCaulay, Doug, 'Report On The Yungngora/Kadjina Station Community Development Programme', Department for Community Welfare, Fitzroy Crossing, 7/2/77.
13. Palmer, Kingsley, 'Land In Aboriginal Religious Belief: Noonkanbah Station, West Kimberley, Western Australia', unpublished report, Perth, August 1978, p.21.

CHAPTER FIVE

1. Transcript of interview by Steve Hawke, November 1978.
2. Quoted from the records of the Court of Disputed Returns in the *Weekend Australian*, 19-20/4/80.
3. ibid.
4. *The Kimberley Land Council Newsletter*, Vol.1 No.1, January 1979, p.1.

5. Minutes of Kimberley Bush Meeting of Noonkanbah Station, Kimberley Land Council, 20-21/5/78.
6. ibid.
7. Howitt, Dr Richard, 'The Corporate Strategies Of C.R.A. Ltd. And Amax Inc.', 1981, p.64, from notes of a field-work interview with P. Purcell, Exploration Manager, Whitestone Petroleum Aust. Ltd, Perth, 8/5/80.
8. Reece, Bob, 'Two Kinds Of Dreaming: Sir Charles Court And The Sacred Goannas Of Noonkanbah', unpublished essay, 1980, p.3.
9. Court, Sir Charles, speech to *Financial Times* seminar, 'Doing Business With Australia: Resource Development Strategies in the 1980s', Sydney, 1976.
10. Reece, op. cit.
11. The *Weekend Australian*, 19-20/4/80, op. cit.
12. Palmer, Ian, *Buying Back The Land: Organisational Struggle and the Aboriginal Land Fund Commission*, Aboriginal Studies Press, Canberra, 1988.
13. ibid.
14. ibid.
15. ibid.

CHAPTER SIX

1. The *West Australian*, 29/9/78.
2. Palmer, Kingsley, 'Land In Aboriginal Religious Belief: Noonkanbah Station, West Kimberley, Western Australia', unpublished report, Perth, August 1978, p.8.
3. ibid, pp.9-10.
4. Howitt, Dr Richard, field notes of interview with Mr P. Purcell, Exploration Manager, Whitestone Petroleum Australia, 8/5/80.
5. Purcell, P., letter to Dr R. Howitt, 19/5/80.
6. Personal communication.
7. Sources: Howitt, Dr R., field notes of interview with Purcell, op. cit, and letter from Purcell, op. cit.; Mines Department files, including letter from M.A. Reynolds, Exploration Manager, Petroleum Division of Amax Iron Ore to Minister for Mines, 17/4/79; *Noonkanbah The Facts*, Government of Western Australia, Perth, September 1980.
8. Transcript of interview by Steve Hawke, November 1978.
9. ibid.
10. Minutes of Kimberley Bush Meeting at Noonkanbah Station, Kimberley Land Council, 20-21/5/78.
11. Transcript of interview by Steve Hawke, 31/5/79.
12. Reynolds, M.A., letter to the Minister for Mines, 17/4/79, Mines Department files, op. cit.
13. ibid.
14. Mines Department files; a chronology of events compiled by the Department in 1980.
15. Palmer, K., op. cit., p.2.
16. Reynolds, M.A., Exploration Manager, Petroleum Division of Amax Iron Ore, letter to D. McCaulay for the Noonkanbah Management Committee, 2/3/79.

CHAPTER SEVEN

1. Erich Kolig, in his book, *The Noonkanbah Story* (University of Otago Press, New Zealand, 1987), deals extensively with both the practice of religion and its physical manifestations in relation to the Noonkanbah people, and does explore the deeper philosophies and motivations. Whilst I have reservations about his work, particularly his treatment of the specifics of the Amax dispute, it does contain interesting and relevant background information. Along with the work of other anthropologists at Noonkanbah, particularly Bindon and Palmer, and more general writings, he provides much of the basis for the following descriptions.
2. Kolig, op. cit., p.63.
3. 'Noonkanbah The Facts', Government of Western Australia, September 1980, p.4.
4. Palmer, Kingsley, 'Land In Aboriginal Religious Belief: Noonkanbah Station, West Kimberley, Western Australia', unpublished report for the Aboriginal Legal Service, Perth, August 1978, p.12.
5. Bindon, Peter, 'Museum Report on Noonkanbah Investigations', unpublished and restricted, 14/6/79, p.15.
6. Kolig, op. cit., p.67.
7. Transcript of interview by Steve Hawke, 1979.
8. Bindon, op. cit., p.13.
9. ibid, p.5.
10. Kolig, op. cit., pp.127-130.
11. Bindon, op. cit., p.12.

12. Transcript of interview by Steve Hawke, 1979.
13. Bindon, op. cit., p.19.

CHAPTER EIGHT

1. Reynolds, M.A., Exploration Manager, Petroleum Division of Amax Iron Ore, letter to Andrew Mensaros, Minister for Mines, Mines Department files, 17/4/79.
2. Reynolds, M.A., letter to the Acting Registrar, Department of Aboriginal Sites at the WA Museum, WA Museum files, 6/4/79.
3. Reynolds to Minister for Mines, 17/4/79, op. cit.
4. Reynolds, M.A., letter to the Under Secretary for Mines, Mines Department files, 24/5/79.
5. Separate notes on the meeting recorded by the Museum and Mines Department officers, held in their respective files.
6. The *West Australian*, 17/5/79.
7. Reynolds to Under Secretary for Mines, 24/5/79, op. cit.
8. Reports held in Mines Department files.
9. Tomkinson, N., Amax Legal Counsel, letter to McDonald, G., Aboriginal Legal Service, 23/5/79.
10. Parks, L.L., Vice-President, Amax Petroleum Division of Amax Iron Ore, telex to Sir Charles Court, copy in Mines Department files, 24/5/79.
11. This quote and the following record of the meeting are taken from a transcript from a tape recording of the meeting at Noonkanbah by Steve Hawke, 30/5/79.
12. Minutes of the Ordinary Meeting of the ACMC, WA Museum files, 1/6/79.
13. ibid.
14. Departmental Memorandum to Andrew Mesnsaros, Minister for Mines, Mines Department files, 28,5,79.
15. Court, C., memorandum to the Under Secretary, Premier's Department, copy in Mines Department files, 3/6/79.
16. Court, C., telex to Arthur Reef, copy in Mines Department files, 5/6/79.
17. Bannister, J., 'Notes for File; Discussions With the Hon. Premier', WA Museum files, 5/6/79.
18. ibid.
19. Bannister, J., memorandum to Dick Old, Acting Minister for Cultural Affairs, copy in Mines Department files, 5/6/79.
20. The *West Australian*, 6/6/79.
21. The Melbourne *Age*, 9/6/79.

CHAPTER NINE

1. This quote and the record of the following discussion at the gate are taken from a transcript from a tape recording at the Noonkanbah boundary gate, Steve Hawke, 15/6/79.
2. Report titled 'Fitzroy River No 1 – Developments In Field June 14-20', Mines Department files.
3. Perth *Daily News* and Melbourne *Age*, 27/6/79.
4. ibid.
5. ibid.
6. The *Daily News*, 18/6/79.
7. Palmer, K., letter to Dick Old, Acting Minister for Cultural Affairs, copy in WA Museum files, 26/6/79.
8. The *West Australian*, 20/6/79.
9. Reynolds, M., affidavit in the Supreme Court of Western Australia, No. 1558 of 1979, 19/6/79.
10. 'Submission on Behalf of the Museum Trustees as Second Defendant', in the Supreme Court of Western Australia, No. 1558 of 1979, undated.
11. Brinsden, J., 'Reasons for Judgement', in the Supreme Court of Western Australia, No. 1558 of 1979, 27/6/79.

CHAPTER TEN

1. The *Daily News*, 28/6/79.
2. The *West Australian*, 29/6/79.
3. File Note of telephone conversation between Ian Crawford, Acting Director, WA Museum, and Peter Jones, Minister for Cultural Affairs, WA Museum files, 4/7/79.
4. The *Canberra Times*, 7/7/79.
5. The *Daily News*, 30/5/79.
6. The Melbourne *Age*, 9/6/79.
7. Telex from the three Fitzroy Crossing DCW District Officers to their Supervisor, recommended for forwarding to the Director, 31/5/79.

8. Tomkinson, N., Amax Legal Counsel, letter to McDonald, G., Aboriginal Legal Service, 22/11/79.
9. Tomkinson, N., Amax Legal Counsel, letter to McDonald, G., Aboriginal Legal Service, 4/12/79.
10. Departmental Memorandum to Andrew Mensaros, Minister for Mines, 4/12/79, and Minister's hand-written note on the Memorandum, Mines Department files.
11. Yungngora Community press release, 6/10/79.
12. McCaulay, Doug, 'Noonkanbah/Millijidee Community Development Project, Fifth Progress Report', Department for Community Welfare, Fitzroy Crossing, December 1979.

CHAPTER ELEVEN

1. Memorandum recording phone call received by the Premier's Private Secretary from Max Reynolds, WA Premier's Department files, 29/2/80.
2. Press release by Dicky Skinner, Chairman Yungngora Community, and Wadgie Thirkall, Chairman Kurnangki Community, 7/3/80.
3. Jones, P., memorandum to Sir Charles Court, Premier's Department files, 10/3/80.
4. ibid.
5. The Melbourne *Age*, 8/3/80.
6. 'Note for file', WA Museum files, 12/3/80.
7. Notes of meeting at Noonkanbah boundary gate, Steve Hawke, 12/3/80.
8. Premier's Department files. (The translations were delivered to the AAPA Commissioner, Terry Long, at the end of that day, and passed by him, to Bill Hassell, to the Premier.)
9. The source of this and following quotes from the meeting is 'Transcript of Tapes Loaned by Mr Ken Colbung. Re Meeting with State Government Ministers at Noonkanbah Station. March 14, 1980', Premier's Department files.
10. Palmer, Kingsley, 'Aborigines and the Land, Go Go Station, Kimberley, Western Australia', unpublished report, Perth, October 1979, pp.2-3.
11. Press release by the Premier, Sir Charles Court, 14/3/80.
12. Yungngora Community, letter to Sir Charles Court, 18/3/80. (Letter not despatched.)
13. The following transcripts from the talks are from a recording by Steve Hawke, 18/3/80.
14. Transcript of interview recorded with Jeremy O'Driscoll, Steve Hawke, 17/12/87.
15. ibid.
16. This quote and the following transcripts are from a recording by Steve Hawke, 18/3/80.
17. Press release by the Premier, Sir Charles Court, 18/3/80.
18. The *West Australian*, 20/3/80.
19. Commonwealth Parliament, The Senate, Hansard, 19/3/80.
20. Chaney, F., telex to Sir Charles Court, Premier's Department files, 19/3/80.
21. ibid.
22. Court, Sir Charles, telex to Senator Chaney, Premier's Department files, 19/3/80.
23. The *West Australian*, 22/3/80.

CHAPTER TWELVE

1. Statement by the Elders of Yungngora Community, 21/3/80.
2. Statement by Yungngora Community, 24/3/80, taken to Perth by Ivan McPhee and Nipper Tabagee.
3. Minutes of the full meeting of the Western Australian Trades and Labor Council, 25/3/80.
4. Joint statement by Sir Lancelot Goody, Roman Catholic Archbishop of Perth, Mr David Oxley, Uniting Church Moderator in Western Australia, and The Most Reverend Geoffrey Sambell, Anglican Archbishop of Perth, 26/3/80.
5. File notes, WA Museum files, 23 – 24/3/80.
6. Memoranda, Jones, P., Minister for Mines, to Premier, and Hassell, W., Minister for Community Welfare, to Premier. Both dated 21/3/80, Premier's Department files.
7. Press release by the Premier, Sir Charles Court, 27/3/80.
8. Reynolds, M., telex to Lloyd Parks, copy in Mines Department files, 27/3/80.
9. Transcript of interview recorded with Brian McGaffin, Steve Hawke, 6/10/88.
10. ibid.
11. Salt, Jeremy, 'Report on the Kimberley Region of Western Australia', United Nations Association of Australia, 1980.
12. The following transcripts from the talks are from a recording by Bobby Kogolo, 29/3/80.
13. The *West Australian*, 31/3/80.
14. The *Daily News*, 28/3/80.
15. The *West Australian*, 2/4/80.
16. Mines Department briefing paper, copy in Premier's Department files, 31/3/80.
17. Briefing paper, Mines Department files, 2/4/80.
18. ibid.

19. The *West Australian*, 2/4/80.
20. Transcript of interview recorded with Jeremy O'Driscoll, Steve Hawke, 17/12/87.
21. 'Report On Visit To Noonkanbah Aboriginal Pastoral Lease Western Australia', Stewart West MHR and John Dawkins MHR, April 1980.
22. The *West Australian*, 3/4/80.
23. ibid.
24. ibid.
25. *Minyarti Wangki Kulkarriyajangka*, Kulkarriya Community School, April 1980. Translated from the Walmatjari.
26. Original translation by Eirlys Richards, adapted by Steve Hawke.

CHAPTER THIRTEEN

1. Press release by the Premier, Sir Charles Court, 2/4/80.
2. Davis, Jack, letter to Steve Hawke, September 1988.
3. Interview recorded with Pat Dodson, Steve Hawke, 18/3/88.
4. Sir Charles Court, on A.M. Current Affairs radio program, Australian Broadcasting Commission, 3/4/80.
5. Press release by the Premier, Sir Charles Court, 6/4/80.
6. ibid.
7. Court, Sir Charles, letter to Malcolm Fraser, Premier's Department files, 11/4/80.
8. Premier's Department files, correspondence, April – May, 1980.
9. ibid, August 1980.
10. ibid.
11. Press release by the Premier, Sir Charles Court, 5/4/80.
12. Press release by the Premier, Sir Charles Court, 6/4/80, op. cit.
13. Court, Sir Charles, letter to Malcolm Fraser, 11/4/80, op. cit.
14. Press release by the Premier, Sir Charles Court, 6/4/80, op. cit.
15. The *West Australian*, 28/3/80.
16. The information regarding Duncan Beaton, and the quote, are from an interview recorded with Bill Grayden, Steve Hawke, 9/11/87.
17. The *West Australian*, 3/4/80.
18. Statement by the Elders of Yungngora Community, 21/3/80.
19. The *West Australian*, 21/4/80.
20. File note, Aboriginal Legal Service, 7/3/80.
21. Interview recorded with Senator Fred Chaney, Steve Hawke, 9/11/87.
22. ibid.
23. Press release by the Premier, Sir Charles Court, 5/4/80.
24. The *West Australian*, 11/4/80.

CHAPTER FOURTEEN

1. The *West Australian*, 22/4/80.
2. Court, Sir Charles, letter to Malcolm Fraser, Premier's Department files, 11/4/80.
3. The *Australian*, 23/4/80.
4. Court, Sir Charles, letter to Max Reynolds, Premier's Department files, 8/5/80.
5. Mensaros, Andrew, Acting Minister for Mines, letter to the Trustees of the WA Museum, WA Museum files, 13/5/80.
6. Interview recorded with Bill Grayden, Steve Hawke, 9/11/87.
7. The *West Australian*, letter to the editor from W.W. Mitchell, 2/8/80.
8. The *West Australian*, 21/4/80.
9. The Melbourne *Age*, 16/5/80.
10. These and following excerpts of the meeting between the Community and Senator Chaney are taken from notes by Phil Vincent of the Aboriginal Legal Service, 18/5/80.
11. 'Report of Operations, E.P.97 Year Four, Third Quarter Ended June 16, 1980', Amax, copy in Mines Department files.
12. Western Australian Parliament, Legislative Assembly, Hansard, 12/8/80.
13. Court, Sir Charles, letter to the Chairman, Yungngora Community, 31/5/80.
14. Elders of Yungngora Community, letter to Sir Charles Court, 9/6/80.

CHAPTER FIFTEEN

1. Press release from Noonkanbah spokesmen, Nipper Tabagee and Alec Buck, 11/6/80.
2. 'Report Of Operations, E.P.97, Year Four, Third Quarter Ended June 16, 1980', Amax, copy in Mines Department files.

3. Tabagee and Buck, press release, 11/6/80, op. cit.
4. Yungngora Community press release, 19/6/80.
5. Amax, Report to 16/6/80, op cit.
6. The *Financial Review*, 1/9/80.
7. The Melbourne *Age*, 17/6/80.
8. Fraser, Malcolm, telex to Sir Charles Court, Premier's Department files, 6/6/80.
9. Court, Sir Charles, telex to Malcolm Fraser, Premier's Department files, 6/6/80.
10. Official transcript of meeting at Derby on 1/7/80, tabled in the Commonwealth Parliament, House of Representatives, Hansard, 19/8/80.
11. ibid.
12. Transcript of speech by Malcolm Fraser in Perth on 6/7/80, tabled in the Commonwealth Parliament, House of Representatives, Hansard, 19/8/80.
13. The *West Australian*, 7/7/80.
14. Federal Department of Industrial Relations, file note, 2/7/80.
15. Skinner, Dicky, Yungngora Community press release, 20/7/80.
16. Hawke, R.J., diary note, 22/7/80.
17. O'Connor, Ray, Acting Premier, letter to the Chairman, Yungngora Community, 22/7/80.
18. ibid.
19. The *West Australian*, 24/7/80.
20. Yungngora Community press release, 19/6/80, op. cit.
21. Jones, P.V., press release, 25/7/80.
22. ibid.
23. The *Daily News*, eyewitness account of journalist Norman Aisbett, 25/7/80.
24. The *Daily News*, 28/7/80.
25. Skinner, Dicky, and McPhee, Ivan, for the Yungngora Community, letter to Gordon Jackson, Chairman, CSR, 30/7/80.
26. The *West Australian*, 28/7/80.
27. The *West Australian*, 30/7/80.

CHAPTER SIXTEEN

1. Rowley, Charles, quoted by Stewart West in the Commonwealth Parliament, House of Representatives, Hansard, 19/8/80.
2. The *Daily News*, 7/8/80.
3. The *West Australian*, 9/8/80.
4. The *West Australian*, 12/8/80.
5. The Melbourne *Age*, 12/8/80.
6. *Minyarti Wangki Kulkarriyajangka*, Kulkarriya Community School, August 1980.
7. ibid.
8. Transcript from a tape recording at Mickey's Pool, Steve Hawke, 12/8/80.
9. *Minyarti Wangki Kulkarriyajangka*, op. cit.
10. Gallagher, Michael, written recollection, 3/4/89.
11. ibid.
12. *Minyarti Wangki Kulkarriyajangka*, op. cit.
13. Gallagher, op. cit.
14. ibid.

CHAPTER SEVENTEEN

1. The *West Australian*, 15/8/80.
2. The *West Australian*, 21/8/80.
3. ibid.
4. In 1979 the Western Australian Government amended the Police Act to make public demonstrations illegal without the written permission of the Police Commissioner.
5. Hagan, Jim, Chairman of the National Aboriginal Conference, transcript of speech at Albert Hall, Canberra, 21/8/80.
6. The *West Australian*, 23/8/80.
7. Hawke, R.J., diary note, 21/8/80.
8. Jones, Peter. 'Statement on the announced decision that a ban will be maintained on the Noonkanbah drilling rig', 22/8/80.
9. Court, Sir Charles, telex to Malcolm Fraser, Premier's Department files, 22/8/80.
10. Court, Sir Charles, letter to Malcolm Fraser, Premier's Department files, 24/8/80.
11. Court, Sir Charles, memorandum to the Ministers for Resources Development, Cultural Affairs and Community Welfare, Premier's Department files, 18/3/80.

12. Court, Sir Charles, telex to Malcolm Fraser, Premier's Department files, 26/8/80.
13. The *West Australian*, 14/8/80.
14. ibid.
15. Colbung, Ken, telegram to the Australian Council of Trade Unions, received 9.15am, 28/8/80.
16. The *West Australian*, 29/8/80.
17. ibid, 29/8/80.
18. ibid, 29/8/80.
19. The *West Australian*, 1/9/80.
20. CSR Limited, press release, 12/9/80.
21. The Melbourne *Age*, 30/8/80.
22. Statement by Yungngora Community, Saturday August 30th, on hearing that drilling had started at Noonkanbah.

CHAPTER EIGHTEEN

1. Court, Sir Charles, press release, 31/8/80.
2. Reynolds, M.A., letter to the Minister for Mines, Mines Department files, 6/11/80.
3. The *West Australian*, 1/9/80.
4. The Melbourne *Age*, 1/9/80.
5. The Melbourne *Age*, 2/9/80.
6. Hagan, Jim, Chairman of the National Aboriginal Conference of Australia, 'Address to the Sub-Commission on Prevention of Discrimination and Protection of Minorities', Geneva, 3/9/80.
7. Vincent, P.J., 'Report On Visit By National Aboriginal Conference Delegation to the United Nations, Geneva, Switzerland, 30 August to 8 September, 1980'.
8. The *Western Mail*, 23/5/81.
9. The *Australian*, 11/9/80.
10. CSR Limited, press release, 12/9/80.
11. Court, Sir Charles, letter to Senator Fred Chaney, Premier's Department files, 10/9/80.
12. Reynolds, M.A., letter to the Minister for Mines, Mines Department files, 6/11/80, op. cit.
13. Western Australian Parliament, House of Representatives, Hansard, 28/11/80.
14. McCaulay, Doug, 'Noonkanbah/Millijidee Community Development Project, Sixth Progress Report', Department for Community Welfare, 24/12/80.

EPILOGUE

1. 'Agepoll', the Melbourne *Age*, 11/10/80.

LIST OF KEY PEOPLE

Note: Unless otherwise specified, information is relevant only to positions held in 1979 and 1980 by the people described.

BANNISTER, John: Director of the Western Australian Museum.

BARR, Gil: State Secretary of the Australian Workers Union.

BERNDT, Professor Ronald: Foundation Professor of Anthropology at The University of Western Australia, widely recognised as one of Australia's most eminent anthropologists. Member of the Aboriginal Cultural Materials Committee constituted under the Aboriginal Heritage Act, and responsible for expert assessments and recommendations relevant to the Act.

BIEUNDERRY, Jimmy: Born in the Great Sandy Desert, resident in Derby. Elected as a member of the National Aboriginal Conference for the West Kimberley in 1977; elected as Co-Chairman of the Kimberley Land Council at its inaugural meeting at Noonkanbah in May, 1978, and Chairman from 1979 to 1980; appointed as an inaugural commissioner of the Aboriginal Development Commission in 1980.

BINDON, Peter: Anthropologist and archaeologist. Worked for the Aboriginal Sites Department of the Western Australian Museum. Author of the reports in May and June 1979 that identified the sites and area of influence of the Pea Hill site complex.

BRIDGE, Ernie: Endorsed Labor Party candidate for the seat of Kimberley in the 1977 State Election; elected as the Member for Kimberley in February 1980. Previous to this a member of the Aboriginal Lands Trust and the Aboriginal Land Fund Commission. Western Australian Minister for Aboriginal Affairs in the Burke and Dowding Governments, 1986 to 1989.

CHANEY, Fred: Liberal Party Senator for Western Australia from 1974. Minister for Aboriginal Affairs in the Fraser Government from December 1978 to November 1980.

COLBUNG, Ken: Chairman of the Aboriginal Lands Trust, Deputy Chairman of the Australian Institute of Aboriginal Studies, and member of the Aboriginal Cultural Materials Committee.

COOK, Peter: Secretary of the Western Australian Trades and Labor Council during 1979 and 1980. Elected as a Labor Party Senator for Western Australia in 1983, and a Minister in the Hawke Government from 1988.

COURT, Sir Charles: Liberal Party Premier of Western Australia from 1974 to 1982. Before becoming Premier he was Deputy Premier and Minister for Industrial Development and the North-West from 1959 to 1971, and Leader of the Opposition from 1971 to 1974.

CRAIG, June: Minister for Lands in the Court Government in 1978.

DAVIES, Ron: Leader of the Western Australian Labor Party Opposition.

DAWKINS, John: Labor Party Member for Fremantle in the Federal Parliament, and a member of the Hawke Cabinet from 1983.

DOWDING, Peter: Elected as the Labor Party Member for the State Upper House seat of North Province in 1980. Later transferred to the State Lower House. A member of the Burke Cabinet from 1983, and Premier of Western Australia from 1988.

FRASER, Malcolm: Liberal Party Prime Minister of Australia from 1975 to 1983.

GRAYDEN, Bill: Minister in the Court and O'Connor Governments from 1974 to 1978 and 1980 to 1983. In March of 1980 he became Minister for Cultural Affairs, with responsibility for the Western Australian Museum, and the Aboriginal Heritage Act.

HASSELL, Bill: Minister in the Court and O'Connor Governments from 1980 to 1983. His Ministerial responsibilities during 1980 included the Department for Community Welfare, the Aboriginal Lands Trust, and the Police.

HAWKE, Bob: President of the Australian Council of Trade Unions during 1979 and 1980. Entered the Federal Parliament at the 1980 election, Labor Prime Minister from 1983.

JOHNSTONE, Murray: The Mines Department officer directly involved at the field level in the Noonkanbah dispute as a departmental and Government representative.

JONES, Peter: Minister in the Court and O'Connor Governments from 1975 to 1983. During 1979 he was Minister for Cultural Affairs with responsibility for the Western Australian Museum and the Aboriginal Heritage Act. In March 1980 he became the Minister for Mines.

LEITCH, Owen: Commissioner of Police in Western Australia.

LYON, Tom: From 1978 until April of 1980 he was in charge of field operations for Amax in the West Kimberley, including the 1978 seismic program and the planned drilling on Noonkanbah. He was responsible for liaison with the Noonkanbah Community.

McLEOD, Don: Involved with the Western Desert and Pilbara Aboriginal people since 1942. Through the Strelley people and their Nomads organisation, became involved with the Noonkanbah Community in 1978, and played an important role as an adviser and participant in events of 1979 and 1980.

McPHEE, Ivan: Member of the Yungngora Community at Noonkanbah. During 1979 and 1980 was the Community Secretary. He often acted as a spokesman in meetings, and represented the Community on tours to Perth and the eastern states in 1980.

MENSAROS, Andrew: Minister in the Court and O'Connor Governments from 1975 to 1983. Minister for Mines in 1979, and Acting Minister for Mines at times in 1980.

MITCHELL, W.W. 'Bill': Public relations consultant closely associated with the Western Australian Liberal Party and the Premier, Sir Charles Court.

MULLER, Friday: An Elder of the Yungngora Community at Noonkanbah. Leader and spokesman for the Community from the late 1960s until 1978. Died in 1981.

NGANAWILLA, Ginger: An Elder of the Yungngora Community at Noonkanbah. Chairman of the Kulkarriya Community School Board from its inception in 1978. Not a public spokesman, but a key leader within the Community. Moved from the main community to establish the Warrimbah outstation in 1982. Died in 1984.

O'CONNOR, Ray: Deputy Premier to Sir Charles Court from 1974 to 1982, and Premier from 1982 to 1983.

OLD, Dick: Leader of the National Country Party for Western Australia, the junior coalition partner in the Court Government, from 1975. Minister for Agriculture in the Court Government, but also the Acting Minister for Cultural Affairs during the crucial period in 1979 when the Museum Trustees were directed to approve the use of land near Pea Hill for drilling.

PARKS, Lloyd: Based in Houston, America, the Vice-President of the Amax Petroleum Division of Amax Iron Ore, with executive responsibility for the Amax oil exploration program in Australia.

RANDOLPH, Peter: Acting Registrar of the Aboriginal Sites Department of the Western Australian Museum.

REEF, Arthur: A senior Vice-President of the Amax Corporation in America.

REYNOLDS, Max: Exploration Manager of the Petroleum Division of Amax Iron Ore. The senior officer of Amax in Western Australia.

RIDGE, Alan: Liberal Party Member of State Parliament for the seat of Kimberley from 1968 to 1980. Minister for Lands from 1974 to 1977, and for Community Welfare with responsibility for the Aboriginal Lands Trust in 1977 and 1978.

SKINNER, Dicky: Member of the Yungngora Community at Noonkanbah. Chairman of the Noonkanbah Management Committee from 1978. Main spokesman for the Community.

TABAGEE, Nipper: Elder of the Yungngora Community at Noonkanbah. Executive member of the Kimberley Land Council since its formation in 1978. The only one of the Noonkanbah Elders who frequently spoke in public and at meetings.

VINCENT, Phil: Aboriginal Legal Service lawyer based in Derby in 1978 and 1979, and in Perth as Principal Legal Officer in 1980. Advised the Yungngora Community from 1978 through 1980, and frequently represented the people in meetings and other forums.

VINER, Ian: Liberal Party Member for the Perth seat of Stirling in the Federal Parliament. Minister for Aboriginal Affairs in the Fraser Government from 1975 to December 1978.

WEST, Stewart: Labor Party Member of Federal Parliament. Opposition spokesman on Aboriginal Affairs in 1980. Member of the Hawke Cabinet from 1983.

WHITLAM, Gough: Labor Party Prime Minister of Australia from 1972 to 1975.

YOUNG, Ray: Minister for Community Welfare in the Court Government in 1978 and 1979.

LIST OF ABBREVIATIONS

AAPA	Aboriginal Affairs Planning Authority
ABC	Australian Broadcasting Commission
ACMC	Aboriginal Cultural Materials Committee
ACTU	Australian Council of Trade Unions
ALFC	Aboriginal Land Fund Commission
ALP	Australian Labor Party
ALS	Aboriginal Legal Service
ALT	Aboriginal Lands Trust
ATSIC	Aboriginal and Torres Strait Islander Commission
AWU	Australian Workers Union
BHP	Broken Hill Pty Ltd
CRA	Conzinc Riotinto Australia. (CRA's exploration work in the Kimberley was carried out by Conzinc Riotinto Australia Exploration).
CSR	Colonial Sugar Refineries
DAA	Department of Aboriginal Affairs
DCW	Department for Community Welfare (Became the Department for Community Services in 1984.)
DNW	Department of Native Welfare (In 1972 it was disbanded, and its functions split between DCW and the AAPA.)
EP	Exploration Permit, followed by a number, as in EP97, designating an area held for oil and gas exploration.
IEDC	International Energy Development Corporation of Australia
KLC	Kimberley Land Council
NAC	National Aboriginal Conference
PGA	Pastoralists and Graziers Association
SES	State Emergency Service
TLC	Trades and Labor Council of Western Australia
WA	West Australia, Western Australia or Western Australian
WAAD	Western Australian Aborigines Department
WAPET	West Australian Petroleum

NOTES ON ABORIGINAL WORDS

The spelling and pronunciation of Aboriginal words are something of a minefield. One can find almost endless styles and variations. Relatively common words such as *gudia* or *Ngarranggani*, and the language names, can be found with as many as eight or nine different spellings.

Generally I have used the spelling system developed for the Walmatjari language by the linguists Eirlys Richards and Joyce Hudson, who worked with Walmatjari people in the Fitzroy Crossing area for many years. This system is described in their book, *The Walmatjari: An Introduction To The Language And Culture*. (Work Papers of SIL-AAB, Series B, Volume 1, Summer Institute of Linguistics, Australian Aborigines Branch, Darwin, 1984.) Variations from this are either in deference to commonly accepted usages, or in direct quotes from other sources; such variations are marked with an asterisk in the glossary.

Where the standard Walmatjari spelling is used the following notes on pronunciation apply.

Vowels:

a	as in cut.
i	as in pit.
u	as in cook.

Consonants:

k, p, and t	In Walmatjari, there are no distinctions between the pairs of hard and soft English consonants *k* and *g*, *p* and *b*, and *t* and *d*. In the spelling of these sounds the letters k, p and t, respectively, are used; but the pronunciation is halfway between the hard and soft English consonants. The one exception made to this rule is where a *k* would normally appear after ng. This is written as *ngg*, as in *murrunggur*, *Ngarranggani* and *Tanggapa*, below. Here, the second *g* is pronounced as a soft *g*, as in *dog*.
ny	as in onion.
rl, rn, and rt	These sounds have no exact English equivalent. They are made with the tongue curled back, and sound similar to *l*, *n* and *t*, respectively, with an *r* immediately before them.
rr	Rolled *r*, as used in Scottish English.

GLOSSARY OF ABORIGINAL WORDS

Bunaba*	Language, tribal group.
Bundarra Goodun*	Place name, site associated with the Pea Hill complex.
Darrugu	Sacred carved stones or wooden boards, associated with particular stories, songs and country.
Djaba*	Language, tribal group.
Gudia*	White person or people.
Irralapajan	Place name, hill north of Pea Hill.
Irrtar	Place name, Kalyeeda Creek.
Jakarra	Skin name, totem.
Jangalajarra	Ngarranggani figure and place name.
Kadjina*	Ngarranggani figure, place name, and community name.
Kakaji	Goanna.
Kalijidi	Place name, St George Range.
Karjunna*	see Kadjina.
Karnakun	Species of bush food.
Kirlilpaja	Species of bush food.
Kirriri	Species of bush food.
Kulkarriya	Place name for the Noonkanbah homestead area, and the name of the Community school at Noonkanbah.
Kumupaja	Species of bush food.
Kurji	Clan name and that clan's traditional country.
Kurliti	Species of bush food.
Looma*	Ngarranggani figure, and name of community.
Maban	Traditional Aboriginal healer, sometimes known as bush doctor or medicine man.
Makarti	Hat.
Malaji	Increase site, where animal and plant species, and properties such as water and fire can be renewed, replenished, increased. (Spelt as *maladji* in some Community statements of 1979 and 1980.)
Mangunampi	Ngarranggani figure.
Marlpaja	Species of bush food.
Marrala	Ngarranggani figure.
Mijirrikan	Place name, waterhole on the Fitzroy River downstream from Noonkanbah.
Minyarti Wangki Kulkarriyajangka	The title of the newsletter published by the Kulkarriya Community School at Noonkanbah. Literal translation – This Is The Word From Noonkanbah.
Murrunggur	The site of an Aboriginal person's spiritual conception, the source of his/her rai.
Nangala	Ngarranggani figure.
Ngarranggani	The conceptual basis of Aboriginal religion, encompassing the creation, the story of the land, the Law, and more; sometimes referred to as the 'Dreamtime' and the 'Dreaming'. Also used to refer to the figures involved in the creation stories, who still reside in the land.
Nyapurru	Skin name, totem.

Nyigina*	Language, tribal group.
Parlil	Place name, Walgidee Hills.
Parrparrkarra	Place name.
Parta	Species of bush food.
Puntirliman	Clan name, and that clan's traditional country.
Raii	Spirit, or essence of human life.
Tamparkutayi	Place name.
Tanggapa	Ngarranggani figure.
Tatju	Place name, hill south of the Fitzroy River. (Also spelt Dadju or Djada.)
Umpampurru	Place name, Pea Hill.
Unyupu	Ngarranggani figure.
Wallangarri	Initiation ritual in the Kimberley.
Walmatjari	Language, tribal group. (The spelling *Walmajarri* has been more widely used and accepted of late.)
Wirrpun	Species of bush food.
Waratea*	Traditional name of country around Millijidee homestead; also the name of a pastoral lease now incorporated into the Millijidee lease, but further south than the country of the same traditional name.
Woradia	*see* Waratea.
Wumina	Ngarranggani figure.
Yungngora*	Ngarranggani figure, place name (Sandy Billabong), and name of the Noonkanbah Community.

*Spelling used is not the standard Walmatjari orthography.

CONVERSION TABLE

1 inch	–	25.4 millimetres
1 foot	–	30.5 centimetres
1 yard	–	0.914 metres
1 mile	–	1.61 kilometres
1 acre	–	0.405 hectares
1 gallon	–	4.55 litres
1 ounce	–	28.3 grams
1 pound	–	454 grams
1 ton	–	1.02 tonnes
1 shilling	–	10 cents
1 pound	–	2 dollars

INDEX

327, 337.

CRA - *see* Conzinc Riotinto Australia Exploration.

Daily News, 164, 207, 263, 270-271.
Department for Community Welfare (DCW), 79, 81, 82, 83, 84, 86-87, 92, 111, 130, 131, 133, 136, 150, 165-166, 167, 168, 169, 180, 186, 188, 190, 316.
Department of Aboriginal Affairs (DAA), 21, 28, 79, 80, 82, 83, 84, 87, 100, 137, 146, 166, 186, 190, 318.
Department of Native Welfare (DNW), 31, 56, 68-69, 70-72, 73, 81, 146.
Dowding, Peter, 170, 174, 195, 254-255, 258, 273, 275, 323, 337.

Electoral Act, 93, 94, 98-99, 206.

Federal Government - *see* Commonwealth Government.
Federation of Land Councils, 310.
Fitzroy Crossing, 12, 13, 16, 20, 24, 29, 31, 36, 38, 45, 46, 47, 48, 50, 51, 56, 57, 59, 73, 74, 76-82, 83-85, 87, 88, 92, 103, 110, 133, 150, 165, 168, 169, 170, 186, 190, 199, 206, 208, 273, 281, 285, 286, 298, 303, 304, 316, 320, 323.
Fitzroy River, 13, 28, 38, 40, 41, 42, 44, 45, 46, 47, 48, 50, 51, 53, 54, 68, 82, 84, 102, 103, 105, 114, 120, 126, 128, 157, 258, 308.
Fraser, Malcolm, 99, 100, 150, 170, 192, 224, 240, 255, 256, 257, 293, 294-295, 297, 298, 299, 307-308, 312-313, 322, 337.

Grayden, Bill, 170, 173, 175, 176-177, 178, 179, 196, 206, 207, 225, 226, 234, 240, 241-243, 244, 253, 255, 260, 266, 267, 291, 293, 299, 314, 323, 337.

Hagan, Jim, 271, 294, 295, 298, 305, 308-309.
Hassell, Bill, 170, 173, 175, 176, 179, 186, 196, 293, 299, 300, 322, 338.
Hawke, Bob, 192, 228, 257, 259, 273, 277, 290, 291, 292, 293, 295, 296, 300, 301, 313, 323, 324, 326, 338.

Jandamarra/Pigeon, 44, 45-46, 47, 50, 327.
Johnstone, Murray, 137, 138-139, 140-141, 146, 147, 152-156, 164, 166, 173, 177, 180, 183, 184, 185, 188, 338.
Jones, Peter, 163, 170, 172, 173, 175, 176, 178, 180, 196, 253, 254, 260, 290, 291, 296, 297, 298, 299, 302, 303, 306, 307, 315, 321, 338.

Kadjina (Karjunna) Community, 78-82, 83, 84, 85, 86, 87, 133, 319.
Kalijidee - *see* St George Range.
Karjunna - *see* Kadjina Community.
Kimberley, 12, 15, 16, 21, 24, 26, 31, 41, 42, 43, 44, 45, 46, 53, 54, 56, 59, 63, 66, 67, 68, 69, 81, 84, 86, 87, 89, 90, 92, 93, 94, 95, 96, 97, 104, 105, 106, 115, 118, 120, 137, 138, 155, 156, 164, 165, 166, 170, 172, 174, 179, 180, 191, 192, 194, 199, 200, 206, 208, 228, 229, 231, 234, 240, 247, 257, 260, 301, 308, 320, 321, 326.
Kimberley Land Council (KLC), 24, 31, 32, 34, 91, 94-95, 107, 108, 133, 144, 165, 172, 180, 200, 208, 227, 228, 229-234, 244, 260, 264, 265, 266, 279, 281, 309, 320, 321.
Kolig, Erich, 62, 63, 79-80, 81, 115, 120, 121, 125-126.

Lake Argyle Diamond Mine, 13, 21, 96, 166, 234, 236, 260, 266, 314, 321.
Land Rights, 21, 79, 92, 94, 99, 100, 164, 165, 199, 207, 223, 225, 236, 240, 244, 252, 266, 267, 319, 323-324.
Lyon, Tom, 106, 107, 109, 110-111, 123, 131, 135-136, 137, 156, 180, 183, 184, 185, 186-188, 190, 198, 199, 200-203, 205, 206, 209, 211, 212, 213, 227, 235, 261, 338.

Marra Worra Worra Aboriginal Corporation, 133, 168, 320.
McLeod, Don, 68, 176, 177, 229, 230-232, 272, 273, 275-276, 299, 310, 338.
McPhee, Ivan, 24, 121, 124, 126, 157, 175, 180, 183, 184, 185, 194, 195, 196, 207, 208, 209, 211, 212, 213, 225, 228, 229, 245, 252, 265, 281, 301, 338.
Mensaros, Andrew, 132, 133, 143, 144, 146, 147, 150, 158, 159, 162, 164, 167, 241.
Mickey's Pool, 38, 128, 278-288, 290, 291, 293, 308, 316, 327.
Millijidee/Station, 28, 38, 79, 80, 81, 86, 89, 95, 105, 114, 166, 279, 319, 323.
Mines Department, 95, 96, 104, 107, 108, 109, 110, 111, 132, 135, 136, 137, 138, 140, 141, 142, 143, 144, 147, 150, 166, 167, 173, 190, 196, 197, 207, 208, 252, 253, 258, 260, 265, 273, 303, 310, 315, 323.
Mitchell, W.W. 'Bill', 243-244, 291, 303, 315, 338.
Mowaljarli, David, 198, 199, 204, 205-206, 207, 228, 235, 236, 245.
Muller, Friday, 24, 26-31, 32, 57, 66, 73, 74, 75, 78, 79, 80-81, 82, 83, 84, 88-89, 105, 107, 108, 109, 110, 111, 132, 225, 310, 319, 338.
Mululby, Bob, 126, 127, 194, 246, 247, 258, 316, 319.

National Aboriginal Conference (NAC), 94, 133, 138, 206, 207, 231, 271, 294, 295, 297, 298, 301, 305, 308, 309, 320, 321.
Nganawilla, Ginger, 48-50, 51-52, 56, 57, 61, 65, 66, 87, 106, 107, 108-109, 174, 181, 186, 189, 190, 193, 213, 282, 319, 338.
Nicki, Mick, 55, 56, 57-59, 73, 85.
Nomads, 87, 227, 253.

O'Connor, Ray, 257, 258, 259, 260, 322, 338.
Old, Dick, 137, 143, 144, 146, 147, 150, 158, 163, 338.
Omen Pty Ltd, 254, 303, 314, 315.

Palmer, Kingsley, 22, 23, 24, 90, 101, 104, 111, 119, 131, 158, 179, 180.
Parks, Lloyd, 136, 167, 172, 197, 207, 208, 240, 338.
Pea Hill (Umpampurru), 14, 15, 38, 96, 114, 120, 121, 123, 125, 126, 128, 130, 131, 142, 143, 157, 165, 172, 173, 180, 194, 225, 226, 237, 245, 252, 254, 257.

Steve Hawke was born in 1959 and grew up in Melbourne. He lived for a year in Tasmania, before heading north for the first time to Darwin in 1978. It was as a journalist for *Nation Review* covering the Noonkanbah dispute at its outset that he first went to the Kimberley in 1978. He worked for the Noonkanbah Community as a media liaison officer through 1979-80.

He has remained living in the Kimberley since 1980, working in a variety of jobs for Aboriginal organisations in the Fitzroy Crossing area, and since 1987, as a consultant on Aboriginal land projects based in Derby.

Photograph by Leslie Corbett